NATIONAL GEOGRAPHIC

TRAVELER

Alaska

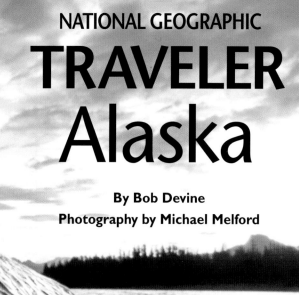

NATIONAL GEOGRAPHIC
TRAVELER
Alaska

By Bob Devine
Photography by Michael Melford

National Geographic
Washington, D.C.

Contents

How to use this guide 6–7 About the author & photographer 8
The areas 41–234 Travelwise 235–265
Index 266–270 Credits 270–271

History & culture 9
Alaska today 10–21
Land & landscape 22–31
History of Alaska 32–39
The arts 40–46

Southeast Alaska 47
Introduction & map 48–49
Cruising through Misty
Fiords 54–55
Feature: Traveling the Inside
Passage 66–69
Train ride: White Pass & Yukon
route 88–89

Anchorage & Mat-Su 91
Introduction & map 92–93
Feature: Buying Alaska
Native art 100–101
Hatcher Pass Drive
114–115

Kenai Peninsula 117
Introduction & map
118–119
Feature: Fishing 128–129
Feature: Bear-watching
134–135
Boat tour on Kachemak Bay
146–147

Alaska Peninsula & the Aleutians 149
Introduction & map
150–151
Feature: Birding on Attu
Island 154
Drive: Kodiak's Chiniak
Highway 160–61

Prince William Sound & around 167
Introduction & map
168–169
Exploring the Richardson
Highway 132–135
Feature: Retreat of the
glaciers 184–85

Interior 189
Introduction & map
190–191
A drive through Denali
National Park 198–201

The Bush 215
Feature: Winter in Alaska
226–229

Travelwise 235
Planning your trip 236
Getting around 236–238
Practical advice 238–240
Hotels & restaurants
241–260
Shopping 261–262
Entertainment 263
Activities 264–265

Index 266–270
Credits 270–271

Page 1: **Climber, Mount McKinley base camp**
Page 2–3: **Prince William Sound near Columbia Glacier**
Page 4: **Totem Bight State Historical Park, Ketchikan**

How to use this guide

See back flap for keys to text and map symbols.

The *National Geographic Traveler* brings you the best of Alaska in text, pictures, and maps. Divided into three main sections, the guide begins with an overview of Alaska today, its history, and culture.

Following are seven area chapters with sites selected by the author for their particular interest. Each chapter opens with its own contents list for easy reference. A map introduces the parameters covered in the chapter, highlighting the featured sites and locating places of interest. Drives and boat trips, plotted on their own maps, suggest routes for discovering the most about an area.

The final section, Travelwise, lists essential information for the traveler—pre-trip planning, getting around, practical advice, and special events—plus provides a selection of hotels and restaurants arranged by area, shops, entertainment and activities.

To the best of our knowledge, information is accurate as of press time. However, it's always advisable to call ahead when possible.

The map inside the front cover will help you orient yourself to the state, while the map in the inside back cover is of the entire Inside Passage.

Color coding

158

Each area is color coded for easy reference. Find the area you want on the map on the front flap, and look for the color flash at the top of the pages of the relevant chapter. Information in **Travelwise** is also color coded to each area.

Visitor information

McNeil River State Game Sanctuary

www.wildlife.alaska.gov/mcneil

🅰 151 F2

✉ 333 Raspberry Rd., Anchorage, AK 99518

☎ 907/267-2182

💲 $$$$$ (non-resident permit) plus application-filing fee, plus air charter

Practical information for most sites is given in the side column (see key to symbols on back flap). The map reference gives the page number of the map and grid reference. Other details are address, telephone number, days closed, and entrance charge in a range from $ (under $5) to $$$$$ (over $25). Other sites have information in italics and parentheses in the text.

TRAVELWISE

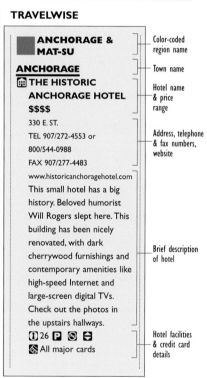

ANCHORAGE & MAT-SU — Color-coded region name

ANCHORAGE — Town name

🏨 **THE HISTORIC ANCHORAGE HOTEL** $$$$ — Hotel name & price range

330 E. ST.
TEL 907/272-4553 or 800/544-0988
FAX 907/277-4483 — Address, telephone & fax numbers, website

www.historicanchoragehotel.com
This small hotel has a big history. Beloved humorist Will Rogers slept here. This building has been nicely renovated, with dark cherrywood furnishings and contemporary amenities like high-speed Internet and large-screen digital TVs. Check out the photos in the upstairs hallways. — Brief description of hotel

🛏 26 🅿 🚭 ♿ — Hotel facilities & credit card details
🅰 All major cards

Hotel & restaurant prices

An explanation of the price bands used in entries (beginning on p. 242) is given in the Hotels & Restaurants section.

REGIONAL MAPS

Point of interest

Drive start point

Road number

Map reference

Important featured site

Important featured town

- A locator map accompanies each regional map and shows the location of that area in Alaska.
- Adjacent regions are shown, each with a page reference.

DRIVING TOURS, BOAT TOURS

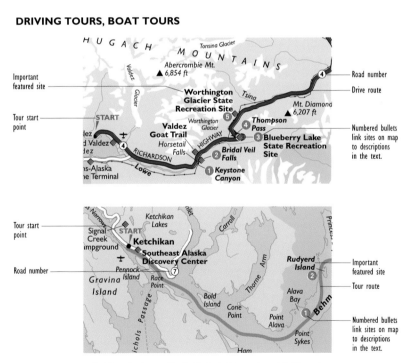

Important featured site

Tour start point

Road number

Tour start point

Road number

Road number

Drive route

Numbered bullets link sites on map to descriptions in the text.

Important featured site

Tour route

Numbered bullets link sites on map to descriptions in the text.

- An information box provides details that include starting and finishing points, places not to be missed along the route, and the time and length of drive.

NATIONAL GEOGRAPHIC

TRAVELER

Alaska

About the author & photographer

Bob Devine writes about the environment, natural history, and outdoor travel from his home in Oregon. His latest book is *Bush Versus the Environment.* The National Geographic has published several of his works, including the *Guide to America's Outdoors: Western Canada* and *Alien Invasion: America's Battle with Non-native Animals and Plants.* He first traveled to Alaska on assignment in 1987 and has since returned as often as possible.

Michael Melford is a renowned photographer whose assignments include both travel and editorial photography. His award-winning work has appeared in many major U.S. publications, including *National Geographic Traveler, Travel and Leisure, Life, Fortune,* and *Newsweek.* He lives with his family in Mystic, Connecticut.

History & culture

Alaska today 10–21
Land & landscape 22–31
History of Alaska 32–39
The arts 40–46

A young dancer in traditional dress

Alaska today

ALASKA. LIKE TOMBOUCTOU, THE VERY NAME EVOKES A LEGENDARY REMOTE-ness. To someone from Peoria or Atlanta or London, Alaska may seem more myth than reality: a wild place inhabited by grizzly bears, moose, and wolves; a dramatic landscape of raw-boned mountains, misty forests, windswept tundra, and glaciers that march into the sea; a realm of snow and ice and perpetual cold; a place peopled by Eskimos and pioneers living off the land.

These things are part of Alaska, but the picture they paint is so incomplete that it does indeed teeter on the edge of myth. Alaska also has espresso stands, farms, Air Force bases, art galleries, suburbs, four-star restaurants, 80°F (27°C) summer days, college basketball tournaments, Internet cafés, bureaucrats, and sand dunes. The reality is that Alaska is a fascinating blend of the wild and the civilized, of the traditional and the

modern, and of many different landscapes and climates.

The basic reason that Alaska has so much wild left is straightforward: It is tough country and few people live there. Though Alaska is by far the biggest state in the Union—well more than twice the size of number-two, Texas—its population is a scant 655,400; more people live in metropolitan Albuquerque. This results in a population density almost a thousand times sparser than, say, New Jersey's.

Alaska does have one bona fide urban area: Anchorage. More than 275,000 people live there in a cityscape familiar to most

Americans: It features skyscrapers, traffic jams, hip clubs, suburban sprawl, fine museums, and many of the other amenities and problems of a city. But even Anchorage is influenced by the proximity of the wilderness. Moose and bears often stroll through backyards. The glacier-streaked Chugach Mountains loom nearby. From the middle of town residents can drive 20 minutes and be in unspoiled forests and mountains.

Living so close to the land results in people also living off the land. Whether an accountant in Fairbanks or a teacher in Juneau, it seems that most Alaskans fish or hunt for food—and many do both. When the salmon are running in summer and fall, plenty of outsiders come to Alaska to hook kings and reds and silvers, but the majority of anglers are residents of the state who are looking to pack their freezers with fillets. Likewise, it's common to hear someone in a fine restaurant in Anchorage talk about getting his moose. A day earlier this person may have been dressed in camouflage instead of a three-piece suit, and instead of carving up a rack of lamb he was carving up the moose he'd just shot.

For some Alaskans those salmon and moose are not just a supplement to food they buy in a supermarket. Thousands of residents in small towns and villages lead subsistence lifestyles, getting the bulk of their food from the land. They not only fish for those prized salmon but for grayling, tomcod, sheefish, eel, and a dozen other species, depending on the region. The list of animals they hunt is equally long, including the obvious, like moose, goose, bear, and caribou, and the surprising, such as beluga whale, seal, porcupine, and walrus. They also trap fox, beaver, marten, and other fur-bearing animals and gather berries, bird eggs, greens, and clams. What some people do for sport, these folks do to live. Many of them wouldn't have it any other way, but many also have little choice, especially given the high cost of living in Alaska (which visitors, too, will certainly notice). Those costs

The mural says "Alaska," but the dress of these youths in Juneau would look right at home anywhere in the United States.

are even higher in the remote villages, where food often costs twice as much as it does in the lower 48.

THE PEOPLE'S LAND

Fortunately for those who use the land for subsistence, sport hunting and fishing, and recreation, the vast majority of Alaska lies in public hands, most of which enjoy at least some protections from development. Large chunks are overseen by the state and by Native organizations, and more than half of the country falls under the steward-ship of the federal government. Unlike many of their counterparts in other states, most Alaskan public lands allow subsistence uses and some sport hunting and fishing. This is true even for Alaska's headliner lands, such as Denali National Park. Visitors often don't realize that its full name is Denali National Park and Preserve. The phrase "and Preserve" is found at the end of

the names of most of the national parks in the state. The areas of Denali designated as preserve are open to subsistence uses and sport hunting and fishing; so, too, are large portions of the park. Only the wilderness section—which includes the main tourism area—is usually off limits. While traveling in the backcountry, visitors may encounter fish nets, traps, and other tools employed by subsistence users. It's important to leave these items undisturbed.

Huge cruise ships, each carrying 2,000-plus passengers, stop at Ketchikan and other Southeast Alaska ports during summer.

NATIVE ALASKANS

Many subsistence hunters and gatherers are Alaska Natives. These indigenous inhabitants constitute about 19 percent of the state's population. Contrary to stereotype, not all Alaska Natives are Eskimos—not even close, though they are the single most

populous Native group. The term "Eskimo" is widely used for the people who live around the west and north coasts and is not considered offensive, but so-called Eskimos think of themselves as belonging to smaller cultural divisions. The two main ones are the Inupiat, who reside on the north coast and on the west coast north of Norton Sound, and the Yupik, who live on the west coast from Norton Sound south to Bristol Bay. Sometimes you'll hear the terms

"Inupiat Eskimo" and "Yupik Eskimo." These peoples further split into smaller groups, such as the Nunamiut, who are, essentially, inland Inupiat.

The vast interior of Alaska and a few bits of the south-central coast are the realm of the Athabascan. These people are related to some of the First Nations of Canada and the lower 48 and sometimes refer to themselves as Indians, though they generally prefer more specific names that describe the small-

er groups to which they belong, such as the Dena'ina, the Ahtna, and the Tanana.

The Alaska Peninsula and the 1,100 miles of islands in the Aleutian chain are the domain of the Aleut, who call themselves the Unangan. Closely related and still lumped together with the Aleut by some observers are the Alutiiq, who occupy the southeast portion of the Alaska Peninsula, the Kodiak Island Archipelago, and Prince William Sound. Finally, there are the Alaska

Float planes can take visitors deep into the wilds, to such places as Kulik Lake in Katmai National Park backcountry.

Natives of the Southeast: the Tlingit, Haida, Tsimshian, and Eyak. They share many cultural traits—though not their languages—with the Northwest Coast Natives of British Columbia and Washington.

As happened with indigenous peoples around the world, the arrival of outsiders was

hard on Alaska Natives. The Aleut were invaded by the Russians in the mid-1700s. These acquisitive and well-armed Europeans and Asians killed most Aleut directly or via disease and starvation and enslaved most of the rest. Aleut numbers plunged from an estimated 20,000 to a tiny fraction of that, and to this day their population remains small. The Russians, as well as American and British whalers in the mid-1800s, also introduced Native Alaskans to alcohol, which has had a profound impact on Native life. Though Native communities have worked hard and have enjoyed some success fighting alcoholism, it still poses a serious problem. Consequently many Native communities prohibit the possession or sale of alcoholic beverages.

Despite these tribulations, many Alaska Natives have improved their lot in recent times. This is largely due to the deal they worked out in 1971, codified by the passage

in Congress of the Alaska Native Claims Settlement Act (ANCSA). This secured extensive subsistence-use rights and formed 12 regional Native and dozens of village corporations that together own 44 million acres (17.8 million ha) of land. These corporations are engaged in fishing, logging, mining, oil production and exploration, health care, and tourism and bring in billions of dollars in revenue. As this suggests, though many Alaska Natives still live close to the

Known simply as "the mountain" to many Alaskans, 20,320-foot Mount McKinley rises above Kettle Lake in Denali National Park.

land, many also work regular jobs, earn college degrees, own and manage businesses, and otherwise participate in modern society.

EUROPEAN INFLUENCE
Despite the impact they had on Alaska, the Russians never settled here in large

numbers—relatively few ethnic Russians live in the state—however, they left behind a sizable number of religious converts whose descendants still attend the state's many Russian Orthodox churches. The main exceptions are the Russian Old Believers, though they don't trace their lineage back to the early Russians; most of the Old Believers came to Alaska in the latter half of the 20th century. Numbering only a few thousand, the majority of them live on the Kenai Peninsula and around Kodiak, where they generally keep to themselves in isolated villages. However, visitors will see Old Believers in stores or operating their fishing vessels, the women wearing ankle-length dresses and caps or scarves and all the men sporting beards.

In the years following the transfer of Alaska from Russia to the United States, almost all newcomers to Alaska were of western European ancestry, particularly

German and Irish. But globalization seems to be bringing diversity to the state in recent years, even if the 2000 census still showed only small numbers of African, Latino, and Asian Americans in Alaska—about 4 percent each.

MAKING A LIVING

All that salmon and moose meat in the freezer notwithstanding, most Alaskans still have to earn a paycheck to pay the bills.

A telephoto lens in combination with guided outings gets you safely near the brown bears in Katmai National Park.

However, due to transportation costs and other difficulties caused by the state's isolation, few large-scale manufacturers other than seafood-processing companies locate in Alaska. The climate and topography preclude other common industries, too, such as agriculture, which is very limited in the

A load of Dungeness crabs (above) arrives for inspection at Petersburg. The trans-Alaska pipeline (opposite) delivers oil some 800 miles (1,280 km) from the edge of the Arctic Ocean to the port at Valdez.

amendment passed by voters in 1976 assures that a percentage of oil and other mineral revenues goes into the Permanent Fund Dividend, which pays an annual dividend to every man, woman, and child living in Alaska. In 2005 each qualified resident received $845.76.

Commercial fishing is a huge industry in Alaska. (Sportfishing also attracts big business.) The ports of Unalaska, Dillingham, Kodiak, Cordova, and other towns near rich fishing grounds are home to thousands of fishing vessels and a good many fish-processing plants. At least half the United States' commercial fish production takes place in Alaska. The state has one of the world's best managed fisheries and has mounted a big campaign to promote wild salmon; farming salmon is currently (and historically) illegal in Alaska.

Tourism is the state's third largest industry and seems environmentally sustainable, despite the occasional overcrowding at popular parks or the air pollution caused by RVs. However, tourism may not be culturally and economically sustainable when it's industrial strength and controlled by outside corporate interests, as is happening in some of the Southeast Alaska ports favored by big cruise ships. Large national and international firms are buying up retail space and hawking glitzy wares to the 5,000-plus passengers getting off the cruise ships every day in summer, and many people feel the change is corrupting the character of those towns.

On the other hand, many Alaskan towns, including some Southeast ports, offer a range of locally owned shops with an array of tour operators who sell their knowledge and love of the land. Instead of offering stuffed grizzly bears for sale, they offer real grizzly bears for viewing, boat tours to offshore wildlife refuges, meetings with noted sled-dog racers, hikes through the rain forest, plane rides over the mountains and glaciers, cultural visits to Native villages, kayaking and canoeing in rivers and along the coast, and many other excursions that celebrate the essence of Alaska. That's a win-win situation for Alaskans and for travelers to Alaska. ∎

state. Other than government jobs, most people work in resource industries, notably oil, fishing, mining, and logging—and tourism, which is a different sort of resource industry but which similarly relies on Alaska's rich natural assets.

Nowadays, oil production is perhaps the state's most famous business, and it puts a lot of money into state coffers (though far more flows to out-of-state interests). It employs several thousand Alaskans and outsiders, and the oil support industries are some of the biggest companies in the state. Oil pumped out of Prudhoe Bay directly benefits every Alaskan: A constitutional

Land & landscape

WILD, UNFORGIVING, AND SPECTACULAR, NATURE'S ATTRIBUTES DEFINE Alaska. In this frontier state that stretches from the Arctic Circle to the Gulf of Alaska and from near Russia to the Coast Mountains of British Columbia, the climate, the terrain, the ecosystems, and the wildlife make themselves felt at every turn. They've become the stuff of legends, humbling even the most cynical of visitors.

HISTORY OF THE LAND

Just as Alaska is a young and dynamic state in terms of its human development, so is it a young and dynamic land in terms of its geology. Floating on the semisolid mantle of the Earth, the Pacific plate is drifting northeast into the North American plate. Being generally denser, the Pacific plate is subducting, or sliding under, the North American plate. Alaska's massive mountains are the result of this tectonic meeting. In fact, many of these mountains are still rising; Mount McKinley, the continent's highest peak at 20,320 feet (6,194 m), yet grows.

This grinding, slow-motion collision of plates also produces earthquakes and volcanic activity. More than 15 active volcanoes simmer along the Alaska Peninsula. Evidence of past eruptions is abundant. For example, the cataclysmic explosion that disintegrated the top of Aniakchak Mountain some 3,500 years ago is apparent in the six-mile-wide (9.6 km), 2,000-foot-deep (610 m) caldera that remains. Nor are major eruptions confined to the distant past. In 1912, Novarupta Volcano shook violently for a week and then blew with a force that could be heard 1,000 miles (1,600 km) away. Its eruption cycle lasted for 60 hours, during which more rock and ash were blasted into the atmosphere than during any other volcanic event in human history, with the exception of the 1500 B.C. eruption of Thíra in Greece.

An even more recent event had a major impact on modern Alaska. At 5:36 p.m. on March 27, 1964, a fault line at the bottom of Prince William Sound spasmed and rocked

Anchorage lies split open after the strongest earthquake in North America's recorded history shook much of Alaska in 1964.

south-central Alaska for three to five minutes with an earthquake that measured 9.2 on the Richter scale—80 times more powerful than the infamous 1906 San Francisco quake. Terra firma suddenly wasn't firm: An island in the sound rose 33 feet (10 m). In some towns streets tilted up like drawbridges. Some coastal flatlands dropped half a dozen feet, allowing seawater to flow across them, eventually killing all the trees. In downtown Anchorage the north side of Fourth Street collapsed and restaurants and stores sank out of sight.

Then came the worst part. Tsunamis spawned by the quake washed ashore. A 70-foot (21 m) wave erased the Native village of

Chenega. In Seward, the quake ignited huge fires in dockside fuel tanks and a tsunami pushed that burning fuel eight blocks inland, causing a flood and a fire at the same time. In Valdez, much of the waterfront slid into the bay and the rest got pounded by a tsunami; the townspeople subsequently abandoned the site and rebuilt in a safer spot 4 miles (6.4 km) away.

Inuit children (above) weather Barrow's Arctic cold clothed in traditional furs. A river laces through a valley in Katmai National Park and Preserve (opposite).

Glaciers are another geologic force in Alaska, gouging out fjords and mountain valleys and releasing meltwater to form rivers and creeks. Unlike the lower 48, where glaciers are an exotic sight in a few high mountains, Alaska's rivers of ice crop up all around from high elevations to sea level; if you count the small ones (though some are larger than Rhode Island), the state contains more than 100,000 glaciers (only 616 are named).

Surprisingly, much of Alaska remained free of ice during the ice ages. The most

significant impact on the area was the result of the worldwide conversion of water into ice, which lowered sea level a few hundred feet. Several times between 10,000 and 40,000 years ago, the shallow ocean floor of the Bering Sea was exposed, creating a broad land bridge linking North America to Asia. North America's first inhabitants are thought to have walked across this land bridge from Siberia.

CLIMATE

There are two take-home lessons about weather in Alaska. Lesson one: It can and does change quickly, so even if you're going on a two-hour outing, be prepared. Carry rain gear and extra layers of clothing almost everywhere. And if you're scheduled to go somewhere in a small plane, realize that bad weather may keep that plane on the ground. By the same token, realize that if you've been dropped off at a wilderness lodge or such by a small plane, you may get stranded at your destination for an extra day or two.

Lesson number two: Alaska is a big state and the weather varies tremendously depending on where you are. More than 2,000 miles (3,600 km) separate Attu, at the western tip of the Aleutians, from the Arctic National Wildlife Refuge, in the northeastern corner of the state. It's about the same distance from Ketchikan, in the southeast, to Barrow, in the northwest. Not surprisingly, their climates differ.

Ketchikan, Kodiak, and the rest of the southern coast lie in the relatively mild maritime zone, warmed by the Kuroshio or Japan Current. Not balmy, mind you, but with highs in the 50s and 60s (10°–20°C) during the summer and with winter temperatures that generally stay on the pleasant side of zero. However, that maritime weather means a lot of moisture; Ketchikan soaks up about 160 inches (4 m) of rain a year and most places get 80, 90, or 100 inches (2–2.5 m) annually. And while a lot of rain falls in winter, plenty falls in summer, too.

Shielded from the moderating influence of the ocean, the Interior experiences weather extremes. Fairbanks occasionally basks in highs of 80°F (27°C) and even 90°F (32°C), with average midsummer highs in

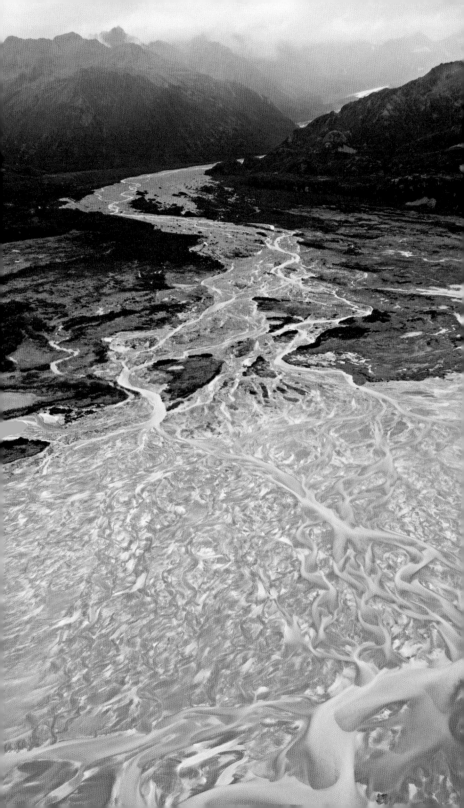

Mount McKinley, North America's highest peak, looms some 18,000 feet (5,486 m) above the valley at its base. Native Alaskans call the mountain Denali, "the high one."

the low 70s. And although summer is the Interior's rainy season, it is usually dry; annual rain totals are a near-desertlike 15 inches (38 cm). In winter the thermometer nose dives. For months the temperature may not rise above zero and sometimes it sits between minus 30°F (–34°C) and minus 50°F (–45°C) for days.

Then there's the Arctic, the northern third of Alaska above the Arctic Circle. In

Barrow, Alaska's northernmost point, the daily low temperature drops below freezing an average of 324 days a year. Traditional fur-lined Inupiat Eskimo parkas are more than a fashion statement here; they're a necessity. Summer highs only creep into the 30s and 40s and it's very dry—about 5 inches (11 cm) of precipitation a year.

No matter where you are in Alaska, in summer you'll be exposed to the midnight sun. The northern part of Earth tilts toward the sun during summer, increasing the daily amount of sunlight the farther north you travel. The Arctic Circle is the line of latitude at which the sun never drops below the horizon on the summer solstice. On the shore of the Arctic Ocean, 250 miles (400 km) north of the circle, the sun will not set for maybe 80 days. In Anchorage, some 350 miles (560 km) south of the circle, the sun still hovers above the horizon for 18 or 19 hours in midsummer; even at 2 a.m. there's the glow of daylight in the sky. The reverse occurs in winter: 80 sunless days on the Arctic Ocean and just 5.5 or 6 hours of sunlight in Anchorage. On the bright side (well, not literally), all that darkness is great for viewing the aurora borealis, or northern lights.

LANDSCAPES

As you'd expect in a land so vast, Alaska has many distinct habitats, from sand dunes to ice fields. However, the state can be broadly divided into three different vegetation zones: coastal rain forest, taiga, and tundra.

Temperate rain forest—courtesy of all the rain—blankets the islands and coast in southeastern and south-central Alaska; it also covera a little bit of the southwest. Temperate rain forest is much less common than tropical rain forest; its rainfall is also generally well distributed across the year.

In Alaska's coastal rain forests, Sitka spruce and hemlock dominate, though other conifers, such as cedars and pines, also show up. These forests are the only ones in Alaska that have trees rivaling the 200- and 250-foot (61–76 m) old-growth denizens of British Columbia, Washington, and Oregon. The damp understory is lush with salmonberry, devil's club, blueberry, columbine, skunk cabbage, ferns, fireweed, huckleberry, and a multitude of other plant species that thrive on moisture.

Inland from the rain forest, on the other side of the coastal mountains, the boreal forest or taiga begins. ("Taiga" comes from a Siberian word for "coniferous forest" and is the more commonly used term.) Taiga covers most of the Interior, though it grades from relatively verdant with 80- and 100-foot (24–30 m) trees in the south to sparse

with 10-foot (3 m) trees at its northern edge, around the Arctic Circle. Spruce is the dominant tree; however, it's not the towering Sitka spruce so common in the rain forest but the more modest white spruce and black spruce. Birch, aspen, tamarack, alder, willow, and balsam poplar add to the mix. In the northern taiga, or where soils are poor or boggy, travelers will see seemingly endless tracts of stunted, spindly black spruce, as if a vast Christmas-tree farm had been sprayed with herbicide.

The tundra is the land above tree line, where the intense cold, short growing season, thin soil, and scouring winds make life impossible for trees. "Above" can mean two things in Alaska: higher elevation or higher latitude. In southern Alaska tree line occurs at 2,000 to 3,000 feet (610–914 m) and tundra takes over higher than that. Traveling north into ever colder climates, the harsh conditions that dictate tree line occur at increasingly lower elevations until, a bit north of the Arctic Circle, tree line is at sea level—in other words, no trees grow on the tundra-covered North Slope, which runs from the Brooks Range to the Arctic Ocean. (Consider the effects of latitude in reverse; in the Colorado Rockies tree line is at about 11,000 feet/3,353 meters.)

At lower elevations and latitudes "moist tundra" is the norm. Hikers in Alaska curse moist tundra, a blend of thigh-high willow and birch thickets with ankle-breaking hummocks of grasses and sedges underlain by standing water and dotted with ponds. Hikers prefer the dry or alpine tundra found on higher ground. Here the hummocks are gone, there's no standing water, and the vegetation is much shorter, often just a few inches tall. At first glance alpine tundra seems barren, but look closely and you'll see a fascinating, colorful plant community working hard to make the most of a short growing season. Depending on the region, alpine tundra may be alive with lupine, crowberry, arctic bell heather, bearberry, mountain saxifrage, wild geranium, moss campion, alpine azalea, cranberry, Lapland rosebay, tundra rose, and the wonderous sky blue of forget-me-not, the Alaska state flower.

Almost anywhere in Alaska, whether rain forest, taiga, or tundra, mountains are part of the picture. Only the extreme north has a sizable expanse flat enough to really qualify as a plain. Even many of the islands in the southeast and the Aleutians feature jagged peaks—natural enough given that those islands are the tops of much bigger mountains whose bottoms are submerged.

The king of Alaska's peaks, and the highest peak in North America, 20,320-foot (6,194 m) Mount McKinley crowns the Alaska Range, which curves through the southern interior of the state. However, McKinley notwithstanding, the most impressive mountains in Alaska are the craggy, snowcapped Wrangell and St. Elias Mountains, neighbors in southern Alaska. In this fastness of lofty summits and mammoth glaciers lie 12 of the 15 highest mountains in Alaska and 10 of the 15 highest on the continent.

The nation's northernmost mountain chain, the Brooks Range, is an older uplift and sports only one peak above 9,000 feet (2,743 m)—9,239-foot (2,816 m) Mount Michelson—yet the length and width of this range is truly Alaska size. More than 100 miles (160 km) broad, the Brooks Range forms a great wall 600 miles (960 km) long, stretching across the state from the Canadian border in the east to the Chukchi Sea in the west. Lying just north of the Arctic Circle, the Brooks Range marks the Arctic Divide, sending rivers off its southern slopes to the Bering Sea and rivers off its northern slopes to the Arctic Ocean.

WILDLIFE

Any discussion of Alaskan wildlife must begin with bears. Some visitors to Alaska hardly go outdoors due to a fear of bear attacks, while other people blithely romp through the woods without giving bears much thought. Both of these extremes are irrational and underscore the importance of getting accurate information about bears in Alaska. The details of dealing with bears can be learned at public lands throughout Alaska *(for information see National Park Service*

A humpback whale lifts its flukes and dives in Glacier Bay. In summer, humpbacks are found all along Alaska's southern coast, especially in the waters of Southeast Alaska.

Though visitors seldom see them, polar bears roam Alaska's Arctic coastlines. They are found most abundantly near the edge of the pack ice, moving seasonally.

brochure *"Bear Safety in Alaska's Parklands," www.nps.gov/akso/bearsafe.pdf*). If you take sensible precautions, both you and the bears will survive your encounters unscathed.

That last statement would not be true if more polar bears lived in the heavily visited parts of Alaska. These cream-furred giants are seriously dangerous and will hunt people. Fortunately, Alaska's polar bears live along the remote western and northern Arctic coasts and spend most of their time out on the sea ice.

Grizzly/brown and black bears also live in Alaska, making it the only state that has all of the North American bear species. (Another bear, the Kodiak bear, is actually a subspecies of the grizzly/brown; it is genetically and physically isolated and has a slightly differently shaped skull.) Visitors often get confused because they hear locals referring to "brown bears," but that's just the common name for grizzlies that live within 100 miles (160 km) of the coast.

Due to their salmon-rich diet, coastal brown bears grow to almost twice the size of their inland brethren, with big males reaching heights of 9-plus feet (2.7 m) and weights of 1,200 pounds (544 kg). Grizzlies, whether brown bears or not, are found throughout almost all of Alaska—on the beaches, in the forests, in the tundra, up in the mountains, and even on many islands. Understandably, the size of grizzlies/brownies scares people, but black bears, though only about a third as large, are at least as dangerous. They generally stick to forested areas. Visitors who want to safely observe either grizzly/brown or black bears will find numerous organized opportunities in Alaska.

Some Alaskans worry more about moose attacks than bears. It's hard for the uninitiated to be concerned about an herbivore, but moose are as big as brown bears, just as fast, more commonly seen, and more temperamental, especially cows with calves.

However, moose are easily dealt with compared to bears: Keep your distance and don't get between cows and their calves; then relax and enjoy watching them munch on willows or stilt around in ponds on those long legs.

Assuming you don't feed or mistreat them, the rest of Alaska's wildlife generally present no cause for concern. On the contrary, watching the many fascinating and beautiful animals that call Alaska home is a highlight for many visitors. From rain forest to Arctic tundra, listen for the thrilling howls of wolves. On steep slopes in the high country look for the brilliant white of Dall sheep, closely related to the bighorns of the lower 48; the males sport curled horns that serve as battering rams during battles over females. On even higher and steeper slopes, scan for the cream color of mountain goats, the champion climbers among hooved animals. In the Interior and way up north, watch for caribou; if you plan carefully, you may be able to see one of the great caribou herds, which number in the tens of thousands.

Not all animals of interest in Alaska wear fur. More than 400 bird species inhabit or migrate through Alaska, including some Asiatic species. Bald eagles are common in coastal Alaska; their cousins, the golden eagles, soar above the Interior tundra looking for marmot and hare. Other avian favorites include trumpeter swans, sandhill cranes, and peregrine falcons.

Take a boat out on the open waters to see puffins, auklets, and huge, raucous nesting colonies of seabirds. Tour boats also allow visitors to explore nearshore environments, which host a dazzling array of marine mammals, including humpback whales, orcas beluga whales, sea lions, walrus, harbor seals, and the perennial crowd favorite, the sea otters.

And one last category of wildlife must be mentioned: biting bugs. Led by Alaska's notorious mosquitoes (and a variety of biting flies), these pests can spoil outings if you're not prepared—and sometimes even when you are. Learn how to handle them, or find out when their numbers peak in the places you want to visit and time your travels accordingly.

PUBLIC LANDS

Visiting the rain forest, taiga, and tundra to see wildlife is made easier by the fact that most of Alaska is public land. The state has the nation's biggest national park, the biggest national wildlife refuge, and the biggest state park. However, be aware that many of these public lands bear little resemblance to their lower 48 counterparts, where visitors often enjoy flush toilets, elaborate visitor centers, extensive trail systems, well-tended campgrounds, and other amenities. Many of Alaska's public lands are raw

wildernesses, with perhaps one visitor center or ranger station on the boundary. For information contact the specific site or the excellent Alaska Public Lands Information Centers *(www.nps.gov/aplic)*.

GUIDED TOURS

Because of the remoteness, the fickle weather, the bears, and all the other rigors of travel in Alaska's outdoors, guided excursions provide a nice complement to independent outings. A wide array of qualified outfits and individuals can take you kayak-

Caribou inhabit much of Alaska. The largest herd, the Western Arctic in northwestern Alaska, numbers close to 500,000 caribou.

ing, fishing, bear viewing, hiking, boating, birding, and flying, whether on a one-hour tour or a two-week expedition. Not only is going with a guide safer, you can learn from these local experts. To choose a good guide, use common sense and recommendations from convention and visitor bureaus and chambers of commerce. Some public lands have lists of authorized outfitters. ■

History of Alaska

MUCH OF ALASKA'S HISTORY HAS REVOLVED AROUND NATURAL RESOURCES. When humans first entered the Western Hemisphere by crossing the Bering land bridge, they probably were hunting mammoths and other game animals. When Europeans first sailed into Alaskan waters, they came seeking the pelts of sea otters and seals. When Americans first came to Alaska in significant numbers, they searched for gold, and later for black gold in the oil fields.

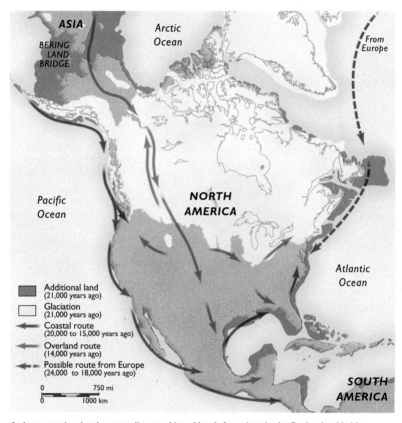

A theory posits that humans dispersed into North America via the Bering land bridge.

Yet along with the fortune hunters came people who settled in Alaska, people looking to establish a new home. Whether Native peoples that have been around for almost 500 generations or recent arrivals, these resident Alaskans are a major part of the state's history, too. They're the ones who build the clan houses, fly the bush planes, populate villages and towns, and skipper small fishing boats.

ALASKA'S FIRST INHABITANTS

Much debate clouds the original arrival of humans in the Americas. The majority view holds that they came between 10,000 and 30,000 years ago, when Ice Age glaciers bound up so much water that sea level dropped about 250 feet (76 m), exposing the shallow ocean shelf in the Bering Strait, where Russia and Alaska are only some 56 miles (90 km) apart. This created the Bering land bridge, though the word "bridge" presents a misleading image because at low water levels the exposed landmass was hundreds of miles wide. This bridge may have been exposed for thousands of years and perhaps more than once. Having been available for so long, it's natural that hunting tribes in Siberia followed their prey across the bridge to Alaska.

Whether some of these first North Americans stayed in Alaska or whether all of them moved south through the Americas and later back to Alaska has been lost in the mists of time. Anthropologists and archaeologists do know that the ancestors of today's Alaska Natives have lived in Alaska for thousands of years. During that time—and perhaps to some degree before arriving in Alaska—they split into a rich variety of linguistic and cultural groups. Some remained nomadic while others settled into permanent villages. They developed increasingly sophisticated techniques for making a living from hunting caribou, catching salmon, harpooning bowhead and beluga whales, and gathering plants from the forest and tundra. Many arts flourished, including sculpting ivory and stone, weaving baskets, story telling, carving totem poles, dancing, and fashioning elaborate masks.

Peter the Great sent Vitus Bering on his first voyage to Alaska.

THE RUSSIANS ARE COMING

In the early 1700s the European powers—mainly Great Britain, France, and Spain—were busy colonizing the world, including North America. They were vaguely aware of the big hole on their maps to the east of Siberia, but they were at war and ignored the area. But Tsar Peter the Great of Russia showed interest. Shortly before his death he sent Vitus Bering to sail east from Siberia's Kamchatka Peninsula. It took a couple of tries and a lot of years, but in 1741 both of the ships in Bering's expedition, after getting separated in foul weather, encountered what is now southern Alaska.

Bering's expedition brought back many pelts, including those of sea otters, which wealthy clients, especially among the Chinese, prized above all others because of the unmatched density of the warm fur. A nice sea otter pelt fetched a price equal to three year's pay for a regular working man. The reports of abundant sea otters attracted *promyshlenniki*—trappers and fur traders who typically took local hostages and forced their fellow tribesmen to buy back the hostages with furs. The promyshlenniki inflicted this cruel system on the Aleut, along with European diseases, and wiped out most of the population. Equally acquisitive but less barbaric Russian fur companies followed and set up operations in Southeast and south-central Alaska.

For several decades the Russians kept the secret of the Alaskan sea otters to themselves, but in the 1770s British and Spanish ships explored Alaska and the word spread. Chasing sea otters, the mythical Northwest Passage (an ice-free shipping route between the Pacific and the Atlantic), political advantage, and scientific information, Europeans made some 200 voyages to Alaskan waters by 1805. Still, under the iron hand of Alexander Baranov (1746–1819), the manager of Alaska operations for the ruling fur-trading Russian-American Company (he came to be called the "Lord of Alaska"), the Russians consolidated and extended their sway in Alaska.

But overhunting caused sea otters and other furbearers to become scarce by the 1820s and 1830s. Coupled with wars and political setbacks at home, the decline in furs caused Russia to gradually lose interest in Alaska. By the 1850s the Russians were ready to sell. (This being the era of colonialism, no one with any power ever questioned the right of the Russians to sell Alaska.) However, they did not want the region to fall into the hands of the British or any of Russia's other European rivals, so, once the U.S. Civil War ended, in 1865, the Russians approached the Americans.

SEWARD'S FOLLY

U.S. Secretary of State William H. Seward and other American political leaders were as eager to acquire Alaska as the Russians were to unload it. Seward was a zealous believer in America's "manifest destiny" to rule over all of North America, even Canada. Other Americans, even those who likewise believed in manifest destiny, disagreed with Seward, pointing to Alaska's remoteness and brutal climate. These critics panned Alaska as "Seward's icebox," "Walrussia," and "Icebergia." And in 1867, when Seward signed the deal with the Russians and paid them $7.2 million, the critics labeled the agreement as "Seward's Folly."

Having closed the deal, the Americans started wondering just what they'd bought. Neither the Russians nor anyone else had explored much beyond the coastline. (The Native peoples who lived beyond the coast knew a little something about what lay in the Interior, but no one asked them.) The new owners didn't even know what to call their new property. Seward chose "Alaska," the Aleut word for "great land." The Aleut had used the term only for what is now the Alaska Peninsula, but Seward adopted it for the entire … the entire what?

The federal government refused to make the land a territory, as happened with lands acquired by previous international treaties, like the Louisiana Purchase. Territorial status would have conferred citizenship upon all the inhabitants and put Alaska on a trajectory toward eventual statehood, and Congress didn't think Alaska rated such treatment. Instead, Alaska's status was left somewhat vague, though clearly it was not bound for statehood and Russians and Alaska Natives were specifically denied citi-

zenship. More than anything the arrangement made Alaska resemble a colony.

For the next few decades, members of the federal government, like the Russians before them, largely ceded day-to-day administration to a fur-trading company: the Alaska Commercial Company, which mainly wanted fur seal pelts (since sea otters were nearly extinct). With fur seal populations in steep decline, the company and the government agreed upon the taking of 100,000 fur seals a year while leaving females and pups. Even with these limitations the company raked in enormous profits.

During those early years of American tenure, Alaska got a visit from someone who couldn't be more different from the seal hunters. Fascinated by glaciers, along with everything else wild, John Muir came north to Alaska, where he knew there were many glaciers. In 1879, he took a ship to Wrangell, in southeastern Alaska, and headed out from there with four Tlingit paddlers and a Presbyterian missionary on what turned into an 800-mile (1,280 km) canoe trip. Among the many grand places they explored was Glacier Bay, where today visitors will find Muir Glacier (not named that

A painting by Edward Leutze depicts the signing of the 1867 treaty that transferred ownership of Alaska from Russia to the U.S.

by Muir). Muir's glowing stories about this journey and an 1880 return trip are said to have launched Alaskan tourism. Within a decade thousands of people had cruised up the Inside Passage to witness for themselves the grandeur of Glacier Bay.

Numerous others, including missionaries and military men, also were exploring Alaska during the 1870s and 1880s, slowly figuring out whether Seward's purchase of

Alaska had been folly or not. They found a diversity of intriguing Alaska Natives, prolific fisheries, ample wildlife, and spectacular landscapes—but all that was overshadowed by the discovery of gold.

GOLD RUSH

When Alaskans talk about *the* "gold rush," they're referring to the stampede of miners to the Klondike that started in 1898. However,

This 1897 play was one of many that fueled the public's fascination with the gold rush.

there were many other significant discoveries of gold, too. Joe Juneau and Richard Harris hit it big at Gold Creek in 1880, at the site of the city that now bears Joe's name. Only that gold required hard-rock mining: Big companies with expensive equipment to drill tunnels into mountainsides and money to build stamp mills and other facilities to extract the gold from the ore were needed at these types of gold strikes. Generally, gold rushes, where thousands upon thousands of people con-

verge on an area, occurred in places where gold had filtered out into streams and could be found by individual miners panning for the yellow metal.

One classic rush took place in Nome, where three prospectors struck gold in 1898 and in 1899 people found gold flakes amid the beach sands on the Bering Sea near town. By the summer of 1900 some 20,000 fortune hunters were camped out on the beach. One prospector found a nugget that weighed 107 ounces—the largest ever recorded in Alaska.

And then there was the Klondike gold rush. The strangest thing about this most extravagant of all Alaskan gold rushes is that the Klondike isn't in Alaska. The Klondike River and its tributary creeks where the gold was discovered lie fully 60 miles (96 km) east of Alaska in Canada's Yukon Territory. This rush became an Alaskan legend because the most popular routes to the Klondike started in and passed through Alaska, and because this rush was *huge*.

Ships carrying news of the Klondike strike—and carrying a ton of gold to drive the point home—arrived in Seattle in July 1897. Because the Klondike was remote and a challenge to reach, July was too late to start out without getting trapped by winter, so people waited until 1898. Come spring some 50,000 gold seekers headed north, with another 50,000 leaving later that year or in 1899. Of those 100,000, only about 30,000 to 50,000 made it to the goldfields. Most of the 70,000 to 50,000 who came up short managed to straggle back to civilization, but a terrible number died trying.

Some of those deaths occurred because there was no obvious best route, so people tried all sorts of ways. One party of 18 New Yorkers decided to cross the Malaspina Glacier, in Southeast Alaska, apparently unaware that it is the largest piedmont glacier in North America, larger than Rhode Island. For an agonizing three months they struggled atop the glacier. One man fell into a crevasse and died; three died in an avalanche. The rest got off the glacier but were utterly lost when winter caught them. They threw together a rickety shelter to wait for spring. Some men went insane with cabin fever and struck out into the teeth of winter to reach the Klondike; they were never heard from again. The seven who survived until spring recrossed the glacier back to where they started, in Yakutat Bay. Only four were alive when a ship found them, and two suffered snow blindness. When the four broken men were dropped in Seattle, an example of irresponsible journalism transformed what should have been a cautionary tale into an inducement to head for

Lindemann or Lake Bennett, where the gold seekers had to build crude boats and float 550 miles (880 km) to the goldfields. Tough, but not as bad as the Malaspina Glacier or some other routes. However, when the tired stampeders topped the 3,739-foot (1,140 m) pass, inside Canadian territory, they were confronted by the Northwest Mounted Police. Originally sent to keep order and make sure customs duties were paid, the Mounties heard that supplies were running

Having rested at The Scales, the last camp on the trail in Alaska, miners bound for Canada's Klondike goldfields labor up the "Golden Stairs" cut into the snow of Chilkoot Pass.

the Klondike: The *Seattle Times* incorrectly reported that the men had returned with half a million dollars worth of gold.

Most stampeders sailed to Skagway or Dyea, neighboring Southeast Alaska towns that competed to be the gateway to the Klondike. From there they made for the goldfields via Chilkoot Pass, a route the Tlingit had been using for centuries to trade with Interior peoples. It required 33 miles (53 km) of steep, difficult hiking to Lake

low in the Klondike. As a result, they began requiring that each person headed for the goldfields bring enough food to last for a year—about a ton. That meant the goldseekers had to go up and down the pass a dozen, maybe two dozen times.

Although the Klondike fields yielded some $300 million in gold, the vast majority of stampeders didn't strike it rich. Some moved on to Nome or some other gold strike. Most went home. But many stayed and made Alaska home; from 1890 to 1900 the state's year-round population doubled from 30,000 to 60,000. This mass migration jump-started the 20th century in Alaska, boosting the building of the railroads, the founding of cities and towns, and the growth of resource industries like fishing and logging. Alaska continued growing steadily, but it didn't experience another great leap forward until World War II.

WORLD WAR II

Few people know that the Japanese invaded Alaska during World War II. Unlike the the Aleutians, and the Japanese hoped an attack on the Aleutians would draw some American forces away from Midway. So on June 3 they bombed Unalaska/Dutch Harbor. They caused some damage and created confusion in the Aleutians, but the tactic didn't work: The Japanese suffered a stunning defeat at Midway.

Partly to save face, the Japanese forces at Alaska's door then invaded two far-western Aleutian Islands, Attu and Kiska, which were undefended and nearly unpopulated. The Japanese built an airfield and bunkers and brought in several thousand soldiers. In

U.S. troops inspect Japanese submarines damaged in the WWII Aleutian Islands campaign.

bombing of Pearl Harbor, the Japanese military actually put troops on the ground and flew the flag of the rising sun over American soil for nearly a year. The invasion did not come as a total surprise. U.S. military planners knew that the westernmost Aleutian Islands lay closer to Japan than they did to Anchorage, and that San Francisco was 1,000 miles closer to Tokyo via the Aleutians than via Hawaii.

The invasion began as a diversion. In early June of 1942 the Battle of Midway was about to begin some 1,500 miles south of response, the Americans island-hopped out to the Aleutians, setting up bases ever closer to Attu and Kiska. American planes repeatedly bombed the two islands and the supply ships coming from Japan, and American ships fought a major engagement with a big Japanese supply convoy in March 1943. But the main battle occurred in May of that year.

On May 11 some 11,000 American troops landed on Attu, which was defended by 2,600 Japanese soldiers. One of the war's most brutal battles ensued, lasting several weeks. In the end all but 28 Japanese were

Workers endeavor to clean a cormorant befouled by the *Exxon Valdez* oil spill.

dead and American casualties reached nearly 4,000. An equally bloody battle seemed inevitable on Kiska, but the Japanese evacuated the island under cover of fog. When American and Canadian troops stormed ashore, they didn't find anyone to fight.

No more combat occurred in Alaska, but war-related development continued apace, notably the construction of airfields and the Alaska Highway, which finally connected Alaska to the lower 48 by road. Even more significantly, the war brought tens of thousands of American troops to Alaska, many of whom fell in love with the Great Land and returned to live there after the war. World War II rapidly transformed Alaska from a frontier backwater into part of modern America, albeit a part that remained a frontier in most ways.

MODERN TIMES

The end of World War II was soon followed by the beginning of the Cold War. With the Soviet Union looming just miles from Alaska, the military presence in Alaska expanded in the decades following World War II. Mostly due to the influx of military personnel and their families, the population of Anchorage jumped from 3,000 in 1940 to about 47,000 residents 11 years later. By 1950 one in six Alaska residents served in the military. All the new residents plus massive military construction and spending gave the Alaskan economy a huge shot in the arm. As a rapidly modernizing region and a vital link in America's national defense, Alaska was declared a state in 1959.

Statehood notwithstanding, Alaska had one more frontier-like boom up its sleeve. In 1968, oil company geologists found a huge oil field on the North Slope, the vast Arctic Ocean coastal plain north of the Brooks Range. Environmental concerns and Native land rights raised serious questions about the development of this field, particularly the construction of the 800-mile (1,280 km) pipeline to Valdez and the subsequent shipping of oil through pristine waters, but the Arab oil embargo in 1973 gave oil advocates just enough of a boost. Buoyed by the resulting oil shortages, Congress authorized the pipeline in a 50 to 49 vote in the Senate on the key legislation. Oil money soon poured into Alaska and into the coffers of the big oil companies—and oil poured into the waters of Prince William Sound when the *Exxon Valdez* ran aground, in 1989. This episode epitomizes the issues that Alaska faces in the 21st century as it tries to balance the use and conservation of its natural resources. ∎

The arts

FOR A STATE POPULATED BY ONLY 655,400 PEOPLE, ALASKA HAS A VARIED AND vibrant arts scene. The visual arts are especially robust, but lovers of music, theater, dance, and literature also will find much to enjoy. Not surprisingly, given the powerful presence of the surrounding landscape, many Alaskan artists pursue themes related to wilderness, wildlife, and the relationship between human beings and the land. Some express these themes through traditional methods; others use cutting-edge contemporary styles. A few leading artists are mentioned below, but they form just a small sampling of the many who have done or are doing fine work.

VISUAL ARTS

The earliest visual artists were the Alaska Natives from past centuries whose names have been lost to time. Most of their work also has been lost, but a few pieces survive in museum collections. The University of Alaska Museum of the North displays several walrus-ivory toys unearthed in an archaeological dig on St. Lawrence Island. Coastal Eskimos have been carving ivory figures since at least 500 B.C.

A new wave of art washed into Alaska when European explorers arrived. Typically an expedition would bring along an artist the way today's travelers bring along a camera, though some of their drawings and sketches have artistic merit and rise above being mere visual recordings. One well-known officially appointed artist was John Webber, who sailed with Capt. James Cook, the renowned British seafarer, on his third and last voyage, from 1776 to 1780. Webber drew and painted landscapes, wildlife, and some of the Alaska Natives he encountered. On that same trip, William Ellis, the surgeon's mate, also painted some of the sights.

The first professionally trained artist to live in Alaska was Sydney Laurence (1865–1940), who went on to become the state's most famous and influential painter. Born in Brooklyn, he roamed the world as a young man, studying painting in Paris and London. Later he used his talents as an illustrator and photographer to capture the Boxer Rebellion in China, the South African Zulu War, and the Spanish-American War.

In 1904 Laurence headed north to Alaska but for several years he eschewed painting in favor of prospecting—even artists can catch gold fever. Necessity rather than artistic passion forced him

World-renowned Tlingit master carver Nathan Jackson adds his own creative flair to traditional totem pole motifs.

back to his brushes; as he frankly put it, "I was broke and couldn't get away. So I resumed my painting." Laurence generally painted traditional, even iconic Alaskan subjects, such as Mount McKinley and trappers. His specialty was large canvases that glorified Alaska's wild landscapes. Today his major works sell for sums well into six figures. Most of his paintings hang in private collections, but the Anchorage Museum of History & Art and the Alaska Heritage Library Museum (also in Anchorage) have good selections; the former devotes an entire gallery to him.

A contemporary of Laurence's who became nearly as famous was Eustace Ziegler (1881–1969), born in Detroit. He began painting at age 7 and by the time he turned 20 he was selling his work professionally. He had plenty to sell, too; from age 20 until just a few months before his death, at age 87, Ziegler produced about 40 paintings a year. The son of an Episcopal minister, Zeigler came to Cordova, on Prince William Sound, at the request of the Episcopal bishop of Alaska to run the Red Dragon, a nonalcoholic social center and mission. Ziegler later went to divinity school and became a priest, returning to Cordova to preside at St. George's Church.

Like Laurence, Ziegler was fascinated by the Alaskan outdoors, but unlike Laurence, Ziegler was equally fascinated by the people of Alaska. He traveled all over via packhorse,

Totem poles, such as this one at Totem Bight State Historical Park in Ketchikan, convey stories via their intricate details.

canoe, riverboat, and dogsled, meeting folks from all walks of life. In an honest, sympathetic style he painted fishermen, prospectors, Native mothers, gamblers, priests, and prostitutes. He also continued his work as a priest until 1924, when a mural commission in Seattle from the Alaska Steamship Company convinced him to commit full-time to painting. Ziegler eventually moved to Seattle, but he returned to Alaska almost every summer to find renewed inspiration.

Fast-forward now to 2005 and a major solo exhibition entitled "Breakup III" at the Alaska State Museum, in Juneau. Museumgoers wander through a dazzling and befuddling series of works fashioned from tape, light, water, space, and video projections, works that invite viewers to interact with and become part of the pieces. The artist is professor Kat Tomka of the University of Alaska, Anchorage, whose mixed-media work has been shown around the world. She is representative of an active contemporary art scene in Alaska that lies at the opposite end of the artistic spectrum from Laurence and Ziegler. Yet even Tomka notes that her love of translucent tape derives at least in part from the waterproof seal-gut parkas used historically by the Aleut, so some connection to the land and people of the Great Land appears even in her avant-garde work.

NATIVE ARTISTS TODAY

Anolic Unneengnuzinna Aalughuk, also known as Ted Mayac, Sr., is an Inupiat Eskimo from King Island, a pinpoint of land about 30 miles (48 km) off the coast of the remote Seward Peninsula. The Inupiat have been carving walrus ivory for thousands of years and Mayac carries on this tradition, with a few innovations in the way he paints his works. After being employed by the Alaska Department of Transportation for 25 years, Mayac retired; he now carves full-time and is active in the King Island community. Inspired by the migrating birds that pass through the island, he shapes incredibly intricate and life-like figures of some 70 different species, often shown engaged in behaviors that reveal Mayac's intimate knowledge of these birds.

James Schoppert, a Tlingit, deeply respected traditional Alaska Native art, yet in his work he liked to use tradition as a departure point and take off in new, sometimes surreal directions. After studying the history of Alaska Native art, Schoppert decided that innovation was itself a tradition among the indigenous peoples of Alaska. His pieces became a bridge between the past and the future.

A multitalented man, Schoppert painted, carved, taught, wrote poetry, and became a leader among Alaska Native artists. He shared his knowledge widely, teaching in places as disparate as the University of Alaska, Fairbanks, and the Fairbanks Correctional Center. He liked to make elaborate masks, which often reflect his sense of humor. One called "Walrus Goes to

Eskimos have been carving animal figures such as this caribou out of walrus ivory for thousands of years.

Dinner" is a walrus face with a fork and spoon for tusks. Another, based on an old Chugach mask with one ear, Schoppert entitled "Art is a One-eared Madman" as a tribute to Vincent van Gogh. Schoppert died in 1992 at the age of 45.

Sonya Kelliher-Combs, born in Bethel in 1969, is a rising young Alaska Native artist whose methods and media at first glance bear little resemblance to anything in her Inupiat Eskimo or Athabascan heritage. (She also is part German and part Irish.) Yet a closer look reveals certain materials and symbols that hark back to her childhood in Nome, where in the

Intricately and boldly patterned, this work in progress by Donald Varnell, an accomplished Tlingit carver from Saxman Village, near Ketchikan, tells a story through symbolism.

summer she labored at a subsistence lifestyle. For example, in her layers of acrylic polymer—the foundation of much of her work—she sometimes implants walrus stomach, a substance used as a window covering in traditional homes because it lets light in and smoke out. She also implants string, beadwork, seal and pig intestines, net, paper, human hair, and other objects. Kelliher-Combs's work is displayed in Alaska's major museums and galleries and has been shown across the United States and in Canada.

One of the most celebrated and unusual media used by Alaska Native artists is the totem pole—a carved log, usually cedar, that often stands 20 or 30 feet (6 or 9 m) high. (The tallest in Alaska towers 132 feet/ 40.2 meters above the village of Kake, on Kupreanof Island.) Totem poles are part of the Northwest Coast Native culture, which includes the peoples of Southeast Alaska: the Tlingit, Haida, Eyak, and Tsimshian. These traditional works of art got their name because they generally include at least one carved figure representing the totem of a clan or other social group, usually an animal such as a raven, wolf, or orca.

Though often quite artistic, totem poles traditionally are not simply works of art. Some are memorial poles, created as a tribute to an important member of the clan upon his death. Others commemorate major events and tell stories and clan histories. There even are "ridicule" or "shame" poles, erected to shame someone; they are taken down after that person atones for his errant ways. Historically, in a general sense totem poles often were used to display the wealth and power of a clan. Incidentally, the saying "low man on the totem pole" is based on a mistaken idea; the lowest figure on a totem pole often is the most important one.

Perhaps the most famous carver of totem poles today is master carver Nathan Jackson, a Tlingit who for several decades has deftly used his adze to shape beautiful poles that are firmly rooted in tradition yet show a creative flair. His poles stand outside in public places, in Alaska's major museums, and in museums in the lower 48, England, and Japan. He represented Alaska at the Smithsonian Festival of American Folklife. Jackson also is known for carving other objects—masks, canoes, and doors— and for his painting and metalsmithing. Yet his greatest accomplishment may be that he helped revive the once languishing tradition of totem pole carving by motivating a new generation of young Southeast Alaska Natives to learn the art.

PERFORMING ARTS

Alaska has little of the urban critical mass typically needed to support high-level performing arts programs, but Anchorage and certain individual groups do provide excellent music, theater, and dance experiences.

It comes as no surprise that Anchorage occupies center stage in Alaska's performing

ing shows as well as the highly regarded Anchorage Symphony Orchestra (which sells out its 2,000-plus-seat theater every year) and the Anchorage Opera.

Independent performing artists and groups also thrive in Anchorage, epitomized by the group Pamyua (pronounced BUM-yo-ah). A high-energy foursome of young Yupik and Inuit performers who got together in 1996, Pamyua has blossomed into one of Alaska's most beloved groups. They're enjoying success beyond the state, too, appearing at world music festivals and winning record-of-the-year honors at the

Renowned Alaska Native musical group Pamyua performs during a celebration for Native American Grammy nominees in New York City, in 2003.

arts scene, being the only municipality in the state that can lay claim to being a big city. Anchorage also has an advantage over other cities: oil money. Through taxes and direct contributions; the oil companies that loom so large in the Alaskan economy have put millions into the performing arts in Alaska, particularly in Anchorage. The city's Alaska Center for the Performing Arts is an outstanding facility that hosts major travel-

Native American Music Awards in 2003—the first Alaskan artists to win it. But labeling their work as "world music" or "Alaska Native music" doesn't fully capture their diversity and creativity. They blend traditional song, drumming, and dancing in an eclectic style that has hints of jazz, gospel, rhythm and blues, funk, hip-hop, and doo-wop. They even include comedy and Yupik storytelling.

A teacher of fiction in the MFA program at the University of Alaska, Anchorage, Jo-Ann Mapson is a best-selling novelist. *Blue Rodeo* **was turned into a television movie (1996).**

For proof that Anchorage doesn't have a monopoly on performing arts in Alaska, one need look no further than the Perseverance Theatre in Juneau. Considered one of the finest regional theaters in the nation, PT, as locals call it, likes to mix challenging classics with innovative and often edgy lesser-known works. Even the classics range widely, from *Death of a Salesman* to *Hair* to a rendition of *MacBeth* set in Tlingit culture and featuring an all-Alaska Native cast. Nonclassics have included a play about the Columbine High School shootings and a musical about the lives of Filipino Alaskans. PT also aggressively premieres new works, such as Paula Vogel's Pulitzer Prize–winning *How I Learned to Drive,* which she wrote and developed while an artist-in-residence at PT.

LITERATURE

More than most, Alaska is the kind of place that inspires people to write, to grope for the words to capture what they see and to express what they feel. Alaska's authors also have used fiction and poetry to examine life in the Great Land. Certainly this is true for Jerah Chadwick, the Alaska State Writer Laureate in 2005, whose spare poems reflect the stark landscape that envelopes his home on the tundra of the Aleutian island of Unalaska. He moved there in 1982 to raise goats, teach, and write poetry, which he does while living in an abandoned World War II compound.

Place plays a central role in *Ordinary Wolves,* too, an extraordinary novel written by northern Alaska resident and photographer Seth Kantner. "An astounding book," writes Barbara Kingsolver. "A magnificently realized story," says the *New York Times Book Review.* Kantner was born and raised in a sod house on the tundra, fishing, trapping, hunting as part of his family's subsistence lifestyle. This novel delves into the tensions between such old ways and modern America.

These themes also are explored in the fascinating chronicles of recent and contemporary life found in the excellent collection of writings in *Authentic Alaska: Voices of Its Native Writers* (1998), edited by Susan B. Andrews and John Creed. And award winner Sherry Simpson gazes deeply at issues facing America's last frontier in *The Way Winter Comes* (1998).

Other notable Alaska writers include Richard Nelson, a former Alaska State Writer Laureate and the author of many books on Alaskan life, most famously *Make Prayers to the Raven: A Koyukon View of the Northern Forest,* which was made into an award-winning public television series; and Jo-Ann Mapson, who has written eight novels, three of them national best sellers.

And finally, Linda McCarriston and Robert Service, both poets, deserve attention for their compositions. McCarriston, a National Book Award finalist and university professor, pursues complex truths about family life, friendship, and children. Service, on the other hand, came to the Yukon around the Klondike gold rush era. Writing poems for the people and not the critics, Service was beloved in his time. Some of his works, such as *The Cremation of Sam McGee* and *The Shooting of Dan McGrew,* are still memorized in classrooms today. ∎

Southeast Alaska is a remote realm of islands, forests, and mountains. Most people visit to see the stunning scenery and the abundant wildlife, and are pleasantly surprised to find appealing towns and a rich human history.

Southeast Alaska

Introduction & map **48–49**
Ketchikan **50–53**
Cruising through Misty Fiords **54–55**
Wrangell **56–57**
Petersburg **58–59**
Sitka **60–65**
Juneau **70–77**
Glacier Bay National Park & Preserve **78–81**
Haines **82–84**
Skagway **85–87**
Train ride: White Pass & Yukon route **88–89**
More places to visit in Southeast Alaska **90**
Hotels & restaurants **242–244**

The bald eagle, ubiquitous along Alaska's southern coastlines

Southeast Alaska

ALASKA'S PANHANDLE, SOUTHEAST
Alaska consists of a narrow strip of mainland and thousands of islands bounded by
British Columbia and the Coast Mountains to the
east and the Pacific Ocean to the west. Only three
towns—Skagway, Haines, and Hyber—connect to
the rest of Alaska by road, but motorists must drive
hundreds of miles through Canada to get to them.

The rest of the Southeast is only accessible by
air or water, but the plane service is decent
and the opportunities to travel by boat are
legendary. This is the home of the renowned
Inside Passage: the route through protected
waters that slaloms among islands almost the
whole length of the Southeast. Every year
hundreds of thousands of visitors, and many
locals, board cruise ships and ferries to travel
all or part of
this scenic waterway.

Mountains, some
rising thousands of
feet right out of the
sea, seem to tower
everywhere. This cool,
wet region is covered by
temperate rain forest, designated as Tongass National
Forest. (The largest national forest in the United States, it covers
nearly 17 million acres—and nearly 80
percent of the Southeast.) With up to
150 inches of precipitation a year in
some places, the verdant forest of spruce-
and-hemlock stands shrouded in mist and
teeming with life—grizzly (inland), brown
(coastal), and black bears, mountain goats,
wolves, Sitka black-tailed deer, and bald
eagles. Five species of salmon swim up
the rivers and creeks to spawn. The ocean
waters also are full of wildlife, including
humpback whales, sea lions, porpoises,
orcas, and sea otters.

Its natural assets would more than suffice, but the Southeast, home to only 60,000
people, also possesses a rich historical and
cultural heritage—from the indigenous
peoples (primarily the Tlingit but including
Haida, Eyak, and Tsimshian) to the later
Russians, Scandinavians, and late 19th-
century gold seekers—that is richly exhibited in excellent museums, art galleries, festivals, and diverse musical offerings. ∎

**Crab pots indicate one of the livelihoods in
the busy fishing town of Petersburg.**

C

Klondike
Gold Rush
at. Hist. Park
Chilkoot
Trail
White Pass Summit
3,292 ft
SOUTH KLONDIKE HWY.
Taiya
River
7 HAINES HWY.
Dyea 98
Skagway
Chilkoot Lake
State Recreation Site
LUTAK
HWY.
Chilkat
Lake
Haines
Chilkat Bald
agle Preserve
Chilkat Inlet

RUSSIA

International
Date Line

CANADA

Anchorage

Juneau

Area of map detail

SOUTHEAST ALASKA

0   40 miles
0   40 kilometers

GLACIER BAY
IATIONAL PARK
AND PRESERVE
(see p. 81)

D

Echo
Cove
Eagle Beach State
Recreation Area
GLACIER/JUNEAU VETERANS'
MEMORIAL HWY.

CANADA

ardslee
Islands
Bartlett
Cove
Gustavus
Point
ustavus
Mansfield
Peninsula

Mendenhall Glacier
Visitor Center
7
Juneau
Auke
Bay
Douglas
Island
Gastineau
Channel

British
Columbia

Hoonah

Chichagof
Island

Pelican

ADMIRALTY ISLAND
NATIONAL
MONUMENT

Pack
Creek

Admiralty
Island

Angoon

Kootznoowoo
Wilderness

E

Kruzof
Island

TONGASS NATIONAL FOREST

Frederick
Sound

Mount
Edgecumbe ▲
3,201 ft
St. Lazaria
Island

Starrigavan
Recreation Area
Sitka

Baranof
Island

Kake

LeConte
Glacier

Petersburg

Wrangell
Narrows
Mitkof
Island
Stikine

To Telegraph
Creek

Kuiu
Island

Kupreanof
Island
7

Point
Baker

Petroglyph
Beach State
Historic Park

Wrangell

Rainbow
Falls Trail

Wrangell
Island

F

Port
Alexander

Etolin
Island
Blind
Slough

Anan Wildlife
Observatory

Coffman Cove

MISTY FIORDS

Stewart
Hyder

NATIONAL

5

Naukati Bay

rince of
Wales
Island

Thorne
Bay

Revillagigedo
Island

MONUMENT

WILDERNESS
Rudyerd
Bay

Iphigenia
Bay

Klawock

Hollis

Kasaan

New Eddystone
Rock

MISTY FIORDS
NATIONAL
MONUMENT

PACIFIC
OCEAN

Craig

Totem Bight
State Historical Site
Ketchikan
7
Herring
Cove

Rudyerd Island
Point Alava

6

Hydaburg

Metlakatla

Annette
Island

Dixon Entrance

Alaska Marine
Highway

ALEXANDER ARCHIPELAGO

WILDLIFE REFUGE

Sitka Sound

Chatham Strait

Stephens Passage

Sumner Strait

Behm Canal

Revillagigedo Channel

PEABODY MOUNTAINS

Icy Strait

Lynn Canal

Favorite Channel

Glacier Bay

Chatham Strait

Lull Island

Cordova Bay

Ketchikan

Ketchikan

🗺 49 E6

**Visitor
information**

www.visit-ketchikan.com

✉ Ketchikan Visitors
Bureau, 131 Front
St.

☎ 907/225-6166 or
800/770-3300

RAIN OFTEN GREETS PEOPLE AS THEY ARRIVE IN THIS famously soggy town, where an average of about 160 inches of rain falls every year. But the sportfishing and wealth of other attractions—both natural and urban—more than compensate for any meteorological inconveniences.

Many visitors come to chase salmon and halibut. The abundance of salmon and timber led to the founding of the town in the 1880s. By the 1930s more than a dozen canneries annually produced 1.5 million cases of salmon, giving Ketchikan its reputation as the salmon capital of the world. Those numbers have declined, but the industry remains an economic mainstay. These days, tourism is a major employer, mostly catering to the approximately 850,000 cruise-ship visitors who arrive each year.

THE WATERFRONT

Ships tie up at the dock beside the **Waterfront Promenade** along Front Street. (The promenade wraps around the **Thomas Basin Boat Harbor,** where the commercial fishing fleet docks.) This is the perfect place to begin a tour of Ketchikan.

Among the first things you'll notice is that dozens of galleries and shops line the streets. Most galleries feature a wealth of locally made art. Many Tlingit, Eyak, Haida, and Tsimshian artists, both traditional and contemporary, work here. World-renowned master carver Nathan Jackson, recipient of a National Heritage Fellowship, has striking totem poles and other carvings on display in galleries, museums, and outdoor public spaces. (For information on all the galleries, ask the visitors bureau for the "Ketchikan Arts Guide.") A good place to start exploring is the historic **Star Building** *(5 Creek St., tel 907/ 225-5954),* which houses two galleries that carry the work of many locals: **Soho Coho** *(tel 907/225-5954)* and **Alaska Eagle Arts** *(tel 907/225-8365).*

The **Southeast Alaska Discovery Center** on the promenade displays a fine collection of Native art. The lobby features three sumptuous totems, one Tlingit style, one Haida, and one Tsimshian. The center presents other aspects of Native life, too; one exhibit re-creates a traditional fish camp and another allows visitors to listen to recordings of Native elders discussing their past and present ways of life. However, the majority of the space is devoted to the natural world and the use of natural resources. The rain forest exhibit comes complete with running water and birdcalls. Interactive exhibits detail all seven of the main ecosystems in the Southeast, from tide pools to alpine tundra.

If in the mood for something lighter, stroll across the street to the **Great Alaskan Lumberjack Show** *(420 Spruce Mill Way, tel 907/225-9050 or 888/320-9049, $$$$$).* Part-show, part-contest, these programs feature highly skilled individuals who compete against each other in numerous events, including sawing, chopping, log-rolling, and the astounding speed climb, in which the contestants ascend very tall poles with monkey-like quickness.

Southeast Alaska Discovery Center
www.fs.fed.us/r10/tongass
✉ 50 Main St.
☎ 907/228-6220
$ $ May–Sept., free Oct.–April

Waterfront diners relish a sunny day in Ketchikan.

Lush vegetation along the trail to Punchbowl Cove in Misty Fiords bears testament to the area's rainfall.

ALONG KETCHIKAN CREEK

Ketchikan's past is conjured up at the **Tongass Historical Museum** (*629 Dock St., 907/225-5600, open daily in summer, Wed.–Sun. in winter, $*), which shares a building with the library on the bank of Ketchikan Creek. Visitors can progress from the town's early incarnation as a Tlingit fish camp through the mining, timber, and fishing eras to the present. A shadier past, of which Ketchikan seems quite proud, can be explored by following the creek downstream for a block and crossing the bridge to Creek Street. The red-light district until the 1950s, **Creek Street** was the place where "both fish and fishermen went upstream to spawn," as the local joke goes. Built on boardwalks above the creek, the district now houses shops, galleries, and restaurants.

A ways up Ketchikan Creek, appropriately on Salmon Street, sits the **Deer Mountain Tribal Hatchery and Eagle Center** (*1158 Salmon Rd., 907/225-6760 or 800/252-5158, open daily May–Sept., $$*). The hatchery supplements the natural king and coho salmon and steelhead and rainbow trout runs in the creek where they have spawned for ages. The coho come up in the fall and winter, but the kings surge upstream in August. The hatchery tour provides information about salmon and takes visitors to see the bald eagles at the adjoining eagle center.

Facing the hatchery from across the creek is the **Totem Heritage Center** (*601 Deermount St., 907/225-5900, open daily May–Sept., Mon.–Fri. rest of year, $$*). The beautiful contemporary totem pole "Raven-Fog Woman," created by Nathan Jackson, stands outside; however, the center focuses on rescuing old, unrestored poles from abandoned Native villages. The center also contains displays of Native beadwork and basket weaving, and sometimes visitors can see artists at work.

TONGASS HIGHWAY

If the beauty and mythology of totem poles capture your imagination, drive 2.5 miles (4 km) south on the shore-hugging South Tongass Highway, and then go left one block on Totem Row (look for the totem poles) to the **Saxman Native Village and Totem Park,** which boasts one

Saxman Native Village & Totem Park
www.capefoxtours.com
☎ 907/225-4846, ext. 103
💲 $$$$. Tickets at gift shop across the street; call for reservations

of the largest collections of standing poles in the world. Note the plain-shafted pole topped by the figure of former Secretary of State William H. Seward—the man who acquired Alaska for the United States. Rumor has it that this is a ridicule pole carved because Seward visited a Tlingit village in 1869 and didn't reciprocate the gifts and hospitality shown him by the villagers. You may look around on your own or you can go on a two-hour tour, which includes watching a traditional dance performance, observing artists at work, hearing stories about the totems, and visiting the tribal house.

About 6 miles (9.6 km) farther south on the highway, turn left on Wood Road and drive a quarter mile to the **Alaska Rainforest Sanctuary.** The 1.75-hour tour leads through a second-growth rain forest and the Eagle Creek Estuary; watch for black bears, bald eagles, seals, and the spawning salmon that entice these birds and animals. The tour also takes in a historic sawmill, resident reindeer, and the working studio of a master carver. The sanctuary has seven zip lines, which enable securely harnessed customers to slide slowly through the treetops 130 feet (40 m) above the forest

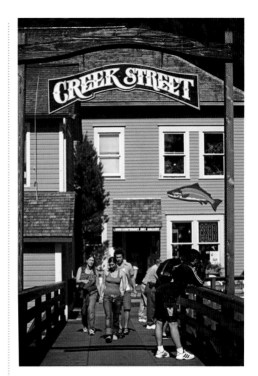

floor. Proceed at your own risk.

More totem poles are on display at the **Totem Bight State Historical Park,** 10 miles (16 km) north of Ketchikan on the North Tongass Highway. A short trail leads through lovely seaside forest to 14 totem poles and a copy of a clan house. A brochure reveals the complexities of art and culture represented. ■

Now home to upscale shops, Creek Street used to be Ketchikan's red-light district.

Alaska Rainforest Sanctuary

⊠ 116 Wood Rd.
☎ 907/225-5503
🕐 Open May–Sept.
$ $$$$$

Totem Bight State Historical Park
www.dnr.state.ak.us/units/totembgh.htm
🅰 49 E6
⊠ 9883 N. Tongass Hwy.
☎ 907/247-8574

Tsimshian of Annette Islands

Unlike the Tlingit, Eyak, and Haida, the Tsimshian people are relative newcomers to Alaska. Their ancestral homeland is in British Columbia, but in the late 1800s a group of Tsimshian led by Church of England missionary William Duncan applied to the U.S. for religious asylum. Granted permission to settle on Annette Island, a few miles south of Ketchikan, some 800 Tsimshian moved there from Old Metlakatla and founded New Metlakatla in 1887. Today the community is just called Metlakatla. In 1891, the U.S. government formally recognized the community and established the Annette Islands Reserve, the only federal Indian reserve in Alaska. ■

Cruising through Misty Fiords

Misty Fiords National Monument is as striking and mysterious as its name suggests. A vista of lofty waterfalls, bald eagles, volcanic plugs, harbor seals, rugged mountains, and lush rain forest unfolds before you as your tour boat delves deep into Misty's 2.2 millions acres, almost all of it wilderness. You'll also likely see bears and salmon and perhaps killer whales, humpback whales, deer, and river otters. Some people cruise round-trip, but most fly back on a floatplane, a wonderful experience in itself.

The calm waters of the Behm Canal reflect the towering splendors of Misty Fiords.

After weighing anchor in Ketchikan, the boat cruises *(for list of tour operators contact Ketchikan Visitors Bureau; see p. 50)* east down Tongass Narrows and out into Revillagigedo Channel. To the south lies Annette Island, the only Native American reservation in Alaska (see sidebar p. 53). At Point Alava the channel turns south and the tour turns north into the monument via **Behm Canal** ①. Handsome Behm Canal is a nearly straight, 100-mile-long (160 km), 2-to-4-miles-wide (3.2 to 6.4 km) natural waterway, framed at this end by low mountains and curtains of hemlock, spruce, and cedar. Scan the tall trees along the shore for eagles and their nests.

After about 8 miles (12.8 km), the boat steers for the western shore and squeezes through the narrows between Revillagigedo (the big island that is home to Ketchikan) and little **Rudyerd Island** ②. Back in the 1920s, a local established a fox farm here—a common enterprise in Alaska at that time, when fox furs were popular. Abundant fish

made feeding the foxes easy. The Great Depression and the fact that southeastern Alaska is a little too warm for foxes brought this and other fox farms to an end. However, their remote locations appealed to bootleggers, who during Prohibition smuggled liquor into the United States from Canada through places like Rudyerd Island.

About 15 miles (24 km) up Behm Canal from Rudyerd Island, **New Eddystone Rock** ③ juts 237 feet (72 m) above the water. A six-million-year-old volcanic plug, the remains of an eroded volcano, this landmark was named in 1793 by Capt. George Vancouver for its resemblance to the lighthouse on Eddystone Rock in the English Channel. (A few years ago a couple decided to have their wedding here, but they forgot to consult a tide table and they were knee-deep in water halfway through the ceremony and had to flee.)

A couple of miles north of New Eddystone the tour turns east into **Rudyerd Bay** ④, one of the gorgeous fjords for which the monument is named. Waterfalls pour off burly granite cliffs, which shoulder in close around this half-mile-wide waterway. A few miles along the boat stops in **Punchbowl Cove** ⑤, facing a sheer, 3,000-foot (914 m) cliff that only a handful of climbers have conquered. Nearby is a pictograph (rock carving) thought to mark the grave of a Tlingit shaman. Several miles deeper into the fjord, **Nooya Creek** ⑥ tumbles into the bay; look for salmon mid-July through September and for the bears, seals, and eagles that come for a fish feed. From way back here in Rudyerd Bay, most boat passengers opt to catch a 30-minute flight back to Ketchikan aboard a floatplane for a uniquely different perspective of the Misty Fiords. ∎

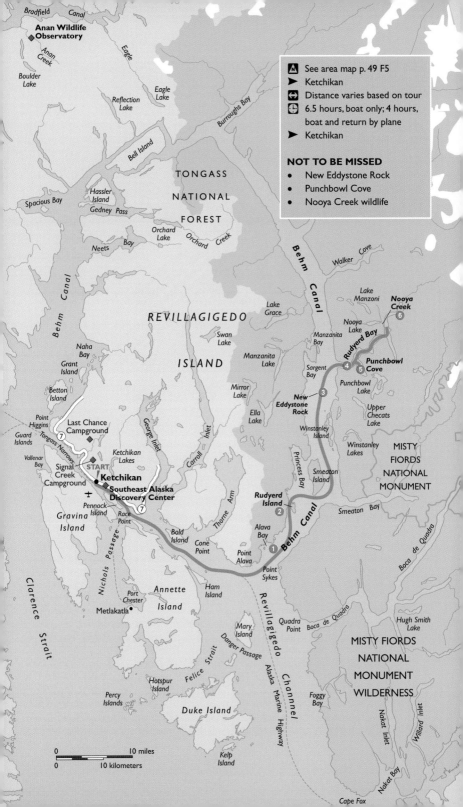

Bradfield Canal

Anan Wildlife Observatory

Anan Creek

Boulder Lake

Eagle

Eagle Lake

Reflection Lake

Burroughs Bay

Spacious Bay

Hassler Island

Gedney Pass

Bell Island

TONGASS

NATIONAL

FOREST

Orchard Lake

Orchard Creek

Neets Bay

REVILLAGIGEDO

Swan Lake

Lake Grace

ISLAND

Naha Bay

Grant Island

Betton Island

Point Higgins

Guard Islands

Vallenar Bay

Signal Creek Campground

Last Chance Campground

Tongass Narrows

George Inlet

Ketchikan Lakes

Mirror Lake

Ella Lake

Manzanita Lake

Carroll Inlet

START

Ketchikan

Southeast Alaska Discovery Center

Pennock Island

Race Point

Gravina Island

Nichols Passage

Bold Island

Cone Point

Thorne Arm

Point Alava

Point Sykes

Behm Canal

Walker Cove

Lake Manzoni

Nooya Creek

Nooya Lake

⑥

Manzanita Bay

Rudyerd Bay

④

⑤ **Punchbowl Cove**

Sargent Bay

③

Punchbowl Lake

New Eddystone Rock

Upper Checats Lake

Winstanley Island

Winstanley Lakes

MISTY FIORDS NATIONAL MONUMENT

Princess Bay

Smeaton Island

Rudyerd Island

②

Alava Bay

①

Behm Canal

Smeaton Bay

Boca de Quadra

Port Chester

Metlakatla

Annette Island

Ham Island

Mary Island

Danger Passage

Quadra Point

Boca de Quadra

Hugh Smith Lake

Clarence Strait

Felice Strait

Hotspur Island

Percy Islands

Duke Island

Revillagigedo Channel

Alaska Marine Highway

Kelp Island

Foggy Bay

MISTY FIORDS NATIONAL MONUMENT WILDERNESS

Nakat Bay

Willard Inlet

Cape Fox

⑦ See area map p. 49 F5

▶ Ketchikan

↔ Distance varies based on tour

⏱ 6.5 hours, boat only; 4 hours, boat and return by plane

▶ Ketchikan

NOT TO BE MISSED
- New Eddystone Rock
- Punchbowl Cove
- Nooya Creek wildlife

0   10 miles

0   10 kilometers

Wrangell

TRAVELERS SEEKING AUTHENTIC SOUTHEAST ALASKA should head for Wrangell. Situated on the northern tip of Wrangell Island, this friendly town of 2,000 is the kind of place where visitors can easily strike up a conversation with someone sitting at a café or watching the fishing boats from the pier. Wrangell also serves as a jumping-off point to the LeConte Glacier, Anan Wildlife Observatory, and the Stikine River—all Southeast treasures.

Wrangell
🗺 49 E5
Visitor information
www.wrangell.com
✉ Wrangell Visitor Center, 296 Outer Dr.
☎ 907/874-3699

Wrangell Museum
✉ 296 Outer Dr.
☎ 907/874-3770 or 800/367-9745
🕐 Mon.–Fri. May–Sept., Tues.–Fri. Oct.–April

The Wrangell Visitor Center is housed in the James and Elsie Nolan Center, most of which is devoted to the **Wrangell Museum.** This museum is much larger and finer than one would expect in a town of this size. It covers the town's unique history; the only town that was governed by four sovereigns—the Tlingit, Russians, British, and Americans. Just inside the museum's entrance stand four of Alaska's oldest carved house posts, fine Tlingit work dating from the late 1700s. The museum also displays photos from the rowdy decades following the 1861 gold rush on the Stikine. One exhibit tells how Wyatt Earp filled in as a deputy marshal for ten days and had to disarm a man whom Earp subsequently recognized as a fellow he'd arrested 20 years earlier in Dodge City.

Connected to the south end of downtown by a narrow footbridge is **Chief Shakes Island** *(end of Shakes St., tel 907/874-3747 or 866-874-2023).* In the bustling harbor this small island is an oasis of calm and reflection as you walk around the **Tribal House** and the **Community House;** contemplate the totem poles that encircle the latter. Aptly, ravens often perch in the trees above the raven totem pole. Scattered about the beach a mile (1.6 km) north of town at **Petroglyph Beach State Historic Site** are artifacts from even older Native inhabitants. Even Native elders don't know the origins of the petroglyphs that are perhaps 8000 years old. Search the boulders and exposed bedrock near the interpretive platform and you may discover as many as 40 of the mysterious rock carvings, including representative figures, like killer whales, and abstract images, like circles and spirals.

South of town thousands of square miles of Wrangell Island await exploration via several trails that spread out from a few decent roads and numerous less-decent logging roads. One of the finest trails, the **Rainbow Falls Trail** *(Tongass National Forest, Wrangell Ranger District, tel 907/874-2323),* starts just 4.5 miles (7.2 km) south of Wrangell on the Zimovia Highway, just opposite the Shoemaker Bay Campground. It winds 0.7 mile (1.1 km) through old-growth forest to 100-foot-tall (30.5 m) Rainbow Falls.

NEARBY ATTRACTIONS
Thirty-five miles (56 km) away, **Anan Creek** holds the title of largest pink salmon run in the Southeast, holding some 100,000 fish. The abundance of fish attracts both brown and black bears to the creek. Visitors can safely view bears snagging salmon from the **Anan Wildlife Observatory** *(Tongass National Forest, tel 907/225-3101, reservations required July–Aug.).*

Many people are equally thrilled by **LeConte Glacier,** a tidewater glacier located in a snowcap-ringed fjord about 25 miles (40 km) north of Wrangell. An extremely active glacier, it routinely calves icebergs. The area is also home to a seal nursery.

The closest natural wonder to Wrangell is the **Stikine River,** a swift, massive, 400-mile-long (643 km) river that drains mountains and glaciers from a vast chunk of British Columbia. A number of tour boats operating

out of Wrangell *(for information contact Wrangell Visitor Center)* offer day trips that pass through country studded with stunning glaciers, icebergs, brown and black bears, moose, spawning salmon, bald eagles, and even hot springs. Hardy travelers can go on an overnight journey 130 miles upriver to **Telegraph Creek,** the only settlement on the Stikine. ∎

Rock carvings thousands of years old lie scattered across Petroglyph Beach.

Petersburg

Petersburg's Norwegian roots and fishing heritage are evident throughout town.

PROUD OF ITS NORWEGIAN TIES, PETERSBURG BILLS ITSELF as Alaska's Little Norway. Indeed, this heritage is displayed in numerous ways, such as the frequent use of the word "Velkommen" by local businesses, the annual Little Norway Festival, the reproduction Viking ship that sits downtown, and the house and building exteriors that feature rosemaling—the colorful, flowing floral painting that developed as a folk art in Norway in the mid-18th century.

Workers at Icicle Seafoods process salmon roe.

However, this tidy town of 3,100 and its splendid natural setting on the northern tip of Mitkof Island (the mountains and narrow waterways reminded Petersburg's founders of the fjord country back home in Norway) offer much more to visitors than Norwegian flavors.

The town's major industry is readily apparent along the waterfront. Three adjacent harbors sheltering hundreds of trollers, gillnetters, long-liners, and other fishing boats make Petersburg a top fishing port. Some of the waterside big seafood-processing plants offer tours *(for more information contact the Petersburg visitor center).*

A block off Middle and South Harbors is **Sing Lee Alley,** the town's historical heart and a pleasant shopping district. Within its few blocks visitors will find **Sing Lee Alley Books** *(11 Sing Lee Alley, tel 907/772-4440),* which sells many Alaskan titles and maps; **Cubby Hole** *(14 Sing Lee Alley, tel 907/772-2717),* for souvenirs brightened by beautiful rosemaling; **Tonka Seafoods** *(22 Sing Lee Alley, tel 907/772-3662 or 888/560-3662, tours Mon.–Sat., $$)*, where you can pick up some smoked salmon to nibble or ship a crate of savory seafood home; and the **Sons of Norway Hall** *(23 Sing Lee Alley, tel 907/772-4575)*, a national historic site built in 1912 on pilings over Hammer Slough. This lovely building and others hanging over the slough offer some of the finest examples of rosemaling in Petersburg.

For learning about the history and culture of Petersburg and vicinity, there's no place better than the **Clausen Memorial Museum.** It houses Tlingit artifacts, a massive lighthouse lens, a dugout canoe, and a stuffed salmon so big that it brings fishermen to their knees in awe; this 126.5-pound (57.4-kg) chinook is thought to be the world's largest salmon ever caught.

MITKOF HIGHWAY

The Mitkof Highway heads south from Petersburg along the scenic Wrangell Narrows and affords easy exploration of some of the outlying parts of Mitkof Island. The first 17.3 miles (27.8 km) are paved and the last 16.5 (26.5 km) are decent gravel. Near Mile 14 the road intersects the **Blind River Rapids Boardwalk.** This quarter-mile (0.4 km) trail crosses muskeg bogs, which cover much of the island, to a favorite fishing spot with the locals. The highway turns inland shortly after the boardwalk and heads southeast. At Mile 16.2, the **Blind Slough Swan Observatory** hosts hundreds of migrating trumpeter swans in late fall; some 50 to 75 stay the winter. In summer, visitors may spy salmon a little downriver—and bears fishing

Public use cabins

If you want a roof over your head (and a solid wall between you and the bears), consider renting a public use cabin. These basic accommodations—usually just bunks for four to six people, a table, some chairs, and maybe a wood- or oil-burning stove—are generally located in remote and scenic places, accessible only by small plane or boat, though a few are along trails or roads. They are very popular and can be reserved up to six months in advance. The Southeast's **Tongass National Forest** *(tel 907/228-6220, www.fs.fed.us/r10/tongass/cabins/cabin_info.shtml)* has more than 170 cabins and shelters. ∎

Whales frequent the waters of Frederick Sound, near Petersburg, in summer.

Petersburg
🅰 49 E4

Visitor information
www.petersburg.org
✉ Petersburg Visitor Information Center, 1st & Fram Sts.
☎ 907/772-4636
🕐 Open daily in summer, Mon.–Fri. in winter

Clausen Memorial Museum
www.clausenmuseum.alaska.net
✉ 203 Fram St.
☎ 907/772-3598
🕐 Open Mon.–Sat. in summer
💲 $

for those spawners. For its last few miles, the highway hugs the eastern shore of the island and looks across at the mouth of the glorious Stikine River (see p. 57). Boat trips can be arranged via tour operators in Petersburg (or Wrangell; see p. 56). ∎

Sitka

Sitka

🅰 49 C4

Visitor information

www.sitka.org

✉ Sitka Convention & Visitors Bureau, Box 1226, 303 Lincoln St., Sitka, AK 99835

☎ 907/747-5940

EVEN BY INSIDE PASSAGE STANDARDS SITKA IS REMOTE because, technically speaking, it's not in the Inside Passage. Of all the southeastern Alaska ports served by the Marine Highway and visited by cruise ships, only Sitka lies on the outside, facing the open Pacific. This means the town occasionally gets hammered by winter storms, but the summer weather is about average for the region.

Sitka was a busy port during the first half of the 19th century, when Novo Arkhangelsk (New Archangel, the early Russian name for what is now Sitka) was the capital of Russian Alaska. The ships coming for sea otter pelts brought merchandise from around the globe and Sitka became, for a New World outpost, a large and sophisticated town by the mid-1830s. One admittedly overheated but not entirely irrational visitor dubbed it the "Paris of the Pacific."

Contemporary Sitka retains many of its past characteristics. This town of 8,800 (the fifth most populous city in Alaska) still features a frenetic port, with a large commercial fishing fleet, hundreds of charter fishing boats, many private boats, and cruise ships visiting several times a week during the summer. And the spice of Tlingit and Russian culture still seasons the town.

CASTLE HILL
Baranof Castle Hill State Historic Site (*between foot of John O'Connell Bridge and back of Harry Race Pharmacy on Lincoln St.*) makes a fine starting point for three reasons: though not even 100 feet (30.5 m) high, Castle Hill provides a 360-degree view of the town and surroundings; it lies between the terrestrial attractions and the marine activities; and it served as the starting point for American Alaska. On October 18,

1867, the Russians lowered their flag here and the Americans raised theirs, signaling the change in ownership of Alaska.

As you stroll around the perimeter, brace yourself for the staggering beauty of Sitka's setting: mountains and forest to the north and east and islands and ocean to the south and west.

St. Micheal's Cathedral, a Russian Orthodox church, sits at the head of Sitka's main drag, Lincoln Street.

Drinking in the scenery will occupy you for a while, but when you eventually set your sights a little lower, you can see the layout of the town. Downtown lies immediately below Castle Hill and consists of just a few square blocks. The clustered part of town fans out a little beyond downtown, but the rest of Sitka, mostly residential, stretches out along the shore for several miles both east and west.

Note the John O'Connell Bridge visitor dock below to the south. Because Sitka lacks a dock that can accommodate large cruise ships, during the summer a fleet of tenders is in perpetual motion ferrying passengers from the ships anchored in the harbor to the O'Connell Dock. You may notice a bumper sticker battle between locals who support expanding the port facilities and those who oppose it. One clever anti sticker reads "Resist Pier Pressure."

LINCOLN STREET & AROUND
Walking from Castle Hill up Lincoln Street, Sitka's main drag downtown, the first street to the left is Katlian Street. Look down and you'll see a building with a striking carved-and-painted entryway, the **Sheet'ka Kwaan Naa Kahidi Tribal Community House** *(200 Katlian St., tel 907/747-7137 or*

The MV *Observer*, a small cruise ship that operates between Juneau and Sitka, eases into the dock in Sitka harbor.

Sitka National Historical Park
www.nps.gov/sitk
✉ 106 Monastery St.
☎ 907/747-0110
🕐 Visitor center open daily; Russian Bishop's House open daily May–late Sept., by appt. Oct.–April
💲 $ (guided tour of Russian Bishop's House)

Alaska Raptor Center
www.alaskaraptor.org
✉ 1000 Raptor Way
☎ 907/747-8662 or 800/463-9425
🕐 Open Sun.–Fri. May–Sept.
💲 $$

888/270-8687)—a modern version of a traditional clan house. The Tlingit name roughly translates to "a house for the people of Sitka." During the summer, visitors can watch a 30-minute song-and-dance performance by the renowned Naa Kahidi Native Dancers, a performance that the local Tlingit say has changed little in thousands of years. The elaborately costumed dancers stage one to three performances daily when large cruise ships are in port. Private shows can be arranged *(contact the community house).*

The blocks of Lincoln Street nearest to the John O'Connell Bridge visitor dock contain many souvenir and luxury shops, but sprinkled among them are some estimable local stores and galleries. The **Artist Cove Gallery** *(241 Lincoln St., tel 907/747-6990)* features the work of local artists and of Northwest Coast and Southeast Native and Inupiat Eskimo artists.

Four blocks from the waterfront, at the confluence with Cathedral Way, Lincoln Street

splits like a river meeting a rock and flows around **St. Michael's Cathedral** *(tel 907-747-8120, open weekdays in summer, donation).* A national historic landmark, this beautiful Russian Orthodox church dates from the mid- to late 1840s. The original building burned down in 1966, but residents saved many of the artifacts from the flames. In 1967, a near-replica of the original was erected on the site and filled with the rescued treasures.

The secular history of Sitka can be explored at the **Isabel Miller Museum** *(330 Harbor Dr., tel 907/747-6455, www.sitkahistory .org, open most days May–Sept., Tues.–Sat. rest of year, donation),* located in Harrigan Centennial Hall near the entrance to Crescent Harbor. The centerpiece of this modest museum is a sprawling detailed model of 1867 Sitka. The old photos are worth a closer look; check out the grinning woman in the pioneer-style full-length dress leading the sprint in an old Fourth of July race. Harrigan Centennial Hall also hosts the esteemed **New Archangel Dancers** *(tel 907/ 747-5516, www.newarchangel dancers.com, summer shows, $)*, women who perform authentic folk dances from Russia.

SITKA NATIONAL HISTORIC PARK

The town's premier historic attraction, Sitka National Historical Park was established to commemorate the Battle of Sitka, an 1804 conflict between the Tlingit and the Russians. The park consists of two sites. The **Russian Bishop's House,** on Lincoln Street between Monastery and Baranof Streets, dates back to 1842 and is one of only four original Russian structures remaining in the Western Hemisphere. Constructed from Sitka spruce, this restored original housed bishops from its completion until 1969. They oversaw an enormous Russian Orthodox diocese that encompassed part of Alaska, Siberia, and reached all the way down the Pacific coast to California. The ground floor displays include elaborate clerical garments and a big brass samovar.

The **Tlingit Fort Site** begins a few blocks from the Russian Bishop's House, at the end of Lincoln Street. The **Visitor Center and Southeast Alaska Indian Cultural Center** contains artifacts that tell the stories of both cultures before and after the battle. Though few in number, the objects are of high quality; note the ceremonial bone dagger inlaid with abalone and the bib made from red, yellow, white, black, blue, and turquoise beads. Native artists work at the center; visitors are encouraged to watch them carve and weave and to talk with them about their art. Outside,

miles of easy trails cut through the park's forests that border Sitka Sound and the estuary of the Indian River. The area south of the estuary features totem poles and the 1804 battle site; the northern area contains picnic areas and the Russian Memorial.

Along the northern boundary of the park perches the **Alaska Raptor Center.** The center rehabilitates and, when possible, releases back into the wild raptors and other birds. In order to educate people about birds of prey, the center makes presentations using their permanent residents, including bald and golden eagles, a peregrine falcon, and a great horned owl.

Just west of the park, the airy confines of the **Sheldon Jackson Museum** house one of the finest Native art collections in southeastern Alaska. During the late 1800s teacher and missionary Rev. Dr. Sheldon Jackson accumulated a vast collection of Native artifacts from all over Alaska—ranging from scary shaman masks and food dishes carved to look like bears to armor made from walrus ivory and mukluks (boots) fashioned from fish skins. Informational panels make the Native way of life emerge from these objects. The Eskimo whaling outfit, for example, a bearded- seal-skin creation that looks like a space suit, is waterproof and airtight. It was worn while butchering whales, which required

Sheldon Jackson Museum
www.museums.state.ak.us
✉ 104 College Dr.
☎ 907/747-8981
🕒 Open daily in summer, Tues.—Sat. in winter
💲 $

Several fine totem poles grace Sitka National Historic Park.

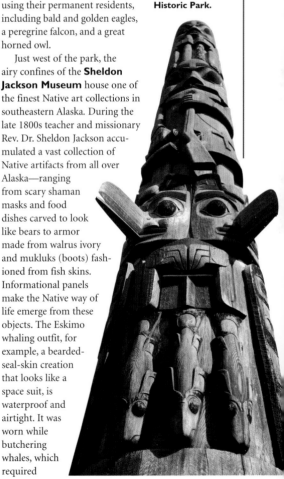

The architectural setting of the Sheldon Jackson Museum complements the collections.

Starrigavan Recreation Area
www.fs.fed.us/r10/tongass
49 C4
Tongass National Forest, Sitka Ranger District, 204 Siginaka Way, Suite 109, Sitka, AK 99835
907/747-6671

wading in icy water because the dead whales were floated in the shallows. The dozens of drawers inside this circular building are a treasure trove of smaller bits and pieces of bygone days.

STARRIGAVAN RECREATION AREA

The Tongass National Forest embraces Sitka. Starrigavan Recreation Area, 7 miles (11 km) north of town on Halibut Point Road, offers an excellent and easily accessible introduction to the land. The area's three trails provide a glimpse of most of the region's main ecosystems; if you want to learn about them in some depth, consider going on one of the guided hikes offered by Sitka tour operators and by the nonprofit Sitka Trail Works *(801 Halibut Point Rd., tel 907/747-7244, www.sitkatrailworks.org).*

The **Forest and Muskeg Trail,** an easy, 0.75-mile (1.2 km) jaunt, winds through spruce-

hemlock forest and along a boardwalk through muskeg (peat bog) populated by a diverse array of tiny mosses and tiny but voracious sundews—carnivorous plants smaller than a dime. At the east end of the trail you can cross the bridge over Starrigavan Creek and start right into the **Estuary Life Trail,** a quarter-mile (0.4 km) boardwalk that slips through the marshes of the creek's estuary. In July, thousands of pink salmon spawn in the creek. If you visit the estuary in the early morning, you'll likely spot a variety of birds and maybe a brown bear or a Sitka black-tailed deer.

Walk about 200 yards (183 m) north from the bird-viewing shelter at the end of the estuary trail and you come to the recreation area's campground. Continue north to the far end, less than a quarter mile (0.4 km), and you'll come to the finest of the three hikes: the **Mosquito Cove Trail.** This 1.25-mile (2 km) loop hugs the beautiful shores of Starrigavan Bay and Mosquito Cove for about 0.75 mile (1.2 km) and then circles back through the heart of the temperate coastal rain forest.

SITKA SOUND

The sound nurtures a rich marine ecosystem. In addition to the charismatic megafauna—whales, seals, sea otters—vast numbers of other creatures favor Alaska's chilly waters, which are among the most productive in the world. You can scuba dive in the sound, but the semi-submersible **M.V. Sea Life Discovery** *(Crescent Harbor or Thomsen Harbor, tel 877/966-2301, www.greenlingenterprises.com, tours May–Sept., $$$$$)* offers a warmer option. Passengers sit in a glass-enclosed hull while a guide provides a running commentary and points out myriad creatures.

The eelgrass beds are home to sunflower stars (sea stars)—which have as many as 24 rays and grow as big as 3 feet (1 m) across—radiant tan-amber-white-bodied lion's mane jellyfish, pipefish, gunnels, red rock crabs, hooded nudibranchs, and orange sea cucumbers. The giant kelp beds harbor northern brown turban snails, shrimp, and northern kelp crabs. Deeper denizens of the sound include scallops, sea peaches, tube worms, and wolf eels.

Hundreds of boats ply Sitka Sound and more distant coastal waters. A large majority of them cater to anglers dreaming of hooking a halibut or a salmon in this fish-friendly habitat. A few boats offer tours of the sound, the coast, and the many islands. Tour offerings vary greatly—from small boats to large cruisers, from one-hour tours to all-day excursions—with something for everyone *(for information contact the Sitka visitors bureau; see p. 60).*

Whichever you choose, no doubt you'll see sea otters floating on their backs, munching shellfish or cuddling their pups. Maybe you'll cruise through the immense shadow of **Mount Edgecumbe,** the 3,201-foot (975.7 m) volcano that looms 10 miles (16 km) west of Sitka on Kruzof Island. (Hardy trekkers can hike and scramble 7 miles/ 11.2 km to its summit; the trail

The M.V. *Sea Life Discovery* semi-submersible provides a scuba-diver's view of a sunflower star.

starts at Fred Creek's Cabin.) You'll typically see at least one humpback whale; the boat captain may cut the engines so you can listen to the humpback's blow.

If the seas aren't rough, the boat may head to **St. Lazaria Island** *(landing not allowed),* which forms part of the **Alaska Maritime National Wildlife Refuge** (see pp. 164–165), a conglomerate of 2,500 coastal islands, spires, rocks, and headlands stretching all around Alaska. The island's 65 acres teem with hundreds of thousands of nesting seabirds in the summer. You'll see kittiwakes wheeling boisterously around the steep cliffs, cormorants spreading their wings to dry, and the ever popular tufted puffins diving for food. ■

Traveling the Inside Passage

Southeast Alaska is a water world. To experience it fully, one must meet it on its own terms, and that means traveling by ship on the Inside Passage. This virtual marine highway stretches some 900 nautical miles (1,667 km) from Vancouver, British Columbia, to Skagway, Alaska, connecting villages, towns, and cities. (See map inside back cover.)

The passage snakes through hundreds of islands, squeezing into straits, narrows, and sounds. The islands buffer these inside waters from the fierce winds and storms of the Pacific Ocean, but navigational challenges abound: summer fog, swift currents, tidal rips, whirlpools, icebergs, sandbars, and suckholes, to name but a few. Despite these hazards, traveling the Inside Passage is one of the great scenic adventures of a lifetime. Travelers instinctively realize this. Maybe 20,000 visitors fly into a typical mainline Southeast port in a year, while some 850,000 arrive by cruise ship.

Some people navigate through the Inside Passage on their own vessels. Others charter a yacht or a cabin cruiser. But those are exceptions. Nearly everyone travels one of three ways: aboard a big cruise ship, aboard a small cruise ship, or aboard the ferries of the Alaska Marine Highway.

BIG CRUISE SHIPS

More than 95 percent of travelers choose to travel the passage aboard big cruise ships—some carry more than 2,500 passengers plus crews. Having become a premier destination, the Southeast attracts ships that are not only large but elaborate, the finest the industry has to offer. They feature health spas, towering atriums, discos, musical shows that take a page from Las Vegas, pools, cabarets, casinos, and those legendary buffets of fine food in quantities that would sink smaller ships.

In addition to all the shipboard activities, most cruise ships offer a smorgasbord of shore excursions, from shopping and bus tours to kayaking and helicopter landings on glaciers. These trips range from a few hours to most of the day, depending on port time, but passengers almost always return to the ship for the night. Given the brevity of shore excursions and the fact that shipboard entertainment is so plentiful, these cruises provide mainly a scenic overview of Southeast Alaska.

The beautiful snowcapped and rain forest–clad mountains of the Inside Passage tower over even the biggest cruise ships.

SMALL CRUISE SHIPS

Small cruise ships get passengers closer to land—literally and figuratively. Depending on the operator, these ships hold anywhere from 10 to 250 passengers. Their smaller size and shallower draft allow the ships to slip into nooks and crannies the big ships can't fit into and they can cruise closer to shore, making wildlife and glacier viewing better.

More important, the focus on board the smaller cruise ships is on Southeast Alaska, not shipboard entertainment. The smaller ships frequently offer talks by expert natu-ralists or Native Alaskans, and they often stop overnight in ports inaccessible to the big ships. The shore excursions tend to visit less traveled places, too. The drawbacks? These boats do not have as many amenities as the big cruise ships (which some passengers may not consider a drawback), and they are often more expensive than the big ships.

ALASKA MARINE HIGHWAY

Recently designated an "All-American Road" by the U.S. Department of Transportation,

the Alaska Marine Highway (AMHS) is the state ferry service. The AMHS takes vehicles as well as passengers on the 11 vessels in its fleet. Visiting 33 communities (10 along the Inside Passage), the marine highway is the way the locals travel; when a high school basketball team plays an away game, they jump onto the ferry. During summer, you can readily tell the independent travelers from the locals: The independents tend to be out on deck with binoculars, scanning for humpback whales, sea otters, bald eagles, and killer whales; locals are more likely to be playing cards or napping.

The mainline vessels can accommodate

450 to 499 passengers and the ships that serve smaller communities hold 150 to 250. Enough ferries ply the Southeast that passengers may get off in one of the major ports and catch another ferry in a day or two—or in a month. Many people set up lodging in several port towns and spend a few days in each, tying this sampler itinerary together with the ferries.

The marine highway is inexpensive compared to the cruise ships, well run, and generally reliable. The ferries even offer a few amenities, like staterooms (more costly, of course), modest restaurants, movies, and

Cruise-ship life while traveling through the Inside Passage offers passengers a feast for the senses. Delicious meals, such as the crusted fresh fish (right), and decadent desserts, such as baked Alaska (left), satisfy even the pickiest gourmand's appetite, while shipboard entertainment and glacial attractions stimulate the mind and body. In Glacier Bay National Park and Preserve, passengers gaze in awe at the Marjorie Glacier (top).

showers. At night some of the passengers who don't have staterooms pitch tents on covered decks; most just slump in the rather comfy chairs or stretch out in sleeping bags on the floor. In summer, reservations are required for travelers with vehicles, and they are advised for people on foot. Book early for vehicles; likewise, cabins go quickly.

See Travelwise (p. 237) for more information on the AMHS. ■

Settled during the gold-rush era, Juneau's downtown is a cornucopia of historic buildings.

Juneau

JUNEAU IS NOT YOUR ORDINARY STATE CAPITAL: NO ROADS connect it to the outside world, bears sometimes wander through town, and its setting is drop-dead gorgeous. Built along the shore of Gastineau Channel, the city backs up against heavily forested mountains that elevate abruptly to heights of several thousand feet—more like the backdrop for a Swiss resort than a state capital.

Juneau

A 49 D3

Visitor information

www.traveljuneau.com

✉ Centennial Hall Visitor Center, 101 Egan Dr.

☎ 907/586-2201 or 888-581-2201

The third largest city in Alaska, Juneau (population 31,000), offers good lodgings, fine restaurants and lively cafés, plenty of cultural activities, and access to a wealth of unparalleled scenery.

HISTORIC DOWNTOWN

History surrounds visitors as they stroll Juneau's downtown. Thanks to good luck and the heroic work of the Volunteer Fire Department, this city never suffered a major fire, as many Alaska towns have. In the seven-block radius of the original downtown, 143 buildings dating from before 1914 still stand—60 of them go back earlier than 1904. As you wander around, note the more than 20

totem poles and other public art in the form of sculptures and murals. And take the time to walk through the adjacent old residential areas up the steep hills, some half dozen blocks above the shore.

Given the importance of government here in Alaska's capital—nearly 45 percent of the locals work for the public—it would be appropriate to begin a tour of Juneau at the **Alaska State Capitol.** Completed in 1931, this unassuming brick-faced building originally housed the territorial legislature, governor, the post office, courts, and numerous other federal and territorial agencies. The second floor displays historical photos.

Delve deeper into Juneau's past at the **Juneau-Douglas City Museum** across Main Street from the capitol. Learn how two prospectors and a Tlingit chief together in 1880 touched off one of the quickest gold rushes ever, with the first boatloads of would-be millionaires arriving about a month after Chief Kowee directed Joe Juneau and Richard Harris to the mother lode above Gold Creek (now Silver Bow Basin). Millions of ounces of gold came out of the ground, but it had to be painstakingly extracted from low-grade ore, which required the efforts of big mining companies rather than independent miners, as evidenced by the museum's elaborate model of the Perseverance Mine. Displays cover many other aspects of Juneau's history, too, from shipwrecks to 19th-century domestic life. And don't overlook the 45-foot (13.7 m) Haida-style totem pole in front of the museum.

Another key element of Juneau's history is evoked a couple of blocks up the hill, on Seventh Street, at the **House of Wickersham,** a state and national historic site. Built in 1898 for a mine superintendent, this handsome house was bought in 1928 by Judge James Wickersham, a prominent Alaska lawyer, politician, judge, author, and historian. Wickersham was instrumental in the effort to make Alaska a territory, which finally succeeded in 1912. Soon after that victory, Wickersham began the drive to make Alaska a state, though he died 20 years before that happened in 1959. The tour of his house details the judge's illustrious past and displays some of his vast collection of Alaskan artifacts plus his personal mementos.

Alaska State Capitol
- 4th & Main Sts.
- 907/465-3800
- Tours Mon.–Sat. June–mid-Sept.

Juneau-Douglas City Museum
www.juneau.org/parksrec/museum
- 155 S. Seward St.
- 907/586-3572
- Open daily in summer, Tues.–Sat. in winter
- $

Wickersham State Historic Site
www.dnr.state.ak.us/parks units/Wickrshm.htm
- 213 7th St.
- 907/586-9001
- Open Thurs.–Tues. Mem. Day–Labor Day
- $

The collections at the Alaska State Museum tell the story of Alaska, the Great Land.

Alaska State Museum

www.museums.state.ak.us/asmhome.html

✉ 395 Whittier St.
☎ 907/465-2901
🕐 Open daily mid-May–mid-Sept., Tues.–Sat. rest of year
💲 $

ALASKA STATE MUSEUM

The Alaska State Museum is a 32,000-object-strong treasure trove of interesting Native artifacts, fine art, and natural history specimens.

The ground floor explores the rich past and present of Alaska's diverse Native peoples—Aleut, Athabaskan, Eskimos, and Northwest Coast Indians. The galleries exhibit rarities such as a belt fashioned from some 200 caribou mandibles and baskets thousands of years old, as well as artifacts of exceptional quality. Consider a contemporary artist's rendition of an Aleut hunting hat, its thin, steam-bent wood tapered like an Olympic cyclist's helmet, the outer surface replete with intricate designs, colorful beads, ivory carvings, and a fringe of sea lion whiskers. Look at the exquisitely fine weaving and elaborate painting on the historical hat on the Kaagwaantaan dancer; experts proclaim it one of the finest spruce-root hats in existence.

The ramp to the second floor circles around a two-story model of a tree topped by an immense bald eagle nest, complete with piped-in eagle calls. Added to over the reproductive lifetime of a pair of eagles, baldies' nests can end up the size of a pickup truck.

The second floor houses some natural history exhibits, but mostly it is devoted to the state's post-European-contact human history, particularly the Russian era. Look for the samovar the size of a potbellied stove and the imperial crest of a double-headed eagle—the symbol of Russian Alaska. The American period galleries examine in great detail the development of the state's natural resources through exhibits on mining, logging, fishing, and oil exploration.

SOUTH FRANKLIN STREET & AROUND

Near the waterfront, numerous shops, restaurants, galleries, bars, and theaters compete for the patronage of visitors. The closer you get to the docks along South Franklin Street, the more you'll see the influence of cruise ships.

On any given summer day four or five ships moor dockside. Tourist dollars are encouraging the growth of new shops and luxury stores; still, many local, distinctly Alaskan businesses remain, some even on South Franklin.

Stop in the old **Senate Building** and browse the art and crafts in the **Juneau Artists Gallery** *(175 S. Franklin St., tel 907/586-9891, www.juneauartists gallery.com).* A block down try the **Decker Gallery** *(233 S. Franklin St., tel 907/463-5536),* which carries work by one of the state's most renowned artists, Rie Muñoz. Authentic Native Alaskan carvings, ivory jewelry, and ceremonial masks can be purchased at **Raven's Journey** *(439 S. Franklin St., tel 907/463-4686).*

MOUNT ROBERTS

Just down the street from Raven's Journey is the **Mount Roberts Tramway,** which hauls passengers up one of Juneau's finest attractions. The tram climbs steeply to the 1,800-foot (548 m) level of the 3,819-foot-high (1,164 m) eponymous mountain that looms over South Franklin Street and Marine Way.

As the tram rises, the views grow from fine to fantastic. The urban Alaska Native Corporation owns the tram, so many employees are Native Alaskans. Sometimes the tram operator will play a traditional drum and sing a song as he takes visitors up or down the mountain. The Native influence continues up top at the tram's terminus: A theater shows a film about Tlingit culture and a gift shop serves somewhat as a museum, where artisans at work are frequently on view. There's also a restaurant with an amazing view and a nature center. But this complex isn't the best thing

about the Mount Roberts Tram. The best thing is Mount Roberts itself.

Beyond the nature center sprawls a network of easy, well-marked trails that lead up the mountain through increasingly sparse forest to a stunning expanse of subalpine and alpine habitat. It only takes 10 to 15 minutes to hike above tree line, where marvelous vistas open up: mountains, waterfalls, and the bodies of water far to the west and south of Juneau. During summer wildflowers blaze from

Mount Roberts Tramway
www.alaska.net/~junotram
✉ 490 S. Franklin St.
☎ 907/463-3412 or 888/461-8726
🕐 Open daily early May–late Sept.
💲 $$$$

Grand views of rugged mountain scenery open up at the top of the Mount Roberts Tramway.

Glacier Gardens
Rainforest
Adventure
www.glaciergardens.com
- ✉ 7600 Glacier Hwy.
- ☎ 907/790-3377
- 🕐 Open daily
  May–Sept.
- 💲 $$$

Mendenhall
Glacier
www.fs.fed.us/r10/tongass
/districts/mendenhall
- 🗺 49 D3
- ✉ Mendenhall Loop
  Rd.
- ☎ 907/789-0097
- 🕐 Visitor center open
  daily May–Sept.,
  Thurs.–Sun. rest
  of year
- 💲 $

the meadows, where hoary marmots graze. Porcupines lumber through the undergrowth, bears occasionally pass through, and mountain goats occupy the highest slopes. If you feel energetic and have proper gear, you can roam for miles—even choosing to return to the city via the 4.5-mile (7.2 km) **Mount Roberts Trail,** which has its trailhead at the end of Sixth Street.

GLACIER/JUNEAU VETERANS' MEMORIAL HIGHWAY

Juneau's one highway, the Glacier/Juneau Veterans' Memorial Highway, may be a dead end, but there are so many worthy sites along the road that motorists won't mind driving up and back. The road starts in downtown as Egan Drive and goes north along Gastineau and Favorite Channels. At Mile 9.3 (as measured from the cruise-ship terminal on South Franklin St.) it officially becomes the Glacier Highway. At Mile 12.1 it technically becomes the Juneau Veterans' Memorial Highway, but most locals still call it the Glacier Highway. By whatever name, the road continues on or near the shore of Favorite Channel and Lynn Canal until it ends 40 miles (64 km) from town at Echo Cove.

The first quarter of this route passes through the Mendenhall Valley, home to Juneau's version of suburbia. At Mile 8, near the Fred Meyer store, there is the **Glacier Gardens Rainforest Adventure.** You can explore 51.5 acres of rain forest with a guide along a 2 mile (3.2 km) loop, but among the big draws here are the acres of flower-intensive gardens. Big conifer trees cut down to maybe 20 feet (6 m) and then rammed upside down into the ground so the root masses stick

up, forming a platform for masses of colorful hanging plants, are the most eye-catching displays.

At Mile 9.3 the south junction of the Mendenhall Loop Road intersects the highway. This road leads 3.4 miles (5.5 km) inland to dead-end at the visitor center at **Mendenhall Glacier,** one of the most popular attractions in all of Alaska. *(To avoid crowds, go before late morning, when tour buses start arriving.)* Spawned high in the mountains by the vast Juneau Icefield, this 12-mile-long (19.3 km), mile-wide (1.6 km) ribbon of blue-and-white ice rumbles to its present terminus—a mile or more across Mendenhall Lake from the visitor center. The glacier has been retreating rapidly,

typically 100 to 150 feet (30.5 to 45.7 m) a year since the 1750s. Unusually hot summers can accelerate the retreat: In 2004 the glacier retreated 600 feet (183 m).

At the **visitor center,** exhibits and a film educate visitors on the mechanics of glaciers, discussing in depth the Juneau Icefield and Mendenhall Glacier. Large panoramic windows allow warm viewing of the glacier. For a closer look, stroll along the easy 0.3-mile-long (0.5 km) **Photo Point Trail** that winds out to the edge of the lake. If you crave an even closer look, take a guided kayak tour on the lake; there's even an outfit that takes people around the lake in a traditional Tlingit canoe. For the closest

look of all, take a helicopter tour and land on the glacier for a guided walk. The copters land well back from the terminus, but the buzz of so many helicopters still annoys many Juneau residents and nature lovers, fueling an ongoing debate about imposing limitations on the whirlybirds.

The area around the glacier is well worth exploring. Right at the end of the parking lot farthest from the visitor center is a platform for watching the sockeye and coho salmon that spawn in Steep Creek in the summer. Be alert, as black bears also are drawn by the fish. Beavers favor the creek, too; look for their dams and lodges.

Nugget Falls gushes down rocky slopes into the lake below Mendenhall Glacier.

Tlingit artistry accents many places in Southeast Alaska, including the Mount Roberts Interpretive Trail, where artist Richard Beasley has carved a totem pole-like figure into a tree.

Opposite: In view of Mendenhall Glacier, outfitters prepare their rafts for a float down the Mendenhall River.

In addition to the path from the visitor center to the lake, five trails provide access to the surrounding landscape. The easy half-mile (0.8 km) **Trail of Time,** a self-guided nature trail, leaves from the center and provides a glimpse of the rain forest. One of the prettiest routes is the 3.5-mile (5.6 km), moderately difficult **East Glacier Loop,** which branches off from the Trail of Time. The loop passes through lush rain forest and at various points offers views of the glacier, Nugget Falls, and alpine slopes frequented by mountain goats.

Back on the Glacier Highway, at Mile 12.4 you will encounter **Auke Bay,** a harbor that has kayak tours, whale-watching trips, and sportfishing charters. Nearby are the University of Alaska Southeast Campus and the terminal for the state ferry. After skirting the bay, the highway turns north and curves along Favorite Channel, sometimes in a canyon of trees, sometimes in the open along the coastline. At times the lofty peaks of the Chilkat Range stab the horizon, 25 to 30

miles (40 to 48 km) to the west. **Inspiration Point** at Mile 18.8 has a scenic view of these peaks.

A sanctuary of peace and quiet awaits at Mile 22.5: the **Shrine of St. Therese** *(tel 907/780-6112).* A retreat for the Diocese of Juneau, the complex of cabins, gardens, walking paths, lodge, and shrine is open to any lodgers or day-trippers "who respect the spirit of the shrine." Walk across the 400-foot (122 m) causeway to tiny Shrine Island to view the beautiful stone chapel.

At Mile 27.7 pull into the main parking lot of the **Eagle Beach State Recreation Area** *(tel 907/465-4563, $),* which includes a ranger station, several trails, and a campground. This area lay beneath thousands of feet of glacial ice until just 250 years ago, so this landscape is quite young. Use the spotting scopes by the interpretive signs to pull in the Chilkats from far across the waters of Lynn Canal or the bald eagles swooping above the estuary fed by Eagle River.

About a quarter mile (0.4 km) farther down the highway, look for the unmarked dirt road to the **Eagle Beach picnic area** *(Tongass National Forest, Juneau Ranger District, tel 907/586-8800).* This less developed area offers great views across Lynn Canal, and many birds favor the nearby tidal flats, including Canada geese, great blue herons, bald eagles, and squawking flocks of gulls.

At Mile 34 a sign warns "Travel Beyond This Point Not Recommended. If You Must Use This Road, Carry Cold Weather Survival Gear." If it's summer and you've got some cool-weather clothing with you, proceed to the end of the highway in Echo Cove, a lovely spot where there's a day-use area and boat launch. ∎

Calving ice from the Johns Hopkins Glacier belly-flops into the waters of a remote inlet of Glacier Bay.

Glacier Bay National Park & Preserve

Glacier Bay National Park & Preserve
www.nps.gov/glba
⛺ 81 & 49 C2
✉ P.O. Box 140, Gustavus, AK 99826; visitor center at Bartlett Cove
☎ 907/697-2230
🕐 Open daily late May—mid-Sept.

Gustavus
⛺ 49 C3
Visitor information
www.gustavusak.com
✉ Gustavus Visitors Assoc., P.O. Box 167, Gustavus, AK 99826

THE HEART OF GLACIER BAY NATIONAL PARK AND PRESERVE is a new land. When Capt. James Cook, the famed British explorer, sailed down this stretch of coastline, in 1778, he encountered a sheet of glacial ice thousands of feet thick and several miles wide. But the little ice age was fading fast, and by 1794, when Capt. George Vancouver passed this way, a 5-mile-long (8 km) bay had appeared—Glacier Bay. The ice continues to melt away: today the deep, double-armed bay cuts 65 miles (105 km) back into the Alaskan mainland.

Near the mouth of the bay, where the ice melted some 250 years ago, mature forest has grown up. At the far end of the bay, where the ice did not recede until much more recently, the early stages of recovery are evident, with colonizing plants like alder and the brilliantly colored fireweed predominating. Scientists and visitors alike can witness the rebirth of a landscape.

The glaciers may have receded, but they hardly have gone away. With 11 tidewater glaciers (glaciers that reach the ocean), most of them actively calving slabs of ice

into the water, the park has one of the highest concentrations of such glaciers in the world. These glaciers are the park's biggest draw. Numerous cruise ships make this bay part of their Inside Passage itineraries. Of course, the overall scenery and the abundance of wildlife certainly share in the spotlight.

Visitors who want to give this 3.3-million-acre park its due should spend a few days here. **Gustavus,** a settlement of about 475, serves as the gateway to the park. Oddly, Gustavus has one of the best airstrips in the Southeast;

it was built as a refueling site during World War II. The airstrip allows Alaska Airlines to make daily summer flights from Juneau, and it also pulls in small planes from various Southeast towns.

Gustavus provides about ten choices of lodging, ranging from nice but simple cabins to pleasant bed-and-breakfasts to one of the finest country inns in Alaska. Amenities include galleries, restaurants, tour operators, and a nine-hole golf course. However, this charming town does not have a main street or a city center. Instead, it lies scattered about the landscape, so visitors need to walk, rent a bike, take a taxi, catch the bus, or rent a car—even though there's only one real road, which is 10 miles (16 km) long.

This road runs from Gustavus into the park, dead-ending in Bartlett Cove, the national park's only developed site and the only other point of entry for travelers heading for Glacier Bay. The Alaska Marine Highway doesn't serve this area, but the privately owned **Gustavus Ferry** *(tel 907/586-8687 or 800/820-2628, $$$$$)* operates between Juneau and Gustavus.

BARTLETT COVE

Wedged into the rain forest on the eastern shore of Glacier Bay, Bartlett Cove is home to **Glacier Bay Lodge,** the only lodging

inside the park. The massive-timbered 56-room lodge provides kayak and fishing-pole rentals and plays host to a small natural history museum and, most important, the headquarters and visitor center of the Glacier Bay National Park and Preserve. This is the place to find out about taking ranger-led hikes and boat tours, getting a campsite, or noting the schedule of

A boardwalk conveys hikers above the soggy rain-forest floor of Bartlett Cove.

evening talks in the auditorium. Near the lodge, the backcountry office dispenses invaluable information for backpackers, kayakers, glacier trekkers, and mountaineers.

There are only three maintained trails in the park. The 1-mile (1.6 km) **Forest Loop Trail** begins at the lodge, swings through a young spruce-hemlock forest dotted with ponds, and then circles back to parallel the beach.

Identifying icebergs

Icebergs are massive floating chunks of ice that have broken off glaciers. In olden days, sailors had names that conveyed their size. For example, if the berg showed about 3 feet (1 m) of ice above water, it was "growler ice," and if it showed 3 to 15 feet (1 to 5 m), it was a "bergy bit." The nature of an iceberg can be discerned by its color. The bluer a berg is, the denser and more compressed the ice; a white berg has large numbers of air bubbles trapped inside it; a greenish black berg is one that calved off the bottom of a glacier. ■

Wildflowers bloom in profusion in June and July. Bears and coyotes sometimes wander the beach; red squirrels and porcupines comb the forest. The same animals may cross your path on the more challenging **Bartlett River Trail,** which starts a little ways up the road from the lodge. This 5-mile-out-and-back (8 km) path passes an intertidal lagoon, forest, and river estuary habitats; it has some muddy spots if rain has fallen, so allow half a day for tromping and savoring. Look for salmon running the river in late summer, and ducks, geese, and waterbirds bobbing in the estuary. Fewer people use the **Bartlett Lake Trail,** whose 6 miles (9.6 km) round-trip are more primitive and demanding, but it's a pretty and tranquil hike to the lake. The trail branches off the Bartlett River Trail.

Hikers can always strike out cross-country but that requires route-finding skills and a lot more effort. The forest undergrowth and the dreaded alder thickets that clog many unforested areas turn cross-country travel from a cheerful outing into an accursed slog. By far the best off-trail opportunity is to go down to the Bartlett Cove dock and walk south along the beach for 6 miles (9.6 km) to **Point Gustavus.** The scenery is delightful and you may spot both marine and terrestrial wildlife. (*Consult park rangers about tides and time trek to take advantage of low tide.*)

THE BAY & GLACIERS
Rewarding as the hikes and views around Bartlett Cove can be, venture farther afield to fully experience the park's grandeur and majesty: the glaciers and bay. Flightseeing opportunities are available out of Gustavus or from distant Southeast towns, and while thrilling, they do not povide provide as intimate viewing experience as boats.

Visitors who want to see Glacier Bay from the water have two main options: kayaks and boats. Kayak rentals are available from the park concessionaire Glacier Bay Sea Kayaks (*tel 907/697-2257, www.glacierbayseakayaks.com*) for day or multiday trips. A limited number of companies are authorized to provide guided kayak excursions (*for information contact park or Gustavus Visitors Association; see p. 78*) within the park. A popular six-hour trip includes instruction before setting off into Bartlett Cove and on to the nearby **Beardslee Entrance,** an enchanting maze of small islands and narrow channels with enticing names, such as Spider Island and Secret Bay.

The tour boat **M.V. *Baranof Wind*** (*Glacier Bay Lodges & Tours, tel 907/264-4600 or 888/229-8687, $$$$$, advance reservations recommended*) doesn't offer as close a communion as do kayaks, but it is much easier on your backside, it delves far deeper into the bay than a kayak day trip, and a naturalist provides a running commentary. By venturing into the backcountry of Glacier Bay, you enter a world of notable distinction. When the park's acres are combined with the undeveloped expanses of its neighbors, **Wrangell-St. Elias** (see pp. 180–183) and Canada's **Tatshenshini-Alsek Provincial Park** and **Kluane National Park,** they form the biggest parkland wilderness in the world.

The glories of that wilderness become apparent during the boat tour: Colonies of cormorants, murres, and puffins throng jagged islands; hulking brown bears fish for salmon at the mouth of creeks; humpback whales spout, slapping the surface with their 15-foot

(4.5 m) flippers and leaping half-way out of the water. Looming to the northwest is the snowcapped Fairweather Range, crowned by 15,300-foot (4,663 m) Mount Fairweather. As the boat slaloms slowly among icebergs of infinite shapes and sizes, you can hear the bergs' air pockets pop and their melting surfaces drip.

Sailing up the West Arm of the bay, you'll soon reach the **Reid Glacier.** It moves an average of 8 feet (2.4 m) a day, making it one of Glacier Bay's fastest-moving glaciers. Next comes **Lamplugh Glacier,** with its castle-like turrets and spires of blue ice. Scores of ice floes carrying seals litter **John Hopkins Inlet.** The boat will eventually head into **Tarr Inlet,** to the far reaches of the West Arm,

and come to rest a quarter of a mile from the furrowed **Margerie Glacier.** This active glacier, some 250 feet (76 m) tall above the surface of the water, commonly calves chunks of ice into the bay, often every few minutes.

Standing on deck, you'll hear what sounds like a rifle shot followed by the sight of a car-size hunk of ice splitting from the glacier face and splashing into the water. This event might repeat numerous times, with the dimensions of the falling ice ranging from dishwasher size to as big as an RV. If you're lucky, an ice hunk larger than a house will flop into the sea, creating a gigantic splash and a thunderous echo that reverberates through the inlet. You'll long for more of this spectacle! ■

Under the right conditions, Lynn Canal assumes the look of a subtle landscape painting.

Haines

HAINES IS LIKE A FAVORITE FLANNEL SHIRT: FAMILIAR, comfy, unassuming. Yet surrounding the town's cozy cafés and little harbor is a landscape of surpassing beauty: snow-dusted mountains, waterfalls, forest, fjords, broad rivers, glaciers, lakes, and wildlife galore. And this landscape gets a mere 60 inches of precipitation a year on average, a relative desert in Southeast Alaska.

The big cruise ships rarely stop here, and it's a long drive from Fairbanks (653 miles, 1,051 km) and Anchorage (775 miles, 1,247 km), so this friendly town of 1,500 people is a delight to explore. The town had its origins as a trading post for the Chilkat and Interior Indians; the first non-natives settled here in 1880. The town grew as it became a mining supply town, and later the only Alaskan site of a U.S. Army post. **Lookout Park,** at the foot of Mission Street, overlooking the harbor and Chilkoot Inlet, makes a good starting point for a walk through historic Haines. From the viewing platforms you can make a 360-degree scan of the area; use the

topographic sign to identify the natural features encircling you.

Head north to Main Street and the **Sheldon Museum and Cultural Center.** The core of the 3,000-item collection comes from the personal stash of Steve Sheldon, who began acquiring things in the early 1900s at age eight. The array of Native artifacts stands out, especially those from the local Tlingit, such as the carved ceremonial hat. But the collection ranges all over, from a lighthouse lens to Chinese camphor-wood trunks brought to Alaska by early traders to a whole corner devoted to Jack Dalton. Dalton was an early resident of Haines; he's most remembered

for his unscrupulous dealings with travelers who needed to use the Dalton Trail—a toll road to the Interior. Later he built a hotel and saloon in town. The museum displays the sawed-off shotgun that he kept loaded with rock salt behind the bar in his saloon.

A very different sort of museum sits a block up Main Street from the Sheldon. The entertaining **Hammer Museum** contains 1,400 hammers and counting. You'll soon realize how much history can be discovered in a hammer. The Tlingit Warrior's Pick "Slave Killer," an 800-year-old hammer found in the ground right under the museum, was used to sacrifice slaves to bury under the cornerposts of new longhouses. Patrons at Harlem's Cotton Club rapped "drink" hammers on the tables as a form of applause. And then there's the autopsy hammer, the Waterford crystal hammer, the Chinese war and Roman battle hammers....

A few blocks from downtown, on the southwest side of Chilkoot Inlet, sprawls the gleaming white, well-kept frame buildings of **Fort William H. Seward National Historic Landmark.** Fort Seward was an active Army outpost from 1904 to 1947. After it was decommissioned, it was turned into the community of Port Chilkoot, which later merged with Haines. Many of the former officers' houses are private homes, but a variety of businesses occupy other buildings in the complex, including the Hotel Hälsingland; **Alaska Indian Arts,** where visitors can watch Tlingit artists at work; **Totem Village,** where you can partake in an evening salmon bake during the summer; and the **Chilkat Center for the Arts,** where the highly regarded Chilkat Dancers perform.

Haines

⛰ 49 C2

Visitor information

www.haines.ak.us

✉ Haines Convention & Visitors Bureau, 122 2nd Ave.

☎ 970/766-2234 or 800/458-3579

🕐 Open daily in summer, Mon.–Fri. in winter

Sheldon Museum & Cultural Center

www.sheldonmuseum.org

✉ 11 Main St.

☎ 907/766-2366

🕐 Open daily mid-May–mid-Sept., Mon.–Fri. in winter

💲 $

Hammer Museum

www.hammermuseum.org

✉ 108 Main St.

☎ 907/766-2374

🕐 Open Mon.–Fri. May–Sept.

💲 $

Alaska Chilkat
Bald Eagle
Preserve
www.dnr.state.ak.us/parks/
units/eagleprv.htm

✉ Haines Ranger
Station, Alaska State
Parks, 259 Main St.,
Haines

☎ 907/766-2292

ALASKA CHILKAT BALD EAGLE PRESERVE

Haines' biggest claim to fame lies northwest up the Haines Highway on the Chilkat River: the 48,000-acre Alaska Chilkat Bald Eagle Preserve. An upwelling of warm water and an exceptionally late salmon run entices more than 3,000 bald eagles to overwinter along the river, primarily between Miles 10 and 26, an area known as the **Valley of the Eagles.** They begin gathering in early October and taper off by February; the best viewing is October through December.

The highest concentrations of eagles are found on the **Eagle Council Grounds,** a stretch of river flats that parallels the highway between Miles 18 and 24. Here, well-developed turnouts with interpretive signs allow easy viewing of these iconic predators catching and eating the spawning chum salmon. The banquet also attracts bears, wolves, and other animals. Numerous operators offer tours *(for information contact visitors bureau; see p. 83)* to this natural phenomenon.

During the summer, you can take a boat up the river and explore the maze of waterways that wind through the bottom-lands. You likely will see moose, often cows with their spindly-legged calves; trumpeter swans; and some of the preserve's resident 200 to 400 eagles.

LUTAK HIGHWAY

Nature lovers may wish to explore the 11-mile (17.7 km) Lutak Highway, which leads north out of Haines to **Chilkoot Lake State Recreation Site.** The first few miles on this shore road yield pretty views of Chilkoot Inlet and rafts of sea ducks bobbing on the water, including handsome harlequin ducks and orange-billed surf scoters. The scenery and the wildlife sightings get even better after the route rounds **Tanani Point** and heads up narrow **Lutak Inlet,** which ends at the outlet stream from **Chilkoot Lake.** Bald eagles, harbor seals, bears feeding on salmon, mountain goats on the slopes above—it's hard to know where to point your binoculars. ■

A single-lane boardwalk leads across the bogs on the trail to the top of Mount Riley.

Historic down-
town Skagway
has become a
shoppers' para-
dise and a magnet
for cruise ships.

Skagway

SKAGWAY IS AN UNABASHED TOURIST TOWN—THE DAILY
summer flood of some 5,000 visitors totally swamps the town's summer population of about 1,800—though with good reason: The town
boasts an impressive array of buildings from the turn-of-the-20th-
century Klondike gold rush era. Much of downtown Skagway is preserved and maintained as part of the Klondike Gold Rush National
Historical Park.

After word of the 1896 gold strike
reached Seattle, in the summer of
1897, hordes of prospectors and
adventurers looking for a gateway
to the Yukon raced to Skagway,
swelling its population from 1 in
1896 up to 10,000 by 1897. In a
few years the gold played out and
Skagway's population plunged to
about 500 by 1902, but many of
the buildings survived. You can
now shop and explore a flamboy-
ant historical era at the same time.

As nearly every visitor to
Skagway arrives via water—either
from a cruise ship, the state ferry,
or the fast ferry from Haines—it
makes sense to start your wander
near the docks. Walk up Congress
Way to the corner of Second
Avenue and Spring Street; the
**White Pass & Yukon Route
railroad depot** (see pp. 88–89)
is here. Continue on Second
Avenue to Broadway, Skagway's
main street. At the corner is the

Skagway
49 C2
**Visitor
information**
www.skagway.com
Skagway Convention
& Visitors Bureau,
245 Broadway
907/983-2854 or
888/762-1898

Part of Klondike Gold Rush National Historical Park, the Red Onion Saloon remains a popular watering hole in the 21st century.

Klondike Gold Rush National Historical Park
www.nps.gov/klgo
✉ 2nd Ave. & Broadway
☎ 907/983-2921
🕐 Open daily May—Sept., Mon.—Fri. rest of year

railroad's old depot, which now houses the visitor center of the **Klondike Gold Rush National Historical Park.** The park service staff answers questions, shows a 30-minute film, and offers 45-minute interpretive tours. Note the reproduction of the *Seattle Post-Intelligencer* for July 19, 1897, that announces the discovery of that seductive yellow metal in the Yukon. In huge bold letters the headline reads "Gold! Gold! Gold! Gold!"

An adjacent part of the visitor center showcases exhibits on the gold rush. Evocative photographs reveal the hardship of the gold rush. One shows dozens of gold seekers on the beach at nearby Dyea with their mountains of gear—gear that needed to be hauled up and over the daunting Chilkoot Trail. The center dis-

plays some of that gear, too, such as dog packs, snowshoes, and, of course, gold pans.

A few steps up Broadway stands the **Arctic Brotherhood Hall** *(245 Broadway)*—reputedly the most photographed building in Alaska. The Brotherhood, a fraternal organization of pioneers, fashioned the facade from thousands of pieces of driftwood. The hall now houses the Skagway Convention and Visitors Bureau; the staff is friendly and you can pick up the excellent and detailed walking-tour map and brochure.

A stroll up Broadway reveals one restored historic edifice after another, including old wooden sidewalks, cabins, and renovated saloons. Many now contain the diamond stores, gift shops, and art galleries aimed at the cruise-ship passengers, but others have

interiors that re-create the buildings' historic use. For instance, the **Mascot Saloon,** at the corner of Third Avenue and Broadway, looks much like it did in 1898, when hard-drinking men bellied up to the bar and downed whiskey—as one of the interpretive signs notes, whiskey was a drink, beer a mere chaser. The Mascot was one of some 70 or 80 saloons catering to the thousands of gold seekers. Lawlessness was rampant; Skagway was reputed to be the roughest place around. "Skagway was little better than a hell on earth," recalled Samuel Steele, superintendent of the North West Mounted Police, after he visited the town in 1898.

After wandering up Broadway, turn right at Seventh Avenue and walk one block to the corner of Spring Street, site of the nicely restored 1899 granite-faced McCabe College building, which now houses city hall and the **Skagway Museum.** Check out the eclectic collection, ranging from a Tlingit canoe to a stuffed brown bear to the July 15, 1898, edition of the *Skagway News,* which reports the gunfight that resulted in the death of notorious Skagway crime boss Jefferson Randolph "Soapy" Smith. (A marker near the corner of First Avenue and State Street commemorates this pivotal event.)

OUTSIDE SKAGWAY

Skagway is set against a backdrop of comely mountains, forest, and rivers. The easiest way to enjoy the scenery is to drive some or all of the **South Klondike Highway.** It's 99 miles (159 km) to the junction with the Alaska Highway, in the Yukon, but within just a few miles the highway climbs into stirring alpine country blessed with waterfalls, lakes, and deep gorges. The British Columbia border and Canada customs await about 15 miles (24 km) from Skagway, just past the 3,292-foot (1,003 m) **White Pass Summit.**

If you'd like to experience what the gold seekers had to face to reach the goldfields, the historic 33-mile (53 km) **Chilkoot Trail** challenges trekkers with a lot of elevation gain. You can get a small taste of the trail by hiking just the first few miles, which are fairly flat and lead through a pretty rain forest along the **Taiya River.** The trailhead is by the bridge over the river, 9.5 miles (15.3 km) out the Dyea Road from Skagway. Also, a local outfit guides hikers 2 miles (3.2 km) on the Chilkoot Trail and then takes them back to the trailhead by rafting down the gentle Taiya. ∎

Skagway Museum
www.skagwaymuseum.org
✉ 700 Spring St.
☎ 907/983-2420
🕐 Open daily May–Sept., varies in winter
💲 $

The White Pass & Yukon Route runs through the high country above Skagway.

White Pass & Yukon route

During the Klondike gold rush, the narrow-gauge White Pass & Yukon route was blasted and chiseled 110 miles (177 km) through the mountains to connect Skagway (which had access to the ocean) to Whitehorse, Yukon (which had access to rivers to the interior goldfields). Today passengers board vintage railcars and travel 20 miles (32 km) to White Pass Summit and back, an extraordinarily scenic three-hour journey. Stand on the outside platforms at either end of the cars; they are great for taking photos and for feeling even closer to the landscape, but be careful—and bring a coat, it gets cold out there.

This trip is very popular, so book well in advance (*White Pass & Yukon Route, P.O. Box 435, Skagway, AK 99840, tel 800/343-7373, www.wpyr.com, 2-3 times daily May–Sept., $$$$$*). The journey starts at the **depot** ❶ on the corner of Second Avenue and Spring Street. The train leaves promptly, so don't be late. For the best views, sit on the left going up and the right coming back.

The train eases out along the east side of town, passing the **Goldrush Cemetery** ❷ at railroad Mile 2.5. Here rest the bones of gold rush gangster Soapy Smith and Frank Reid, the man who shot him, as the interpreter will explain over the speakers. (There are also roving interpreters, who

move through the cars answering questions and pointing out some of the sights.)

Continuing above the Skagway River, steadily gaining elevation, the train chugs up to **Denver** ❸ at Mile 5.8. On morning runs hikers often get off here to head up the **Denver Glacier Trail.** Hikers and backpackers can flag down the train to get a ride back to town in the afternoon. At Denver you'll see an old red caboose that can be rented through the Forest Service for overnight stays. The train crosses the Skagway East Fork River and then about a mile later reaches **Rocky Point** ❹, which yields tremendous views down the valley to Skagway, the harbor, and beyond.

The hardship of gouging this route out of these rugged mountains is grimly memorialized at Mile 10.4 at Black Cross Rock. A blasting accident buried two workers under the 100-ton (90.7 tonne) hunk of black granite by the tracks; altogether 35 laborers died during the two years of construction. Hundreds of horses used to haul equipment also perished, earning one area along the route the nickname "Dead Horse Gulch." On the brighter side, a profusion of waterfalls decorates the route as it proceeds, topped at Mile 11.5 by the spectacular **Bridal Veil Falls** ❺, fed by the glaciers on Mount Cleveland and Mount Clifford.

At Mile 16, just before entering **Tunnel Mountain** ❻, the train crawls across a bridge 1,000 feet (305 m) above Glacier Gorge; anyone afraid of heights should not look down. Shortly after the long tunnel, at Mile 17, arguably the finest vista of the

route appears: **Inspiration Point** ❼. The views down the valley stretch to Skagway, to the Lynn Canal, and to the Chilkat Range, some 20 miles (32 km) farther south. Finally, after much huffing and puffing, the engines pull the railcars up to their destination, **White Pass Summit** ❽, 2,865 vertical feet (873.3 m) higher than sea level, where the train started. ∎

▲ See area map p. 49 C2
► Starts in Skagway
↔ 40 miles round-trip
⏱ 3 hours round-trip
► Skagway

NOT TO BE MISSED
- Rocky Point
- Bridal Veil Falls
- Inspiration Point

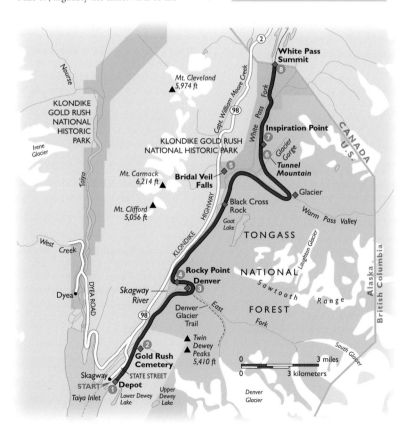

More places to visit in Southeast Alaska

Putting in for a paddle to Admiralty Island to watch the brown bears at Pack Creek

ADMIRALTY ISLAND NATIONAL MONUMENT

The Tlingit call Admiralty Island Kootznoowoo, which means "fortress of the bears," for good reason: More than 1,500 brown bears call this lush island home that works out to about one per square mile. The population remains high due to the heavily forested habitat and the abundant supply of food protected by the **Kootznoowoo Wilderness,** part of Admiralty Island National Monument.

The monument's most famous attraction is **Pack Creek,** where many of the 1,000-pound (453 kg) bears congregate during the summer to feast on spawning salmon. This is one of Alaska's most renowned bear-viewing sites and a permit system is in place to protect people and bears. Make plans well ahead, as these permits get snapped up quickly. Many visitors go on organized tours, most of which are run out of Juneau, only 15 miles (24 km) north of the monument.

The monument also features soaring rain forest, one of southeastern Alaska's greatest concentration of nesting bald eagles, and coastal waters favored by humpback whales. A number of Juneau companies run sea-kayaking trips along Admiralty's shores. The famous freshwater Cross-Admiralty Canoe Trail also allows people to canoe and kayak across the island.

🅰 49 D3 ✉ 8461 Old Dairy Rd., Juneau, AK 99801 ☎ 907/586-8790, www.fs.fed.us /r10/tongass/districts/admiralty

TATSHENSHINI & ALSEK RIVERS

The Tatshenshini and Alsek Rivers meander through the largest designated wilderness area on the planet: the combined acreages of **Tatshenshini-Alsek Provincial Park, Kluane National Park, Wrangell-St. Elias National Park and Preserve** (see pp. 180–183), and **Glacier Bay National Park and Preserve** (see pp. 78–81). The only practical way to venture across this pristine expanse is by river.

The put-ins for rafts and kayakers are along the Haines Highway. A few hardy souls take on the Alsek River, which in its upper stretch has challenging whitewater and one set of rapids that requires a helicopter portage. Most people start on the Tatshenshini River, which has a few Class III and IV rapids but nothing too daunting. The Tat joins the lower Alsek, below all the rapids, and flows through Glacier Bay National Park to the take-out at Dry Bay. Trips generally run 11 to 12 days and take rafters past 14,000-foot (4,267 m) peaks, prime grizzly country, and glaciers. Unless you're a river rat and a wilderness veteran, go with an organized tour. 🅰 48 A2–B2 ✉ Glacier Bay National Park and Preserve, P.O. Box 140, Gustavus, AK 99826 ☎ 907/697-2230, www.nps.gov/glba

YAKUTAT

This out-of-the way coastal town of 680 is flanked by the **Russell Fiord Wilderness** and the southern end of **Wrangell-St. Elias National Park and Preserve** (see pp. 180–183). Visitors come for the legendary sportfishing (salmon and halibut but also Situk River steelhead), the surfing (Yakutat's big waves and miles of sandy beaches have made it the state's surfing capital), and the magnificent beaches, mountains, glaciers, lakes, and wildlife. 🅰 48 A1 ✉ Greater Yakutat Chamber of Commerce, Yakutat, AK 99689 ☎ 907/784-3933, www.yakutatalaska.com ■

Among the state's fastest growing areas, Anchorage and the adjoining Matanuska-Susitna Borough predictably offer many urban amenities. That said, this is still Alaska, so expect to find abundant natural attractions to complement the cityscapes.

Anchorage & Mat-Su

Introduction & map 92–93
Anchorage 94–99
Turnagain Arm 102–106
North Anchorage 107–109
Mat-Su Borough 110–113
Hatcher Pass Drive 114–115
More places to visit in Anchorage
    & the Mat-Su Borough 116
Hotels & restaurants 246–250

The vista from Flattop, a popular hiking destination just east of Anchorage

Anchorage & Mat-Su

OF ALL THE PLACES IN THIS DISTINCTIVE STATE, ANCHORAGE AND THE Matanuska-Susitna Borough will feel most familiar to travelers from the lower 48. An old one-liner quips that "Anchorage is only 20 minutes from Alaska." While that's a bit harsh, it's true that most of Anchorage consists of subdivisions, office buildings, fast-food restaurants, parks, and all the other development typical of 21st-century America. This is increasingly true of the Mat-Su Borough, too, where sprawling cities like Wasilla are looking more like California suburbs every day and outlying areas are turning into bedroom communities from which people commute to Anchorage.

Hiking the Rainbow Creek section of the Turnagain Arm Trail, high above the Seward Highway and Turnagain Arm

fine art galleries to scenic bike paths. The pretty downtown is largely free of chain stores and strip malls and is an appealing place to stroll while shopping and sightseeing. Up in the Mat-Su Borough, whose heart

Yet these urban outposts have their attractions, and travelers would be wise to sample them. For a city still visited by bears, Anchorage offers plenty of civilized amenities, from excellent museums to trendy bars, music festivals to innovative restaurants,

To Denali National Park and Preserve

Iditarod National Historic Trail

Yentna

Susitna

Will

Valley

NANCY L
STATE REC. A

•Susitna

Susitna

Susitna

Susitna

Little

SUSITNA FLATS
STATE GAME
REFUGE

Beluga

Alaska Aviation Heritage Museum
Tony Knowles Coastal Trail

Fire Island

Cook Inlet

Po
Ma

Chugach State P
Headquart

Chickaloo
Bay

KENAI NATIONAL
WILDLIFE REFUGE &
WILDERNESS AREA

△
A

△
B

lies about 40 miles north of Anchorage, civilization has taken a different form. The Mat-Su emerged in the 1930s as an agricultural region, the only one of any size in Alaska. This heritage remains strong today, as visitors will notice when driving the back roads past horse ranches, red barns, and gardens that boast those famously large midnight-sun veggies.

Those curious about what came before the ranches, art galleries, and, yes, fast-food joints will find a rich human history. It began with the Dena'ina, an Athabascan people, who inhabited the Anchorage area and most of the Mat-Su core. Captain Cook sailed by in 1778, and Russian settlers drifted in before the end of the 18th century.

Various gold rushes, including minor ones near Anchorage and in the Mat-Su Borough, brought more people during the late 1800s and early 1900s. After that the railroad, pioneering aviators, the military buildup sparked by World War II, and the oil boom of the 1970s took Anchorage and the Mat-Su into modern times.

And, despite that old joke, Anchorage and the Mat-Su are indeed part of Alaska. The region teems with outdoor activities and outstanding natural features. Visitors will find long wilderness hikes, fishing, winter sports, boating, glaciers, beluga whales, wetlands busy with birds, lofty mountains, alpine meadows painted by wildflowers, moose on the loose, and scenery galore. ∎

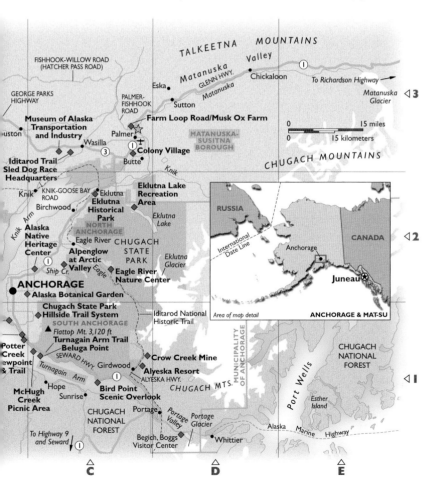

Anchorage

Anchorage
◪ 92 B2
Visitor information
www.anchorage.net
✉ 524 W. 4th Ave.
☎ 907/276-4118 or 800/478-1255

INHABITED BY NEARLY 280,000 PEOPLE, ANCHORAGE IS BY far Alaska's largest city. Travelers who have been out in the wilds may experience culture shock when they encounter its skyscrapers and trendy bars. Certainly, after cooking over a campfire for a week, visitors can find it disorienting to sit down in an elegant restaurant and dine on free-range chicken stuffed with prosciutto, spinach, caramelized onions, and Romano cheese. Bewildered as they may be, however, travelers who have been roughing it are often ready to indulge in urban pleasures. Anyone who has been camping in Alaska's wet and cold regions will also appreciate the mild and often dry summer weather in this city that gets only about 16 inches of precipitation a year. The relatively gentle climate is one of the factors that have led so many people to settle here.

Civilized amenities notwithstanding, the great outdoors is never far away. For example, nearly every city resident has a tale to tell of his or her encounter with a bear or a moose here in town. (Happily, nearly 100 percent of these meetings end without any harm.) Visitors and residents alike also appreciate the fact that even when they're stuck in a traffic jam or coming out of shopping malls, the views of the mountains that ring the city provide relief from the visual nightmare of urban sprawl. Of note, here salmon enter city streams to spawn. At lunchtime downtown workers, some dressed in suits, take their fishing rods to Ship Creek's renowned fishing hole and, amid office buildings and the port's industrial zone, reel in 30-pound kings before returning to their desks.

Ship Creek curves along the northern edge of downtown from Knik Arm up through the port. The fishing hole, near the railroad depot, is a good place to start a city tour. Those eager to see spawning salmon can walk about half a mile east along Ship Creek Avenue to a bridge at the **Salmon Viewing Area.** Downtown lies

Downtown Anchorage represents Alaska's only big-city skyline.

Anglers line Ship Creek, in the shadow of downtown Anchorage.

Saturday Market
- ✉ 3rd Ave. between E & C Sts.
- ☎ 907-272-5634
- 🕐 Closed mid-Sept.– mid-May

Oscar Anderson House
www.anchoragehistoric.org
- ✉ 420 M St.
- ☎ 907-274-2336
- 🕐 Closed mid-Sept.– June
- 💲 $

on higher ground, a couple of blocks south up Port Access Road. The area of most interest to travelers is bordered by Second Avenue on the north, Ninth Avenue on the south, M Street on the west, and Gambell Street on the east.

On a Saturday or Sunday in summer, between 10 a.m. and 6 p.m., stop by the **Anchorage Market & Festival,** better known as the Saturday Market. This is not a farmers' market so much as an outdoor bazaar where more than 300 local merchants sell such wares as jams and jellies, smoked salmon, ivory jewelry, carved wooden moose heads, pottery, fur coats, coonskin (and skunkskin) caps, and duct-tape wallets. Street performers lend a festive air; occasionally a phalanx of bagpipers will march up one of the walkways, noisily parting the crowds. Most of the food stalls

sell such Alaska treats as halibut fritters, salmon quesadillas, and Kachemak Bay oysters.

HISTORIC ANCHORAGE
Anchorage is fairly new as cities go. Many of its older buildings were destroyed by the 1964 earth-quake, but visitors still find rem-nants of the past scattered around downtown. At the corner of Fourth Avenue and D Street is the **Wendler Building,** distin-guished by a sidewalk statue of Balto, a famous sled dog that led the heroic Serum Run to Nome; each March mushers start the Iditarod here. Among the city's oldest buildings, it's the only one with a corner turret. At 420 M St., the **Oscar Anderson House,** built in 1915, is the first proper frame house in Anchorage. Now a museum, it displays many of the Anderson family's original belong-

ings. Another cluster of homes constructed in the early 1900s graces the neighborhood bounded by First and Third Avenues and F and Christensen Streets.

Just west of the historic neighborhood, on Second Avenue, the **Tony Knowles Coastal Trail** begins its 11-mile (17 km) meander along Cook Inlet. Runners, cyclists, in-line skaters, and people just out for a stroll flock to this scenic path that largely follows the shoreline on the western edge of town to **Kincaid Park.** Look for whales, particularly off the trail just outside downtown, and also watch for other wildlife, including moose, as you head south from Point Woronzof around Kincaid Park. On a clear day you may spot Mount McKinley to the far north and Mount Susitna (the "Sleeping Lady") to the west.

GALLERIES & MUSEUMS
Art lovers will find plenty to browse in the dozens of downtown galleries. Try to attend a **First Friday Art Walk**, held between 5:30 and 7:30 p.m. on the first Friday of the month, when dozens of galleries, shops, and restaurants offer food, drink, live music, and appearances by exhibited artists *(the Anchorage Daily News prints a map/guide).*

For outstanding photos and paintings of traditional Alaska subjects, try **Stephan Fine Arts Gallery** *(600 W. 6th Ave., tel 907/ 274-5009 or 800/544-0779),* which carries Thomas Mangelsen's distinctive bear photos.

At the other end of the art spectrum is the nonprofit **International Gallery of Contemporary Art** *(427 D St., tel 907/ 279-1116).* Recent displays included a video installation of a lady applying red lipstick and a collection that chronicled an artist's

hip-replacement surgery, making art of his blood, X-rays, bone fragments, and related paraphernalia.

Aurora Fine Art Gallery *(406 G St., corner of 5th Ave., tel 907/274-0234)* offers a blend of traditional and contemporary styles, epitomized by the "totemic design" pieces by Marilyn Kaminsky Miller sometimes carried by the shop. Miller takes classic Native subjects and nature scenes and renders them in imaginative form via copper, aluminum, and raku-fired clay.

For something different, check out the scintillating array of handblown glass at the **Alaska Glass Gallery** *(423 G St., tel 907/279-4527).* This bright space packed with radiant, vividly colored glass sculptures is reminiscent of a sunlit coral reef. But be careful—the gallery is tight.

To browse art you wish you could buy, visit the **Anchorage Museum of History & Art.** Though the official state museum

Anchorage Museum of History & Art
www.anchoragemuseum.org
✉ 121 W. 7th Ave.
☎ 907/343-4326
🕐 Closed Mon. & Tues. mid-Sept.–mid-May
💲 $$

Giant veggies

Veggies love the land of the midnight sun. With TLC and 18 to 20 hours a day of energizing sunshine, vegetables in the Mat-Su Borough balloon to preposterous sizes. Backs strain to lift 60-pound zucchini. Pulling 20-pound carrots from the ground qualifies as an upper-body workout. One bunch of Swiss chard topped out at nine feet—tall enough to qualify as a tree. The Olympics of big produce is the Giant Cabbage Weigh-off at the Alaska State Fair, where the winner harvests $2,000. The current record cabbage tipped the scales at 105.6 pounds. ∎

Landscapes in the Anchorage Museum of History & Art capture Alaska's natural beauty.

Alaska Experience Center

www.alaskaexperiencetheatre.com

✉ 705 W. 6th Ave.

☎ 907/276-3730 or 877/276-3730

💲 $$

is in Juneau, the capital, this larger, expanding museum covers all of Alaska, serving as a de facto second yet equally fine museum. The main floor devotes six galleries to works from the time of European contact to modern days. It opens with an engraving of a Prince William Sound man done in 1784 by Captain Cook's expedition artist and devotes much wall space to massive landscapes by such acclaimed Alaska painters as Sydney Laurence.

Native art and other objects depicting the lives of Alaska's many indigenous peoples fills the **Alaska Gallery,** which occupies the second floor. This permanent exhibit takes visitors from prehistoric times up to Alaska's present, and docents offer gallery tours four times daily in summer. Visitors aren't likely to miss the cutaway diorama of an Aleut house or the full-size section of the trans-Alaska oil pipeline. But take time to look at the little things, too, such as a photograph taken in 1908 in Nome of men in white top hats herding reindeer through town during a parade.

Just west of the Town Square

fountains and flowers are four venues that showcase what Alaska has to offer. *Aurora— Alaska's Great Northern Lights (Sydney Laurence Theatre, Alaska Center for the Performing Arts, 621 W. 6th Ave., tel 907/263-2993, closed early Sept.–late May, $$)* is a 40-minute show of aurora borealis photos set to music. The **Alaska Experience Center** has two offerings: *Alaska the Greatland* and an earthquake exhibit. The former is a lavish 40-minute film about the state shown on a vast, wraparound dome screen. The earthquake exhibit features a quake simulator, interactive displays, photos, and a movie about the devastating 1964 quake. Aimed primarily at children, the **Imaginarium** *(737 W. 5th Ave., tel 907/276-3179, $)* science center hosts exhibits on Arctic ecology and Alaska marine life, as well as a bubble lab and planetarium.

A store as unusual as its name, the **Oomingmak Co-op** *(609 H St., tel 907/272-9225 or 888/360-9665)* sells sweaters, hats, baby booties, and other clothing hand-knitted by Native craftspeople using qiviut, the ultrawarm inner hair of musk oxen.

Beyond downtown there are places worth seeking out. Inside a Wells Fargo Bank building, the **Heritage Library Museum** (*301 W. Northern Lights Blvd., tel 907/265-2834, closed Labor Day–Memorial Day*) boasts one of the city's largest collections of Native artifacts and artwork by several of Alaska's masters. The museum centers on the first floor, but you'll find other items in elevator lobbies throughout the building.

GARDENS & PARKS

For a glimpse of native flora, stroll the **Alaska Botanical Garden** (*4601 Campbell Airstrip Rd., tel 907/770-3692, $*), especially the **Wildflower Trail** and **Lowenfels Family Nature Trail.** Along the former you'll see bluebell, fool's huckleberry, wild geranium, chocolate lily, and other blooms. The latter will lead to a creek that hosts spawning king salmon in the summer. Watch for moose and bears in this 110-acre spruce-and-birch woodland.

Chugach State Park

www.dnr.state.ak.us/parks /units/chugach

🅰 93 C1–C2

✉ Potter Section House, Mile 115.2, Seward Hwy.

☎ 907/345-5014

To understand how important aviation has been and continues to be in Alaska, visit the **Alaska Aviation Heritage Museum** (*4721 Aircraft Dr., tel 907/248-5325, closed Tues., $$*). The museum's collection of 26 aircraft includes such rarities as a 1944 Grumman Widgeon amphibious plane and a Stinson L-1 Army reconnaissance plane, the only one of its kind still fit to fly. An observation platform overlooks the huge floatplane base on neighboring Lake Hood, constantly abuzz with small aircraft.

A couple of miles east of the botanical garden lies the western boundary of **Chugach State Park,** Anchorage's half-million-acre backyard playground. Locals make about a million visits a year to hike, ski, climb, raft, fish, pick berries, canoe, and otherwise enjoy this wild sanctuary. You could spend a week deep inside this wilderness inhabited by bears and wolves or simply drive 20 minutes from downtown, walk a short trail, and be treated to a 360-degree panorama of the city, Cook Inlet, and mountains. ∎

Cyclists pause at an overlook on the Tony Knowles Coastal Trail to admire views of icy Cook Inlet.

Buying Alaska Native art

All over Alaska, even in remote locations, visitors will encounter shops selling traditional Alaska Native art. The variety is wonderfully overwhelming, reflecting the different styles, themes, traditions, and media that have developed in different regions. Travelers will see the fine beadwork on moose hide characteristic of Athabascan tribes, the etched walrus ivory produced by Eskimos, and the intricately carved and brightly painted headdresses of the Tlingit, to name a few.

Along with the variety, the high-quality craftsmanship and natural materials that go into Native art will delight visitors. These diverse cultures have spent thousands of years refining their traditional arts, and genuine Native art is dazzling. However, not all the items advertised in shops as "Native" art are genuine. Each year collectors spend millions of dollars on Native art, and the temptation to cash in on that hot market has given rise to unscrupulous imitators, such as carvers who substitute resin for soapstone. The authenticity of a pair of $15 earrings may not matter to a buyer (then again, it may), but travelers paying hundreds or

thousands of dollars for a work of Native art likely want to ensure it's the real McCoy.

How to know? Perhaps the easiest way is to look for the "silver hand" sticker, which bears a hand symbol and the words "Authentic Native Handicraft from Alaska." While intended to guarantee that items for sale were made by a Native Alaskan, it does not, of course, guarantee quality. The method also isn't foolproof, as stickers can be transferred and not all genuine pieces bear the silver hand.

Probably the surest approach, short of personally knowing the artist, is to buy from a reputable shop. This isn't intuitive if you're an outsider, but one good bet is to patronize gift shops at museums and cultural centers. For example, shops at the Alaska Native Heritage Center, in Anchorage, and the Alaska State Museum, in Juneau, are well known for Native artwork. A less obvious choice, but one renowned for both authenticity and good value, is the gift shop at the Alaska Native Medical Center, in Anchorage. For advice regarding reputable shops at other museums and cultural centers, contact the Alaska State Council on the Arts *(411 W. 4th Ave., Suite 1E, Anchorage,*

AK 99501, tel 907/269-6610 or 888/278-7424, www.eed.state.ak.us/aksca).

When visiting an unfamiliar shop, ask about an item's origins or request written proof of its authenticity. If the salesperson claims a seal figurine was made of walrus ivory by a Yupik on St. Lawrence, ask the clerk to write that claim on your receipt. Carefully inspect the material from which artwork is made. For example, genuine soapstone can be distinguished from resin by its cool feel (resin is warmer) and its weight (soapstone is heavier). A brochure outlining such identification methods is available from the Alaska State Council on the Arts *(www.ftc.gov/alaska)*.

If worse comes to worst and you are scammed, lodge a complaint with the Federal Trade Commission *(tel 877/382-4357, www.ftc.gov)* or the Alaska Attorney General's Office *(tel 907/269-5100, www.law .state.ak.us/consumer)*. ∎

Opposite: A Tlingit ornamental visor. Right: Dorica Jackson, the wife of famed Tlingit carver Nathan Jackson, colors a totem pole made by her husband. Below: An artisan at the Alaska Native Heritage Center sands a soapstone figure.

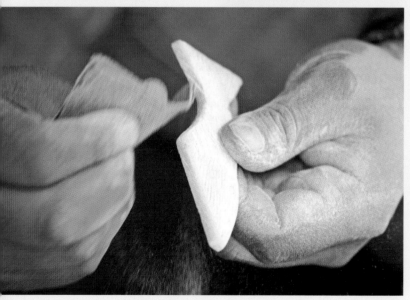

Turnagain Arm

Chugach State Park
www.dnr.state.ak.us/parks
/units/chugach
🅰 92 C1–C2
✉ Potter Section House, Mile 115.2, Seward Hwy.
☎ 907/345-5014

MILEPOSTS
Milepost references correspond to actual mileage signs along the road, which are calculated from Seward—the town that gives the highway its name.

Opposite: Birders and othernature lovers visit Potter Marsh and scan the wetlands for the birds and spawning salmon that frequent the area.

THE OFFICIAL BOUNDARIES OF THE MUNICIPALITY OF Anchorage extend far south and southeast of the city proper, encompassing small towns, rural areas, and vast wilderness expanses. The sprawl continues to roll southward down the Seward Highway, along the northeast shore of Turnagain Arm, the southern branch of Cook Inlet. The highway twists and turns for some 50 miles south of downtown to where Turnagain Arm ends and the Kenai Peninsula begins.

The Seward Highway forms the backbone of south Anchorage. All attractions lie along this shore-hugging highway, either off the handful of short side roads or along trails that start from the side roads or highway. This guide covers the 43 miles (70 km) between urban Anchorage and the tip of Turnagain Arm—named for Capt. James Cook's 1778 need to once again turn his ship around when he discovered the passage did not go through.

Potter Marsh, as residents call it, is the most scenic and accessible part of the **Anchorage Coastal Wildlife Refuge.** Officially named the Potter Point State Game Refuge (*Alaska Department of Fish & Game, tel*

907/267-2556), the marsh lies at Mile 117.4, less than 10 miles (16 km) south of downtown. Watch for moose browsing amid willows that line the short drive leading to the trailhead parking lot—they'll sometimes feed in the marsh, too.

Bring binoculars to scout for birds along the quarter-mile interpretive boardwalk. During spring migration—roughly late April to mid-May—large flocks of waterfowl throng the marsh. Though early summer sees fewer birds, a number of species do come to nest on the refuge, including bald eagles, arctic terns, and, most conspicuous, lesser Canada geese. Seeing a dozen fuzzy goslings paddling along behind mama goose is a highlight for many visitors. In late July and August masses of migrating shorebirds pause here on their way south.

CHUGACH STATE PARK
As one drives south from Potter Marsh, the sheer scenic power of this stretch of the Seward Highway hits home. Immediately to the right are the waters of Turnagain Arm. Here, at the wide base of this ever-narrowing wedge of water, it's about 10 miles (16 km) across to the majestic Kenai Peninsula. To the left are the peaks and forests of **Chugach State Park,** punctuated by rocky cliffs, creeks, and waterfalls. For information about the state park's

Ice worms

Thanks to Robert Service's humorous poem, "The Ballad of the Ice Worm Cocktail," many people think the ice worm is about as real as the unicorn or the jackalope. But ice worms do exist, though not typically in cocktails. About half an inch long and as husky as a piece of thread, ice worms came by their common name because they do, indeed, inhabit ice, living just beneath the surface of glaciers. Scientists have yet to understand how these creatures thrive in the extraordinary cold. ■

The Seward
Highway skirts
the shore of
Turnagain Arm,
offering stunning
views of the
surrounding
mountains.

many offerings, pull in at Mile 115.2 and visit its headquarters, housed in the historic **Potter Section House** *(closed weekends),* home to a crew of railroad workers in the old days.

A few hundred feet down the highway is the turnoff to **Potter Creek Viewpoint & Trail.** (The state park administers this pullout and other turnouts, viewpoints, and trails down to Girdwood.) Stroll over to the platform here for fine views, enhanced by spotting scopes and informational signs. Travelers looking for a short hike will enjoy the 0.4-mile **nature trail.** Those looking for a longer hike have also come to the right place, as this is the northernmost trailhead for the **Turnagain Arm Trail** (formerly the Old Johnson Trail).

This is among the state's most beloved trails, used heavily by locals. For 9.4 miles (15 km) it parallels the highway, offering grand vistas across Turnagain Arm, slipping through thick spruce forests, and crossing cool creeks. Due to its south-facing slope and sun exposure it's also one of the first places in the area where snow melts and wildflowers erupt in the spring. After a modest initial climb, the route remains fairly level and easy until the last 2 miles, which are moderately difficult. Hikers short on time or who want to start somewhere besides Potter Creek can choose from two entry points on the way to trail's end at Windy Corner.

One of those intermediate entry points is at **McHugh Creek Picnic Area** (Mile 111.9), but trail access isn't the only reason to stop here. The picnic area offers three successively higher parking lots *(fee)* with increasingly expansive views. The second lot features a viewing platform, wildlife interpretive signs, and spotting scopes. Survey the mountains beyond Turnagain Arm or swivel the scopes around and scan steep slopes to the east for Dall sheep—mountainsides above this stretch of highway are among the best places in Alaska to spot these snow-white relatives of bighorn sheep. Interpretive signs cover subjects ranging from moose stomachs to the history of the railroad.

A mile and a half farther, off the west side of the highway, is **Beluga Point,** another pullout with great views of the arm and scopes with which to watch Dall sheep. As its name suggests, the point is also a great spot to observe the beluga whales that cruise these waters following coho salmon runs in mid- to late August. Though their numbers have dropped, these small white whales that always seem to be grinning still swim by on occasion. *(Warning: Never walk out onto mudflats that are uncovered at low tide—neither here at Beluga Point nor anywhere along*

Turnagain Arm. What looks like solid ground may turn out to be quicksand; people have gotten stuck and drowned as the tide rapidly rolled back in.)

Watching a rising tide may sound as exciting as watching paint dry, but when observed from a safe distance, the tide at Turnagain Arm can be a thrilling sight. The arm experiences one of the world's broadest tidal fluctuations—up to 35 feet between low and high tides. As that enormous mass of incoming water squeezes into the narrowing confines of the arm, it creates a tidal bore—a rush of water some six feet high. The arm is one of only two places in the U.S. where this phenomenon occurs—the other is Knik Arm, the branch of Cook Inlet that lies north of Anchorage.

Perhaps the best site from which to behold the tidal bore is **Bird Point Scenic Overlook,** (Mile 96.5), where interpretive signs explain the tide changes, and a handsome network of stone paths and platforms overlooks the arm. About 45 minutes after low tide in Anchorage, plus or minus 30 minutes, the growling wall of water will sweep past the point. (Of course, depending on conditions, the wave may be as puny as six inches and that growl may be more of a purr.) The tidal bore stretches all the way across the arm and travels ten to 15 miles (24 km) an hour. Sometimes locals actually surf the wave.

Between Miles 95.3 and 92.5, on the west side of the highway, you'll encounter five scenic turnouts that feature enough interpretive panels to constitute a museum. Stop and learn about the area's prehistory, the abandoned gold rush town of Sunrise, ways in which the 1964 earthquake and tidal wave reshaped Turnagain

Arm, and the method used by local Dena'ina Athabascan to hunt belugas. (At low tide hunters would place an upside-down tree trunk in the mudflats, hide atop it as the tide rolled back in, then harpoon a passing beluga. The men attached the harpoon point to air-filled bladders that would slow the beluga till fellow hunters in kayaks could catch it.)

Bird Point Scenic Overlook provides an opportunity to see the dramatic tidal bores that sweep across Turnagain Arm.

Crow Creek Mine
www.akmining.com/mine/crow.htm
- 93 C1
- ✉ Crow Creek Rd.
- ☎ 907/278-8060
- ⏱ Closed mid-Sept.– mid-May
- 💲 $

Portage Glacier & Portage Valley
- 93 D1
- ✉ Begich, Boggs Visitor Center
- ☎ 907/783-2326
- ⏱ Open daily summer; Winter hours vary

ALYESKA HIGHWAY

At Mile 90 motorists reach Girdwood Junction, though Girdwood is nowhere in sight. The reason is that the town was so damaged by the 1964 earthquake and tidal wave that its citizens decided to rebuild 2 miles up the Alyeska Highway—the spur road running northeast from the junction.

Up the Alyeska Highway, just shy of the new Girdwood, Crow Creek Road forks off to the left. Three miles (5 km) up this deeply rutted gravel road is the **Crow Creek Mine.** From the 1890s to the 1940s, this productive mine yielded tons of gold. Eight original buildings filled with mining artifacts are open. Though fairly ramshackle, the site is probably an accurate reflection of the mine's rough-hewn past. Gold still flows down Crow Creek, and visitors

can rent a pan and bucket, listen to the attendant's brief instructions, then try their luck.

A mile farther the highway ends at **Alyeska Resort** *(tel 907/754-1111 or 800/880-3880, www.alyeskaresort.com),* a ski area, with offerings for summer and winter fun. Turn left on Arlberg Road and continue past the condos and vacation homes about a mile to the resort's Alyeska Prince Hotel. Behind this luxurious hotel, you can catch a tram to the 2,300-foot level of Mount Alyeska. From here you can enjoy the fantastic views over basic food at a cafeteria or indulge in fine, four-diamond dining and the incredible setting at the Seven Glaciers Restaurant. Visitors who have made prior arrangements can paraglide down instead of taking the tram. Other summer activities include hiking, mountain biking, and berry picking.

PORTAGE

At Mile 78.9 on the Seward Highway travelers arrive at the **Portage Glacier** and **Portage Valley,** the southernmost attractions in the Municipality of Anchorage. Turn onto the spur road that heads east toward the glacier and Whittier. As you drive along Portage Creek through this lovely valley framed by mountains and glaciers, you'll pass a number of campgrounds and hiking trails. Just past the 5-mile mark, turn right and stop by the **Begich, Boggs Visitor Center,** an elaborate facility with ample exhibits. From the glassed-in viewing room you can admire icebergs bobbing about in Portage Lake, though the glacier itself has receded out of sight. Consider taking a guided boat tour to its face. ■

North Anchorage

Once motorists headed north on the Glenn Highway clear the urban core of Anchorage, most speed up to 65 and don't slow down till they reach the Knik River and enter the Mat-Su Borough, about 30 miles (48 km) up the road. That's fine if you're late for a wedding, but travelers should tarry a bit. North Anchorage harbors several intriguing cultural and historical sites and offers a wealth of natural beauty and outdoor activities. The Glenn Highway ties the area together.

Alaska Native Heritage Center

www.alaskanative.net

🗺 93 C2

✉ 8800 Heritage Center Dr.

☎ 907/330-8000 or 800/315-6608

💲 $$$$

ALASKA NATIVE HERITAGE CENTER

On the city outskirts, at Mile 4.4, take the Muldoon Road exit north and follow signs to the Alaska Native Heritage Center. *(Free shut-tles also available from several downtown locations, midtown, and Spenard near airport.)* This is an excellent place to learn about Alaska Native culture and history. Although it displays wonderful

MILEPOSTS

All Glenn Highway milepost references mark the distance from the highway's origin in downtown Anchorage.

A Tlingit dancer dons traditional garb for a performance at the Alaska Native Heritage Center.

The Alaska Native Heritage Center serves as a doorway to the region's rich cultural legacy.

Eagle River Nature Center

www.ernc.org

🅰 93 C2

✉ 32750 Eagle River Rd.

☎ 907/694-2108

🕐 Open daily Summer & Tues.–Sun. May & Sept.

💲 $$

artwork and historical artifacts, the center is emphatically not a museum. People representing 11 Native cultures gather here to preserve their traditions and educate others about them.

Staff greet visitors at the Welcome House. From there a half-mile trail leads around a small lake to several "village" sites, each depicting a particular culture or a group of similar cultures. Tours leave every half hour. Villages include an underground community house built in Inupiaq and St. Lawrence Yupik styles, as well as a large clan house that reflects Southeast Native traditions.

The **Hall of Cultures** brims with art and crafts, both historic and contemporary. Stop by the tables at which Native artists from around the state create their works while chatting with visitors. Many of the works are for sale. The **Gathering Place** hosts Native storytellers, dancers, athletes, and other performers.

Exit the Glenn at Mile 6.1 and head east on Arctic Valley Road, which climbs a steep, gravelly route for 7 miles to **Alpenglow at Arctic Valley** *(tel 907/428-1208)*, a ski resort favored among locals for blueberry picking in late summer and fall, as well as excellent hiking. Strong hikers can likely make the 3.5-mile round-trip climb of **Rendez-vous Peak** in two to three hours, but should allow an extra hour to loll atop the 4,050-foot (1,234 m) summit and feast on the scenery.

EAGLE RIVER NATURE CENTER

Those who crave hiking with a dose of education should take the Eagle River exit (Mile 13.4) and turn right on Eagle River Road. Follow this road east through a bedroom community for a few miles till you're alongside a pretty river hugged by burly mountains. At the end of the road, 12.5 miles (20 km) from the Glenn, you'll find the Eagle River Nature Center.

This small nature center features nice displays and a helpful, friendly staff that conduct daily nature walks in summer. The picnic area provides a scope with which to watch wildlife and savor the incredible natural setting. Get a trail map and choose from among several excellent hikes.

The **Iditarod National Historic Trail** (aka Crow Pass Trail), one of Alaska's most storied multiday routes, winds 27 miles (43.5 km) from the center to the end of Crow Creek Road, above Girdwood. Watch for grizzlies, glaciers, moose, beavers, Dall sheep, mine ruins, peaks, and pristine forest. The first 4.5 miles from the center are easy to moderate.

The Eagle River Nature Center features a network of hiking trails and viewing platforms.

Eklutna Historical Park
www.eklutnainc.com

⚑ 93 C2
☎ 907/688-6026
⊕ Closed mid-Sept.–mid-May
$ $$

At the other end of the scale is the center's **Rodak Nature Trail,** a gentle, 0.75-mile (1.2 km) interpretive loop along a creek past beaver- and salmon-viewing decks. From this trail hikers can follow the Eagle River along the 3-mile **Albert Loop Trail** *(except when portions are closed to allow bears to fish for salmon).*

EKLUTNA

In this Athabascan village, just west of Mile 26.5, you'll find **Eklutna Historical Park,** an unlikely blend of Native and Russian Orthodox spiritual traditions. Filled with about 80 brightly colored spirit houses, the Athabascan cemetery dates to at least 1652, and probably has been in use for a thousand years. Also on the grounds is the 1870 **St. Nicholas Russian Orthodox Church.** Native touches in the building's design speak to its largely Athabascan parish.

Head east from Eklutna and follow signs 10 miles (16 km) up a slow, curving road to the campground and day-use area at **Eklutna Lake Recreation Area** *(tel 907/688-0908).* Carved by the retreating Eklutna Glacier, this piney valley and 7-mile lake welcome boaters, fishers, hikers, mountain bikers, ATV riders, and horseback riders. ■

Mat-Su Borough

Mat-Su Borough
🗺 93 D3
Visitor information
www.alaskavisit.com
✉ Mile 35.5, Parks Hwy.
☎ 907/746-5000
🕐 Closed mid-Sept.– mid-May

THE MATANUSKA-SUSITNA BOROUGH IS ALASKA'S BREAD-basket—not that that's saying much in this state of unforgiving weather and equally harsh soil. The Mat-Su Borough, as Alaskans call it, does have a relatively mild climate and some flat land suitable for farming, but the region also contains huge mountains, glaciers, broad braided rivers, and vast expanses of bear- and wolf-laden wilderness.

The Mat-Su's reputation as an agricultural region stems largely from a decision made by the Roosevelt Administration during the Great Depression, when Midwestern farms were failing by the bushel. The government recruited 203 families whose farms had gone under and in 1935 transplanted them to the Mat-Su. They struggled terribly at first, but enough of these colonists (the project was called the Matanuska Colony) perse-vered, eventually developing a viable farming community. Today the Mat-Su is better known as an outdoor-activity destination and the site of burgeoning bedroom communities for Anchorage, less than an hour's drive south.

The vast Mat-Su's geographic boundaries are wildly arbitrary. The borough covers a 24,683 square miles (63,930 sq. km) area that reaches north even into Denali National Park—more than 200 miles from its southern boundary, defined by Cook Inlet and Knik Arm. For the purposes of this book the three other mar-gins are Matanuska Glacier to the east, the Susitna River to the west, and Hatcher Pass Road (see p. 114–115) to the north. At about 30 by 100 miles, that's plenty big enough.

Palmer
🗺 93 C3
Visitor information
✉ 723 S. Valley Way
☎ 907/745-2880
🕐 Closed weekends mid-Sept.–mid-May

PALMER
The 1935 colonists set down roots in Palmer, so it's an appro-priate place to begin a journey

through the Mat-Su Borough. Start at the **Palmer Visitor Information Center, Museum & Chamber of Commerce** (*723 S. Valley Way, tel 907/745-2880*), which serves as a fount of

tourist information and houses a small history museum dedicated to the Matanuska Colony. Whipsaws, scythes, and clothes wringers all testify to the colonists' backbreaking work. The collection's dogsled and ice chisel remind visitors that these farmers also had to cope with unfamiliar conditions. Don't miss the gorgeous community garden.

A short walk from the visitor center is the **Colony House Museum,** former home of Oscar and Irene Beylund; it has been restored to look as it did between 1935 and 1945. The Beylunds' furnishings and personal possessions evoke the early days of the colony, but what really animates this museum are its guides. Most are descendants of original colonists and a few are original colonists who came here as children. They bring personal knowledge and passion to their discussions of life in the colony.

Across the street is the **Colony Inn.** Built in 1935, the building was a teacher dormitory through the 1960s. Today it's an elegant small inn and restaurant.

Colony House Museum

🅰 93 C3
✉ 316 E. Elmwood Ave.
☎ 907/745-1935
🕐 Open daily May– Aug., & by appt. rest of year)
💲 $

Fall colors illuminate the view along the Glenn Highway.

Visitors to the Musk Ox Farm can get a close look at these quintessential arctic beasts— and vice versa.

Musk Ox Farm
www.muskoxfarm.org
🅼 93 C3
☎ 907/745-4151
🕐 Closed mid-Sept.– early May
💲 $$

A block east, at the corner of E. Elmwood Avenue and S. Denali Street, is **United Protestant Church,** otherwise known as the "Church of a Thousand Trees" or "Church of a Thousand Logs." Colonists built this church between 1935 and 1937, using logs even for the striking altar. The church is still in use, so visit it respectfully.

For another dose of colonial history, head south on the Glenn Highway about a mile to **Colony Village** *(2075 Glenn Hwy., tel 907/745-4827, closed Sun.)* on the Alaska State Fairgrounds. The village comprises a collection of relocated historic buildings. If it's late August or early September, you can eat corn dogs and ride a roller coaster at the state fair.

Back roads vein the valley, crossing farmland established by colonists. Where better to loop among the farms than on **Farm Loop Road?** From Palmer, head north on the Glenn a few miles and turn west onto Palmer-Fishhook Road, the turnoff to Hatcher Pass, at Mile 49.5. Drive

1.4 miles, turn right onto the Farm Loop, and follow it for 3 miles (4.8 km) past fields dotted with horses and traditional barns, ending at Mile 50.7 of the Glenn.

Half a mile south off the Glenn, a short spur road leads west to the **Musk Ox Farm** *(watch for signs).* Musk oxen are fascinating creatures, though they neither have musk glands nor belong to the ox family. At a half ton, their most noticeable feature is their shaggy coat. These long guard hairs protect musk oxen from frigid climes in their native habitat—far north regions such as Greenland. In fact, the farm's animals are descendants of 34 oxen brought from Greenland in the 1930s to replace the Alaska musk oxen, which had been hunted out by the 1860s. Today some 4,500 musk oxen roam wild in Alaska.

The replacement musk oxen weren't brought over primarily for conservation reasons, though. They were intended to provide Native Alaskans with a cottage industry. Beneath a musk ox's guard hairs is a woolly undercoat called qiviut, said to be eight times warmer than sheep's wool yet very silky and lightweight. Farm staff comb out the qiviut once a year and send it to Native weavers, who in turn make scarves, hats, and other garments from this marvelous hair.

The gift shop sells a variety of qiviut products; even if you don't buy anything, at least feel the material. Beside the shop is a small musk oxen museum, a place to browse while waiting for tours, which leave every half hour. Each tour includes a close look at these critters.

WASILLA

Centered 10 miles (16 km) west of Palmer via the Palmer-Wasilla or Parks Highway is Wasilla. Resist the urge to hit the gas and put this town in your rearview mirror, as there are a few worthwhile sights. Start on Main Street at the **Dorothy Page Museum** (*323 N. Main St., tel 907/373-9071, closed Sept.–April, $*), amid the remnants of old town Wasilla, a block north of the Parks Highway. This small facility offers rotating exhibits and interpretive displays about early pioneer life.

Turn off the Parks at Neuser Drive (Mile 47), and follow signs about a mile to the **Museum of Alaska Transportation & Industry** (*3800 W. Museum Dr., Mile 47, Parks Hwy., 907/376-1211, closed Mon., $$*), a large facility with a split personality. Inside the main building are orderly exhibits on bush pilots, cherry vintage cars, and the hang glider one Robert Burns used to sail down from the summit of Mount McKinley. Outside, however, looks like a junkyard, though visitors enjoy wandering amid the jumble of boats, police cars, helicopters, ambulances, and military jets.

Wasilla is a center for dog mushing and the Iditarod. On Knik-Goose Bay Road you'll find the **Iditarod Trail Sled Dog Race Headquarters** (*Mile 2.2, tel 907/376-5155 or 907/248-6874*) and the **Knik Museum & Sled Dog Mushers' Hall of Fame** (*Mile 13.9, Knik-Goose Bay Rd., tel 907/376-7755 or 907/376-2005,*

A statue outside the Iditarod Trail Sled Dog Race Headquarters pays tribute to the sport's dogs and mushers.

closed mid-Sept.–June). Both present exhibits and artifacts related to mushing and that most venerable of all sled dog races, the Iditarod. Some Wasilla-area mushers, including four-time Iditarod champion Martin Buser, offer tours of their kennels. You can chat with these mushers about the history of the sport, the rigors of the race, and their training methods. Best of all, you can pet sled dogs and cuddle puppies. ■

Wasilla
🅰 93 C3
Visitor information
✉ 415 E. Railroad Ave.
☎ 907/376-1299
🕐 Closed mid-Sept.–mid-May

Hatcher Pass Drive

Hatcher Pass Road runs from the low country by the Matanuska River to the low country by the Susitna River, along the way winding through the handsome high country of the Talkeetna Mountains. The route's higher elevations receive lots of snow, which often closes the midsection of this route from October through early July. In summer the road is suitable for most vehicles, although the middle 25 miles are gravel and sometimes narrow and bumpy, so slow down and enjoy the views. For general info, contact the Mat-Su Convention & Visitors Bureau *(tel 907/746-5000)* or Alaska State Parks *(tel 907/745-3975)*.

The route begins 7.5 miles (12 km) north of downtown **Palmer** at Mile 49.5 (as measured from Anchorage) on the Glenn Highway. Turn west on Palmer-Fishhook Road (aka Fishhook–Willow Road) and follow it north through farm country. At Mile 8.5 take the turnout for the **Little Susitna River ❶**, a frothy waterway that rushes down from Mint Glacier.

The next 5 miles (8 km) feature half a dozen turnouts from which you can savor the Little Susitna and tundra-covered mountains in every direction. This beautiful stretch ends at a parking area for the **Gold Mint Trail ❷**. Here the road parts ways

with the Little Susitna. To see more of the river, hike this gently sloping trail through the waterway's striking alpine valley. It's about 8 miles (12.9 km) to **Mint Glacier.**

After a sharp turn at the Gold Mint parking area, the road climbs steeply west. At Mile 14.6, Archangel Road, a rough spur best left to 4WD and mountain goats, leads north to a trailhead for **Reed Lakes.** Parking for the **Fishhook Trail** is right off the main road at Mile 16.4.

At Mile 17 visitors approach the spur to **Independence Mine State Historical Park ❸** *(tel 907/745-2827 or 907/745-3975, www.dnr.state.ak.us/parks/units/indmine.htm,*

Historic buildings and tundra-covered slopes grace the route through Hatcher Pass.

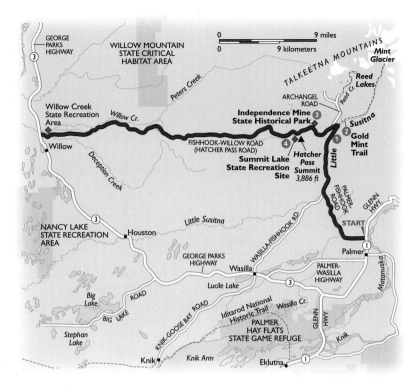

WILLOW MOUNTAIN STATE CRITICAL HABITAT AREA

0   9 miles
0   9 kilometers

TALKEETNA MOUNTAINS

Mint Glacier

Reed Cr. Lakes

Peters Creek

ARCHANGEL ROAD

Willow Creek State Recreation Area

Willow Cr.

Independence Mine State Historical Park ➌

Susitna

Willow

Deception Creek

FISHHOOK-WILLOW ROAD (HATCHER PASS ROAD)

Summit Lake State Recreation Site

Hatcher Pass Summit 3,886 ft

➍

Little

➊ Gold Mint Trail
➋

PALMER-FISHHOOK ROAD

GLENN HWY.

NANCY LAKE STATE RECREATION AREA

Little Susitna

Houston

WASILLA-FISHHOOK RD.

START

Palmer

Matanuska

GEORGE PARKS HIGHWAY

Wasilla

PALMER-WASILLA HIGHWAY

BIG LAKE ROAD

Big Lake

Lucile Lake

KNIK-GOOSE BAY ROAD

Iditarod National Historic Trail

Wasilla Cr.

GLENN HWY.

Stephan Lake

PALMER HAY FLATS STATE GAME REFUGE

Knik

Knik Arm

Eklutna

Knik

closed mid-Sept.–mid-June, $). While individual prospectors panned for gold flakes down in the creeks, the big outfits opted for hard-rock mining in the mountains, searching for the mother lodes that spawned those flakes. At its peak, in the early 1940s, the Independence Mine employed more than 200 workers, an easy number to imagine when you tour the mess hall, cookhouse, bunkhouses, commissary, assay office, and other buildings that comprise this sprawling complex. Visitors can wander around on their own, peer through a few windows, and peruse the interpretive signs, but it's better to take one of the informative guided tours, which go inside several of the buildings.

At Mile 18.9 the road peaks at 3,886-foot (12,870 m) **Hatcher Pass Summit.** Trails fan out from the parking lot, letting you roam the alpine slopes and soak up the views. Similar landscapes and views await at Mile 19.3; park at **Summit Lake State**

🅰 See area map pp. 92–93 B3–C3
▶ Palmer
↔ 49 miles (78 km) one way
🕐 2–3 hours plus stops
▶ Junction of Parks Hwy., 70 miles (112.7 km) north of Anchorage

NOT TO BE MISSED
• Little Susitna River
• Independence Mine
• Hatcher Pass Summit

Recreation Site ➍ and stroll around the lake or up to the bluff.

From the summit the road narrows and winds steeply down for about 7 miles (11.2 km) before running straight and flat. Despite a few good views, the occasional beaver pond, and glimpses of Willow Creek, this section of road, particularly the last 10 or 15 miles, is just another pretty drive. ■

Just outside Anchorage, this trail summits Flattop Mountain, in Chugach State Park.

More places to visit in Anchorage & Mat-Su

CHILKOOT CHARLIE'S

Known affectionately as Koot's, this huge bar/restaurant/nightclub features three stages and 15 bars. While largely a loud, raucous, hormone-charged anarchy of young singles, it's stranger than that. The bartenders and staff wear odd costumes, and customers sit on padded tree stumps and beer kegs. Many of the bars are themed, such as the **Swing Bar,** a 1940s send-up complete with big band music, martinis, and black-and-white TVs. Other themes are truly bizarre, such as the **Russia Room** and the **Soviet Walk,** which, respectively, go for a tsarist ambience and the feel of a Soviet subway. Somehow Koot's get such big-name bands as the Beach Boys, Metallica, and Bon Jovi to play here. It was named America's best bar in 2000 by *Playboy* magazine—nota Nobel Prize, but hey, it's a bar. ✉ 1071 W. 25th Ave., Anchorage ☎ 907/279-1692, www.koots.com

CHUGACH STATE PARK HILLSIDE TRAIL SYSTEM

Hikers rave about this deservedly popular network of trails in Chugach State Park, on the east side of Anchorage just 20 minutes from downtown. Perhaps nowhere else in the U.S. can you travel from skyscrapers to wilderness in less time. Short spur roads off Hillside Drive lead to major access points where visitors can park and start tromping: **Prospect Heights,** off O'Malley, and **Glen Alps,** off Upper Huffman. From Glen Alps, for example, you can take a 3.5-mile (5.6 km) round-trip trail (1,550-foot/4,724 meter elevation gain) to the top of **Flattop Mountain**—a moderate climb but for a slippery scramble up the steep last stretch. Rewards include panoramic views of Anchorage, Cook Inlet, the Kenai Peninsula, and even the distant Alaska Range. Pick up a copy of the park's Hillside Trail System map/brochure. ⚠ 93 C2 ✉ Chugach State Park ☎ 907/345-5014, www.alaskastateparks.org 💲 $ (parking)

MR. WHITEKEYS' FLY BY NIGHT CLUB

This club is even stranger than Koot's. It's owned and operated by a former Chilkoot Charlie's employee known only as Mr. Whitekeys. The Fly by Night showcases such top acts as Dr. John, Riders in the Sky, Mose Allison, and Clarence "Gatemouth" Brown. The club also offers what it terms "gormay kweezeen," which includes "the finest selection of Spam entrées you'll find anywhere in the world." (Ask about the Spam thing; it's a running joke with deep Alaska roots.) But the Fly by Night's true claim to fame is its nightly show. In summer the club presents the *Whale Fat Follies,* a sharp-tongued, insightful, hilarious, and often raunchy revue that skewers all things Alaska and costars a tap-dancing outhouse. The club bills it as "the Alaska show that the Department of Tourism does NOT want you to see." ✉ 3300 Spenard Rd., Anchorage ☎ 907/279-7726, www.flybynightclub.com 🕐 Closed Sun. & Mon. & Jan.–March ■

The Kenai Peninsula is a microcosm of Alaska, possessing nearly all of its virtues: Native cultures, abundant wildlife, ocean and coastal settings, Russian and pioneer history, mountain wilderness, urban amenities, and plenty of outdoor activities.

Kenai Peninsula

Introduction & map 118–119
Seward 120–123
Kenai Fjords National Park
    124–127
Kenai National Wildlife Refuge
    130–131
Kenai & vicinity 132–133
Homer 136–140
Across Kachemak Bay 141–145
Boat Tour Kachemak Bay
    146–147
More places to visit on the Kenai
    Peninsula 148
Hotels & restaurants 250–254

An array of colorful flies reveals the fishing frenzy that grips the peninsula.

Just outside Seward, Fox Island straddles the broad mouth of Resurrection Bay.

Kenai Peninsula

TO SAY THE KENAI PENINSULA "HAS IT ALL" MAY SOUND LIKE A CHAMBER OF commerce pitch, but it's true. Its diverse attractions include the dramatic Kenai Fjords National Park, noteworthy art galleries, some of the state's fine.st canoeing, world-class museums, islands thick with nesting seabirds, intriguing reminders of Russia's affair with Alaska, an enormous national wildlife refuge, a glacier visitors can stroll up to, luxurious wilderness lodges, hundreds of miles of beautiful coastline, top-notch restaurants accessible only by boat, and world-renowned fishing for salmon, halibut, and other species.

The Kenai, as Alaskans call it, is a roughly oval peninsula that juts southwest into Cook Inlet. About 51,000 people live here, 6,800 in Kenai, the peninsula's largest town. The peninsula's northern boundary is just 52 miles from Anchorage, connected by the pretty Seward Highway, and residents of the state's biggest city often head to the Kenai for recreation. It's a large peninsula, about the size of West Virginia, although some 40 percent is covered by lakes, rivers, and vast wetlands. All that fresh water in proximity to the salt water that virtually surrounds the peninsula largely accounts for the fishing mania that grips the Kenai.

The first peoples to settle the peninsula were Athabascan in the north and west and Alutiiq, or Aleut, in the south and east. Next came the Russians, whose influence

has been particularly strong. The town of Kenai was founded in 1791 by Russian fur traders, and many place names (e.g., Kasilof and Kalifornsky) speak to the peninsula's Russian past. Still living in small pockets around the Kenai are Old Believers, a traditional Russian Orthodox people who dress in old-fashioned garb and speak Russian as well as English.

As in much of the state, the Kenai's modern growth was boosted by the discovery of gold (around 1850) and oil and gas (around 1960). Today the oil and gas industry (offshore in Cook Inlet), commercial fishing, and tourism are the economic mainstays.

The Seward Highway leads, not surprisingly, to Seward and Resurrection Bay. The peninsula is otherwise accessible along the 143 miles of the Sterling Highway, which branches west off the Seward through Kenai National Wildlife Refuge and national forest lands, threads the main population centers of Kenai and Soldotna, and then continues south along the Cook Inlet to the storied end of the road at Homer and the land across Kachemak Bay. ■

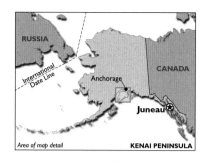

RUSSIA

CANADA

International Date Line

Anchorage

Juneau

Area of map detail

KENAI PENINSULA

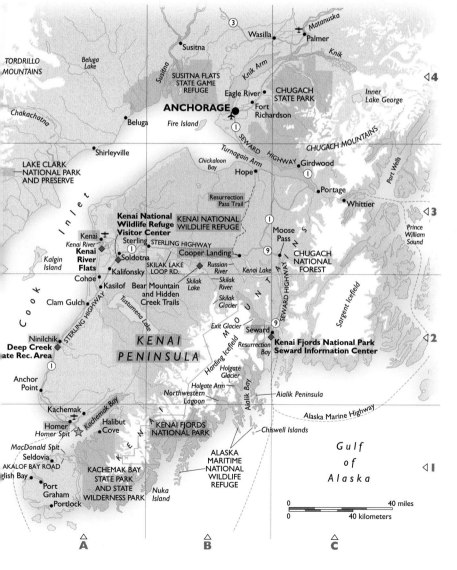

Downtown Seward is a pleasant mix of shops and historic buildings.

Seward

Seward
⚑ 119 C2

Visitor information
www.seward.com

✉ Seward Chamber of Commerce–Convention & Visitors Bureau, 2001 Seward Hwy.

☎ 907/224-8051

🕑 Closed weekdays Labor Day–Mem. Day

Alaska SeaLife Center
www.alaskasealife.org

✉ 301 Railway Ave.

☎ 907/224-6300 or 800/224-2525

$ $$$$

THE SEWARD HIGHWAY IS A HARD ACT TO FOLLOW. HEADING south through the Kenai Peninsula, this All-American Road, Alaska Scenic Byway, and USFS Scenic Byway slips through the dramatic forest and mountains of the Chugach National Forest, passing whitewater creeks, hanging glaciers, and moose stilting through beaver ponds. But when motorists reach the end of the road, in the city that gave the highway its name, they'll find that Seward and environs more than live up to the scenic byway's promise.

Seward overlooks Resurrection Bay, a svelte finger of the Gulf of Alaska. Framed by rugged peaks and dark spruce forest, the town comprises a pleasantly rustic port of about 2,500 residents, roughly divided into two parts: the relaxed, older downtown and a busy cluster of new development around the small boat harbor a mile north.

THE WATERFRONT

One fairly recent development has taken center stage in Seward: the **Alaska SeaLife Center,** one of the state's top museums and research institutions. The center is devoted to wildlife rehabilitation, understanding Alaska's marine ecosystems, and communicating

that understanding to the public. If that sounds too stuffy, not to worry. Sure, the museum presents plenty of serious information about current research on the Bering Sea and ongoing ramifications of the *Exxon Valdez* oil spill. But the SeaLife Center also knows how to elicit a "gee whiz."

Large underwater viewing galleries let visitors press their faces against the glass to watch harbor seals and sea lions zip by with astounding speed and grace. In the Discovery Pool, kids can run their fingers over sticky sea anemone tentacles or a sea star's smooth arms. In the aviary, watch as seabirds stand atop the rocks and flap vigorously to pump an insulating layer of air into their down feathers. Kneel for an underwater view of tufted puffins and pigeon guillemots stroking around beneath the surface.

During the day, listen for special announcements, such as a sea lion training session that visitors can watch from an overhead viewing deck. Don't worry, the sea lions aren't being prepped for some exploitative aquarium show; these sessions foster safe handling when the pinnipeds are moved or vets care for them. As trainers approach, the sea lions whack their flippers against the fence and scamper around like excited puppies, clearly eager to play.

Take a **behind-the-scenes tour** *(reservations required)* to learn even more fascinating facts. For example, did you know that octopuses crave stimulation and contact? In the labs, staffers tell visitors all about these intelligent animals while feeding them by hand. On daily **Encounter Tours** *(summer only)*, you may get the chance to confirm staffers' claims that octopus suckers feel soft, like a baby sucking a thumb —albeit a hundred times stronger.

Video monitors offer a closer look. Since the center is the state's primary marine mammal and seabird rehabilitation facility, the cast of animal characters continually changes. One day you may witness blood being drawn from a puffin, another day anesthesia being administered to a sea otter.

From the SeaLife Center, a paved shoreline path runs east along the waterfront, then strikes out north along the bay about a mile to the small boat harbor, passing through a couple of parks on the way. Scattered along the trail are interpretive displays on a wide variety of topics, such as rain forest flora, commercial fishing, and the history of the Alaska Railroad (whose southern terminus is in Seward, near the north end of the path).

DOWNTOWN

Immediately north of the SeaLife Center is downtown Seward, a compact district that measures about half a dozen blocks east to west and maybe three blocks north to south. Fourth Avenue serves as the main drag. Though you'll find a few gift shops and hotels, downtown is not a tourist mecca; many of its restaurants, clothing stores, and the like are geared toward locals, making them all the more appealing to travelers eager to sample a slice of Alaska life.

Visitors may want to stop in at the **Seward Community Library**—to check out not a book but paintings by leading

Seward Community Library
www.cityofseward.net/library/
✉ 238 5th Ave.
☎ 907/224-3646
🕐 Closed Sun.

Catch of the day: Halibut and salmon hang from the dock in Seward.

Resurrection Bay Galerie
www.alaskafinearts.com
✉ 500 4th Ave.
☎ 907/224-3212
🕐 Closed Mon.

Caines Head State Recreation Area
www.dnr.state.ak.us/parks/units/caineshd.htm
✉ Alaska State Parks, Kenai/PWS Area Office
☎ 907/262-5581

Alaska artists, a collection of Russian icons, or the original Alaska flag, designed in 1927 by a boy from a local orphanage. From Memorial Day through Labor Day you can plunk down $3 to see a video of the harrowing 1964 Good Friday earthquake, which hit Seward hard.

Delve further into local history by respectfully wandering the corridors of the historic **Van Gilder Hotel** (308 Adams St., tel 800/204-6835), which boasts an extensive collection of photographs. Be sure to read the captions. For example, the text beside a photo of the 1941 downtown fire reveals that soldiers stationed in town took a military approach to extinguishing the blaze. Unfortunately, when they dynamited the building in which the fire started, the explosion blew flam-

ing debris all over town. Even more history awaits at the **Seward Museum** (336 3rd Ave., tel 907/224-3902), which houses Native and pioneer artifacts.

Next door to the museum, get a taste of contemporary Seward life at **Resurrect Art Coffee House Gallery** (320 3rd Ave., tel 907/224-7161), run out of a historic former Lutheran church. A favorite local hangout, it offers espresso, tasty pastries, and a healthy helping of local art, ranging from simple crafts to expensive paintings. You'll find a bigger dose of fine art at **Resurrection Bay Galerie.** Don't be fooled by its location in a somewhat disheveled historic house; this top-drawer gallery displays serious contemporary paintings and sculpture. Some of the prices are serious, too, costing more than your two-week Alaska vacation.

OUTSIDE SEWARD
A couple of miles south on the shore road is **Lowell Point State Recreation Site.** This 20-acre spread offers beach access to Resurrection Bay, but it is better known as a jumping-off point for kayak trips on the bay. It's also the trailhead for a 4.5-mile (7.2 km) hike to **Caines Head State Recreation Area.** The scenic route follows the western shore along a beach framed by forested mountains. Check with park staff to time the hike properly, as portions are only passable at low tide.

At the recreation area explore Fort McGilvray, a now abandoned strategic command center built during World War II to protect the Port of Seward at a time when Japanese forces had landed on the Aleutian Islands. Take a flashlight and wander through the subterranean maze of passageways and rooms or enjoy tremendous views

Mt. Marathon race

Most people wouldn't look at a 3,000-foot-plus (915 m) peak and think, *Let's run up and down that mountain as fast as we can!* Then again, most people aren't from Seward. Every July 4th since 1915, runners starting at sea level in downtown Seward have raced 1.5 miles (2.4 km) up Mount Marathon and 1.5 miles back down. The slopes are so steep in spots that contestants must use their hands to haul themselves up. Add to that gullies, loose shale, ice, and snow, and it's no wonder that bloodied knees are par for the course. The record is 43 minutes 23 seconds. The race has become a major event that draws 900 participants (the maximum allowed) and thousands of onlookers from all over Alaska and beyond. ∎

from former artillery batteries atop the 650-foot promontory.

A mile north of downtown is the **Seward Small Boat Harbor,** its west side flanked by relatively new development—upscale restaurants, galleries, hotels, and shops. The docks are thick with sportfishing charter outfits. Stroll through here as the boats return to watch anglers string up huge halibut. The docks also house the Kenai Fjords National Park Seward Information Center (see p. 124), as well as several outfitters that offer kayak and boat tours of Resurrection Bay and the park. ■

A playful Steller sea lion swooshes past delighted visitors at the Alaska SeaLife Center.

Tour boat passengers hope for a glimpse of calving ice from one of the park's grand glaciers.

Kenai Fjords National Park

Kenai Fjords National Park
www.nps.gov/kefj

- 119 C2
- Seward Information Center, 1212 4th Ave., Seward
- 907/224-7500
- Closed weekends Labor Day–Oct., closed in winter

KENAI FJORDS IS A PRIMORDIAL PLACE. NATURE IN THE RAW. A world where you can witness fundamental geological processes in action. Except for a fringe of temperate rain forest, the park is a rugged land of rock and ice—especially ice, which sheathes a large majority of its 607,805 acres. The Harding Icefield alone buries more than half the park beneath hundreds and thousands of feet of ice. Tour the park to be transported back to the ice ages.

Visiting Kenai Fjords is no walk in the park, so to speak. With the exception of those visiting Exit Glacier, few people venture into this unforgiving landscape on their own—nor should they, unless they know what they are doing. Fortunately, a cadre of experienced tour operators have set up shop in the gateway town of Seward. The Park Service also offers a handful of guided tours.

Start your visit at the **Kenai Fjords National Park Seward Information Center,** at Seward's small boat harbor. Though it's small and lacks the museum-like displays of some national park visitor centers, it

does screen several good films about the park in its small auditorium. Stop by to learn about the park's scenic wonders and abundant wildlife. Also pick up a list of authorized tour operators; many boat trips provide Park Service interpreters.

Dozens of these operations are run out of a row of buildings adjacent to the information center. Stroll the district for brochures and ask staff for tour specifics. Decide if you want a flightseeing trip, a scenic boat tour, a fishing trip, a kayaking expedition, a glacier trek, etc. Do you want to explore for three hours or three days? Do you want minimal guidance—say, a charter boat that will drop you off in a wilderness cove and come back for you in a week —or a full-service tour in a heated boat with lunch and drinks?

The quickest means to a literal overview of Kenai Fjords is in a small plane or helicopter. Though you won't see things up close— unless you arrange a glacier landing—you will see remote spots that boat tours can't reach. Within minutes you'll be buzzing above the 300-square-mile

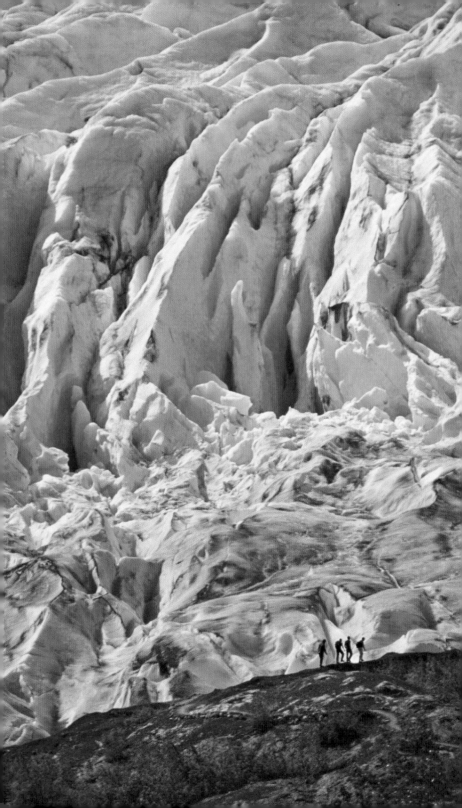

Harding Icefield, skimming over blinding snowfields and aqua crevasses. Watch for the stony tips of mountains that just peek above the ice like gasping swimmers; the Eskimos call these *nunataks,* or lonely peaks.

Here, hundreds of inches of annual snowfall compact into dense ice that fuels 32 distinct glaciers. However, these rivers of ice are retreating faster than they're being replenished, as happened in the last ice age, when withdrawing glaciers left behind the deep, narrow, U-shaped fjords that give the park its name.

These sublime fjords are best approached from the sea. Most visitors choose one of several scheduled power boat tours, whether aboard a smaller vessel with 20 passengers or a multi-deck cruiser with 120. Others opt for guided kayak trips, boating out to a drop-off point for a day trip rather than paddling all the way out from Seward—a rigorous, multiday adventure.

The boat tours range from three-hour loops of Resurrection Bay to day trips lasting nearly ten hours. To fully appreciate the park, choose at least an eight-hour voyage. Those with deep pockets and the desire to roam the park's far reaches can arrange multiday charters, including a stay at a wilderness lodge. Whichever tour you choose, dress warmly—hat, gloves, layered long underwear, and a rainproof jacket and pants. It'd be a shame to spend your tour holed up belowdecks.

Typical full-day trips start along the western shore of Resurrection Bay, where you'll spot bald eagles, dozens of sea otters, and perhaps a passing orca (killer whale). At the mouth of the bay, take note of the murky water —a mix of glacial silt and abun-dant phytoplankton, the base of a rich food chain that produces tons of krill and attracts hungry humpback whales.

Farther out lie the **Chiswell Islands,** among the few easily accessible areas of the **Alaska Maritime National Wildlife Refuge** (see pp. 164–165). These grassy sea stacks host a Steller sea lion rookery, as well as thousands of nesting kittwakes, murres, and tufted and horned puffins.

At the far end of the route, boats head up Aialik Bay and Holgate Arm, stopping about a quarter mile from the towering face of **Holgate Glacier.** Drifting amid gleaming icebergs may seem reward enough for the long trek, but everyone is waiting for one more treat. They want to see and hear this tidewater giant calve an ice chunk as big as a house. Most settle for a car-size piece, accompanied by a loud report and monumental splash.

Exit Glacier, the only part of the park accessible by road, is a 12-mile (19 km) drive from Seward. Stop at the Nature Center to learn about the glacier or sign up for a guided hike. An easy, half-mile (0.8 km) trail leads to the face of the glacier, but admire it from behind the warning signs—in 1987 a visitor was killed by calving ice.

Consider slogging up the steep **Overlook Loop Trail** a half mile for a close-up view of the glacier's crevassed north side. A side trail, on the return trip, follows Exit Creek back to the center. Hardier hikers might tackle the challenging **Harding Icefield Trail,** a 6-mile (10 km) round-trip that gains 3,000 vertical feet (914 m). *(Check with rangers; trail can be snow-bound into summer.)* Watch for black bears and mountain goats, and feast on incredible views of the ice field and environs. ■

**Opposite:
The massive
fissured flank
of Exit Glacier
dwarfs a group
of passing hikers.**

Fishing

One summer afternoon in 2004, Nevadan Don Hanks was on a charter fishing boat in Kachemak Bay when he felt a powerful tug on his line. When he was done reeling in, he'd landed a behemoth of a halibut. Back on the dock in Homer, the monster weighed in at a whopping 352.6 pounds (159.9 kg). That was a happy day for Hanks, and not just because he had a big fish to brag on. It turned out that his halibut was worth $51,298. Even a fish as tasty as halibut isn't normally worth $146 a pound, but Hanks's catch of the day also happened to be the winning entry in Homer's Jackpot Halibut Derby.

Consider that Homer, a gem of a town that had plenty of fine choices for a municipal motto, proudly branded itself "The Halibut Fishing Capital of the World." As you drive along the Homer Spit, you run a gauntlet of charter-fishing offices, each wallpapered with photos of grinning anglers standing beside considerably larger halibut.

The Seward Silver Salmon Derby—one of several on the peninsula and dozens statewide—epitomizes the lust for Alaska salmon, especially king (chinook), red (sockeye), and silver (coho). The latter is the focal point of the derby, which celebrated its

The Homer Jackpot Halibut Derby is just one symptom of the sportfishing madness that grips this state. Residents and visitors alike fish till they drop, from the banks of wilderness rivers above the Arctic Circle to Ship Creek in downtown Anchorage. They fish out of swanky $500-a-day lodges and they fish out of old canvas tents. They fish for grayling, Pacific cod, steelhead, rockfish, Dolly Varden, lake trout, lingcod, whitefish, northern pike, and rainbow trout. But most of all, they fish for halibut and salmon.

The obsession with halibut and salmon is most pronounced on the Kenai Peninsula.

50th anniversary in 2005. Thousands of anglers come to town, jamming the hotels and camping out on the waterfront. They wouldn't think of throwing back the biggest silver salmon—worth $10,000—but $50,000 goes to whomever lands the silver that bears the grand-prize tag. Tags on other released fish correlate to a new Ford Explorer and a Hawaiian vacation.

Extensive regulations govern the Seward derby. The last line of the weigh-in rules warns that "any evidence of fish tampering will result in permanent disqualification." Alaska may be a laissez-faire state, but fish

Opposite: Beneath his beard, local fisherman Jack Spangler is smiling about catching this king salmon. Above: Anglers work the Kenai River near Cooper Landing. Left: Sockeye on their way to someone's grill. Below: Combat fishing near the confluence of the Kenai and Russian Rivers.

tampering … now, that's a serious matter requiring strict regulation.

The most egregious example of Alaska's over-the-top fishing culture is "combat" fishing, which occurs during major salmon runs along easily accessible rivers, most notably the Kenai. Battling for position, plagues of anglers crowd the riverbanks, sometimes literally elbow to elbow. If you're an angler yourself, morbidly curious or just bored, this is a phenomenon well worth watching. Just don't stand too close to all those folks casting into the river or you may get hooked for real. ∎

**Kenai National
Wildlife Refuge**
http://kenai.fws.gov
 119 B2–B3
✉ Headquarters &
    Visitor Center, Ski
    Hill Rd., Soldotna
☎ 907/262-7021

Kenai National Wildlife Refuge

IT STARTED WITH MOOSE. TO PROTECT THESE SPLENDID beasts and their habitat, the federal government in 1941 designated a large tract of land as the Kenai National Moose Range. In 1980 the boundaries of this protected area were expanded and the name was changed to the Kenai National Wildlife Refuge. Today the refuge sprawls across nearly two million acres, encompassing more than half of the Kenai Peninsula.

The peninsula's abundant moose are fun to watch, but motorists should beware these big animals lumbering across the roads.

The 1980 changes reflected a sophisticated understanding of ecosystems and a recognition of the need to set aside entire landscapes to protect resident species. In habitats ranging from ice fields to alpine tundra to low-elevation lakes to rivers to spruce-birch forest, this refuge shelters not just moose but wolves, brown and black bears, Dall sheep, sandhill cranes, lynx, caribou, bald eagles, wolverines, trumpeter swans, and beavers, among other species.

Start your visit at the Soldotna **visitor center,** which can be hard to find. At Mile 96.1 of the Sterling Highway, turn onto Funny River Road and immediately turn right on Ski Hill Road, before you reach the RV park or building supply store. Drive 0.8 mile and you're there. Browse the center's dioramas and wildlife films or take the 0.75-mile (1.2 km) **Keen Eye Trail,** which leads through spruce-birch forest to an observation platform and spotting scope at Headquarters Lake.

The refuge may not be the "Land of 10,000 Lakes," but in an area 27 times smaller than Minnesota, it boasts some 4,000 lakes, and countless wetlands, rivers, and creeks. No wonder moose love it and anglers flock here. South of the Sterling Highway, which bisects the refuge, lies a scattering of small lakes amid two big lakes, **Skilak** and **Tustumena**—the latter one of Alaska's largest, at 117 square miles (303 sq. km). But true lake country lies north of the highway, where thousands of small lakes bump one another. All this makes for great canoeing—so great that the **Kenai National Wildlife Refuge Canoe Trail System** has been dubbed a National Recreation Trail.

This trail consists of two subsystems: The 60-mile-long (97 km) **Swan Lake Canoe Route**

links 30-some lakes and is perfect for day trips, while the 80-mile-long (129 km) **Swanson River Canoe Route,** which connects 40 lakes and 50 miles (80 km) of river, is better suited to multiday adventures. Here, you'll pass shores lined by spruce and birch where moose feed in the shallows, swans glide by, and loons sound their plaintive calls. Perhaps you'll spot a coyote trotting through a meadow or a river otter snaking down a mudbank. Because this is true wilderness, even day trips require caution and experience. Guided trips are available.

For a drier experience, drive east on the Sterling Highway to Mile 75.5 and the west entrance to the **Skilak Lake Loop Road.** This 19-mile gravel road branches off the highway and skirts Skilak Lake, passing through the **Skilak Wildlife Recreation Area,** before rejoining the highway at Mile 58. Views extend beyond the lake to the southern part of the refuge, where the husky Kenai Mountains dominate the horizon. Flowing from those peaks is the Skilak River, fed by the Skilak Glacier, which in turn stems from the Harding Icefield, shared by the refuge and Kenai Fjords National Park (see pp. 124–127).

Most of the refuge's maintained trails branch off the loop road. **Bear Mountain Trail,** a moderate 1.6-mile (2.5 km) round-trip, promises views of the Kenai Mountains and frequent wildlife sightings, including the eponymous bears. **Hidden Creek Trail,** a moderate-to-difficult 2.6-mile (4 km) round-trip, winds through the scene of the 1996 Hidden Creek Fire, where wildflowers thrive and the open landscape yields long views west across Cook Inlet to the volcanoes of the Aleutian Range. ■

Berry heaven

The Kenai Peninsula is blessed with soaring mountains, prolific salmon runs, sumptuous forests, and a lovely coastline, as well as a diverse abundance of edible berries. Pickers will find some old favorites, such as blueberries and raspberries. They'll find somewhat more exotic species, too, such as high-bush cranberries, currants, and salmonberries. And they'll find species few people have ever heard of, such as nagoonberries, watermelonberries, and cloudberries. To find out when and where to pick, and to make sure you know how to avoid poisonous berries, contact the University of Alaska, Fairbanks, Cooperative Extension Service office in Soldotna (tel 907/262-5824.) ■

Views along the Skilak Lake Loop Road take in the majestic Kenai Mountains.

Kenai

🗺 119 A3

Visitor information

www.visitkenai.com

✉ Visitors & Cultural Center, 11471 Kenai Spur Hwy. at Main

☎ 907-283-1991

🕐 Closed weekends mid-Sept.–mid-May

Kenai & vicinity

STRATEGICALLY SITUATED ON A BLUFF ABOVE THE MOUTH of the Kenai River, Kenai has long attracted residents and visitors. For centuries the Dena'ina people lived in the area, subsisting as fishers, hunters, trappers, and farmers. In 1791 Russian fur traders built a fort here, making it the second permanent Russian settlement in Alaska. Just six years later at the Battle of Kenai, the Dena'ina defeated the Russians, and the site declined to the status of a minor trading post.

Characteristic onion domes atop the Holy Assumption of the Virgin Mary Church testify to Kenai's Russian Orthodox roots.

The Americans built Fort Kenay here in 1869, two years after purchasing Alaska from the Russians. In the 1880s fish canneries put Kenai on the map, and the discovery of major oil and gas fields in Cook Inlet in the 1950s consolidated Kenai as the largest and most industrial of the peninsula's cities. Still, its population is a mere 7,000, while its scenic setting befits a resort town more than an industrial city.

Start at the edge of Old Town Kenai at the **Kenai Visitors & Cultural Center.** The staff at this handsome complex will load you up with tourist information, and the center also serves as a museum. Take time to browse its excellent collection of Native artifacts and items from the Russian and American eras, as well as noteworthy temporary exhibits, such as wildlife art by major American painters.

The center offers a walking-tour map of **Old Town,** which comprises a few blocks between the highway and the mouth of the river. Steer toward the three robin's-egg-blue onion domes atop the **Holy Assumption of the Virgin Mary Russian Orthodox Church.** The first church on this site was built by a Russian monk in 1845, the present church in 1894. Tours are available of this domed building, one of the state's oldest Orthodox churches and a National Historic Landmark. A block away is **St. Nicholas Chapel,** a traditional Orthodox chapel made of logs.

On the fringes of Old Town, off Mission and Riverview Roads, are viewpoints of the river, the canneries, the Kenai Mountains to the east, and Cook Inlet and the Aleutian Range to the west. One of the overlooks features an interpretive sign about beluga whales, which sometimes swim past. Blue-gray when born, belugas are bright white as adults, making them easier to spot. For a closer look at the water, head down Spruce Street to **Kenai Beach Dunes,** a fine beach backed by low sand dunes on the north side of the river mouth.

South of downtown off Bridge Access Road are the **Kenai River Flats,** which encompass some 3,000 acres of marsh on either side of the Warren Ames Bridge. The flats offer outstanding wildlife-watching, particularly in spring. A great variety of waterfowl favor the area, notably the thousands of snow geese that congregate here in mid-April to feed during their migration to Siberia. In May and early June caribou slip into the flats to calve, and visitors may spot baby caribou testing out their spindly legs. In spring and summer, when the candlefish and salmon are running, hungry harbor seals and belugas swim upriver to feed just off the flats.

To experience a fusion of past and present Kenai, drive to **Kenai Landing** *(2101 Bowpicker Lane, tel 907/335-2500),* at the end of Cannery Road on the finger of land that extends north into the mouth of the Kenai River. This ambitious development converted

existing cannery buildings into a complex that includes a hotel, a restaurant, galleries, a theater, a museum, an indoor warehouse market with dozens of vendors, a waterfront promenade, a nature trail, and a boat launch and dock. Developers even restored part of the cannery to process sockeye and coho salmon on a small scale, allowing visitors to watch this traditional process—and sample the tasty end product. ■

Kenai River Flats
www.wildlife.alaska.gov
▲ 119 A3
☎ Alaska Dept. of Fish & Game: 907/262-9368

A visitor to Clam Gulch collects the key ingredients for a tasty chowder.

Bear-watching

Ten people stand very quietly on a slope overlooking the river, all eyes on an approaching grizzly. Walking on all fours along, the huge male comes within 100 feet (30.5 m)— much closer than recommended in literature on bear safety, given that a bear can run 100 feet in less than three seconds. For a moment the grizzly pauses right below the group, and then, to the relief of its watchers, it wades into the river, a salmon dinner on its mind.

Other grizzlies *(Ursus arctos)* are already out in the water, fishing, and the two juveniles in this big male's path aren't about to tangle with him. They move aside. About 50 feet from the bank, the dominant bear finds a spot to his liking atop the rim of a six-foot-high rocky ridge that spans the river, creating a barrier over which migrating salmon must jump. He crouches at the edge of the cascade, facing downstream, and waits. Suddenly, a ten-pound coho launches itself over the barrier, but this salmon isn't destined to reach its spawning grounds. With unnerving quickness the grizzly pivots and snatches the fish out of the air. Ripping off strips of flesh, the bear devours the salmon rapidly and readies itself to catch the next unlucky fish.

For hours this group of people watches that big male and the 15 to 20 other grizzlies working this stretch of river. Some of the bears fish below the falls in the shallows, splashing around as they try to pin elusive salmon with their five-inch claws. A sow and her two small cubs lurk around the edges of the prime fishing grounds, looking for opportunities to fish—or to grab leftovers—without exposing the cubs to attack. With so many bears in such a small area, disputes are inevitable. Every so often the bears woof and grunt at each other, and occasionally things escalate to roars and bluff charges.

Because these folks are on a reputable, organized bear-watching trip, they aren't taking any greater risk than someone who goes rafting or flightseeing. Were they on their own, it would be foolhardy to get so close to a bunch of hungry bears, but these excursions operate under tight safety restrictions laid down by the government agency that oversees the public land where the bear-watching takes place. (Almost all organized bear-watching occurs on national park or national forest land.) The trips are led by experts who know how to behave around bears and who make sure tour par-

Opposite: Before the salmon start running, bears often graze on grass.
Below: Grizzlies are excellent anglers, but they don't practice catch-and-release.
Bottom: Small groups size up the bears at Hallo Bay, in Katmai National Park.

ticipants follow the rules established for everyone's safety. And for that rare confrontation, these guides come prepared with guns, pepper spray, or flares, depending on the person and place.

Licensed guides typically schedule bear-watching trips around salmon runs in summer and early fall, when bears predictably congregate. Trips are available at many sites in the southern parts of coastal Alaska.

Homer is the most popular jumping-off point. Bear-watching is especially popular in **Katmai National Park, Tongass National Forest,** and the **McNeil River State Game Sanctuary** (run by the Alaska Department of Fish and Game). There's a lottery system at McNeil River, where reservations can be hard to get, so plan well in advance.

Information about most of the major bear-viewing sites is available at www.nps .gov/aplic; click on "bear viewing." Be aware that these trips are expensive, but be aware, too, that watching an 800-pound (300 kg) grizzly from 100 feet (30.5 m) is an experience you won't soon forget. ∎

Fishing boats, water taxis, and tour boats throng the harbor on Homer Spit.

Homer

THE HOMER REGION HAS RELATIVELY SLEEPY ORIGINS. For millennia Native peoples came here in search of shellfish. Russian fur traders also passed through. True settlement only began after the Americans bought Alaska, in 1867, when coal was discovered nearby and railroaded to ships at the end of the Homer Spit. A community formed around the docks, but was abandoned in 1907. The coal industry collapsed over the following decade. Homer remained a remote outpost until the Sterling Highway arrived, in the early 1950s.

Homer
🅰 119 A1
Visitor information
www.homeralaska.org
✉ Homer Chamber of Commerce, 201 Sterling Hwy.
☎ 907/235-7740

The road initiated Homer's modern phase. Not that a million people flocked here—even today the population is a mere 5,332—but newcomers kept trickling in, and a diverse lot at that: artists, charter boat captains, '60s dropouts, restaurateurs, Russian Old Believers, naturalists, and shopkeepers. Homer richly deserves its reputation as an eclectic community.

This town at the end of the road has also attracted travelers,

leading, though, as this elaborate high-tech facility is a natural history and cultural museum, not a place to find out where to get a good seafood dinner. Visitors enter through massive sculpted metal doors with handles shaped like kelp.

The center has a specific mission: to study the **Alaska Maritime National Wildlife Refuge** and share its findings with the public. This unusual refuge comprises a constellation of 2,500 far-flung islands that host marine mammals and some 40 million seabirds—more than in the rest of North America put together. Jump at any opportunities to boat out to one of the refuge islands.

If you miss a boating adventure, at least go to the **Seabird Theater,** near the visitor center entrance—the next best thing to observing a seabird nesting colony on one of the islands. Towering above theatergoers are realistic-looking, guano-stained artificial rocks, inhabited by more than 120 sculpted puffins, auklets, cormorants, and other birds. At the press of a button, the colony seems to spring to life, as huge screens overhead and amid the rocks erupt in a swirl of seabirds, real enough to make you duck. Shrill birdcalls fill the room and you may even catch a whiff of a seabird colony.

Other appealing, often interactive exhibits further explore the natural history of the islands, while several rooms are devoted to humans' ongoing relationship with the refuge. A full-size talking model of an Aleut trapper tells how foxes were introduced to the islands and ended up doing great harm to resident seabirds. In a re-created field biologist's tent, talk-

Alaska Islands & Ocean Visitor Center
www.islandsandocean.org
✉ 95 Sterling Hwy
☎ 907/235-6961
🕐 Open daily summer, Tues.–Sat. Labor Day–mid-May

drawn by the magnificent scenery —a gorgeous bay, glaciers, volcanoes, plentiful wildlife, forests, and an enchanting coastline. For those eager to explore farther afield, the town has become a jumping-off point for boat and plane travel into the wilds across Kachemak Bay (see pp.141–145) and to the far side of Cook Inlet.

ALASKA ISLANDS & OCEAN VISITOR CENTER

One of Homer's newest and more impressive attractions, the Alaska Islands and Ocean Visitor Center greets motorists as they enter town along the Sterling Highway. The term "visitor center" is mis-

Narrow Homer Spit lights up Kachamak Bay.

Bunnell Street Gallery

www.bunnellstreetgallery.org

✉ 106 W. Bunnell St., Suite A

☎ 907/235-2662

🕐 Closed Sun. in winter

ing figures of Olaus Murie and other famed early naturalists share tales of their exploration of the refuge.

When you finally emerge from the center, consider a hike along the trails that run from there down through Beluga Slough to **Bishop's Beach,** a nice spot for a stroll during low tide. As you watch for shorebirds, don't neglect the stunning backdrop of mountains that frame the bay. Up the beach on the edge of town is the Bishop's Beach Picnic Area.

GALLERIES & MUSEUMS

In town, but still with a view over Kachemak Bay, is the **Bunnell Street Gallery.** This nonprofit institution occupies Homer's largest and oldest commercial building, the Inlet Trading Post, which used to sell hardware to homesteaders. In the gallery's main room—an airy space with a grand piano—visitors can catch monthly shows, often of a single artist who may be local, from elsewhere in Alaska, or occasionally from out of state. The emphasis is on cutting-edge contemporary art. In the back room, browsers can contemplate the works of some 40 artists, many of them local.

While considered one of the state's finest galleries, the Bunnell Street Gallery faces stiff competition from galleries along Pioneer Avenue, less than a mile uphill (Homer boasts one of the state's leading art communities). The cluster of three shops on East Pioneer between Svedlund Street and Kachemak Way is known as **Gallery Row.** In a light, bright space at 475 E. Pioneer Ave., **Fireweed Gallery** (tel 907/235-3411, closed Sun. except in summer) features a wide range of high-end Alaska work, from grand oil paintings to serigraphs to turn-of-the-century-style engravings. Also look for the unusual, such as wildlife sculpture fashioned out of fossilized whale flipper finger bones and the popular, whimsical work of Don Henry, a local artist whose work is displayed in public venues around town. Henry creates figures, such as an eagle or a palm tree, out of found metal objects—for the most part, old kitchen utensils.

Next door to Fireweed, at 471 E. Pioneer, is **Ptarmigan Arts** (tel 907/235-5345) where the variety is dazzling: fiber art, paintings, hats, glass, gold and silver jewelry, and ceramics. Across the street, at 448 E. Pioneer, is **Picture Alaska Art Gallery** (tel 907/235-2300), which displays fine art, top-notch crafts, and a collection of 350 vintage photos of Alaska. It also sells art supplies and, in The Upstairs Boutique, women's clothing.

Gallery Row and several other galleries around town celebrate

Inside the museum, just behind the ticket counter, is a large space devoted to temporary exhibitions, which have included animals sculpted from willow twigs and plankton art. The main floor displays artifacts that evoke the lives of Natives, homesteaders, and commercial fishers. A video shows Native hunters in a kayak stalking a seal. Natural exhibits include a beaked whale skeleton, a four-foot-wide king crab, and a feed from a live cam-

Pratt Museum
www.prattmuseum.org
✉ 3779 Bartlett St.
☎ 907/235-8635
🕐 Closed Mon. mid-Sept.–mid-May, & Jan.
💲 $$

Homer's passion for the arts on the first Friday evening of every month by opening their doors to showcase new works. Many of the featured artists are present to discuss their work and, like everyone else, to sample the drinks and hors d'oeuvres.

The Pioneer Avenue area is also home to the **Pratt Museum,** one of Alaska's best small museums, which specializes in the region's natural history, human history, and culture. Start outside in the native plant garden and at the Harrington Cabin.

era mounted on Gull Island. Visitors can pan and zoom the camera for a closer look at this bird colony out in Kachemak Bay. Downstairs, a feed from another live camera focuses on grizzlies fishing for salmon along the McNeil River.

OUTDOORS HOMER

For the best views in Homer, drive (or bike, if you've got strong legs) to the top of the plateau that rises more than 1,000 vertical feet above town. To get there, head east on Pioneer Avenue, which

Homer's Pratt Museum highlights the region's human and natural history.

Moose still meander through Homer's residential neighborhoods.

Carl E. Wynn Nature Center
www.akcoastalstudies.org/wynn.htm
☎ Center for Alaskan Coastal Studies: 907-235-6667
⏱ Closed Labor Day —mid-June
💲 $$

soon turns into East End Road. Continue about a mile out of town to East Hill Road, turn left, and climb steeply until you intersect Skyline Drive. A left turn on the gravel road will take you past luxury homes and the magnificent views that lured those homeowners up here.

If you turn right on E. Skyline and drive 1.5 miles, you'll reach the **Carl E. Wynn Nature Center,** affiliated with the Center for Alaskan Coastal Studies. Its 140 acres shelter meadows brimming with wildflowers, spruce forest, and a migration corridor for moose and black bears. Visitors can solo hike the trails that crisscross the center or join a guided hike.

Finally, don't miss the **Homer Spit,** the literal and figurative end of the road (the Sterling Highway ends at the tip of the Spit) where the town began. This legendary 4.5-mile sand-and-gravel finger juts

southeast midway across beautiful Kachemak Bay. The spit is the heart of Homer, as close to a downtown as Homer comes. In summer it's jammed with cars, trucks, RVs, cyclists, and pedestrians. People come to stroll the beaches, browse the galleries, eat at the restaurants, fly kites, kayak in the bay, knock back a beer at the Salty Dawg, drop a hook in the Fishing Hole, get an ice cream cone, watch the sea otters, camp, or stay at the Land's End Resort.

Most of all, people visit the spit to go boating, as this is the jumping-off point for commercial fishing boats and sportfishing boats are for hire; tour boats, water taxis, and the Alaska state ferry also stop here. Every day hundreds of anglers dreaming of beefy halibut and king salmon clamber aboard dozens of charter boats and motor out to the bay and Cook Inlet. Most come back smiling. ∎

Across Kachemak Bay

THIS ALLURING SLICE OF ALASKA DOESN'T HAVE A NAME, so most people refer to it as "across Kachemak Bay," or simply "across the bay." Broadly, the area includes everything on the 20-by-60-mile protrusion of land at the southwestern tip of the Kenai Peninsula, bounded by Kachemak Bay to the north and the Gulf of Alaska to the south. The southern and western portions of this area are hardcore wilderness that few people reach, so typically "across Kachemak Bay" means the coastal areas nearer Homer and the closer parts of the Interior within 400,000-acre Kachemak Bay State Park.

Kenai Peninsula Tourism Marketing Council
www.kenaipeninsula.org
✉ 35477 Kenai Spur Hwy., Ste. 205, Soldotna
☎ 907/262-5229

Even the more accessible area is pretty remote, reachable only by boat or small plane. Civilization is limited to two small towns, Seldovia and Halibut Cove, and a sprinkling of houses, cabins, and lodges. Otherwise, the region is a realm of fjords and secluded coves backed by forests and glacier-striped mountains.

To reach your destination quickly, or for an overview of the bay, take a small plane, perhaps a flightseeing trip. But for a closer look, take a boat. For more information on boat and plane service, contact the Homer Chamber of Commerce *(tel 907/235-7740, www.homeralaska.org).*

The **Center for Alaskan Coastal Studies** *(tel 907/235-6667, www.akcoastalstudies.org)* offers excellent boat tours with land segments (see pp. 146–147). Once or twice a week in summer a state ferry *(tel 907/465-3941 or 800/642-0066, in Homer tel 907/235-7099 or 800/382-9229, www.ferryalaska.com)* makes the 75-minute run to Seldovia, stays there about four hours, then returns to Homer. Several smaller water taxis based in Homer will take passengers to points across the bay. A few fit folks paddle across the bay in kayaks, but it's a long, sometimes rough trip. Far more people contact kayak outfitters across the bay and start from

there, skimming along the shore or out to Gull Island for a look at this raucous seabird nesting site.

The most popular vessels are three boats out of Homer that make daily trips across the bay in summer. Two of the boats are

Seldovia's tiny commercial district consists of a handful of businesses, including Herring Bay Mercantile.

operated by Central Charters *(tel 907/235-7847 or 800/478-7847, www.centralcharter.com)*. The **Danny J** *(fare)*, a 34-passenger fishing boat, stops at Halibut Cove twice a day. The noon departure does a little touring, around Gull Island, and allows passengers 2.5 hours to wander Halibut Cove. The 5 p.m. departure gives people three hours in town, half of which many folks spend at the famed Saltry restaurant. Central Charters also operates the larger (and warmer, with ample inside seating) **Discovery** *(fare)*, which makes a six-hour run to Seldovia, touring the coast, then spending about three hours in town.

Rainbow Tours *(tel 907/235-7272, www.rainbowtours.net)* runs the **Rainbow Connection** *(fare)*,

Wilderness lodges

Alaska has more than its share of bears, cold, mosquitoes, rain, isolation, and other qualities that make camping tough. In other words, there's a definite market niche for wilderness lodges, and Alaska has hundreds of them. Some are basic, some are luxurious, and many fall in between, but they all provide safety and comfort deep in the wilds. Most also provide expertise, equipment, and guides for outings. A majority are geared mainly to anglers and hunters, but more and more lodges cater to guests who want to go hiking, watch wildlife, and savor the scenery. Several of the state's finest wilderness lodges lie across Kachemak Bay from Homer. *(Homer Chamber of Commerce Visitor Information Center, tel 907/235-7740, www.homeralaska.org)*. ∎

a 99-passenger vessel that does a daily nine-hour excursion to Seldovia, taking the scenic route down and lingering in town for about seven hours.

When visitors first cruise into **Halibut Cove** (population 26), they quickly realize this is no ordinary remote Alaskan village. Passengers can't help but notice that some of the town's dwellings are log mansions, not log cabins. Once ashore, they discover another odd feature: no roads. Not only are there no roads into town, but no roads, period. Residents get around by kayaking or taking a skiff across the lagoon on which the town is centered or by strolling the raised boardwalk that follows the shoreline. Visitors are welcome to wander the dozen blocks of private boardwalk between 1 p.m. and 9 p.m., provided they respect residents' privacy.

The first place most visitors encounter is **The Saltry** *(reservations required; contact boat tour office)*—one of Alaska's best restaurants. In the early 1900s three dozen herring salteries operated in Halibut Cove, swelling the town's population to around 1,000. Alas, the salteries overfished the herring, the fishery collapsed, and all the salteries shut down. By the mid-1900s the population could be counted on two hands, but the setting slowly drew artists and a smattering of others back to the cove. Today the town hosts several lodges, bed-and-breakfasts, and cabins; a boat-builder; commercial fishers; a Morgan horse farm; and even a day spa in summer.

More than half of the cove's residents are artists, some quite well known. Visitors can browse their work in the **Experience Fine Art Gallery** *(tel 907/296-2215)*, a co-op that shows only local artists. The **Cove Gallery** *(tel 907/296-2207)* is owned by Diana Tillion, a highly regarded artist who does her painting with octopus ink, drawn from the creatures with a hypodermic needle. And then there's Alex Combs's studio, which he often leaves open even when not around. Visitors are invited to take any pottery or paintings they like and leave what they consider fair payment.

The town of Halibut Cove abuts **Kachemak Bay State Park** and dozens of miles of developed hiking trails. As most trailheads are only reachable by boat, water taxis often drop off and pick up hikers. A fairly easy, rewarding route is the **Grewingk Glacier Lake Trail,** 3 miles (4.8 km) one way from the Glacier Spit Trailhead to the shore of Grewingk Glacier Lake. You walk along the beach, through forest,

Wilderness lodges overlook Kachemak Bay's lushly forested south shore.

Halibut Cove
119 A1
Visitor information
www.halibutcove.com
509/548-2193

Kachemak Bay State Park
www.alaskastateparks.org
119 A1
Halibut Cove Ranger Station: 907/235-6999 (summer), Dept. of Natural Resources: 907/269-8400 or 907/262-5581 (rest of year)

Black Kittiwake

Bald Eagle

Lynx

Wolves

Orca

Dall Porpoise

Aleutian Tern

Red-Faced Cormorant

Tufted Puffin

Sandhill Crane

Common Murre

Sea Otter

Ancient Murrelet

Horned Puffin

Chinook Salmon

Eider Drake

Painted Anemone

Yellow Zoanthid

RESIDENTS OF KACHEMAK BAY

Orange Ochre Starfish

Sunflower Starfish

Painted Star

Pacific Herring

Brown Bear

Moose

Harbor Seal

Western Sandpiper

The town across Kachemak Bay is **Seldovia,** a fishing village of 263 with maybe another 100 outside of town. Seldovia actually has a few roads, even a paved **Main Street.** On a small hill above Main Street is the modest **St. Nicholas Russian Orthodox Church,** built in 1891, a reminder that Russian fur traders settled here some 135 years ago. Also on Main Street, across from the harbor, are the small museum, visitor center, and gift shop of the **Seldovia Village Tribe.** At the southern end of Main on Seldovia Slough you can see a remaining section of the old boardwalk that used to rim much of the harbor; much of the town was destroyed by the 1964 earthquake. Along with the arrival of the highway in Homer, the quake knocked Seldovia from its position as the economic powerhouse of lower Cook Inlet, and it has remained sleepy ever since—much to the delight of most of its current residents and visitors.

Behind the school, at the end of Spring Street, the well-marked **Otterbahn Trail** leads 1.2 miles (2 km) past a lagoon to **Outside Beach,** a great place to beachcomb while admiring Kachemak Bay and the trio of volcanoes across Cook Inlet. Check a tide table before leaving, as access from Outside Beach can be cut off at high tide. If you have a vehicle, drive out the unpaved **Jakolof Bay Road,** a scenic route that curves east along Kachemak Bay for 13 miles before becoming impassable. At Mile 7.5 steps lead down to **McDonald Spit,** a 1.5-mile-long sandy finger that points into Kachemak Bay and is favored by marine life and birds. Over the last few miles of road you can clamber down to Jakolof Bay, known for its fine tide-pooling. ■

Seldovia

⚓ 119 A1

Visitor information

www.seldovia.com

☎ 907/234-7803

and across rocky terrain to the lake for a grand view of the glacier. Bring a map and talk to park staffers before setting out. For a stiffer challenge, ask about the **Poot Peak Trail** to the lower summit *(only technical climbers should attempt upper summit).*

Tours of the bay reveal its wildlife, striking scenery, and fascinating natural history.

Boat tour on Kachemak Bay

KACHEMAK BAY AND THE COASTAL LANDS ON ITS SOUTH SIDE ARE WILD and vast—it would take a lifetime to know this region intimately. But the staffers at the Center for Alaskan Coastal Studies *(tel 907/235-6667, www.akcoastalstudies.org)* have spent cumulative lifetimes plumbing the mysteries of this place, and through their expertise, they can help day-trippers at least make the area's acquaintance. In summer the center offers a daily tour, the most complete of which is the ten-hour guided combo tour *(fare)*, which includes a boat trip out of Homer, time at the center's field station, a hike, kayaking, and the boat ride back to Homer.

The journey begins in the **harbor** near the end of Homer Spit, amid the hundreds of commercial fishing and sportfishing boats. The no-frills vessels the center uses for its tours are just like the charter boats, only they're not packed with anglers hankering for halibut. Watch for sea otters as the boat motors out the mouth of the harbor.

You'll reach **Gull Island** ❶ in just 30 minutes. The boat may spend an equal amount of time slowly circling these few acres of rock, because in summer Gull Island hosts thousands of nesting seabirds, mostly black-legged kittiwakes and common murres, as well as tufted and horned puffins, cormorants, guillemots, and gulls.

From Gull Island it's about a mile to the center's **Peterson Bay Coastal Science Field Station** ❷, nestled amid spruce on a hill overlooking Peterson Bay. If weather allows, visitors sit on the deck of the log building for a briefing by the naturalist. As much of the hike will involve tide-pooling, the group first visits touch tanks, where you can see and handle such intertidal critters as a fish-eating sea star (starfish), a decorator crab, and a gumboot chiton. Watch for a while and you'll see slo-mo action, perhaps a sunflower star chasing a sea urchin at a pace approaching that of dripping ketchup.

As you begin the **forest hike** ❸, notice yurts scattered around the grounds; some are available for overnight rental. Plant diversity along this trail is high since it marks a transition zone between coastal forest and interior boreal forest. As you near the water, the trail tiptoes through a ghost forest of dead spruce, killed when the 1964 earthquake dropped the land six feet, allowing seawater to flow into the forest.

The trail emerges on the cobble shore of **China Poot Bay** ❹, where the retreating tide reveals a mysterious world of tide pools. For an hour or two the group peers into crevices and under rocks, ferreting out such intertidal life as anemones, clams, limpets, yellow snail eggs, and an occasional octopus.

Back at the center, the group gathers for kayak lessons, and after 30 minutes of instruction everyone is ready for the guided paddle. Sometimes tours head out to Gull Island, other times deeper into **Peterson**

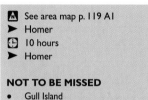

⚠ See area map p. 119 A1
► Homer
🕐 10 hours
► Homer

NOT TO BE MISSED
- Gull Island
- Peterson Bay Field Station
- China Poot Bay

Gull Island is a nesting ground for gulls, kittiwakes, and graceful cormorants.

Bay ❺, where you'll spot sea otters and an oyster farm that thrives in these clean, cold waters. After two to three hours, kayakers return to the center's dock, switch to a bigger vessel, and return to Homer. ∎

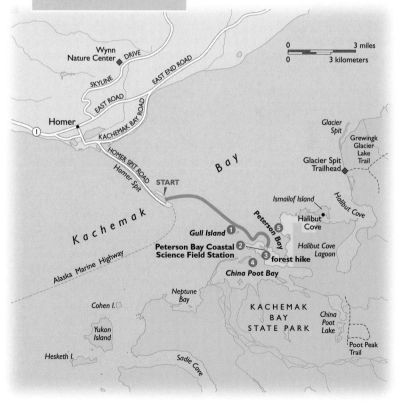

Mount Iliamna looms over the oft-photographed Russian Orthodox church in Ninilchik.

More places to visit on the Kenai Peninsula

COOPER LANDING

Cooper Landing isn't so much a town as an area. Sure, you'll find lodges, cafés, and shops scattered for several miles along the Sterling Highway, about ten miles west of its junction with the Seward Highway. And visitors can check out the modest **Cooper Landing Museum,** which covers local human and natural history, and the **K'beq Footprints Heritage Site,** where local Dena'ina Athabascan offer interpretive walks and display artifacts that speak to their culture. But Cooper Landing is really about Kenai Lake, the Upper Kenai River, and the Kenai's confluence with the Russian River, all within a few miles of town.

Several outfits run guided rafts down the gentle **Upper Kenai,** with a few Class II rapids to stir the blood. Watch for moose, bald eagles, grizzlies, and waterfowl. One outfit offers sea kayak tours of **Kenai Lake,** framed by forest and mountains. And a lot of companies take anglers out on the river in drift boats, as its confluence with the **Russian River** is one of the world's great fishing hot spots during summer salmon runs.

This is combat fishing, where boats crowd in and anglers stand elbow to elbow. To reach the fiercest fighting, take the **Russian River Ferry** *(fare)*, a cable ferry that crosses to the opposite bank of the Kenai River, world-renowned for its red (sockeye) salmon run. ⚠ 119 B3 **Visitor**

Information Cooper Landing Chamber of Commerce & Visitors Bureau ☎ 907/595-8888, www.cooperlandingchamber.com

NINILCHIK

This small town (pop. 783) sits on the Sterling Highway, where the Ninilchik River flows into Cook Inlet. Anglers come to fish at **Deep Creek State Recreation Area,** where charter boats chase salmon and halibut. Others just poke around the weathered waterfront community, check out historic buildings, or grab seafood at a café with a water view. A highlight is the handsome **Russian Orthodox church,** built in 1901 on a high point above Ninilchik. ⚠ 119 A2 ☎ 907/567-3571, www.ninilchikchamber.com

RESURRECTION PASS TRAIL

Running 38 miles (61 km) between Cooper Landing and Hope through a section of **Chugach National Forest,** this trail is among the best in south-central Alaska. Though a two- to four-day trek, it's a relatively easy grade on a well-maintained trail. You'll cross beautiful forest and alpine tundra and maybe see moose, bears, Dall sheep, and mountain goats. Lucky hikers will spot wolves and caribou. Along the way are rental cabins; these are extremely popular in summer, so reserve about six months ahead. ⚠ 119 B3 ☎ 907/224-3374, www.fs.fed.us /r10/chugach/seward ∎

The Alaska Peninsula and Aleutian Islands form a nearly 1,500-mile (2,414 km) arc that stretches southwest into the Pacific Ocean. This wild realm is home to abundant wildlife and a hardy and intriguing culture.

Alaska Peninsula & the Aleutians

Introduction & map 150–151
Lake Clark National Park & Preserve 152
McNeil River State Game Sanctuary 153
Katmai National Park & Preserve 155–157
Kodiak Island archipelago 158–159
Drive: Kodiak's Chiniak Highway 160–161
Aleutian Islands 162–163
Alaska Maritime National Wildlife Refuge 164–165
More places to visit on the Alaska Peninsula & in the Aleutians 166
Hotels & restaurants 254–255

Salmon fillets drying in the open air near Lake Clark

Alaska Peninsula & the Aleutians

THE REMOTEST PARTS OF THIS RUGGED, WINDSWEPT AREA ARE JUST A couple hundred miles from Russia, nearer to Asia than the rest of Alaska. Even the areas closer to the state's more developed areas are, with a few exceptions, wild places rarely touched by human feet. Anyone willing to venture here will find a realm of stark, pristine beauty.

The Alaska Peninsula and the 1,100-mile-long string of Aleutian Islands follow the westward curving Ring of Fire, a chain of volcanoes that frames most of the North Pacific. This northern arc—the spine of southwestern Alaska—contains more than 60 fire-breathing mountains, many still active. The subduction of the North Pacific plate beneath the North American plate along the 25,000-foot-deep Aleutian Trench accounts for all the tectonic activity.

Despite the eruptions, earthquakes, and tsunamis generated by these volcanoes, not to mention the frequent cyclonic storms that blast this region (bring your foul weather gear), life thrives here. Tens of millions of seabirds come to nest; more than half a million northern fulmars rear their young on Chagulak Island (the largest known colony in the world), and miniscule Kaligagan Island hosts more than 100,000 tufted puffins, the state's largest

colony. Large mammals, including caribou, arctic foxes, moose, wolves, and, most famously, the huge brown bears of Kodiak Island and Katmai National Park and Preserve, roam the land. The waters host an abundance of large marine mammals, including humpback, beluga, bowhead, and gray whales; orcas; northern sea lions; walrus; and sea otters. There are also vast numbers of fish.

The plethora of fish and wildlife long ago attracted the Unangan people, popularly known as Aleut, who settled most of the 200-plus Aleutian Islands, and the Alutiiq people, who mainly came to Kodiak Island and the Alaska Peninsula. They lived off this

Area of map detail

SOUTHWEST ALASKA

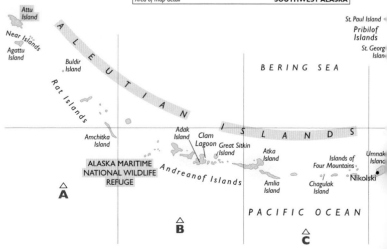

The scenic but rugged terrain of Unimak Island challenges even the hardiest hikers.

harsh but rich land for millennia until Russian fur hunters arrived in the 1700s. These trappers devastated both the sea otters and the Unangan, whose population plunged from perhaps 20,000 to maybe a few thousand. The sea otters have largely recovered but the Unangan have not. The number of Aleut stands at roughly 8,000 today and they live on only five islands. Yet the fascinating legacies of both the Unangan and the Alutiiq have survived and can be seen in southwestern Alaska today. The U.S. impact on this area has been felt mostly in two ways: the commercial fishing boom and the little-known but vital World War II battles fought in the Aleutians. ■

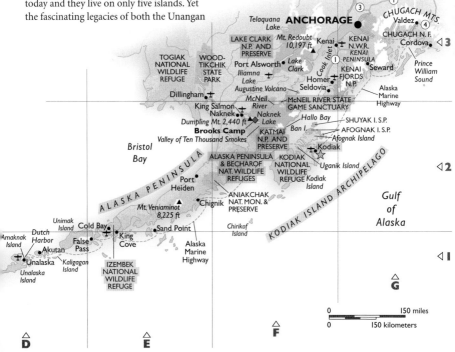

Lake Clark National Park & Preserve

Lake Clark National Park & Preserve
www.nps.gov/lacl

🅼 151 F3

✉ Field Headquarters, 1 Park Pl., Port Alsworth

☎ 907/271-3751 (superintendent), 907/781-2218 (Port Alsworth)

AT MORE THAN FOUR MILLION ACRES, NEARLY TWICE THE size of Yellowstone, Lake Clark National Park and Preserve is big. It encompasses tremendous diversity, from two 10,000-foot volcanoes to a coastline dotted with seabirds to dense spruce forests, where wolves and bears roam, to 40-mile-long Lake Clark to whitewater rivers to an Arctic-tundra-like plateau favored by caribou.

Access to the park is primarily by chartered aircraft. A few people boat to the coastal section, but most arrive via floatplanes that land on the lakes or in wheeled planes that land on gravel bars or beaches. This wilderness park demands respect; prepare thoroughly and be sure your skills and fitness are up to the challenging environment, or go with a guide.

Port Alsworth, the little settlement on Lake Clark, is home to the Park Service's field headquarters. From here, the easy and maintained **Tanalian Falls Trail** passes through a forest of birch and spruce, skirts ponds and bogs, paces the frothy Tanalian River to Kontrashibuna Lake, and ends 2.5 miles (4 km) later at the waterfall. Keep an eye out for Dall sheep on the high slopes, moose in the ponds, and bears everywhere. The **Telaquana Trail** also provides an undeveloped route from Lake Clark to Telaquana Lake. If you want to hike elsewhere, be ready to bushwhack and use a GPS instrument or a map and compass.

Many visitors navigate the park via water, most often in inflatable kayaks and canoes, which must be brought in. Paddling any of the long, large, unspoiled lakes—**Turquoise, Twin, Two,** and **Upper** and **Lower Tazimina** to name but a few—is a quintessential Alaska experience. ∎

A relaxing soak soothes aching muscles after a long day of hiking in Lake Clark National Park.

McNeil River
State Game Sanctuary

Campers find refuge in their tents along the McNeil River.

McNEIL RIVER IS ARGUABLY THE BEST SPOT IN THE WORLD to watch brown bears. Three factors account for what is possibly the greatest concentration of brown bears on Earth: good salmon runs, an excellent fishing area where low falls and rapids slow the migrating salmon, and the lack of other excellent fishing areas nearby.

McNeil River is very difficult to reach, however. Only 150 to 250 permits a year are issued to the area; a lottery decides the winners. If you are one of the lucky few, you must pay several hundred dollars for the permit, charter a plane to the sanctuary, bring your own camping gear, and hike 2 miles (3.2 km) (sloshing through creeks and crossing mudflats) to a 10-by-10-foot (16-m-by-16-m) gravel pad. Here you stand with ten other visitors and an armed Fish and Game naturalist for six to eight hours, often in the rain and cold.

The rain and the expense are soon forgotten when a thousand-pound boar grizzly lumbers by, usually a mere 75 feet (23 m) away. Or when a sow and her two rambunctious cubs show up to snag a few fish. You'll typically see several dozen bears in the course of a day. The record for the most in sight at one time is 72, most of them within 200 feet (61 m).

You also will appreciate the scenic sanctuary, lying in the shadow of Augustine Volcano. You'll probably see red foxes, harbor seals, and bald eagles, and may sight moose, wolves, and caribou. But the bears are the true attraction at McNeil River.

Incidentally, the safety record is perfect. Since restrictions were applied in the 1970s, no visitor has been mauled or killed and no bears have had to be shot. ■

McNeil River State Game Sanctuary
www.wildlife.alaska.gov
/mcneil

🅰 151 F2

✉ Permits: Alaska Dept. of Fish & Game, Wildlife Conservation, McNeil River State Game Sanctuary, 333 Raspberry Rd., Anchorage, AK 99518

☎ 907/267-2182

💲 $$$$$ (non-resident permit) plus application-filing fee & air charter

The recognizable horned puffin, a frequent visitor to Attu, delights bird-watchers.

Birding on Attu Island

Eurasian siskin. Siberian blue robin. Oriental turtle-dove. Asian brown flycatcher. The avid birder who sees that roll call of species immediately envisions a magical place: Attu, the westernmost island in the Aleutians, 1,000 miles from mainland Alaska and continental North America.

Attu is hallowed ground for birders: It is one of the best places to spot birds that can be added to a North American life list. In order for a bird to be placed on the list, it must be spotted in North America, and according to the boundaries drawn by the American Birding Association, Attu is in North America (but it's very close to Asia).

So, if a Eurasian siskin is spotted on Attu, it can go on the list. If the bird is spotted in Asia, where it is quite common, it can't go on the list. That's the primary reason people are willing to brave the often miserable weather and spend thousands of dollars to get to Attu to view bird species that they could much more easily and cheaply see in Asia. Between the storms that blow Asian species onto Attu and migration routes that pass over the island, 30 to 35 Asian species are often sighted in a typical two- to four-week season.

A few pioneering birders began going to Attu in 1977, and organized birding trips soon followed. They landed at an airstrip left over from World War II and set up camp on the southeast part of the island. During the day, the birders would fan out to the coast, tundra, bay, freshwater marsh, and other habitats. Then they'd wait. When a rarity was spotted, word went out over the group's radios and other birders rushed to the site. From 1977 to 2000, more than a thousand birders made the trip to Attu.

Since 2000, Attu is only accessible by boat—and finding a boat that will cut through the stormy North Pacific isn't easy. Beginning in 2006, the *Spirit of Oceanus* (*Victor Emanuel Nature Tours, tel 800/328-8368, www.ventbird.com*) and the **M.V. Skimus** (*High Lonesome Bird Tours, tel 520/458-9446 or 800/743-2668, www.hilonesome.com*) will make the trip to Attu. ∎

Katmai National Park & Preserve

**Katmai National
Park & Preserve**
www.nps.gov/katm
- 151 F2
- Visitor information: Headquarters, P.O. Box 7, King Salmon
- ☎ 907/246-3305

KATMAI'S NEARLY 4.1 MILLION ACRES OFFER ENOUGH
scenic splendors, get-away-from-it-all tranquillity, and wildlife viewing to satisfy the most demanding lover of the outdoors. But this park has two additional special features: volcanoes and brown bears. Fifteen volcanoes rise in the park, some of them still steaming. In the lands below roam some 1,500 to 2,000 brown bears, one of the continent's largest protected populations of these storied predators.

The only way to reach Katmai is by plane. Most people arrive on scheduled jets from Anchorage, which land in **King Salmon,** a bush town just outside the park's western border that houses park headquarters and a visitor center. From there you either take a floatplane *(daily flights June–mid-Sept.)* or drive 10 miles (16 km) to Lake Camp and boat east on 50-mile-long (80 km) **Naknek Lake** to Brooks Camp.

Brooks Camp is the park's hub and a busy place during the summer. It has a visitor center, a lodge (Brooks Lodge, see p. 254), a campground, limited food service, equipment rentals, and guide services. Several nice day hikes start in the camp, but even these short hikes require standard wilderness precautions. The summer skies above Katmai are clear and sunny only about 20 percent of the time, and it can drizzle for days, so be prepared. And don't forget those 1,500 brown bears; travelers are strongly urged to attend the park's brief program on bear safety.

The moderate 4-mile (6.4 km) (one way) trail to the 2,440-foot (744 m) summit of **Dumpling Mountain** starts in the Brooks Camp Campground. An overlook at the 1.5-mile point provides fine views of Naknek Lake and distant volcanoes. Forge ahead and you'll enjoy dense forest, alpine meadows, and even finer vistas from the top. Ranger naturalists also lead guided hikes out of Brooks Camp.

Every visitor to Katmai should take the eight-hour round-trip park bus tour along the 23-mile

**More interested
in salmon, brown
bears at Katmai
ignore photographers crowding the viewing
platforms.**

The raw, isolated beauty of Hallo Bay, on the Katmai coast, entices lovers of wildlife and pristine lands.

(37 km) dirt road to the **Three Forks Overlook** above the **Valley of Ten Thousand Smokes** (*reservations recommended July–Aug.*). This broad valley was devastated by the 1912 eruption of Novarupta Volcano (see sidebar opposite), which buried the previously verdant landscape under as much as 700 feet (213.5 m) of volcanic debris—ash, pumice, and rock. Robert Griggs, who stood above the valley in 1916 and beheld the innumerable steam vents, wrote "the whole valley as far as the eye could reach was full of hun-

dreds, no thousands—literally tens of thousands—of smokes curling up from its fissured floor." Thus, the valley's name. The smoke is gone now, but the moonscape remains.

Hardy hikers can take the steep, strenuous 1.5-mile (2.4 km) **Ukak Falls Trail** from the overlook down to and across the valley floor, where the turbulent **Ukak River** network has carved deep gorges in the packed ash. The **Three Forks Convergence** area, where the Ukak and its tributaries meet, is particularly scenic.

A rain of ash

In 1912 Novarupta exploded with a fury ten times more powerful than the 1980 eruption of Mount St. Helens. Gas, pumice, and ash belched from the belly of the Earth and darkened the sky over most of the Northern Hemisphere. More chilling than any facts is the first-person account of an Aleut fisherman trapped in the vicinity: "We are waiting for death at any moment. We are covered with ashes, in some places ten feet and six feet deep. Night and day we light lamps. We cannot see the daylight ... and we have no water. All the rivers are ... just ashes mixed with water. Here are darkness and hell, thunder and noise. It is terrible. We are praying." ■

BEAR VIEWING

No visitor to Katmai should miss watching brown bears snag migrating salmon at **Brooks Falls,** a half-mile (0.8 km) hike from Brooks Camp. Across a floating bridge, an elevated viewing platform enables visitors to safely observe the bears fishing from as close as a 100 feet (30.5 m). During peak season—especially during the big sockeye run, in July—space on the platform is at a premium; rangers limit each person to an hour, and visitors often wait in long lines to get a place on the platform. A second viewing platform is located on the Brooks River where it empties into Naknek Lake.

There's never a crowd problem at **Hallo Bay** on Katmai's coast. Since 1994 **Hallo Bay Bear Lodge** *(tel 907/235-2237, www.hallobay.com, 5-hour to 7-day trips May–Sept., $$$$$)* has brought eight to ten guests at a time to its remote camp to walk among the brown bears. No platforms, no shotguns. A guide simply takes four or five people out to mingle with the bears. Safety comes from the guide's deep understanding of bear behavior and the operation's scrupulous efforts to keep bears from becoming human oriented—and, as a last resort, flares. In 12 years there has never been a bear attack and flares have only been used four times. Seeing brown bears 50 feet away in an utterly wild setting is a sublime experience. ■

Kodiak Island archipelago

Kodiak Island

🏕 151 F2

Visitor information

www.kodiak.org

✉ Kodiak Island Convention & Visitors Bureau, 100 Marine Way, Suite 200, Kodiak

☎ 907/486-4782 or 800/789-4782

🕐 Daily Mem. Day– Labor Day, Mon.– Fri. rest of year

A thick under-story of devil's club carpets the rain forest.

THE 16 MAJOR ISLANDS AND MANY SMALLER ONES OF THE Kodiak Island archipelago sprawl across the Gulf of Alaska for 177 miles. Kodiak Island accounts for nearly three-quarters of the archipelago's dry land; it's the second largest island in the U.S. (Hawaii's Big Island is larger). Though this wild and windswept island realm is most famous for its numerous hulking brown bears, ironically it is also the most accessible and developed part of southwestern Alaska.

KODIAK ISLAND

The commercial fishing center of **Kodiak,** population 6,200, is by far the largest city in the archipelago (and the entire southwest of Alaska, for that matter); travelers can get here via jet flights or the state ferry. About 100 miles (160 km) of scenic gravel roads fan out from Kodiak, making up the only road system in the region.

Begin your tour down on the docks. The **Star of Kodiak,** the last Liberty Ship built during World War II, sits moored near the visitor center. After a 1964 tsunami wiped out much of downtown and several canneries, the mothballed ship was towed up to Kodiak to serve as a fish-processing plant. It's now the home of a seafood corporation.

Kodiak's extensive Russian past is on display at the **Baranov Museum,** just a little down from the Liberty Ship. The oldest Russian building in the United States, it was built in 1808 by the Russian-American Company to store sea otter pelts. Inside is a wealth of artifacts from the Russian era, including some dazzling Easter eggs. The museum also houses exhibits about the archipelago's indigenous peoples and the American years. Flip through the dozens of albums containing archival photos.

The Russian influence is further evident a block away at the **Holy Resurrection Russian Orthodox Church** (385 Kashavarof St., tel 907/486-3854, tours available), the third orthodox church built on this site; the first was in 1794. From the blue cupolas to the ornate interior, this 1945 structure is a visual feast. Continue northeast another block and you'll come to a lovely chapel and **St. Herman Theological Seminary** (414 Mission Rd., tel 907/486-3524), one of only three Russian Orthodox seminaries in the United States.

The history of Native life in the archipelago is full and rich as well; the Alutiiq have lived here for more than 7,500 years. The **Alutiiq Museum and Archaeological Repository** (215 Mission Rd., tel 907/486-7004) has gathered more than 100,000 artifacts that evoke the past lives of the Alutiiq and other Eskimo groups, though only a modest portion of the vast collection is displayed. Meander past seal-gut parkas, ceremonial masks, harpoons, kayaks, knives, fine woven baskets, and much more.

To sample some recent history, drive northeast on Rezanof Drive (which turns into Monashka Bay

Road) and go almost 4 miles (6.4 km) to **Fort Abercrombie State Historical Park** (1400 Abercrombie Dr., tel 907/486-6339). The old concrete bunkers of this World War II–vintage artillery emplacement are interesting, but the views of the sea and the sightings of sea otters, puffins, whales, and other wildlife keep most people enthralled. The park also has a campground, picnic areas, and trails through lush forest to the rugged shoreline.

KODIAK NATIONAL WILDLIFE REFUGE

The 1.9 million roadless acres of Kodiak National Wildlife Refuge occupy the southwest two-thirds of Kodiak Island, all of **Uganik** and **Ban Islands,** and a chunk of **Afognak Island.** The 2,300 resident brown bears are Kodiak brown bears, a subspecies of the brown bear. Guides and air taxis take visitors to view bears on the refuge; they're easy to find in July and August when the salmon runs are peaking. Be sure to look beyond the bears: The refuge is a scenic blend of mountains, open tundra, deep fjords, and much more wildlife.

SHUYAK ISLAND & AFOGNAK ISLAND STATE PARKS

The archipelago's outer islands are difficult to reach, but worth the effort. Two remote state parks, 47,000-acre Shuyak Island State Park and 75,000-acre Afognak Island State Park, both reward hardy travelers with a healthy dose of scenery. If you prefer the comforts of home, **Afognak Wilderness Lodge** (tel 907/ 486-6442, www.afognaklodge.com) is located inside Afognak and affords some of the finest marine mammal sightings in Alaska. ■

Baranov Museum
www.baranov.us
✉ 101 Marine Way, Kodiak
☎ 907/486-5920
🕐 Open daily in summer, Tues.–Sat. rest of year, closed Feb.
💲 $

Kodiak National Wildlife Refuge
http://kodiak.fws.gov
🅰 151 F2
✉ 1390 Buskin River Rd., Kodiak
☎ 907/487-2600 or 800/408-3514

Shuyak Island & Afognak Island State Parks
www.dnr.state.ak.us/parks
🅰 151 F2
✉ 1400 Abercrombie Dr., Kodiak
☎ 907/486-6339

Kodiak's Chiniak Highway

This route traces the scenic northeastern shore of Kodiak Island, slaloming around three deep bays before swinging east to end at Cape Chiniak and Cape Greville. It passes through a variety of landscapes, including temperate rain forest, alpine meadows flush with wildflowers in the spring and summer, rolling tundra, stands of alder and cottonwood, and coastlines subject to pounding waves and turbulent tides. Motorists also will encounter bits of rural Alaska amid the wilderness, such as a roadhouse, a winery, and, incongruously, some cattle and bison ranches. The first 12.8 miles (20.6 km) of the highway are paved; the last 30 (48 km) are decent gravel.

The back roads of Kodiak beckon visitors to explore and experience the island's beauty.

The drive begins at the corner of Marine Way and Rezanof Drive in **Kodiak ❶** *(for information, contact Kodiak Island Convention & Visitors Bureau; see p. 158).* Head southwest on Rezanof, which soon turns into the Chiniak Highway. At Mile 2.4, enjoy the panorama that opens up at **Deadman's Curve** of Kodiak Harbor, Chiniak Bay, and some of the archipelago's many islands.

Back on the highway, turn left at Mile 4.4 into the **Buskin River State Recreation Site ❷** *(tel 907/486-6339, www.dnr .state.ak.us/parks/units/kodiak/buskin.htm).* This is the most popular fishing site on Kodiak Island's road system; big runs of sockeye and silver salmon migrate up the river in summer. Beachcombers will see plenty of bald eagles, too, swooping down to get their share of the salmon.

About half a mile (0.8 km) farther down is the turnoff for **Anton Larsen Bay Road,** a 11.7-mile (18.8 km) spur that leads north past the island's golf course and along the western shore of **Anton Larsen Bay,** a pretty fjord with a large island at its mouth. At Mile 6.6 on the highway you'll see the largest U.S. Coast Guard station in America; more than a thousand people work here. A quarter mile (0.4 km) past the station's entrance the highway comes to **Womens Bay ❸,** which the road skirts for several miles. The bay was so named because Alutiiq women went there to hunt, fish, and gather food.

At the head of the bay, near Mile 10, the highway bridges the mouth of **Sargent Creek,** where in the fall emperor geese come to winter. A quarter mile (0.4 km)

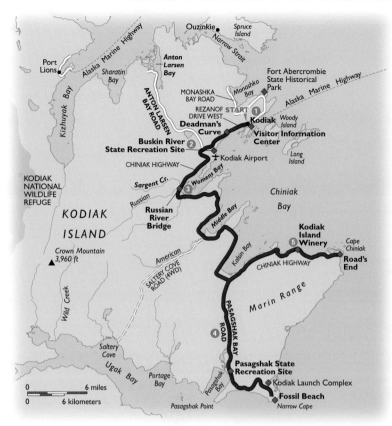

later, stand on the **Russian River Bridge** and watch spawning salmon *(Aug.–Sept.)*. The wildlife theme continues from about Mile 19 to Mile 21.5, where eagles and the occasional eagle nest can be seen in the cottonwood trees along **Middle Bay.**

The route's major junction occurs at Mile 30.6, where the **Pasagshak Bay Road** ④ cuts due south for 16.5 miles (26.5 km). This road leads to two unusual sites for rural Alaska. First, the Kodiak Launch Complex, a state-of-the-art private aerospace facility that launches rockets for commercial and military interests *(the site is not open to the general public).* Secondly you'll find **Fossil Beach,** where rocks contain fossilized seashells.

Retrace your route to the Chinak Highway, where at Mile 36.7 the **Kodiak Island Winery** ⑤ *(tel 907/486-4848, tours daily),* makes for a most unexpected sight.

🅜	See area map p. 151 F2
▶	Kodiak
↔	85.6 miles (138 km), out and back, not counting spur roads
🕓	4 hours plus stops
▶	Kodiak

NOT TO BE MISSED

- Buskin River State Recreation Site
- Pasagshak Bay spur
- Kodiak Island Winery

It makes award-winning wines and champagnes from organic fruits and berries. If you want a meal to go with your tipple, at the road's end you'll find, logically enough, **Road's End** *(Mile 42.4, tel 907/486-2885),* a traditional Alaskan roadhouse known for its pies. ∎

Standing near the Unalaska's Russian Orthodox Church of the Holy Ascension, a crabber shows off catch.

Unalaska Island

🅰 150 D1

Visitor information

www.unalaska.info

✉ Unalaska/Port of Dutch Harbor Conv. & Visitors Bureau, 15 S. Fifth St.

☎ 907/581-2612 or 877/581-2612

Museum of the Aleutians

www.aleutians.org

✉ 314 Salmon Way

☎ 907/581-5150

🕐 Open daily in summer, Tues.–Sat. rest of year

💲 $

Aleutian Islands

A SUBMERGED VOLCANIC MOUNTAIN RANGE RISES OUT OF the North Pacific to form the Aleutian Islands, a string of more than 200 islands and tiny islets in a 1,100-mile arc that curves west toward Russia and Japan from the tip of the Alaska Peninsula. The confluence of the mild Kuroshio or Japan Current and the frigid Bering Sea creates a great deal of rain, fog, wind, and storms, which, along with the forbidding isolation, may account for the fact that only about 8,000 people live in the Aleutians. More than half live on Unalaska Island.

The town of Unalaska on Unalaska Island is the hub of Aleutian life. Fewer than ten of the Aleutians are populated, even by tiny villages. Many islands are part of the **Alaska Maritime National Wildlife Refuge** (see p. 164–165) and brim with seabirds and marine mammals.

The state ferry makes a twice-monthly visit to Unalaska and provides the least expensive way to get an extensive look at the Aleutians. Passengers can board in Kodiak (or from Homer or Seldovia on the Kenai Peninsula) and spend three to four days cruising down the Alaska Peninsula and out the Aleutians as far as Unalaska. Get out the binoculars and scan the water for sea otters, sea lions, harbor seals, porpoises, and whales, including humpbacks, grays, minkes, and orcas. Scan the rocky coastline and islands for the dozens of species of seabirds. Or just sit back and drink in the misty headlands, barrel-chested cliffs, tundra-greened islands, and volcanic cones—assuming you're not awash in fog. Once in Unalaska you can look around town for about 5.5 hours before the ferry heads back north, or stay for a while and then fly out.

UNALASKA ISLAND

Many people refer to the town of **Unalaska** as "Dutch Harbor," but Dutch Harbor is actually only the name of the harbor. Though the town's permanent population is about 4,350, there are probably twice that many people here during the peak fishing season, roughly November to April, when transient fishermen and cannery workers arrive and things get pretty rowdy. The town actually straddles two islands: Unalaska and close neighbor Amaknak; they're connected by a 500-foot (152.4 m) span officially called the Bridge to the Other Side.

For an overview, start at the impressive **Museum of the Aleutians** on Salmon Way. This 9,400-square-foot (873 sq m) facility covers the islands' native culture, the Russian era, and the Aleutian campaign during World War II. The museum also conducts summer archaeological digs. There are 25 known Unangan prehistoric village sites within 3 miles (4.8 km) of the museum; the oldest, **Unalaska Bar,** dates back 9,000 years, making it one of the oldest sites in Alaska. Visitors are welcome to help with these excavations.

Unalaska's downtown national historic landmark and the outstanding symbol of the Russian era is the **Russian Orthodox Church of the Holy Ascension.** The current wooden church topped by two blue cupolas was completed in 1895, but the first church on this site dates back to 1825. Inside is a superb collection of hundreds of significant icons, artworks, and artifacts.

More recent history is evident at the **Aleutian World War II National Historic Area.** It's a little-known fact that a bloody battle of the Pacific Theater was fought between Allied forces and the Japanese on Attu, the westernmost Aleutian island. A World War II–era building near the airport harbors a visitor center-museum where you can learn

Leftovers at Unimak's World War II airfield, the first for wheeled aircraft in the Aleutians

about this year-long struggle that began with the bombing of Unalaska. Stroll the grounds of Fort Schwatka, the coastal defensive post on Amaknak Island, and note the **S.S. Northwestern,** which lies half submerged in nearby Captain's Bay.

VISITING OTHER ISLANDS

Nearby islands offer a wealth of birding, fishing, hiking, whale-watching, and other opportunities. Contact the Unalaska visitors bureau for information on tour and charter-boat operators or how to get around on your own. ■

Aleutian World War II National Historic Area
www.nps.gov/aleu
✉ Visitor center near airport
☎ 907/581-9944
🕐 Open daily in summer, Tues.–Sat. rest of year

Alaska Maritime National Wildlife Refuge

http://alaskamaritime.fws
.gov or
www.islandsandocean.org

🏔 150 AI–CI

✉ Alaska Islands &
Ocean Visitor
Center, 95 Sterling
Hwy., Homer

☎ 907/235-6961

🕐 Closed Sun.–Mon.
Labor Day–mid-May

Alaska Maritime National Wildlife Refuge

THE 4.9-MILLION-ACRE (16,190 SQ KM) ALASKA MARITIME National Wildlife Refuge consists of more than 2,500 islands, reefs, islets, spires, and coastal stretches scattered all around Alaska. The bulk of the refuge, however, lies along the Alaska Peninsula and in the Kodiak archipelago, the Pribilof Islands, and, especially, the Aleutians.

Most of the units in the refuge are difficult and expensive to reach, involving the chartering of small planes and boats. But there are three sites in southwestern Alaska where a relatively modest outlay departs Homer and Seldovia *(every two weeks Apr.–Oct.)* for Kodiak and then heads out along the Alaska Peninsula and down the Aleutians as far as Unalaska, passing many refuge holdings on

Hundreds of thousands of fur seals breed on the Pribilof Islands.

of money can bring you face to face with this striking refuge. You'll be treated to breathtaking landscapes and an astonishing wealth of wildlife, notably millions of seabirds and many species of marine mammals.

KODIAK TO UNALASKA

The Alaska Marine Highway state ferry **Tustumena** (see p. 237)

the way. During the summer, refuge naturalists travel on the *Tustumena;* they give presentations and answer questions.

The voyage takes three to four days and the seas can be rough, but a passenger without a vehicle and no cabin can sometimes get a ticket from Homer to Unalaska for a few hundred dollars. You'll probably want to take a plane

back, but it's still a bargain. Once in Unalaska you can go out to nearby parts of the refuge with one of the town's many tour operators (contact Unalaska/Dutch Harbor Convention & Visitors Bureau; see p. 162).

ADAK ISLAND

Lying 350 miles (563 km) west of Unalaska, half of Adak Island is a wilderness section of the maritime refuge. This exceedingly remote place is accessible by twice-weekly flights from Anchorage and by roads and trails established when Adak was home to a big naval base and a city of 6,000 people. The base closed in 1997 and now only 69 people live there, giving it something of a ghost-town feel. Stop at the refuge headquarters in town to find out how to explore this starkly beautiful place, with its 2,000-foot (609 m) sea cliffs and mountains greened by alpine tundra.

Don't miss the 6-mile (9.6 km) **wildlife drive** around pretty **Clam Lagoon,** where you should spot sea otters, seals, and all sorts of birds, including sought-after Asian rarities (see p. 154). At **Finger Bay,** a dramatic, fjord-like cut in the island, you can take an easy, 1-mile (1.6 km) hike up to and along **Lake Betty.** Right outside of town are the black sands of **Kuluk Bay beach,** a good place to watch seabirds and, if it's reasonably clear, to gaze 20 miles (32 km) across the water to the 5,704-foot (1,739 m) volcano that is neighboring Great Sitkin Island.

ST. PAUL ISLAND

To go from remote to even more remote, head about 200 miles (322 km) north of the Aleutians into the Bering Sea to the **Pribilof Islands,** the biggest of

which, **St. Paul,** is about 8 by 14 miles (13 by 22 km). PenAir (tel 800/448-4226, www.penair.com) flies from Anchorage to St. Paul several times a week. Almost all visitors go on a package tour through St. Paul Island Tours (tel 877/424-5637, www.alaskabird ing.com), an outfit run by the Unangan (Aleut) people, who make up almost the entire population of the Pribilofs (the largest Aleut population in the world). All visitors stay at the basic, bathroom-down-the-hall King Eider Hotel; there are no other lodgings and no camping.

The knowledgeable guides show you wildflower-bedecked tundra, blue arctic foxes, reindeer, nesting puffins and other seabirds, but most of all they take you to the fur seal rookeries. About 800,000 of these husky seals come to the Pribilofs every summer to breed—the largest such gathering in the world. From observation blinds you can watch mothers nursing pups, males fighting over females, and all the rest of this raucous scene. ■

Getting a close-up of the sea birds on the Pribilof Islands.

Adak Island
http://alaskamaritime.fws .gov
🄰 151 B1
✉ Aleutian Islands Unit NWR, 146B Seawall Rd., Adak
☎ 907/592-2406 (summer), 907/235-6546 (rest of year)

More places to visit on the
Alaska Peninsula & in the Aleutians

ALASKA PENINSULA & BECHAROF NATIONAL WILDLIFE REFUGES

These neighboring refuges on the Alaska Peninsula, administered as a single unit, more than live up to their status as a refuge for wildlife. Sea otters, falcons, moose, sea lions, wolves, waterfowl: The diversity and numbers are staggering. A 10,000-head barren-ground caribou herd spends much of its year in these refuges. Most of the salmon that constitute the Bristol Bay fishery, the richest salmon fishery in the world, spawn in streams that originate on refuge lands. And the numbers and size of the brown bears are legendary.

The combined 5.5 million acres (22,260 sq km) of these refuges also contain smoldering volcanoes, the second biggest lake in Alaska, rugged coastline, windswept tundra, and rushing rivers, as well as some unusual geological features. At **Gas Rocks,** near Mount Peulik, underground gases continuously seep through cracks in the granite. About a mile away stand the rare and otherworldly **Ukinrek Maars—**

rounded craters created in 1977 during a series of eruptions. **Castle Cape Fjords** is a jumble of towering rock spires composed of contrasting light and dark layers so distinctive that sailors use the rocks as a navigational aid.

Despite their myriad attractions, the refuges are little visited. They are challenging to reach, hard to get around in, completely undeveloped, and the mercurial weather. Staff at the refuges' King Salmon Visitor Center *(King Salmon airport)* can suggest ways to visit. King Salmon, though a town of only 400, offers a fair selection of lodging, stores, and restaurants (and several bars), as it's the main gateway to the Alaska Peninsula.

🅰 151 F2 ✉ King Salmon Visitor Center ☎ 907/246-4250 (visitor center), http://becharof.fws.gov or http://alaska peninsula.fws.gov

IZEMBEK NATIONAL WILDLIFE REFUGE

Izembek is indeed a haven for a lavish assortment of wildlife. Gray and minke whales cruise nearshore waters; sea otters, sea lions, and seals inhabit the coastline and nearby islands; salmon galore spawn in Izembek streams; caribou herds migrate through in fall, with hungry wolves in tow; and brown bears mass to gorge on the salmon. But Izembek is most famous for the enormous flocks of migrating waterfowl and other birds that come to feed on some of the world's largest eel-grass beds, found in 150-square-mile (388.5 sq km) **Izembek Lagoon.**

Izembek is reasonably accessible. Scheduled flights and the state ferry go to **Cold Bay,** a small town beside the refuge that has some visitor facilities and the refuge headquarters. If you rent or bring a car, you can bounce around the 40 miles (64 km) of gravel roads that fan out into parts of the 417,533-acre (16,900 sq km) refuge. 🅰 151 D1–E1 ☎ 907/532-2445 or 877/837-6332, http://izembek.fws.gov ∎

Halibut fever

Every summer halibut fever rages across Alaska. Small halibut are the tastiest, but many anglers lust for the trophy fish—a desire whose flame is fanned by halibut derbies, where the largest fish of the season earns thousands of dollars for the lucky angler. The current world-record fish, caught in the Dutch Harbor area (on Unalaska Island), weighed 459 pounds (208 kg). The previous record halibut was a 395-pounder (179 kg) also hooked around Dutch Harbor, but that angler, Mike Golat, almost lost the record. Rules declare that the halibut has to be gaffed—landed with a hook—not shot, but gaffing and hefting a fish that size into Golat's little skiff would have swamped. So, quick-thinking Golat landed the fish by towing it all the way to shore. ∎

Renowned for two of Alaska's premier wild places—Prince William Sound and Wrangell–St. Elias National Park and Preserve —this region has few settlements. Of them, one was built on copper, one on fishing, and one on oil.

Prince William Sound & around

Introduction & map 168–169
Valdez 170–171
Cordova & Copper River Delta
172–175
Prince William Sound 176–177
Drive: Exploring the Richardson
Highway 178–179
Wrangell–St. Elias National Park
& Preserve 180–183
McCarthy/Kennicott 186–187
More places to visit around
Prince William Sound 188
Hotels & restaurants 255–257

Bush planes take visitors on flightseeing excursions or drop them at wilderness campsites.

Prince William Sound & around

THIS SWATH OF SOUTH-CENTRAL ALASKA ENCOMPASSES A STRIKING BLEND of land and sea. The land is a vast and diverse expanse of spruce lowlands, rain forest, majestic rivers, and high country rife with towering peaks and massive glaciers; it supports plentiful wildlife. Land meets sea at Prince William Sound, a roughly 30-by-70-mile (48 by 112 km) offshoot of the Gulf of Alaska. The sound is a wonderfully irregular world of lushly forested islands, fjords that slash deep into the mainland, jagged peninsulas, and deep waters teeming with life.

Humans have lived off the bounty of land and sea in this region for millennia. The 13.2 million acres (5.3 million ha) of Wrangell–St. Elias National Park and Preserve were and still are home to the Ahtna, an interior Athabascan people. Prince William Sound lies in the traditional territory of the Alutiiq, the coastal dwellers whose strongholds were on Kodiak Island and the Alaska Peninsula to the southwest. The Eyak, a small indigenous group, live around the Copper River Delta, with one

foot in the Wrangell–St. Elias area and one in Prince William Sound.

Europeans arrived in 1778, when Captain Cook sailed into the sound, which he dubbed Sandwich Sound. By the time Cook's expedition got back to England the Earl of Sandwich (Cook's patron) had fallen into disrepute, and the editors of Cook's maps changed the name to honor the king's third son, who later became King William IV. The major influx of outsiders occurred in the late 1890s, when the Klondike gold

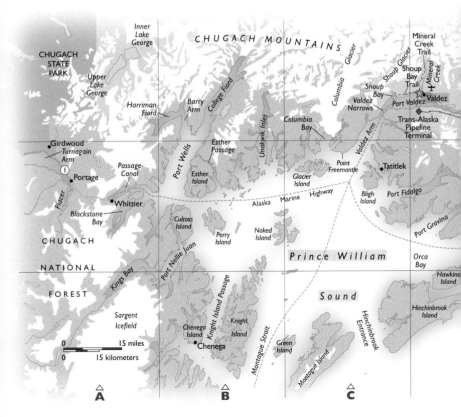

Adventurous visitors climb the Root Glacier in Wrangell–St. Elias National Park.

rush brought fortune seekers into the Port of Valdez and north through what is now the Wrangell–St. Elias area. But copper had a more lasting impact on Wrangell–St. Elias.

From 1906 to 1938 the Kennecott Mines Company (later renamed Kennecott Copper Corporation) operated in what is now the middle of the national park; at one point it was the richest copper mine in the world.

Prince William Sound has also gained a place in history. The 1964 Good Friday earthquake, the most violent quake ever recorded in North America, had its epicenter here. The shock waves and the tsunamis that followed pounded the area, leveling villages and the city of Valdez, which was rebuilt later on higher ground 4 miles (6.4 km) from its original site. And on March 24, 1989, coincidentally also Good Friday, the oil tanker *Exxon Valdez* ran aground and spilled 10.8 million gallons of crude into the sound. Cleanup efforts and the passing years have erased visible signs of the spill; restoration and environmental monitoring efforts continue today. ■

To McCarthy/ Kennicott, Copper Center, and Tetlin N.W.R. (see map on p. 183)

WRANGELL-ST. ELIAS NATIONAL PARK AND PRESERVE ◁ **3**

RICHARDSON HIGHWAY

4

Copper

Bremner

Trans-Alaska Pipeline

CHUGACH MOUNTAINS

CHUGACH NATIONAL ◁ **2**

FOREST

Rude

Childs Glacier

Million Dollar Bridge

Sheridan Mountain Trail

Sheridan Glacier

rca Inlet Cordova

10

COPPER RIVER HIGHWAY

Haystack Trail

Copper River Delta

Alaganik Slough

◁ **1**

Gulf of Alaska

△ **D**   △ **E**

Kayak Island

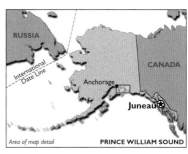

RUSSIA

CANADA

International Date Line

Anchorage

Juneau★

Area of map detail   **PRINCE WILLIAM SOUND**

Commercial fishing boats crowd the mooring piers of Valdez harbor.

Valdez

HISTORICALLY, VALDEZ SHOULD BE THOUGHT OF AS TWO cities—the one prior to Good Friday 1964, and the one since then. Before 1897 Valdez amounted to little, but that year some 7,000 gold-crazed greenhorns inundated Valdez in a mostly doomed effort to reach the Klondike goldfields. A modest town grew up in the ensuing decades, especially after the Richardson Highway linked the Port of Valdez to the Interior, but on Good Friday 1964 a massive earthquake and consequent tsunamis obliterated much of that Valdez.

Valdez
⚐ 168 D3
Visitor information
www.valdezalaska.org
✉ Valdez Convention & Visitors Bureau Visitor Information Center, 200 Fairbanks St.; or visitor center, 200 Chenega St., Valdez
☎ 907/835-4636 or 800/770-5954
🕐 Open daily April–Sept., Mon.–Fri. rest of year

Citizens rebuilt the town on higher, more stable ground 4 miles (6.4 km) to the west. Growth accelerated rapidly after the oil industry and the trans-Alaska pipeline came to Valdez in the 1970s. Today Valdez is a prosperous city of 4,450 that serves as not only a terminal for oil tankers but also a recreation hub for sportfishing, kayaking, flightseeing, river rafting, hiking, winter sports, wildlife viewing, and boat tours of the sumptuous eastern end of Prince William Sound.

Start your tour downtown at the **Valdez Museum,** a well-organized facility on Egan Drive that does a fine job of displaying its mix of Native, gold rush, early settlement, and oil industry artifacts. Spend some time looking at the evocative photos of the stampeders struggling to the goldfields; then read the quotes from contemporaries, like the one who wrote: "Think of a man hitching himself to a sled, putting on 150 pounds, and pulling that load from 7:00 a.m. till 2:00 p.m., eating frozen bread and beans and drinking snow water for lunch, then walking back the distance of 10 miles. If this is not turning yourself into a horse what is it?"

The history lesson continues at **Remembering Old Valdez** *(436 Hazelet St., tel 907/835-5407, open daily mid-May–early Sept., by appt. rest of year, $),* a modest outlier of the museum that lies four blocks south. As the name indicates, this annex recalls pre-earthquake Valdez. A scale model faithfully details the town's appearance, right down to the window design on the Alaskan Hotel. Check for yourself: Carefully examine photos of Old Valdez on the walls and compare them with the model. Don't miss the harrowing video of the earthquake.

The trans-Alaska pipeline and its terminal can be seen across the bay from Valdez, but not visited; instead, take the multimedia tour of the pipeline at **Prince William Sound Community College** *(303 Lowe St., tel 907/834-1600, $).* For a real-life view of the oil tankers loading up, albeit from 3 miles (4.8 km) away, stroll out the **Dock Point Trail,** a three-quarter-mile (1.2 km) loop that starts at the east end of the small boat harbor, across from the boat ramp.

If your taste runs to waterfalls and a dramatic canyon, go west on West Egan Drive to Mineral Creek Road. **Mineral Creek Trail** at the end of the road leads 1.75 miles (2.8 km) up to the canyon's end and an abandoned gold stamp mill. For a very long day hike or an overnight trip, cross Mineral Creek on West Egan and head out the 9-mile (14.4 km) **Shoup Bay Trail.** The first three miles (4.8 km) to Gold Creek are easy, but the next 6 miles (9.6 km) grow increasingly

steep and rugged. Those who reach the bay earn views of a nearby kittiwake rookery and Shoup Glacier.

A few miles out of town, at the airport complex, the superb **Maxine & Jesse Whitney Museum** is said to be the largest private collection of Native art and artifacts in Alaska, plus trophy-class mounts of Alaska's large mammals. The pieces are elaborate and reward close inspection. If the museum isn't too busy, a staff member may give you a personal tour. Don't miss the fantastic parkas, like the one made from 40 murre breasts with wolverine lining. The highlight of the museum, however, is the room filled with scrimshaw— birds, dolls, ships, whales, and other figures exquisitely carved by Native artists using walrus ivory. ∎

Bridal Veil Falls cascades down Keystone Canyon, outside Valdez.

Valdez Museum
www.valdezmuseum.org
✉ 217 Egan Dr.
☎ 907/835-2764
🕐 Open daily mid-May–early Sept., Mon.–Sat. rest of year
💲 $

Maxine & Jesse Whitney Museum
www.pwscc.edu
✉ 303 Valdez Airport Rd.
☎ 907/835-8931
🕐 Open daily in summer
💲 $$

Angling for a prize catch, fishermen head upriver along a slow, smooth stretch of the Copper River.

Cordova & Copper River Delta

NESTLED AT THE BASE OF THE TEMPERATE RAIN FOREST and glacier-clad mountains on Orca Inlet, Cordova is known for its famously tasty Copper River wild salmon. The town's population of 2,300 just about doubles in the spring and summer, when outsiders come to fish the rich fishing grounds at the mouth of the Copper River and work in the seafood-processing plants.

Cordova

⚠ 168 D2

Visitor information

www.cordovachamber.com

✉ Cordova Chamber of Commerce, 401 1st St., Cordova

☎ 907/424-7260

Cordova Historical Museum

www.cordovamuseum.org

✉ 622 1st St.

☎ 907/424-6665

🕒 Open daily Mem. Day–Labor Day, Tues.–Sat. rest of year

$ $

The Copper River Delta measures about 60 miles (96 km) wide at the mouth and includes 700,000 acres (283,300 ha) of mudflats, willow-lined sloughs, creeks, ponds, and grassy wetlands that moose, bears, and river otters call home. And up to five million shorebirds refuel here during spring and fall migrations, inspiring the annual renowned shorebird festival (around first week of May).

HARBOR WALK

In a fishing town like Cordova, the natural place to start a tour is the harbor. Begin at the **Prince**

William Sound Science Center (300 Breakwater Ave., tel 907/424-5800, www.pwssc.gen.ak.us, closed Mon.–Fri.), which sits on the dock near the mouth of the harbor. Its deck offers stunning views of the harbor. In addition to all the fishing boats, you may spot sea otters; hundreds of them live in Orca Inlet. Primarily a research and education facility, the center runs a limited community education program of field trips, lectures, and science projects open to the public.

From the center, stroll along Breakwater Avenue, which runs

above the north side of the harbor. You'll pass the **Anchor Bar & Grill** (*207 Breakwater Ave., tel 907/424-3262*), a hard-core fisherman's hangout where you can soak up some serious local flavor. At the end of Breakwater, turn right on North Railroad Avenue, the harbor's east side. You'll pass a couple of canneries, where workers in white smocks and rubber boots may be taking a break outside.

After a long block, turn right on Nicholoff Way, which skirts the south side, of the harbor. Near the corner, stop at **Baja Taco** (*tel 907/424-5599*), a little joint with a view where locals and visitors alike gaze at the harbor while munching fish tacos. The whole café used to be in the red school bus that now houses the kitchen. A couple of buildings down is the **Ilanka Cultural Center** (*110 Nicholoff Way, tel 907/424-7903*), which serves the Native village of Eyak. Its small but elegant museum displays, among other things, a purse made of swan's feet and one of the world's few complete killer whale skeletons.

DOWNTOWN

Cordova's downtown consists of a few square blocks just east of the harbor; much of the action takes place on First Street. The **Orca Book & Sound Company** (*507 1st St., tel 907/424-5305*) is a good small book and music store; it also exhibits local art and houses the **Killer Whale Café** (*tel 907/424-7733*) in the back, a local favorite known for its cheesecake and biscuits and gravy. Farther down the street two more hard-boiled bars sit side by side: the **Alaskan Hotel & Bar** (*600 1st St., tel 907/424-3288*) and the **Cordova Hotel & Bar** (*604 1st St., tel 907/424-3388*).

Wild salmon

Alaska is bullish on wild salmon. Its commercial wild salmon fishery is the largest in the world, hauling in more than 160 million salmon a year. The state currently doesn't allow fish farming, and it passionately promotes the health, economic, and conservation benefits of wild salmon. In fishing towns like Cordova, bumper stickers and signs in windows promote wild salmon. The **Alaska Seafood Marketing Institute** (*tel 800/478-2903, www.alaskaseafood.org*) is the source for all things salmon: a buyer's guide, recipes, a summary of the salmon's life cycle, and much more. ■

GETTING TO CORDOVA

Cordova is only reachable by sea or air. The state ferry system runs a ship from Valdez several times a week, and jet airplanes make scheduled flights.

Copper River Delta
🅰 169 E1

A couple of buildings down, browse through the **Cordova Historical Museum.** It covers in depth the 196-mile (315 km) railroad that was miraculously built in the early 1900s from the copper mines in Wrangell–St. Elias through forbidding mountains to the Port of Cordova. A little bit of everything else Cordovan is also displayed: photos of the Iceworm Festival, an Eyak dugout canoe, a small

The multitude of spawning sockeye contribute to the Copper River's renown as a salmon fishery.

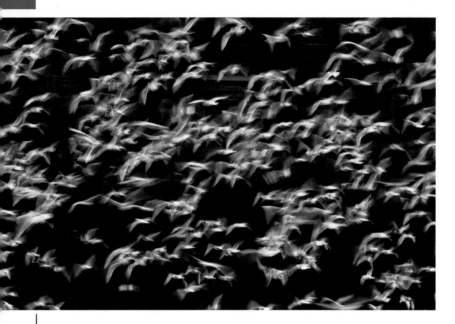

The sights and sounds of millions of shorebirds fill the Copper River Delta during migration.

Visitor information
www.fs.fed.us/r10/chugach cordova

✉ Cordova Ranger District, Chugach National Forest, 612 2nd St., Cordova

☎ 907/424-7661

painting by Sydney Laurence (Alaska's most celebrated landscape artist), and commercial fishing gear.

A block east of the museum, housed in the historic courthouse and post office building, is the Cordova Ranger District Office of the Chugach National Forest. This office oversees the Copper River Delta and can provide a wealth of information. Some people flightsee over the delta and the mountains behind it, which makes for an exhilarating hour. But most people take advantage of the improbable 48.8-mile (78.5 km) **Copper River Highway** that traverses the delta. Copper River/Northwest Tours (tel 907/424-5356) runs a bus tour out the highway, or you can rent a car and do it yourself.

COPPER RIVER HIGHWAY
Mile 0 is at the state ferry terminal, on the north side of Cordova. Follow Ocean Dock Road, which turns into First Street, through

town; First Street becomes the Copper River Highway as it leaves town. Around Mile 7 the highway goes through what locals call **"the gap,"** emerging from the mountains and forest into the open country of the delta, characterized by some spruce and hills but mostly flat wetlands greened by alder, willow, and grass. Moose, bears, beavers, and trumpeter swans—5 to 10 percent of the world's trumpeters nest here, some 100 to 150 overwinter—populate the next few miles. At Mile 10.5, Forest Service interpretive signs discourse on the delta and the national forest.

Three miles (4.8 km) later a 4-mile (6.4 km) spur road leads to the **Sheridan Glacier** and the **Sheridan Mountain Trail,** a strenuous hike that wends past waterfalls to a picturesque alpine basin. This is also the access road for Alaska River Expeditions (tel 907/424-7238 or 800/776-1864, www.alaskarafters.com, late May–Sept., $$$$$), a Cordova outfit

that takes visitors to the glacier, puts them in rafts in the iceberg-littered terminal lake, leads them down the river through Class II and III rapids, and then floats them through the delta to the highway take-out.

Back on the highway, a side road at Mile 16.8 dead-ends at **Alaganik Slough,** a classic stretch of delta made accessible by an elevated and signed board-walk. Bears, eagles, gulls, and other animals come to feed on the spawning candlefish in the summer. The **Haystack Trail,** departing the highway at Mile 19.1, is another easy boardwalk trail. It curves 0.8 mile (1.3 km) through spruce-hemlock forest to the top of a knoll that looks out over the delta and the Gulf of Alaska beyond, an excellent viewpoint for spotting moose, trumpeter swans, and bears.

At Mile 26.7 the highway starts crossing the main channels of the **Copper River** on bridge after bridge. Be careful in fall and winter at the pullouts: The wind howls down this corridor so powerfully then that it can knock a person over. After about a dozen miles, the highway swings north through cottonwood forests along the east bank of the river and ends at Mile 48.1, at the **Million Dollar Bridge.** It actually cost $1.4 million in 1910 to build this 1,550-foot-long (472 m) bridge. It was part of the railroad between Cordova and the Kennecott copper mines, but the 1964 earthquake caused its collapse. Repairs made it passable in 2005, but it doesn't go anywhere—yet. This is the road Cordovans are fighting about.

Walk through the little campground beside the bridge to the river bank. The **Childs Glacier** lies on the other side, a quarter mile (0.4 km) away. This active glacier frequently calves massive ice slabs, sometimes sending sizable waves across the river to the bank where visitors stand. Stay on high ground. ■

A maze of waterways and marshes, the vast Copper River Delta drains the Wrangell and Chugach Mountains.

Prince William Sound

Prince William Sound

 168 B1–D1

Visitor information

www.valdezalaska.org

✉ Valdez Convention & Visitors Bureau Visitor Information Center, 200 Fairbanks St.; or visitor center, 200 Chenega St.

☎ 907/835-4636 or 800/770-5954

PRINCE WILLIAM SOUND IS ONE OF THE MOST BEAUTIFUL bodies of water in the world. Its jumble of islands and 1,500 miles (2,414 km) of ragged coastline, with hundreds of coves, bays, lagoons, narrows, and deep fjords, provide plenty of opportunities to explore. The surrounding land has been graced with thick rain forest, tidewater glaciers, and the craggy Chugach Mountains. Exploring the sound by ferry, tour boat, private charter, or kayak is an Alaska must-do.

WESTERN SOUND

The gateway to the western sound is **Whittier,** a truly odd town. To reach it by car, you travel through a tunnel shared by trains (see sidebar below), and almost all of the community's residents live in a couple of concrete high-rises built in the 1950s. But Whittier is only about 60 road miles (96 km) from Anchorage, so many people wishing to see Prince William Sound come here. Numerous tour boat, charter-fishing, and kayaking operators stand ready to take visitors out for three hours or for the whole day. Ferry service is also very popular out of Whitter.

Large or small, most tours either head into **Blackstone Bay,** just south of Whittier, to watch several active tidewater glaciers calving great hunks of ice into the sea, or they head northeast up to **College Fjord, Barry Arm,** and **Harriman Fiord,** where dozens of glaciers await. Some tours ease through **Esther Passage,** which narrows to a few hundred yards at some points. Throughout this western region lofty glacier-fed waterfalls tumble into the sound, bears fish along the shores, mountain goats gambol on the upper mountain slopes, and orcas, humpback whales, sea otters, and sea lions swim the blue depths.

Tour vessels and itineraries vary widely. The Greater Whittier Chamber of Commerce *(www .whittieralaska.com)* lists outfitters operating out of Whittier.

EASTERN SOUND

Valdez (see pp. 170–171) is the gateway to the sound's eastern half. A full-day boat tour out of Valdez may cruise west through the upper reaches of **Valdez Arm,** staying about 200 yards (183 m) off the forested northern shore. Dozens of waterfalls course down slender channels through

Anton Anderson Memorial Tunnel

To link by rail the military bases in Anchorage and Fairbanks to an ocean port (Whittier) during World War II, Army engineers blasted a 1-mile (1.6 km) tunnel through Begich Peak and a 2.5-mile (3.6 km) tunnel through Maynard Mountain. In 2000, the tunnel was made passable for cars. Organized caravans of cars take turns with trains, easing over the recessed tracks at 25 mph, passing dripping rock walls in the dimly lighted tunnel—definitely not a drive for claustrophobics. Occasionally you hear the roar of the giant fans that clear fumes from the tunnel. Try not to think about the signs that say "Evacuate to Safe House only when strobe light flashing." ∎

the green tundra on the steep mountain slopes, sometimes ending with a swan dive off a sheer cliff. A raft of about 40 sea otters floats by, its occupants grooming, cuddling their pups, and eating off their midsections while floating on their backs.

Just past Shoup Glacier, the boat enters the **Valdez Narrows,** a passage between two fingers of the mainland that squeezes down to 600 yards (548 m) across. The white heads of mature bald eagles dot the tops of shoreline spruces and you'll spy a couple of bulky eagle nests. With binoculars you can see mountain goats near the snow line high on the slopes. Black bears often patrol the shores through here.

As the boat rounds Point Freemantle and steers northwest toward Columbia Bay, icebergs begin to appear, evidence that the boat is nearing its main quarry:

the **Columbia Glacier.** Almost 450 square miles (1,165 sq km) in area, 34 miles (54.7 km) long, and more than 3,000 feet (914 m) thick, the Columbia is one of the largest and most active glaciers in the Northern Hemisphere. The boat slows as the captain picks a path through the glacial castoffs, some the size of houses and others ferrying harbor seals. The boat stays about half a mile (0.8 km) from the 3-mile-wide (4.8 km), 300-foot-tall (91.5 m) terminus so people can safely watch as giant slabs of ice calve with loud, gunshot-like cracks into the water, sending up huge splashes.

On the return journey, you will see hundreds of raucous sea lions in a crowded colony, colorful tufted puffins diving for food, more waterfalls and icebergs, more mountain goats, humpback whales, and orcas. The list goes on and on. ■

Sea kayaking is a popular activity in Prince William Sound, where new vistas open around each bend.

Exploring the Richardson Highway

The scenic Richardson Highway connects Prince William Sound to points north. Tracing an old gold rush route, the road follows a dramatic river up into the coastal mountains and then follows a succession of pretty rivers down the mountains to the flatlands of the Copper River Valley. Known as Alaska's first road, the Richardson was initially called the Valdez to Eagle Trail. The highway eventually ends in Fairbanks; this drive ends at the Edgerton Highway.

The view from Thompson Pass (top) stretches for miles; in summer, the tundra here blooms in a riot of color (above).

Keep in mind as you drive that the mileposts along the Richardson were erected prior to the 1964 quake that leveled Old Valdez and forced the town to a new site 4 miles (6.4 km) farther away. So when you see, for example, the mile marker at Thompson Pass and it says "26," that means you're 26 miles (41.8 km) from Old Valdez but 30 miles (48.3 km) from New Valdez.

About 9 miles (14.5 km) out of Valdez, the Richardson comes alongside the **Lowe River** and paces this braided waterway east for several miles. Around Mile 13, the highway swings northeast and enters the narrow confines of **Keystone Canyon** ❶. Seemingly at every bend waterfalls cascade from towering cliffs into the Lowe. Turn out at Mile 13.4 to contemplate **Horsetail Falls** and about half a mile (0.8 km) later to savor **Bridal Veil Falls** ❷. At Bridal Veil stretch your legs along the 2.5-mile-long (4 km) **Valdez Goat Trail.** Once named the Military Trail, it traces an old Native route that figured prominently in getting gold seekers and military personnel from the coast to the Interior. There's an overlook a quarter of a mile (0.4 km) up the path. At Mile 16.4 there's an outfitter who runs raft trips through Keystone Canyon.

At Mile 18.8 the highway seriously starts climbing and after a few miles rises above tree line into the alpine tundra. At Mile 24 a 1-mile (1.6 km) dirt road leads to **Blueberry Lake State Recreation Site** ❸, which has a campground, picnic tables, and

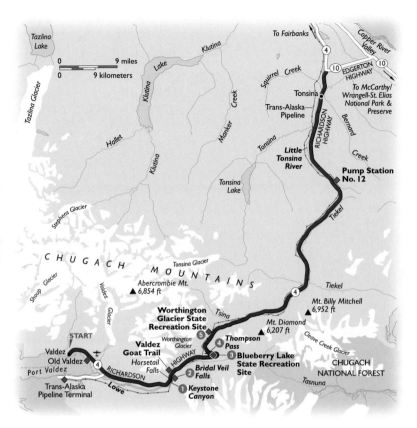

fine fishing. Scan the lake and ponds for trumpeter swans.

Two miles (3.2 km) farther the road reaches its highest point, 2,678-foot **Thompson Pass** ❹. It's one of the snowiest places in Alaska. It once got 62 inches (1.5 m) of snow in a day and almost 1,000 inches (25.4 m) one winter. Stroll through the tundra and enjoy the grand views. At Mile 28.7 stop at the **Worthington Glacier State Recreation Site** ❺. There's a little visitor center, interpretive panels, and a paved trail that leads the short distance to the face of the glacier.

For the next 40 miles (64 km) or so dozens of turnouts allow you to stop and gaze at the mountains, the rivers, and the waterfalls. Watch for wildlife, too, especially in the backwater areas from about Miles 53 to 58, where moose and beavers abound. At Mile 64 the trans-Alaska pipeline meets the

> ▲ See area map p. 168 D1–D2
> ► Valdez
> ⟷ 82.5 miles (from Old Valdez)
> ⊕ 2 hours plus stops
> ► Edgerton Highway junction
>
> **NOT TO BE MISSED**
> • Keystone Canyon
> • Thompson Pass
> • Worthington Glacier

highway and at Mile 64.7 you can pull off at **Pump Station No. 12** and read about this famed oil conduit. From there the highway runs along the **Little Tonsina** and **Tonsina Rivers.** This drive ends at Mile 82.5, where the Edgerton Highway, the gateway road to McCarthy (see pp. 186–187) in the heart of Wrangell–St. Elias National Park and Preserve, meets the Richardson. ■

A boulder riding a glacier down from the Bagley Ice Field.

Wrangell–St. Elias National Park & Preserve

HULKING MOUNTAINS, GLACIERS THE SIZE OF GREAT Smoky Mountains National Park, abundant wildlife, active volcanoes, rugged Gulf of Alaska coastline, boreal forest, tundra, frothing rivers, and very little evidence of civilization: This park epitomizes wild Alaska. And Wrangell–St. Elias is big; by far the largest park in the United States, it could swallow six Yellowstones.

Wrangell–St. Elias National Park & Preserve
www.nps.gov/wrst
🅐 169 E3 & 183
✉ Mile 106.8 Richardson Hwy.
☎ visitor center: 907/822-5234
🕐 Visitor center open daily in summer, Mon.–Fri. rest of year

The park's **Headquarters Visitor Center** in the little community of Copper Center on the western edge of the park is a good place to start an exploration of Wrangell–St. Elias, but don't let its familiar atmosphere mislead you into thinking it is like national parks in the lower 48. Sure, it offers tidy displays on ecology, friendly rangers ready to answer questions, and a 20-minute film, **"Crown of the Continent."** But outside these walls lie 13.2 million acres (5.3 million ha) of wild Alaska. There isn't even a campground and there are very few established trails. The one outpost of civilization deep in the park is the enclave of McCarthy/Kennicott (see pp. 186–187). One of those rare trails is the **paved path** behind the visitor center. This half-mile (0.8 km) loop along the lip of the ridge has many interpretive signs and affords great views of the park's spruce plain and the massive Wrangell Mountains beyond, including three volcanoes—

Mount Drum, Mount Wrangell, and Mount Blackburn.

VISITING THE BACKCOUNTRY

Only well-equipped backcountry veterans should bushwhack into Wrangell–St. Elias on their own, and even they should consult with rangers prior to slipping into the wilderness. Everyone else can venture in via the Nasbena and McCarthy Roads or with the help of the numerous guide services that operate out of McCarthy/Kennicott, the handful of tiny towns scattered along the highways that skirt Wrangell–St. Elias's western boundary, and Yakutat in the park's far southeast. The main gateway communities are Glennallen, Copper Center, and Chitina *(Greater Copper Valley Chamber of Commerce, tel 907/822-5555, www.traveltoalaska.com).*

To taste that delicious backcountry without struggling across creeks and up mountains for days, take a plane. Air charters will drop small groups at remote sites, landing on riverside gravel bars, on strips left behind by abandoned mining operations, on mountain slopes (the less vertical ones), and even on glaciers. You disembark with your gear and wave as the small plane takes off—the last vestige of the outside world you'll see for a while. You might pitch your tent amid the wildflowers of the alpine tundra or beside a lake on which car-size icebergs bob. Some sites even have cabins. At the appointed time the following day—or the following week, or whenever—the plane will return.

For those who want to wing it but not overnight in the park, flightseeing tours provide an overview of this rough-hewn landscape usually reserved for mountain climbers atop a summit. Four major ranges meet in Wrangell–St. Elias, producing an uplift that includes 9 of the nation's 16 highest peaks, led by 18,009-foot (5,489 m) Mount St. Elias. The plane might fly past the tendrils of steam that often rise from Mount Wrangell, one of North America's largest active volcanoes; or fly over glaciers, its shadow a speeding speck of black rippling across the gleaming whiteness of the snow and ice below; or maybe fly low along the broad, braided path of one of the big rivers that surge seaward from the high country.

Those rivers provide another avenue through the backcountry. Outfitters offer raft trips ranging from half a day to a couple of weeks down the **Copper, Kennicott, Chitina, Nabesna,** and **Nizina Rivers.** Some of these involve bucking-bronco rides through Class IV rapids.

GETTING TO WRANGELL-ST. ELIAS

The primary airports that serve Wrangell–St. Elias are Gulkana, Chitina, and McCarthy; you can also fly into Tok in the north and Glennallen, Valdez, Cordova, and Yakutat in the south.

Hikers drink in the scenery of the Jumbo Mine area in Wrangell– St. Elias.

Others feature calm floating more oriented to fishing or watching for moose.

Some river runners cater to kayakers, too, though arguably the best kayaking awaits in the coastal waters of **Icy Bay** and **Yakutat Bay** in the extreme southeast corner of the park. Paddlers can poke around in the nooks and crannies of these bays and spot bald eagles, Dall porpoises, the pied plumage of a harlequin duck, and brawny Steller sea lions, which can weigh as much as a Ford Escort.

Visitors who don't want to take on the backcountry by themselves or use a guide service still can penetrate the tough hide of the park by driving either the McCarthy Road (see pp. 186–187) or the Nabesna Road. Unpaved and rough in spots, even these roads present challenges—nothing about Wrangell–St. Elias is easy—but at least they give travelers a glimpse of the park's interior. And each road provides access to jumping-off points for further exploration.

NABESNA ROAD

The 42 miles (67.6 km) of the Nabesna Road start in the town of **Slana** on the northern boundary of the park *(Mile 59.8 on Glenn Hwy., aka Mile 65.2 on Tok Cutoff).* Be sure to ask about current road conditions at the Slana Ranger Station *(tel 907/822-5238, late May–early Sept.)*; sometimes weather makes this potholed byway impassable. Even when conditions are good, ordinary cars typically can get only to Mile 29, after which 4WD and high-clearance vehicles are advisable.

The route begins in the black-spruce flats, home to numerous winged species, from mosquitoes to the northern hawk owl. Around Mile 7 **Rufus Creek** slides along the north side of the road while the gathering braids of the **Copper River** flow along the south side. These waterways herald the wet country soon to appear, a world of ponds and lakes backed by mountains on the north, south, and east. Watch for moose feeding on aquatic plants. These horse-size members of the deer family plunge their heads into the water and bite off submerged vegetation, then raise back into the air and chew as water drains off their faces and, if male, massive antlers.

There are primitive campsites at Miles 16.6 and 16.7 with picnic tables, but the real attraction is the sweeping view, which encompasses Kettle Lake, 14,163-foot (4,317 m) Mount Wrangell, 9,240-foot (2,816 m) Tanada Peak, and 16,237-foot (4,949 m) Mount Sanford. At Mile 29, the turn-around point for motorists without a rugged vehicle, stretch your legs by hiking along **Trail Creek.** There's no well-defined trail, but it isn't too hard to walk

north along the creek bed; you can go for days if you want. **Lost Creek,** at Mile 31, offers a similar opportunity and takes hikers to a few lakes and a spring.

During the last third of the drive the mountains start squeezing in; at this point the gravel road begins developing its own rugged topography, getting bumpier and dipping through creeks in imitation of the land around it. As the road veers south and grinds into the former mining settlement of **Nabesna** you are confronted by a sky full of mountains. This is the end of the road; for 200 miles (322 km) to the south sprawls the vast wilderness of Wrangell–St. Elias. ■

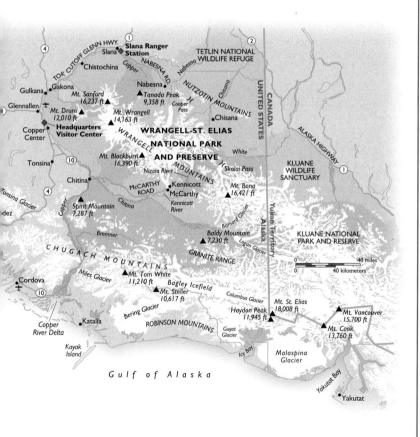

Retreat of the glaciers

If Jane and John dig out the slides of their 1963 Inside Passage cruise, they could show you a striking shot of the terminus of the Mendenhall Glacier looming within 500 or 600 yards (457–549 m) of the visitor center. But if they visited the Mendenhall today, they'd be shocked to see that the glacier is now a mile from the big viewing windows at the visitor center.

Glaciers all over Alaska are receding. Occasionally a renegade surges forward, but Bruce Molnia, a research geologist with the U.S. Geological Survey, estimates that 99 percent of the state's glaciers below a mile (1.6 km) in elevation are in recession. These Alaskan glaciers have been pulling back since the end of the little ice age, around 1850, but a major study published in *Science* in 2002

found that the melting has increased substantially over the past half century and accelerated greatly since the 1990s. The Mendenhall retreated some 600 feet (183 m) in 2004 alone—more than four times its average yearly retreat. Glaciers advance and retreat for a variety of natural reasons, but this mass retreat does not fit previous patterns. One popular theory among scientists studying Alaska's glaciers is global warming.

Glaciers are receding because they're melting. And the low-elevation portions of glaciers—which include about 80 percent of the state's total glacial ice—are melting all over, not just at the terminus; glaciologists talk about glaciers "thinning." In that 2002 study published in *Science*, the researchers tracked 67 Alaska glaciers. They discovered that from the mid-1950s to the mid-1990s,

an estimated 480 cubic miles (2,000 cubic km) of ice melted off those glaciers and flowed into the ocean. It may be hard to visualize a cubic mile of water, but it's a lot. Now consider that Alaska contains about 50,000 to 100,000 glaciers (though some are quite small), that an estimated 99 percent of the low-elevation glaciers are melting, and that about 85 percent are doing so rapidly. The glaciers of coastal Alaska, the Yukon, and British Columbia could release more meltwater into the oceans than the glaciers of any other region on Earth, even Antarctica, which harbors 90 percent of the planet's ice.

The *Science* paper notes that dwindling Alaska glaciers may contribute enough freshwater to the sea to raise the global sea level a fraction of an inch a year. Insignificant? Not when you consider that the rate may accelerate; that many glaciers and ice sheets around the world are likewise melting and may soon melt faster; and that even a rise of a few inches can cause widespread damage. ■

The weight of the Rainbow Glacier created a bowl-shaped depression (left), revealed once the glacier retreated. Tourists admire the snout of Portage Glacier (below).

The generous front porch of the Kennicott Glacier Lodge provides far-reaching views.

McCarthy/ Kennicott

🅰 183

Visitor information

www.traveltoalaska.com

✉ Greater Copper Valley Chamber of Commerce, Glennallen

☎ 907/822-5555

Kennecott National Historic Landmark

www.nps.gov/wrst

✉ Visitor center, Kennecott Mines

☎ 907/554-2417

🕐 Open daily Mem. Day–Labor Day (visitor center)

McCarthy/Kennicott

LONG BEFORE PEOPLE STARTED COMING TO WRANGELL–ST. Elias National Park and Preserve to find wildness and scenic beauty, they came for copper. Between 1911 and 1938, 100 million to 200 million dollars worth of copper ore was dug out and processed in the Kennecott mines, deep in the middle of what is now the national park. Today the site is preserved as Kennecott National Historic Landmark.

The settlement that grew up around the mine, Kennicott, is essentially a ghost town now. (The mining company misspelled the name of the explorer, Kennicott, after whom the mines were named.) Five miles (8 km) away, however, tiny McCarthy thrives. The McCarthy Road from Chitina, on the park's western boundary, is one of only two roads that penetrate Wrangell–St. Elias (for Nabesna Road, see pp. 182–183).

Probing 60 miles (96.5 km) into wilderness, the **McCarthy Road** is a legend in Alaska. It's dirt, it's narrow, it's rutted, it crosses 240 feet (73 m) above a river on an old one-way bridge, and it runs on top of an abandoned railroad bed from which old spikes and metal debris will surface to bite car tires. Most rental car contracts prohibit customers from driving on this road. Yet thousands of people make this drive every year and love it.

The decor at the McCarthy Lodge is classic Alaskan.

GETTING TO MCCARTHY

You can drive yourself to McCarthy; however, Backcountry Connection *(tel 907/822-5292 or 866/582-5292, www .alaska-backcountry-tours.com)* runs shuttle vans to the town. You can also fly into McCarthy.

McCarthy Road doesn't *quite* reach McCarthy. It stops at the Kennicott River, where you must park *(fee)* and cross the channels of the river via two footbridges. Once across, walk the mile (1.6 km) to McCarthy, turning right at the fork about a quarter mile (0.4 km) up the road, or take one of the fairly frequent shuttle vans *($)*.

McCarthy developed as the supply and recreation center for the miners, meaning it had a few stores and plenty of saloons and brothels. It's a quieter place these days, with a few restaurants, hostelries, and private residences, many in historic buildings. Just as you enter town, drop by the little **McCarthy-Kennicott Museum.** The collection focuses on the mining days, but has lots of displays about the miners' lives outside the mines, such as a program for the 1929 Fourth of July festivities, which included a nail-driving contest for "Ladies" and a 50-yard (46 m) dash for "Fat Men." McCarthy also houses several tour operators, who will take visitors flightseeing, river rafting, horseback riding, mountain biking, and backpacking.

Catch a van *($)* up to the mill buildings of **Kennicott Mines.** A brochure for a self-guided tour of the landmark is available at the Kennecott Visitor Center; however, the only way to see the interior of some of the mill buildings is with an organized tour *(ask at the visitor center or in McCarthy).*

The main bit of life left in Kennicott, beside the landmark, is the historic **Kennicott Glacier Lodge** *(tel 907/258-2350 or 800/582-5128, www.kennicottlodge .com, open in summer),* a fine place to stay, eat, or put up your feet on the 180-foot-long (54.8 m) front porch while savoring views of the Kennicott and Root Glaciers. If you'd like a closer look, the easy to moderate **Root Glacier Trail** runs alongside the glacier for about 1.5 miles (2.4 km). For a lung-busting trek, tackle the steep, 9-mile (14.5 km) round-trip **Bonanza Mine Trail,** which offers stunning views. ∎

More places to visit around Prince William Sound

COPPER CENTER

Founded in 1896, this town of 445 souls on the western edge of Wrangell–St. Elias National Park and Preserve was the first non-Native town in south-central Alaska. During the big gold rush around the turn of the 20th century, would-be miners heading for the Klondike via Valdez Glacier staggered into Copper Center when they came down out of the mountains.

Whether for a bed, a meal, or a drink, most of those stampeders eventually found their way to the Blix Roadhouse. The Blix was replaced in 1932 by the **Copper Center Lodge** (*tel 907/822-3245 or 866/330-3245, www.coppercenterlodge.com*); listed on the National Register of Historic Places, this appealing two-story log building still caters to travelers. (Locals favor the restaurant as well.) Order a halibut sandwich and you'll get what seems like a pound of fish; as in many local Alaska eateries, the portions appear to be geared to people who work hard and burn a lot of calories.

Next door, the **George I. Ashby Memorial Museum** (*contact lodge, open daily June–mid-Sept., donation*) fills the rooms of two historic log buildings. The contents of the first building cover a little bit of everything: pioneer history, local Alaska Native culture, and the outdoors. It is a pretty low-key place—note the drawer labeled "Rocks and Stuff"—but amid the traps, rifles, and old mining tools are some intriguing historic photos and letters. The second building is devoted to the 1898 Alaska gold rush. ⚑ Map p. 183 **Visitor information** ✉ Greater Copper Valley Chamber of Commerce, P.O. Box 469, Glennallen, AK 99588 ☎ 907/822-5555, www.traveltoalaska.com

KAYAK ISLAND

This long, slender island lies just southeast of Prince William Sound, outside its protective bosom and exposed to the open Pacific. Sticking out as it does, Kayak Island was the first place in the state that Vitus Bering encountered during his 1741 voyage of discovery for Russia. However, neither Bering nor the island deserve their reputations as the person and place for the first European contact with Alaska. A subordinate of Bering's, Aleksey Chirikov, commanding a second vessel that got separated from Bering in bad weather, actually ran into Alaska a day or so earlier.

But even if its historical reputation drops a notch, Kayak Island remains an alluring hideaway with both scenic beauty and a wealth of wildlife. Few people visit, though it can be reached by plane from Cordova, 62 miles (100 km) away. (You can also travel by boat from Cordova, but the 16-hour journey sometimes encounters rough seas.)

Walking the shoreline of Kayak Island can be a treasure hunt: All sorts of flotsam drifting on the Pacific—rubber duckies, running shoes, glass fisherman's floats, and even the classic messages in bottles—washes up on the island's southwest-facing beaches. **Visitor information** ✉ Cordova Ranger District, Chugach National Forest, P.O. Box 280, Cordova, ☎ 907/424-7761, www.fs.fed.us/r10/chugach/cordova

TETLIN NATIONAL WILDLIFE REFUGE

Most of the refuge's 730,000 acres (295,400 ha) are wet. During migration, its untold numbers of ponds and lakes host multitudes of waterfowl, as many as 100,000 sandhill cranes, and many other birds. Moose, grizzlies and black bears, caribou, wolves, and other wildlife also use the refuge. Tetlin is tough to penetrate, but starting about 30 miles (48 km) southeast of Tok the Alaska Highway skirts the refuge for about 65 miles (105 km). With seven pullouts featuring interpretive signs, this stretch of highway serves as an unofficial tour route. The refuge visitor center is located at Mile 1229. ⚑ Map p. 183 **Visitor information** ✉ Refuge headquarters, Tok ☎ 907/883-5312, http://tetlin.fws.gov ■

The Interior is Alaska's heart. Relatively few towns and roads interrupt this vast wilderness of mountains, rivers, forest, and tundra, but the presence of Fairbanks and Denali National Park open the Interior to visitors.

Interior

Introduction & map 190–191
Talkeetna 192
Denali Highway 193
Denali National Park & Preserve 194–197
Drive: A drive through Denali 198–201
Nenana 202
Fairbanks 203–208
Chena Hot Springs Road 209–210
Steese Highway 211–212
Elliott Highway 213
More places to visit in Alaska's Interior 214
Hotels & restaurants 257–259

A Siberian husky, the ubiquitous sled dog

Interior

THE INTERIOR REMAINS A RAW WILDLAND DOTTED BY A FEW VILLAGES whose residents live close to the land. It is this wildness that draws most visitors, whether to behold Mount McKinley, watch grizzly bears, camp in Denali National Park, or canoe pristine rivers. Travelers want to see what the early Koyukon Athabascan saw—the landscape and wildlife that sustained Natives thousands of years ago and, in a less tangible way, continues to sustain us even in these modern times.

Along the Elliott Highway motorists often spot moose feeding in roadside ponds and lakes.

Bounded by ocean on three sides, with most of its population, economic activity, and visitors sticking close to salt water, Alaska in many ways feels like a coastal state. But far inland from the Pacific Ocean, the Arctic Ocean, and the Bering Sea, within the coast ranges, sprawls the Interior—Alaska's heartland. While it includes features reminiscent of the state's coastal areas, such as brawny mountains and massive glaciers, the region also offers distinctive traits.

Taiga—subarctic boreal forest dominated by white spruce—covers much of the northern Interior. Unlike southern Alaska's stately coastal forests, taiga is sparsely vegetated and consists of modest trees, mostly spruce, that top out between 30 and 40 feet (9 and 12 m)—half that in the poor soil of the so-called "drunken forests." The Interior also features enormous expanses of tun-

dra—windswept slopes and soggy plains devoid of trees and blanketed by a complex blend of ground-hugging plants.

Humans have inhabited the Interior for millennia. First came the Athabascan, who led nomadic or seminomadic lives, following caribou herds and setting up summer fish camps by salmon rivers. (Interestingly, their languages are closely related to those of the Apache and Navajo.) Though to a lesser degree than coastal Alaska Natives, Athabascan did have contact with Russian fur traders, starting in the 1820s; many worked as contract trappers for the Russian-American Company.

Modern settlement of the Interior didn't really get started until 1902, when a gold strike brought thousands of people to the Fairbanks area, quickly establishing that city as the region's hub. In 1923 completion of the 470-mile (755 km) Alaska Railroad, from Seward to Fairbanks, further opened the Interior to development. A sizable military buildup began during World War II, and the Prudhoe Bay oil discovery and pipeline boom followed in the 1960s and 1970s. Between 1967 and 1969, the population of Fairbanks and environs alone grew from 40,000 to 65,000. ■

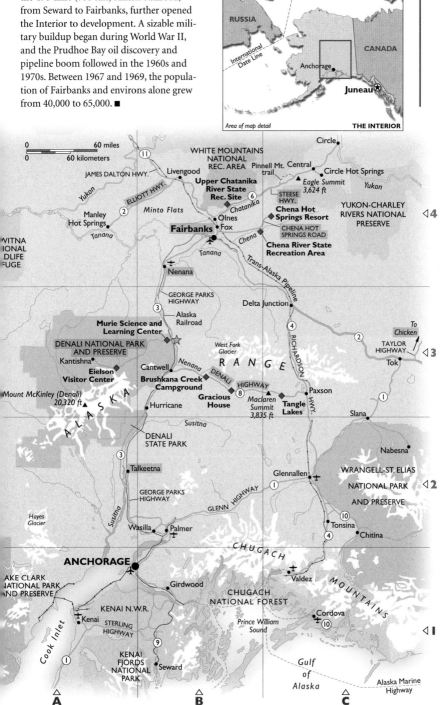

RUSSIA

International Date Line

Anchorage

CANADA

Juneau

Area of map detail

THE INTERIOR

0   60 miles
0   60 kilometers

Circle

WHITE MOUNTAINS NATIONAL REC. AREA

JAMES DALTON HWY.

Livengood

Pinnell Mt. trail

Central

Circle Hot Springs

Upper Chatanika River State Rec. Site

Eagle Summit 3,624 ft

Yukon

Yukon

ELLIOTT HWY.

Chatanika

STEESE HWY.

YUKON-CHARLEY RIVERS NATIONAL PRESERVE

Manley Hot Springs

Minto Flats

Olnes

Chena Hot Springs Resort

Tanana

Fairbanks

Fox

CHENA HOT SPRINGS ROAD

WITNA IONAL DLIFE FUGE

Tanana

Chena

Chena River State Recreation Area

Nenana

Trans-Alaska Pipeline

GEORGE PARKS HIGHWAY

Delta Junction

Murie Science and Learning Center

Alaska Railroad

RICHARDSON

To Chicken

DENALI NATIONAL PARK AND PRESERVE

Kantishna

West Fork Glacier

R A N G E

TAYLOR HIGHWAY

Eielson Visitor Center

Cantwell

Nenana

DENALI

Tok

Mount McKinley (Denali) 20,320 ft

Brushkana Creek Campground

HIGHWAY

Paxson

Hurricane

Gracious House

Maclaren Summit 3,835 ft

Tangle Lakes

Slana

A L A S K A

Susitna

DENALI STATE PARK

Nabesna

Talkeetna

Glennallen

WRANGELL-ST. ELIAS NATIONAL PARK AND PRESERVE

GEORGE PARKS HIGHWAY

GLENN HIGHWAY

Tonsina

Hayes Glacier

Susitna

Wasilla

Palmer

Chitina

ANCHORAGE

CHUGACH

Valdez

MOUNTAINS

AKE CLARK IATIONAL PARK ND PRESERVE

Girdwood

CHUGACH NATIONAL FOREST

Cordova

KENAI N.W.R.

Prince William Sound

Kenai

STERLING HIGHWAY

Cook Inlet

KENAI FJORDS NATIONAL PARK

Seward

Gulf of Alaska

Alaska Marine Highway

A

B

C

Talkeetna

The homey West Rib Pub & Café serves a mouthwatering musk ox burger.

TALKEETNA IS A PERFECT ANTIDOTE TO THE HARRIED modern American lifestyle. This town of some 850 souls features log homes, cafés that serve musk ox burgers, an airstrip that calls to mind an unkempt gravel road, and a laid-back attitude. Folks often stroll around town instead of driving. Talkeetna's end-of-the-road character is enhanced by the fact that it indeed lies at the end of the road—a 14.3-mile (23 km) spur that branches off the Parks Highway at Mile 98.7.

Talkeetna
🗺 191 A2
Visitor information
www.talkeetnachamber.org
✉ Talkeetna Chamber of Commerce
☎ 907/733-2330

The spur emerges on Village Park at the head of **Main Street.** Among the mix of businesses and homes is the historic **Talkeetna Roadhouse** (*tel 907/733-1351, www.talkeetnaroadhouse.com*), where for decades travelers have stopped for a meal, a room, or one of its storied cinnamon rolls. Among several Main Street galleries and gift shops, **Talkeetna Artisans** (*tel 907/733-4222,*

www.tartgallery.com) sells works beyond typical Alaska art fare.

Main Street and the alleys north and south of it comprise the **Talkeetna Historic District** (*Talkeetna Historical Society, tel 907/733-2487*), which includes 16 buildings on the historical society's walking-tour map. Learn even more at the **Talkeetna Historical Society Museum** (*alley S of Main & B Sts., tel 907/733-2487*).

An outfitters' hub, Talkeetna is especially busy in summer. Bush pilots offer flightseeing trips around Denali National Park (some even land on glaciers; see pp. 194–197), while local river trips take in the scenery and wildlife here at the confluence of the Talkeetna, Susitna, and Chulitna Rivers. Or consider taking a ride on the **Hurricane Turn,** a flag-stop train that ambles back and forth between Talkeetna and the Hurricane Gulch area. ∎

Sheldon to the rescue

In the mid-1900s, bush pilot and Talkeetna resident Don Sheldon ferried researchers and climbers to high-elevation glaciers on Mount McKinley, routinely making landings few other pilots would attempt. He shone in risky situations and rescued many a lost hiker and imperiled mountaineer. One story recounts the time a boat capsized in the Susitna River, leaving five passengers clinging to rocks in the rapids. Sheldon reportedly landed upriver in a floatplane, drifted down the rapids, grabbed one of the men, and delivered him to safety. He repeated the risky maneuver four more times, rescuing all five men. ∎

Denali Highway

TRAVELERS EXPECTING THE DENALI HIGHWAY TO RUN through Denali National Park will be disappointed, as this road lies southeast of the park. But drivers who realize that and approach the highway for its own considerable charms will enjoy the ride. Note that 112 of the highway's 134 miles (216 km) are unpaved, dusty, bumpy, and potholed in sections. Note, too, that no towns or service stations line this route—only a handful of traditional Alaska roadhouses and lodges. In a pinch, motorists can get a flat fixed or fuel up at one of the lodges, but prudent travelers should be prepared for back-road driving conditions.

Bureau of Land Management Glennallen Field Office
www.glennallen.ak.blm.gov
🅰 191 B3
✉ Mile 186.5 Glenn Hwy., Glennallen
☎ 907/822-3217

Starting from **Cantwell,** on the Parks Highway, motorists will enjoy a few miles of pavement before the road turns to gravel. After a few miles you'll encounter the **Nenana River** and follow it upstream about 15 miles (24 km), with plenty of chances to canoe or kayak. For creekside camping, turn in at Mile 30 to Brushkana Creek Campground, which offers 18 first-come, first-served sites. Pullouts along the next 10 miles (16 km) offer fine views of the West Fork Glacier and several prominent Alaska Range peaks.

At Mile 52.8 travelers come to **Gracious House** *(tel 907/333-3148 or 907/259-1111 in summer —allow ten rings for this radio phone, www.alaskaone.com/gracious),* one of those down-home, do-it-all Alaska lodges where you stride through the log doorway beneath a caribou rack to get a room, a meal, a flightseeing trip, a hunt, air taxi service, a tent site, a tow, and more.

Along much of the route, particularly between Miles 75 and 90, wetlands invite travelers to break out the binoculars and look for trumpeter swans, moose, and river otters. Keep those binocs handy for the pullout near Mile 98, as well as the pullout atop 3,835-foot (1,169 m) **Maclaren Summit,** the second-highest

road pass in the state. When you've had your fill of sweeping views of the mountains and the Maclaren and Susitna River valleys, carefully scan the slopes for passing caribou and grizzlies.

If you'd like to venture into the surrounding wilds, there's no better place than the **Tangle Lakes,** around Mile 112. Try the **Tangle Lakes Lodge** *(Mile 113 Denali Hwy., tel 907/822-4202)* or the **Tangle River Inn** *(Mile 115 Denali Hwy., tel 907/822-3970 or 907/895-4022 in winter)* for canoeing, fishing, and bird-watching. Just past the lakes you'll return to pavement and cruise past more grand views to the end of the road at **Paxson,** on the Richardson Highway. ∎

Canoes are a great way to explore the Tangle Lakes.

Denali National Park & Preserve

Denali National Park & Preserve
www.nps.gov/dena

🅰 191 A3, 197, & 199
✉ Mile 237 Parks Hwy.
☎ 907/683-2294
$ $$

Greater Healy/Denali Chamber of Commerce
www.denalichamber.com
☎ 907/683-4636

DENALI IS BIG, NOT ONLY IN THE AGGREGATE—AT MORE than 6 million acres (2.4 million ha), it's larger than Vermont—but in its particulars. Glaciers dozens of miles long. Rivers a mile wide. Moose that stand seven feet (2.1 m) at the shoulder. And, above all, 20,320-foot (6,194 m) Mount McKinley, the continent's highest point. Locals simply call it "the mountain." More than 2 million of its acres are wilderness, and nearly all of the remaining 4.2 million acres likewise show little evidence of human presence. It's no wonder grizzly bears and wolves thrive here.

The presence of bears, wolves, and big game animals such as caribou, Dall sheep, and moose was a key to establishment of the park. For thousands of years Athabascan had hunted in the area but with a light touch that maintained healthy wildlife populations. Things changed in 1903, however, with the discovery of gold near the mountain. As gold seekers rushed in, market hunters followed and began killing game at an unsustainable pace to provide meat to the stampeders.

Charles Sheldon, a pal of Theodore Roosevelt's and an avid outdoorsman, came out to do some noncommercial hunting and was disgusted with the slaughter being perpetrated by the market hunters. He worked tirelessly to create a national park that would protect the wildlife. Sheldon attained his goal in 1917, when President Woodrow Wilson signed a bill to set aside the region as Mount McKinley National Park, handing the pen he used to one of the delighted onlookers—Sheldon himself.

ORIENTATION

As Denali is so big and wild, the park is more difficult to tour than, say, Yellowstone or the Great Smoky Mountains, but with a little effort casual visitors can make Denali's acquaintance. The park comprises two main areas: the front country and the backcountry. Closed to private vehicles, the backcountry takes in most of the park. Just one road, the **Park Road** (see pp. 198–201), accesses this wilderness, and visitors can travel it via shuttle buses. (Because this is Alaska's most popular national park, with some 400,000 annual visitors, the Park Service had to restrict private vehicles to protect the park's natural resources.) To fully experience Denali, travel this road at least halfway.

The front country holds its own charms, evident even amid the sprawl of roadside services near the entrance. Note the promenade above the rushing Nenana River and views from some of the restaurants and hotels. Several tour operators offer guided excursions into the park and surrounding wildlands via plane, helicopter, raft, jet boat, 4WD vehicle, bus, and foot.

Flightseeing trips are an especially popular, though pricey option. These excursions in small planes tour the park and, weather permitting, circle the mountain. (Many flightseeing outfits are based in Talkeetna; see p. 192.)

Opposite: Mount McKinley dominates this section of the Alaska Range.

Buzzing around Mount McKinley like a fly around an elephant offers a visceral sense of its magnitude. At 20,320 feet (6,194 m), it's the undisputed champion of North America. While that leaves it almost 9,000 feet (2,743 m) short of Mount Everest in elevation above sea level, McKinley looms 6,000 feet (1,829 m) taller than Everest when measured from its base. In fact, McKinley's 18,000-foot (5,486 m) vertical rise above the surrounding plain is among the world's highest.

VISITOR CENTER

Travelers get their bearings 1.5 miles into the park at the **Denali National Park Visitor Center.** Opened in 2005, this handsome structure doubles as a natural history museum. Check out visually stunning films on the big screen in the spacious theater. Elsewhere in the visitor complex you'll find a bookstore/gift shop, a food court, and the railroad depot. Interpretive hikes and a shuttle bus to the park kennel leave from here. But don't expect to board Fido at this kennel; it's for the park's sled dogs,

which rangers use to patrol Denali in the winter. In summer the rangers stage sled demonstrations three times a day.

The center also houses the **Murie Science & Learning Center** *(tel 907/683-1269 or 866/688-1269, www.denaliinstitute.org).* While many of its programs are aimed at school groups and teachers, a fair number are offered to casual visitors. Go behind the scenes to learn about current park research efforts. Twice a day in summer the center conducts the three-hour class "Wildlife Tracker: Science of Predators & Prey." The truly gung ho can sign up for three- to five-day field seminars on such topics as the wolves of Denali, high-country wildflowers, and glaciers of the Alaska Range.

HIKING

Though the backcountry offers few established trails, hikers can choose from a variety of well-maintained trails in the front country. Denali is so wild that even in the front country you need to watch out for wildlife—particularly bears and moose. Of course, that means wildlife-watching opportunities abound. If it's a bear or a moose, watch from a safe distance—the Park Service recommends a minimum of 25 yards (23 m) for a moose (double that if it's a cow with calves) and 300 yards (275 m) for a bear. Rangers advise maintaining that 25-yard minimum even for large docile mammals, for their protection and comfort. Stretch that to at least 100 yards (90 m) for nesting raptors or in the proximity of large mammal dens.

While the **Savage River Loop Trail** (2 miles/3.2 km round-trip) begins at Mile 14.8 on the Park Road, all other trails start at or near the visitor center. The easiest of these is the **Taiga Trail** (2.6 miles/4.2 km round-trip), which winds through subarctic forest and connects with three other trails.

Perhaps the most popular hike is the **Horseshoe Lake Trail** (1.4 miles/2.3 km round-trip), a gentle, scenic route that meanders past a river, creek, ponds, and the eponymous lake. All that water hosts plenty of life, from tiny flowers to beaver, muskrat, ducks, and moose.

Those with strong legs and a lot of energy should consider the **Mount Healy Overlook Trail** (4.5 miles/7.2 km round-trip from Taiga Trail or 5.5 miles/8.9 km round-trip from the visitor center), which passes through the park's primary habitats and ends atop a ridge with views of the front country. To reach the trailhead from the visitor center, walk about half a mile on the Taiga Trail. From the overlook, watch for grazing Dall sheep and soaring hawks, eagles, and falcons. ■

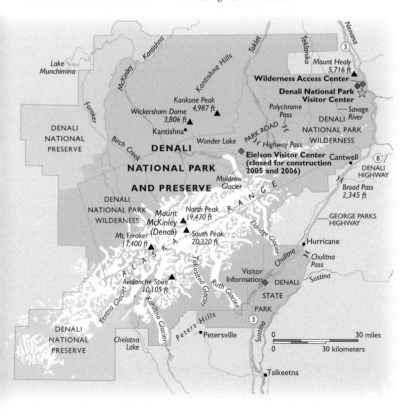

A drive through Denali National Park

The 92-mile (148 km) Park Road extends into Denali's otherwise wild heart. It slips through spruce and aspen forests, tightropes along mountainsides above broad river valleys, crosses vast expanses of alpine tundra, and provides ample opportunities to view the park's resident wildlife. So popular is this drive that in 1972, when the Parks Highway opened, the Park Service closed most of the road to private vehicles to prevent continual traffic jams; access beyond the first 15 miles (24 km) is by shuttle bus only. Some visitors may chafe at the lack of freedom, but the restricted access also protects park resources and enhances the visitor experience. Passengers are free to hop off the bus at certain spots, see the sights, then (space permitting) take a different bus either farther into the park or back to the entrance. If you do opt for a walkabout, be prepared to spend at least an hour in the wilderness. At a minimum, carry rain gear and insect repellent and know the ABCs of dealing with bears.

A park-operated shuttle bus rolls along the restricted road through Polychrome Pass.

For information and to catch a bus, head to the **Wilderness Access Center ❶**, a half mile from the park entrance. While travelers *can* make reservations at the WAC, in busy summer season it's best to make reservations weeks or even months ahead *(tel 907/272-7275 or 800/622-7275, www .nps.gov/dena or www.reservedenali.com)*.

The park offers a range of travel options. First decide whether you want a tour bus or shuttle bus. Tour buses provide full service and popular itineraries. For example, the Tundra Wilderness Tour features a naturalist guide, a box lunch and drinks, pickup at places besides the WAC, and service to and from the Teklanika or Toklat Rivers (Mile 31.3 or Mile 53). That said, it costs much more than a round-trip shuttle to Toklat.

While shuttle buses are billed as no-frills transportation, most drivers are quite knowledgeable about the park and will share information and answer questions. Visitors can choose from a list of half a dozen distances and destinations, ranging from a two-hour round-trip that turns around at Mile 15 to a 13-hour round-trip that goes to the end of the road, at Mile 92. For the best views, grab a window seat that will face south when the bus is on the road.

The first 15 miles (24 km) of road to Savage River is paved, skirting the base of **Healy Ridge** and threading two river val-

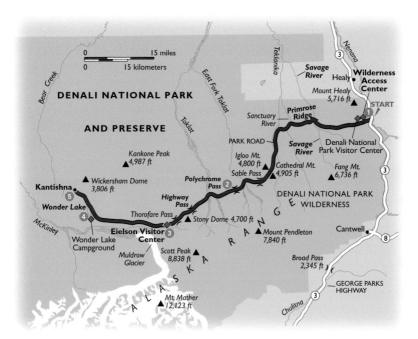

leys. At first, views are limited by trees as the bus passes through bottomland taiga—subarctic evergreen forest. But after a few miles the road climbs, and the predominant white spruce and accompanying aspen, paper birch, and balsam poplar diminish in both number and stature. Higher elevations bring successively harsher growing conditions and sparse vegetation. Watch for snowshoe hare; during spikes in their population cycle these rabbits with oversize feet can be spotted every few hundred yards. You also may glimpse their most notorious predator, the lynx. On a clear day near Mile 9 you may spot the tip of Mount McKinley peeking over closer mountains, though it's more than 70 miles (113 km) away!

At Mile 14.7 the **Savage River** marks the boundary between the park's front country and backcountry. Here, buses pass a checkpoint beyond which private vehicles (with some exceptions) are not permitted, and pavement gives way to gravel. For the next 8 miles the road parallels **Primrose Ridge,** mostly above the tree line in the tundra. Passengers enjoy unobstructed views of the mighty Alaska Range, about 15

- See area maps pp. 191 A3 & 197
- ► Wilderness Access Area
- 94 or 184 miles round trip
- 5 to 13 hours
- ► Wilderness Access Area

NOT TO BE MISSED
- Mount McKinley
- Polychrome Overlook
- Wonder Lake
- wildlife

miles (24 km) to the south. Open views of the river valleys and tundra-covered slopes promise excellent wildlife-watching opportunities. Grizzlies may pop up just about anywhere. Both shuttle and tour buses stop long enough to allow passengers to watch and photograph animals, though drivers may not bother if the critter is just a dot on a hillside a mile away.

The stretch from Savage River to Polychrome Pass, at Mile 45.9, offers even better odds for spotting the park's charismatic megafauna. Soon after bridging the

Sanctuary River at Mile 22, the road turns south and runs about 17 miles (27 km) along the Teklanika River to Sable Pass. A wolf pack roams this river valley, and people have spotted wolves near or even on the road. Moose favor ponds and willow thickets in the forested bottomland. Scan surrounding snowline slopes for Dall sheep; passengers often spot herds grazing on precipitous meadows as casually as cows feed on Wisconsin flatland. Sheep also frequent mineral licks at the spring. Though grizzlies range widely and unpredictably, sows and their cubs have been repeated visitors over the years around **Sable Pass** (Mile 39.1). Also favoring the pass is another wolf pack—one of 14 packs that roam the park.

While wildlife often vies with scenery for visitors' attention, the dramatic landscape takes center stage as the road rises from the East Fork Toklat River to **Polychrome Pass** ❷. Passengers uneasy about heights may feel the urge to flee their south-facing seats as the narrow road negotiates dizzying drop-offs, although the views usually keep even white-knuckled passengers in those coveted seats. Everyone can breathe easy and savor the vistas as buses linger at the Polychrome Pass rest stop. In addition to the mountains, sprawling river valleys, and glaciers, visitors are treated to an overlook of the orange-, yellow-, red-, purple-, black-, and white-banded Alaska Range foothills for which the pass is named.

Both wildlife and scenic beauty abound along the 20 miles (32 km) from Polychrome Pass to the Eielson Visitor Center. Amid open tundra the road crests **Highway Pass**—at 3,980 feet (1,213 m) the highest point on the road, with a panorama to match its lofty status. Watch for soaring golden eagles and scan nearby rock piles for the pikas and marmots those eagles are hunting. Also scope out the ridgetops and remnant snowbanks, where caribou hide to escape swarming bugs.

The **Eielson Visitor Center** ❸ is all about location, location, location. *(Closed for reconstruction. Scheduled to reopen by summer 2008, new Eielson will feature exhibits, short interpretive trail, ranger desk, and guided outings.)* From this perch, visitors get a top-to-bottom view of Mount McKinley—

Above: The Kantishna Roadhouse is one of three lodges at road's end. Opposite: Backpackers head toward Polychrome Pass.

that is, if the weather cooperates. Summer showers account for most of the park's 16 inches (41 cm) of annual rainfall, and clouds often obscure all or part of the mountain, even on fairly clear days. But if you beat the one-in-three odds of seeing the summit, the view will knock your socks off.

From Eielson the road descends along the Thorofare River, past the Muldrow Glacier, then follows the McKinley River to **Wonder Lake** ❹. Watch for moose in the roadside ponds—not to mention beaver, muskrat, and waterfowl. At Mile 84.6 most buses take the short spur to **Wonder Lake Campground,** a beautiful spot to picnic or hike. This is the closest (27 miles/43 km) the road comes to Mount McKinley.

A few buses continue to **Kantishna** ❺ (Mile 91), a mile from road's end. This area was absorbed into the park in the 1980 expansion—along with some 4.2 million other acres (1.7 million ha). Several pre-existing privately owned lodges remain here, deep in the otherwise lodgeless park. These provide a more comfortable alternative for visitors who long to be in the backcountry but prefer not to camp. ■

Nenana

Nenana

🗺 191 B4

Visitor Information

✉ Parks Hwy., Nenana

☎ 907/832-5435

🕐 Closed weekends Labor Day–Memorial Day

NOWADAYS MOST TRAVELERS ZOOM BY NENANA (POP. 549) as they drive the Parks Highway, but this small town has a history. A traditional Athabascan gathering place, it served as a construction base for the Alaska Railroad in the early 1900s. In 1923 President Warren G. Harding drove a golden spike here to celebrate the railroad's completion. The town still serves as a port for tugs and barges that ply the Tanana and Yukon Rivers, bringing supplies to remote villages during the brief thaw. Though it offers no grand attractions, this sleepy old berg does claim a few interesting sites.

Marking the visitor center, the tugboat *Taku Chief* plied the Tanana and Yukon Rivers for three decades.

Nenana City Office

www.nenana.org

☎ 907/832-5441

Just off the highway, motorists encounter the visitor center, in a beflowered, sod-roofed log cabin. Beside it sits the colorful *Taku Chief*, a tug that worked the rivers for more than 30 years. Head down the five or six blocks of A Street, the main drag, and you'll find a variety of down-home businesses, such as the **Rough Woods Inn** *(2nd & A Sts., tel 907/832-5299)*, a lodge and café known for its pie and home to Alaskan Wood Carvers.

At the junction of A and Front Streets lies the **Alaska State Railroad Museum** (aka Alaska Railroad Depot), a small affair housed in the 1922 depot. In addition to train artifacts, the museum displays items relating to Native and gold rush history. Check out the photo of Frank Bateau in harness pulling his own sled; he didn't let the fact that he couldn't afford dogs stop him.

Four blocks east is the **Alfred Starr Nenana Cultural Center** *(415 Riverfront, tel 907/832-5520, closed in winter)*, built in 1998 to showcase local Native history and culture. The center overlooks the Tanana River. Sit out on its deck a while to watch the tugs and barges that travel as far as 1,400 miles (2,250 km) to provide a lifeline to remote villages. Just upriver, fish wheels scoop the day's catch from the current. ■

Nenana Ice Classic

Since 1917 Alaskans have wagered on the exact time the icebound Tanana River at the town of Nenana will break up. Each winter, Nenana residents erect a large tripod on the frozen river and run a line from the tripod to a clock in a building on shore. When the ice breaks up—usually in late April or early May—the tripod falls and stops the clock, determining the winning time. Between Feb. 1 and April 5, some 300,000 tickets are sold all over Alaska *(www.nenana iceclassic.com)*. Each sells for $2.50. Fifty-one percent of the money goes to the winner(s) and 49 percent goes to local nonprofits, minus administrative costs incurred by the residents. ■

Fairbanks

FAIRBANKS SERVES AS INTERIOR ALASKA'S HUB, GATEWAY, supply center, and de facto capital. But despite being the state's second largest city, Fairbanks has a population of only 29,954. Of course, that's relatively huge in this vast, sparsely settled region; thus, Fairbanks hosts the region's main university, major shopping centers, big festivals, and lion's share of cultural institutions. Because the city is small in absolute terms and surrounded by thousands of square miles of near-wilderness, residents have remained tied to the land in ways seldom found among urban dwellers in the lower 48.

Fairbanks is set along the Chena River near its confluence with the mighty Tanana, in the vicinity of turn-of-the-20th-century gold strikes. While this suggests careful site selection, truth is the location was an accident. City founder, mayor, and notorious wheeler-dealer (many say criminal) Capt. E.T. Barnette had planned to build a trading post farther up the Tanana, but the stern-wheeler carrying Barnette and his supplies couldn't make it any farther up the Chena. Barnette was effectively stranded in the middle of nowhere—the site of present-day downtown Fairbanks. That was in 1901. Gold was discovered in the surrounding hills the following year, and the ensuing rush turned Barnette's accidental trading post into a thriving city of thousands by 1905, with electricity, schools, police and fire departments, a library, a three-story "skyscraper," and 33 saloons in the space of four blocks. The town diversified enough to weather the inevitable bust of the gold rush and has since held its position as the Interior's leading city.

In light of Fairbanks's history, visitors should start downtown

At the center of Fairbank's Golden Heart Park, *The First Unknown Family* commemorates the first people to cross the Bering land bridge from Asia to Alaska.

Fairbanks
191 B4
Visitor information
www.explorefairbanks.com
550 1st Ave.
907/456-5774 or 800/327-5774

on the **Chena River** at the **Log Cabin Visitor Information Center,** a historic white spruce, sod-roofed cabin in the shadow of the Cushman Street Bridge. Though downtown isn't posh, it is a pleasant place for a walk or alfresco dining at a restaurant overlooking the river—assuming it's a typically sunny summer day and not a February afternoon when the high temperature is -30° F (-34° C). From the visitor

paddle past the city and country-side, along the way taking in various Alaskan traditions, including a sled dog demon-stration, a bush plane show, and a guided walking tour of **Chena Indian Village.**

The coolest spot downtown is the **Fairbanks Ice Museum** (*500 2nd Ave., tel 907/451-8222, www.icemuseum.com*), which centers on a 20° F (-7° C) exhibition space filled with creative

Sculptures from the World Ice Art Championships remain gloriously frozen through summer in the frigid interior of the Fairbanks Ice Museum.

center you can step over to neigh-boring Golden Heart Park, take the footbridge across the Chena, or stroll the promenade that fol-lows the river along First Avenue. Active travelers may opt to rent a canoe or kayak and paddle along the river through downtown.

Hundreds of visitors explore Fairbanks and the Chena aboard the riverboats *Discovery II and III*—that is, hundreds of passen-gers per 3.5-hour trip on either of these stern-wheelers (*1975 Discovery Dr., two blocks N of airport, tel 866/479-6673, www .riverboatdiscovery.com, closed mid-Sept.–mid-May*). The ships

ice sculptures. Venture inside or admire pieces from the heated viewing area. Every March, the city hosts the **World Ice Art Championships** (*www.icealas ka.com*), during which sculptors from around the globe fashion both realistic and abstract pieces, some more than 20 feet (6 m) tall. The best pieces are moved to the museum for summer viewing. A large-screen slide presentation shows the artists at work.

West of town on the south bank of the Chena lies **Pioneer Park** (*2300 Airport Way, tel 907/459-1087, www.co.fairbanks .ak.us/Parks&Rec/PioneerPark*).

Known until 2001 as Alaskaland (and still called that by most locals), this 44-acre (18 ha) spread is a combination historical museum, theme park, community center, tourist trap, and city park. The Alaska Native Village & Museum explores the Athabascan era, while the early days of settlement are presented in various ways at Pioneer Hall, Wickersham House (home of James Wickersham, Alaska's first territorial judge), a refurbished railroad car used by President Harding, the Pioneer Air Museum, and the Rusty Heurlin exhibit, which features a narrated tour of the gold rush. The historical highlight is the stern-wheeler *Nenana,* a massive, beautifully restored riverboat that steamed the Yukon from 1935 through the mid-'50s. In addition to its historical aspects, Pioneer Park contains, well, just about everything: art galleries, a salmon bake, a carousel, miniature golf, gold panning, a church, picnic grounds, a 384-seat theater, a saloon, a dance hall, bike rentals, an operating railroad, and eateries and gift shops galore.

In the midst of Fairbanks, flanked by subdivisions and malls, sprawls an almost 1,600-acre (648 ha) oasis called **Creamer's Field Migratory Waterfowl Refuge** *(Farmhouse Visitor Center, 1300 College Rd., tel 907/452-5162, www.creamers field.org).* During the spring (April & May) and fall (Aug. & Sept.) migrations, ducks, geese, and swans rest and eat here before continuing their long flights. From the trails and raised platforms that overlook the field or through a spotting scope at the visitor center, you can watch waterfowl feeding and squabbling. Migrating sandhill cranes also flock here, dipping their four-foot-tall (1.2 m) frames to load up on grain, especially during the annual Tanana Valley Sandhill Crane Festival in August. Watch patiently and you may spot some of the predators that stalk waterfowl, including peregrine falcons and red foxes.

Five easy trails, ranging from a quarter mile (0.4 km) to 2 miles (3.2 km), lead deeper into the refuge. From the **Seasonal Wetlands Trail** hikers can spot shorebirds and wood frogs, while on the **Farm Road Trail** you may encounter basking woodchucks or hunting northern harriers and American kestrels. The **Boreal Forest Trail** *(brochure available*

The soaring architecture of the expanded Museum of the North echoes Alaska's grand landscape.

at visitor center) leads through taiga, a habitat that covers much of the Interior. Look for hare, moose, and a host of wildflowers, including wild roses, dwarf dogwood, white violets, and calypso orchids. At the southeast corner of the refuge is a visitor center for the **Alaska Bird Observatory** *(tel 907/451-7159, www.alaskabird.org),* which operates a banding station here. Call to learn more about a banding demonstration or to accompany the resident biologist on a net check.

UNIVERSITY OF ALASKA

The University of Alaska, Fairbanks, boasts several attractions, starting with the acclaimed **Museum of the North** *(907 Yukon Dr., tel 907/474-7505, www.uaf.edu/museum, $$).* As you enter the museum, pause to admire the hilltop views; on a clear day the Alaska Range saws the horizon. While you're out there, study the shimmering white curves of the museum's exterior. Greatly expanded between 2002 and 2005, the musem is noted for stunning new architecture that echoes those jagged mountains, and suggests glaciers, the northern lights, and even the tail of a sounding whale.

The expanded interior enables display of long-stored treasures.

The riverboat *Discovery II* paddles along the Chena River past Fairbanks and environs.

Take, for example, the newly opened **Rose Berry Alaska Art Gallery,** with soaring ceilings and curved walls—it's like being inside a glacier. This gallery highlights Native artwork and classic Alaskan landscapes that have been languishing in storage. Another new venue is the **Arnold Espe Auditorium,** which will open with two highly recommended multimedia programs: *Dynamic Aurora*, about the northern lights, and *Northern Inua*, showcasing the remarkable athletes at the World Eskimo Indian Olympics.

While enjoying the new, don't neglect the old; the **Gallery of**

Alaska holds the heart of the collection and is the best Alaska primer provided by any museum. See if you don't feel a shiver as you approach Otto, the nine-foot (2.7 m), 1,250-pound (560 kg) brown bear—stuffed, of course— that guards the entrance. Behind this awesome beast are five galleries, each of which presents the human and natural history, art, and contemporary life of one of the state's five geographic regions. Venture into the **Western & Arctic Coasts Gallery** for a gander at an Inupiaq umiak—an open boat made of walrus hide— and watch a video of Eskimos in an umiak hunting whales amid icebergs. Slowly circle the voluptuous sculpture of a polar bear, fashioned from bronze with a marbled patina. Contemplate the "Dinosaurs of Alaska," the world's largest collection of high-latitude dinosaurs and related vertebrates. Then…well, just keep going and you'll end up with a rounded view of the western and Arctic Coasts. Visit the other four regional galleries for a thorough overview of Alaska.

While the Museum of the North is UA's big draw, the campus does hold other attractions, such as the **Georgeson Botanical Garden** *(117 W. Tanana Dr. on W end of campus, tel 907/474-1944, www.uaf.edu/snras/gbg, closed in winter).* The expected floral fireworks certainly bring people to the garden, but more interesting is its position as the hemisphere's northernmost botanical garden. Learn how Alaska's plants adapt and thrive in the land of the midnight sun and frigid winter. Starting around mid-July visitors can gawk at 30-pound (14 kg) beets, cukes the size of third graders, 80-pound (36 kg) cabbages, and other

Striking sandhill cranes are among the many bird species that stop by Creamer's Field Migratory Waterfowl Refuge.

monster veggies that 21 hours of sunlight a day can foster.

In summer the university offers guided tours of certain research facilities. Visitors can learn about the aurora borealis and earthquake tremors at the **Geophysical Institute** *(903 Koyukuk Dr. on W end of campus, tel 907/474-7558, www.gi.alaska .edu)* or the potential effects of global warming on Alaska and other northern lands at the **International Arctic Research Center** *(W end of campus, tel 907/474-7558, www.iarc.uaf.edu).* The most popular of these tours takes visitors through LARS— the **Large Animal Research Station** *(2220 Yankovich Rd., just N of campus, tel 907/474-7207, www.uaf.edu/lars).* Expecting cows and horses? Remember, you're only 200 miles (320 km) from the Arctic Circle; the large animals at this facility are caribou, reindeer, and musk oxen.

Visitors will get a wonderfully close look at these distinctive far-north critters, as tour guides answer questions and share facts. Among the things you'll learn: Caribou and reindeer are the same species, but after 10,000 years of separation—caribou in North America and reindeer in Europe—they've developed slight

differences (e.g., caribou are a bit taller and reindeer sport more white patches). Caribou and reindeer have hollow hairs, which insulate them during the bitter northern winters and add buoyancy to safely cross rivers. The clicking you hear from the legs of caribou and reindeer is a special tendon that helps propel their feet forward, saving precious energy during long migrations.

The station's musk ox bulls weigh up to 700 pounds (315 kg), are very aggressive, and sometimes even charge four-wheelers, so LARS staffers use a big tractor when they need to enter the pen. On the other hand, fuzzy little musk ox calves are about as cute as any animal on Earth. Perhaps that explains why musk ox moms nurse their young even after they've grown into 200-pound (90 kg) yearlings. This practice has its perils—cows' nipples are buried deep in folds of warm skin, and nursing 200 pounders sometimes shove so hard to suckle that they lift mom's hindquarters clear off the ground.

SLED DOGS

Fairbanks visitors can also visit various outfits that care for sled dogs. One of the best tours features Mary Shields and her dogs in a two-hour program she calls **Alaskan Tails of the Trail** *(for directions and transportation call 907/457-1117, www.maryshields .com).* Shields is the first woman to finish the Iditarod, the grueling 1,050-mile (1,690 km) sled dog race, and she has run dog teams all over Alaska and even in Siberia. She limits visitors to 20 at a time and invites them not only into her kennels but also up to her log home to chat about sled dogs and her profession. ■

Chena Hot Springs Road

THE 56.6 MILES (91 KM) OF CHENA HOT SPRINGS ROAD
brim with scenery and wildlife. That alone merits a drive along this
route, a local favorite. But there are two additional reasons. One,
as the name reveals, is the delightful hot springs at road's end and
the elaborate resort that has grown up around the steaming waters.
The second attraction is the Chena River State Recreation Area—
254,000 acres (102,870 ha) of forest, mountains, rivers, and tundra
that flank the road for nearly half its length.

Chena Hot Springs Road branches
east off the Steese Highway (see
pp. 211–212) just north of Fairbanks. The first couple of dozen
miles are pleasant but unremark-
able: rural homes, farms, woods,
a few streams. The reasons to
stop and tarry start at Mile 26.1,
when the road enters the **Chena
River State Recreation Area.**
A mile later motorists approach
Rosehip State Campground, the
first of three campgrounds in the
recreation area. Even if you don't
camp at this pretty riverside site,
take the short **Rosehip Campground Nature Trail.** Signs
along the path explain such
things as forest succession and
river erosion, and it's a good
place to spot wildlife.

At Mile 38, just shy of First
Bridge, you'll find a picnic table
at a pullout that also provides
river access for canoeing and
kayaking, popular pastimes in the
recreation area. The area offers
many good access points, making
it easy to plan just the right trip.
While the upper reaches of the
Chena include Class II rapids,
this lower stretch is pretty
smooth. Exercise reasonable caution, however, the current can be
swift, the water is cold, and trees
often block sections of the channel. Paddlers have excellent odds
of seeing moose and beaver—or

**Toasty hot springs
await weary
motorists at
road's end.**

**Chena River
State Recreation
Area**
www.dnr.state.ak.us/parks
/units/chena
🗺 191 B4–C4
✉ Mile 26.1 Chena
Hot Springs Rd.
☎ 907/451-2705

Above: Someone used this sign on the Chena Hot Springs Road for target practice. Right: A hiker savors the scenery of the Chena River State Recreation Area.

at least signs of beaver, such as a dam or lodge.

Around Mile 39, just beyond Second Bridge, is the Tors Trail State Campground. Riverside sites amid tall spruce and birch draw people here, as does another boat access point, but the main attraction is the **Granite Tors Trail.** Strong hikers can complete this moderate-to-difficult 15-mile (24 km) loop in a day, though many prefer to overnight along the trail. Starting in the forest, the trail soon strikes out across alpine tundra, wildflowers in the foreground, huge mountains in the background. The trail is

From the campground, Chena Hot Springs Road follows the river north, passing ponds and marshes favored by moose, beaver, and muskrat. At Fourth Bridge, around Mile 49, a short side road leads to parking for the **Angel Rocks Trail,** a scenic 3.5-mile (5.6 km) loop past massive tors. Those seeking a strenuous trek can branch off about 2 miles (3 km) from the trailhead on the **Angel Rocks to Chena Hot Springs Trail.** This leads to a ridge and follows cairn after cairn. The 360-degree views are fantastic. So is the fact that the trail ends at **Chena Hot**

Chena Hot Springs Resort
www.chenahotsprings.com
191 C4
Mile 56.6 Chena Hot Springs Road
907/451-8104 or 800/478-4681 (U.S. only)

indistinct in places, and hikers must navigate by rock cairns—easy in clear weather but a challenge in mist or rain. Midway through the hike you'll cross the **Plain of Monuments,** an expanse of tundra dotted with tors—granite outcrops that range from a few feet to 100 feet (30 m) high. Formed underground tens of millions of years ago, these pinnacles were exposed as surface materials eroded away. Grizzlies roam the tundra, so watch for them—and watch out for them.

Springs Resort, where relief awaits cold hands and tired legs.

A soak in Rock Lake, hot tubs, or the indoor pool is a must, but the resort also offers lodging, camping, a restaurant, rafting, mountain biking, dogsledding, fishing, gold panning, canoeing, and tours of the **Aurora Ice Museum,** where everything—the furniture, drinking glasses, even the bar—is made of ice. Most people also opt to visit the eponymous hot springs at Mile 56.6, road's end. ∎

Steese Highway

The sun sets well after midnight in summer along the Steese Highway.

SCENERY, WILDLIFE, HISTORY, BUSH TOWNS, HOT SPRINGS—travelers have many options along the Steese, which runs northeast from Fairbanks to Circle. The first 53 miles (85 km) of this 161-mile (260 km) road are paved, the next 73 mostly gravel but wide and easygoing. But the remaining 35 miles are narrow and winding. One 117-mile stretch lacks gas stations, so fill up before you start, and then refill in Central or Circle before turning back.

Upper Chatanika River State Recreation Site
🅐 191 B4–C4
☎ 907/451-2705 (Alaska Dept. of Natural Resources PIC, Fairbanks)

The Steese is a beautiful drive through the hills and mountains in fall (late Aug.–early Sept. this far north), when the trees and tundra turn yellow and red. However, the first few miles pass bland development, so scoot out of town. Just past Mile 8 is a pullout where visitors can walk right up to the **trans-Alaska oil pipeline** *(tel 907/278-1611, www.alyeska-pipeline.com)*. A visitor center opens in summer.

A mile farther is the exit to **Gold Dredge No. 8** *(1755 Old Steese Hwy. N, tel 907/457-6058, www.golddredgeno8.com)*. To reach it, turn left on Goldstream Road, then left on the Old Steese Highway. From its construction days in 1928 till its retirement in 1959, this 250-foot-long (76 m), five-story dredge crawled across this landscape, creating its own water channel and processing so many tons of rock that it produced more than 7.5 million ounces of gold. Though the dredge is privately owned, the Park Service has declared it a National Historic Mechanical Engineering Landmark.

More evidence of golden days awaits at Mile 28 in the **Chatanika Gold Camp** *(tel 907/389-2414 or tel 907/479-0554, www.fegoldcamp.com)*, site of the historic Fairbanks Exploration Company camp, built in the 1920s to support nearby dredging. Now it's a rustic restaurant, bar, and hotel. On Sundays the

TRAIL INFORMATION
For information on Davidson Ditch, Nome Creek Valley Gold Panning, Twelvemile Summit, and Pinnell Trail & Eagle Summit, contact Alaska Bureau of Land Management, www.ak.blm.gov, tel 907/474-2251 (Northern Field Office, Fairbanks).

staff stokes a huge coal-fired cookstove for a breakfast buffet. Half a mile down the highway lies the **Chatanika Lodge** *(tel 907/389-2164),* a motel, store, restaurant, and saloon that's a lively gathering place for both locals and travelers; the entrance and walls brim with antlers and trophy heads.

Here the road paces the pretty Chatanika River, a rapids-free Class II stream that's a favorite among canoeists. At Mile 39, the **Upper Chatanika River State Recreation Site** offers a good put-in point at the pleasant campground. For longer paddles, put in at any of several roadside sites farther upriver; check water levels with the Fairbanks office of the state Department of Natural Resources before setting out.

Ditches are not usually big tourist draws, but at Mile 57.3 you

may want to stop at the **Davidson Ditch Historical Site.** Built in 1925 to provide water for the area's floating gold dredges, the 83-mile (134 km) channel carried up to 56,100 gallons a minute. From this same turnoff (U.S. Creek Road) motorists with 4WD can cross steep hills about 7 miles to the **Nome Creek Valley Gold Panning Area,** one of several places along the Steese that allow recreational panning.

At 3,190-foot (972 m) **Twelvemile Summit Wayside** (Mile 85.5), hikers have access to one of Alaska's finest trails: the **Pinnell Mountain National Recreation Trail.** For 27 miles (43 km) it passes through wildflower-strewn alpine tundra, along mountain ridges that yield views of the White Mountains and Alaska and Brooks Ranges, and through habitat favored by animals from pikas to wolves. A day hike up just the first couple of miles is rewarded with alpine vistas. The trail emerges at a parking area at Mile 107.5 on the Steese. Hike to **Eagle Summit,** less than a mile from this parking lot, to see gorgeous wildflowers.

At Mile 127.5 the road eases through small-town **Central** (pop. 102), whose services cater to the busy mining district that surrounds it, as well as travelers. The **Circle District Historical Society Museum** *(tel 907/520-5312)* covers both natural history and mining, past and present.

The Steese ends at **Circle** *(Visitor information: Yukon Trading Post, tel 907/773-1217; HC Company Store, tel 907/773-1222),* an even smaller town than Central. On the west bank of the Yukon, this town serves as the jumping-off point for summer river traffic, including riverboats and jet boats. ■

One of several historic gold dredges that once mined ore throughout the Interior

Elliott Highway

THE ELLIOTT SLIPS ALONG HILLSIDES AND RIDGETOPS, 191 A4–B4
serving up views of boreal forest, mountains, rivers, and wildlife.
Starting 11 miles (18 km) north of Fairbanks at the Steese Highway
junction, near the town of Fox, this route runs 152 miles (245 km)
into the wilds. The first 73 miles (118 km), to the Dalton Highway
junction, are paved, but the last 79 miles (127 km) are gravel, narrow, and winding. Gas is available at Mile Fox 66 and at road's end,
but there's little else along this remote road, so prepare accordingly.

**Caribou aren't
the only species
whose migratory
route crosses
Interior Alaska.**

Just how remote is suggested at Mile Fox 9, where you'll spot the sign Olnes City (POP. 1). While Olnes wouldn't even rate its own sign in, say, southern California, it's the third largest town on the Elliott. (The biggest, Manley Hot Springs, is a metropolis of 73.)

For a short walk or weeklong backpack, pull off at Mile Fox 27.7 and the **Wickersham Dome Trailhead** (*contact Fairbanks BLM office, tel 907/474-2200*). This path leads to a network of trails in the **White Mountains National Recreation Area,** but even a 20-minute walk will take you above the tree line to wildflower meadows and mar-velous vistas. Much of the drive is also above the tree line, so motorists won't miss out.

At Mile Fox 66 the road enters the tiny town of Livengood (pop. 29), an old mining settlement that offers services at the North Country Mercantile. Seven miles farther the Dalton branches north, looking like the main highway; turn southwest to con-tinue on the Elliott. Beyond Mile Fox 85 the views open up on the White Mountains, Tanana River, Minto Flats, and Alaska Range.

At road's end lies **Manley Hot Springs.** The old resort has shut down, but people still enjoy soaking in the springs, a short walk from the small campground. The center of life in this village is the historic **Manley Roadhouse** (*tel 907/672-3161*), which has been serving travelers and locals since 1906. Grab a bite, have a beer, or arrange for a cabin, and then talk it up with the miners, road crews, trappers, and other folks who live in the bush. ∎

More places to visit in Alaska's Interior

CHICKEN
Hundreds of miles into Alaska's outback, Chicken is a famously eccentric hamlet of 21 people—maybe three times that when miners hit town in summer. Legend has it the town was established as Ptarmigan in 1903, but townsfolk changed the name to Chicken (a synonym for ptarmigan) since it was easier to spell. There are no phones (cell service is spotty) and no flush toilets, but

days it offers fabulous views of Mount McKinley and its Alaska Range entourage of snowcapped, jagged peaks. Many argue that the vistas from pullouts at Mile 134.7 and Mile 162.4 of the Parks Highway (which cuts through the state park from Mile 132.2 to Mile 168.5) are the finest roadside views, bar none, of the mountain and the range. Other pullouts in this area also offer excellent views.

Far up the Taylor Highway, the town of Chicken occupies a few scattered buildings.

there is a post office, which gets mail on Tuesdays and Fridays, weather permitting. Stop by the **Chicken Mercantile** for some of Sue Wiren's mythic cinnamon rolls, homemade pie, and—wait for it—chicken soup. Be sure to check out **Pedro Dredge No. 4.** If all that driving seems a bit much, at least read the NSFAQ (not-so-frequently asked questions) on the town's colorful website *(www.chickenalaska.com).* Also visit the Chicken Center *(www.chickenak.com)* for info on guided tours of town. 191 C3

DENALI STATE PARK
Overshadowed by its celebrated neighbor to the north, this 325,240-acre (131,720 ha) state park also warrants attention. On clear

A number of trails run through the park. Many are backpacking routes, though casual day-hikers can certainly hike a few miles up and back on these longer trails. Try the first 3 miles (4.8 km) of the **Little Coal Creek Trail,** which leaves from the parking lot at Mile 163.8 of the highway. One beautiful and easy day hike is the 4.8-mile (7.7 km) **Byers Lakeshore Loop,** which begins at Byers Lake Campground and circles the lake. A quarter mile (0.4 km) north of Byers Lake is the **Alaska Veterans Memorial/ POW-MIA Rest Area.** A small visitor information center is staffed in the summer. ▲ 191 A2 ✉ Alaska State Parks, Mat-Su/CB Area ☎ 907/745-3975, www.dnr.state.ak.us /parks/units/denali1.htm ■

The Bush comprises the wilderness and villages that lie beyond cities, beyond roads, beyond ferries—the rule in this massive state, not the exception. It is also the part of Alaska most visitors never see.

The Bush

Introduction & map 216–217
Dillingham & vicinity 218–219
Bethel & vicinity 220
Nome & vicinity 221–222
Kotzebue 223
Dalton Highway 224–225
Kobuk Valley National Park 229
Gates of the Arctic National Park & Preserve 230–231
Arctic National Wildlife Refuge 232
Barrow 233
More places to visit in the Bush 234
Hotels & restaurants 259–260

A walrus skull rests amid tundra wildflowers in the lush, remote Pribilof Islands.

Walrus congregate at the Walrus Islands State Game Sanctuary, in Bristol Bay off Dillingham.

The Bush

TRAVELERS CAN DELVE DEEP INTO THE WILDERNESS AT DENALI NATIONAL Park. They can get off the roads and ride the state ferry to distant communities in Southeast Alaska. They can jet 500 miles (800 km) from the mainland and land at an isolated Aleutian Islands town like Unalaska/Dutch Harbor. By lower 48 standards, these places are indeed remote. But the Bush takes remoteness to a whole different level. It is what lies beyond those relatively accessible parts of Alaska.

Hogatza. The Kilbuck Mountains. Flat. The Kogoluktuk River. Sleetmute. Marys Igloo. Platinum. Thunder Mountain. Oliktok Point. Red Devil. Shaktoolik. Wild places and villages few travelers have heard of and fewer still have seen. Vast expanses where grizzlies, moose, and wolves outnumber people. Settlements inhabited by 200 to 300 Natives and maybe a handful of non-Native get-away-from-it-all types. This is the Bush.

Residents in most Bush villages lean heavily on subsistence lifestyles. They hunt moose, walrus, caribou, geese, beluga whales, bears, ducks, seals, and bowhead whales; trap beavers, mink, otters, wolverines, and hare; gather berries and wild onions; and fish for just about everything. Many also earn money as commercial fishers, hunting and fishing guides, summer firefighters, miners, and government workers, and by making and selling Native crafts.

No hard-and-fast boundaries define the Bush. Roughly, it includes the western half of mainland Alaska and the northeastern quadrant—about three quarters of the state. This vast region encompasses a range of ecosystems, though most of it falls under the two broad categories of tundra or boreal forest, each laced with mountain ranges. It also features a long, complex coastline that fronts the Bering Sea, the Chukchi Sea, and the Beaufort Sea, a part of the Arctic Ocean.

By definition the Bush is not connected to the rest of the state by road or railway, with the exception of the Dalton Highway, built to serve the Arctic oil fields at Prudhoe Bay. People travel by boat along the coast, up the rivers, and across the watery coastal plain of the Yukon-Kuskokwim Delta. To reach anywhere else, they fire up the props on those small planes.

Casual visitors almost always travel to the region by plane, which generally makes the Bush an expensive destination. That said, daily jet service from Anchorage does serve several larger Bush towns. Flying into these few hubs (versus chartering a flight to more remote regions) or simply driving the

Dalton Highway are the most practical and least expensive means of transportation to Alaska's outback. Many areas are also accessible by boat.

The larger towns offer lodging, restaurants, grocery stores, and tour operators, mostly geared to anglers and hunters. While smaller villages usually lack such visitor amenities, they sometimes let travelers sleep in their schools or some other government building (though it may be on the floor). ■

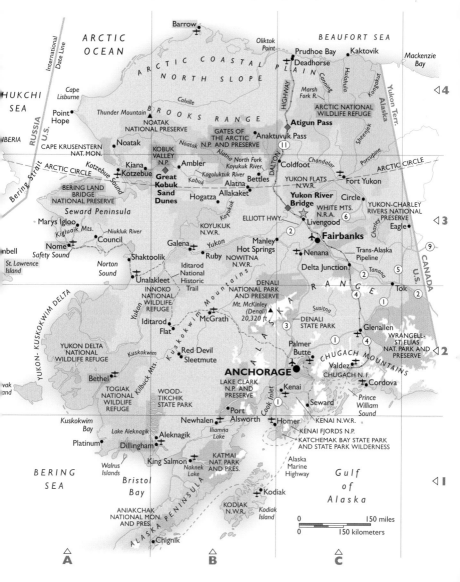

Dillingham

△ 217 B1

**Visitor
information**
www.dillinghamak.com
✉ Seward & D Sts.
☎ 907/842-5115
🕐 Closed weekends

Dillingham & vicinity

IF YOU LIKE FISH, DILLINGHAM IS YOUR TOWN. THIS IS THE
harbor for the Bristol Bay commercial sockeye salmon fishery, one of
the world's most productive. Dillingham also offers outstanding
sportfishing opportunities; guides, charter boats, and wilderness fishing lodges abound. The town has plenty to offer non-anglers, as well,
serving as a jumping-off point to several prime wilderness and
wildlife areas. Though a working town with a utilitarian ambience,
Dillingham does offer basic services for travelers, such as hotels,
restaurants, and stores.

**A male walrus
proudly displays
his tusks, which
he uses to dig
mollusks from
the ocean floor.**

**Togiak National
Wildlife Refuge**
http://togiak.fws.gov
△ 217 A2
✉ Information: 6 Main
   St., Kangiiqutaq
   Bldg.
☎ 907/842-1063

Your first stop should be the
library, at the corner of Seward
and D Streets—not to check out
a book but to stop at the visitor
center and **Sam Fox Museum**
*(tel 907/842-5610, closed week-
ends)*, which share a building
with the library. The small museum focuses on local history, particularly that of the Yupik
Eskimos. It also serves as an art
gallery of sorts, displaying traditional and contemporary Native
arts and crafts. Visitors can buy
carved ivory, masks, Eskimo
dolls, and other arts and crafts at
several stores in town.

For a look at present-day
Dillingham, stroll down to the
harbor, where hundreds of small
fishing boats crowd the docks—
when not out fishing, of course.
To learn more about the industry,
ask the visitor center about a tour
of one of several **commercial
salmon canneries.**

Those wanting to explore outdoors might consider the **Togiak
National Wildlife Refuge.** At
4.3 million acres (1.7 million ha),
this wilderness of lakes, rivers,
mountains, and coastline is huge;
while its eastern boundary lies
just 3 miles (4.8 km) west of
town, the western boundary is
some 130 miles (210 km) away.
To navigate this expanse, almost
all travelers enlist the help of
guides. Rafting tours often start
on headwater lakes and drift the
waterways for several days. Most
trips are geared to fishers or
hunters, though sightseers and
wildlife watchers will also enjoy
themselves, assuming they don't
mind roughing it. The refuge
shelters moose, wolves, otters,
and brown and black bears. The
nearly 200,000 caribou of the
Mulchatna and Nushagak Peninsula herds visit the refuge, while
whales, sea lions, seals, and more
than a million seabirds frequent
the 600-mile (965 km) coastline.

Winding north from Dillingham is one of the Bush's rare

roads, a **scenic byway** that leads 25 miles (40 km) to the village of **Aleknagik** and the southern end of **Lake Aleknagik.** Ten miles (16 km) up the lake is the southern border of **Wood-Tikchik State Park**—at 1.7 million (688,500 ha) acres, the country's biggest state park. Visitors can reach the park via charter boat out of Aleknagik or from Dillingham via the Wood River, although especially when the salmon are running and eagles, brown bears, river otters, kingfishers, foxes, and other critters gather along with the anglers to feast on the fish.

Wildlife-watchers on the lookout for something different may want to take a floatplane or charter boat from Dillingham to **Round Island,** the heart of the **Walrus Islands State Game Sanctuary,** in northern Bristol

Wood-Tikchik State Park
www.dnr.state.ak.us/parks/units/woodtik.htm
🗺 217 B2
☎ Dillingham Ranger Station: 907/269-8698

most people fly to one of the big lakes in a floatplane and then take a guided raft, canoe, or kayak trip through the network of lakes connected by rivers. The park is a transition zone. To the east you'll find wooded and wet lowlands, while the western reaches feature tall peaks, alpine valleys, and fjord-like arms of lakes that reach deep into the mountains. The wildlife-watching is excellent, Bay. The rugged little island is home to walrus. Some 8,000 blubbery, tusked male walrus haul out on the beaches each year. You'll also find some 250,000 seabirds, hundreds of Steller's sea lions, and red foxes. Special permits are required, and conditions can be tough, so consult thoroughly with the Fish and Game folks before putting this trip on your itinerary. ■

Dillingham derives its living from the sea.

Walrus Islands State Game Sanctuary
☎ Alaska Dept. of Fish & Game, Div. of Wildlife Conservation: 907/842-1013

Bethel & vicinity

Bethel

🅰 217 A2

**Visitor
information**

www.bethelalaska.com

✉ 192 Alex Hately St.

☎ 907/543-2911

**Yupiit Piciryarait
Cultural Center
& Museum**

✉ 420 Chief Eddie
Hoffman Hwy.

☎ 907/543-1819

🕐 Closed Sun. & Mon.

$ $

VISITORS ARE OFTEN SURPRISED AT HOW BIG BETHEL IS. ITS population ranges between 6,000 and 8,000, depending on the season. It also hosts the third busiest airport in Alaska, with daily jet service from Anchorage and squadrons of small planes from dozens of nearby villages; the town is the transportation and supply hub for much of western Alaska. However, Bethel retains the off-the-grid, ramshackle feel of a Bush community. Some residents of this predominantly Native town still wear traditional Yupik Eskimo clothing, such as caribou-skin parkas and sealskin mukluks. Yet Bethel definitely exists in the 21st century: You can get a latte in a dozen different places, and locals include Albanians, Filipinos, and Koreans who have come to work here, many as cab drivers—a surprising number for a place that only has a couple of dozen miles of road.

**Spectacled eiders
nest at the Yukon
Delta National
Wildlife Refuge.**

**Yukon Delta
National
Wildlife Refuge**

http://yukondelta.fws.gov

🅰 217 A2

☎ 907/543-3151

🕐 Closed Sun.

To learn about the history and contemporary culture of the Yupik/Cupik and Dene, drop by the **Yupiit Piciryarait Cultural Center & Museum.** One of its three galleries houses a permanent collection of Native art and artifacts, while the two others offer changing exhibits. The gift shop sells local Native art and crafts.

Bethel's big attraction is the vast **Yukon Delta National Wildlife Refuge,** where glacial silt deposited over the millennia by the Yukon and Kuskokwim Rivers has created the second largest delta in the U.S., exceeded only by the Mississippi. Most of the refuge comprises wet tundra mixed with ponds, lakes, rivers, and creeks. Caribou, lynx, bears, wolves, polar bears (along the coast), and musk oxen (on Nunivak Island) roam the refuge, as do millions of birds. Call to arrange a guided tour. ∎

Nome & vicinity

A waterfront boardwalk harks back to Nome's frontier origins.

UNLIKE MOST BUSH TOWNS, NOME DIDN'T START AS A Native settlement. Born abruptly after the discovery of gold in 1898, it was initially named Anvil City, after the gold strike in Anvil Creek. By the summer of 1900 some 20,000 people had arrived in this remote boomtown on the Seward Peninsula at the edge of the Bering Sea. Though gold mining remains big business around Nome, the rush is long past and the population now stands at about 3,500—still big enough to make this town the hub of northwestern Alaska.

Of all the Bush communities, Nome is the one most geared to travelers who aren't hunters or anglers. In fact, enough package tours come to town that sometimes all the hotels are filled, so reserve early. Nome is unique among Bush locales because about 300 miles (483 km) of decent gravel roads fan out along the coast and up into the tundra-covered mountains of the peninsula. Properly informed and prepared, visitors can rent a car and tour around on their own.

Start at the visitor center, on Front Street, the town's main drag, which runs along the Bering Sea. The center's resources and staff are exceptional and extend well beyond the usual help with lodging or restaurants. They can hook you up with just the right tour guide or provide maps and handouts for you to go it alone, whether you're looking

Nome
🗺 217 A3
Visitor information
www.nomealaska.org/vc
✉ 301 Front St.
☎ 907/443-6624
🕐 Open daily late May–mid-Sept., weekdays only rest of year

Carrie M. McLain Memorial Museum
- ✉ 200 E. Front St.
- ☎ 907/443-6630
- ⏱ Closed Sun. & Mon. mid-Sept.–late May

Board of Trade Ivory Shop
- ✉ 212 Front St.
- ☎ 907/443-2611

Arctic Trading Post
www.nomechamber.org /arctictrading.html
- ✉ Front & Bering Sts.
- ☎ 907/443-2686

Chukotka-Alaska Store
- ✉ 514 Lomen Ave.
- ☎ 907/443-4128

for historic gold dredges (or currently operating ones), good fishing holes, or rare birds. Pick up the walking-tour map, which emphasizes historic sites, though most gold rush buildings have burned down or been destroyed by storms.

Steps from the visitor center, in the basement of the library building, is the **Carrie M. McLain Memorial Museum,** which focuses on early Bering Strait–area Eskimo life, the gold rush, and the 1925 diphtheria epidemic. The latter ended after the heroic delivery of serum to Nome by dogsled from Nenana, 650 miles (1,050 km) away—an event that inspired the renowned Iditarod Sled Dog Race, which starts in Anchorage and ends in Nome every March. Don't miss the museum's outstanding collection of historic photos.

Polar bears & pack ice

While visitors associate grizzlies and black bears with Alaska, fewer realize the state also harbors polar bears. That's because visitors rarely see one, which is just as well, as they are far more dangerous to humans than are the two other bear species. A few thousand polar bears spend some of the winter on the northwestern and northern Alaska coasts, ranging south as far the Yukon-Kuskokwim Delta, but during the summer—when most visitors are around—the bears are roaming the pack ice far to the north. Some scientists worry that polar bears may be among the early victims of global warming, as the ice pack on which they spend most of their lives is melting. ∎

Nome is an excellent place to buy Native art and crafts, notably carved ivory, a specialty of northwestern villages. Try the **Board of Trade Ivory Shop** and the **Arctic Trading Post.** Another shop, the **Chukotka-Alaska Store,** carries not only Alaska Yupik products but also Siberian Yupik works and other Russian wares—a reminder that Nome is only 161 miles from Siberia.

Three main roads pierce the wilds of the Seward Peninsula: the Nome-Council, Nome-Taylor (Kougarok), and Nome-Teller. The 72-mile (116 km) **Council Road** heads east along the Bering Sea for about 30 miles (48 km), then veers inland northeast to the Niukluk River. In early summer, as ice floes break up, marine mammals and birds congregate in the leads (gaps in the ice); look for ringed seals, eiders, harlequin ducks, and arctic and Pacific loons. Twenty-two miles (35 km) from town is **Safety Sound,** a hot spot for waterfowl and seabirds, including such Asian strays as the Mongolian plover. Gold rush cabins in Council augur the end of the road.

The 86-mile (138 km) **Kougarok Road** runs north into the ruggedly handsome **Kigluaik Mountains,** which invite hiking. Note the remains of the Wild Goose Pipeline, built—but never finished—to supply water to the early gold mines (*refrain from disturbing site*). Scan roadside cliffs for nesting golden eagles, peregrine falcons, and gyrfalcons and watch for grizzlies. Beyond Mile 80 the road can be rough.

Wending its way northwest to the village of Teller, the 72-mile (116 km) **Teller Road** is another good birding route and may yield glimpses of reindeer and their herders, as well as musk oxen. ∎

Kotzebue

JUST AS EXTREME WEATHER SHAPES THE TUNDRA, FORCING plants to hug the ground for dear life, so the harsh Arctic climate has shaped Kotzebue. Perched on the tip of a narrow, 3-mile-long (4.8-km) spit that juts into a sound on the Chukchi Sea, this town of 3,130 hardy residents—80 percent of them Inupiat Eskimos—takes some serious weather hits. Accordingly, its buildings are low-lying and solidly built—aesthetics take a backseat to practicality. Yet a close look at Kotzebue and its environs reveals much beauty in its people and their art and in the minimalist Arctic landscape.

Kotzebue
⚠ 217 A3

Visitor information
www.cityofkotzebue.com
✉ 258A 3rd Ave.
☎ 907/442-3401

Kotzebue is a jumping-off point for visits to the dunes in Kobuk Valley National Park.

Scheduled to open by 2008, the **Northwest Arctic Heritage Center** will reveal the beauty of Inupiat Eskimo art and culture. This major venture of the Western Arctic Parkland Service (National Park Service) will also showcase the grandeur of nearby Park Service lands.

Those public lands include Kobuk Valley National Park (see p. 229), Noatak National Preserve, and Cape Krusenstern National Monument. Stop by the NPS **Visitor Information Center** in Kotzebue to learn about these utterly untamed places.

Most of the few visitors to **Noatak National Preserve** traverse its 6.3 million acres (2.5 million ha) by rafting down the Noatak, a Wild and Scenic River. Except for a few rough stretches, the long voyage—up to three weeks—is a gentle float, but its remoteness dictates using a guide. (*Contact preserve for approved raft and floatplane operators.*) The stark tundra and mountains are home to grizzlies, wolves, gyrfalcons, and swans. Between April and August you may catch sight of the huge western Arctic caribou herd.

From Kotzebue it's only 10 miles (16 km) by plane or boat to **Cape Krusenstern National Monument.** While most folks venture here to look for rare birds blown in from Asia, encounter musk oxen or marine mammals, or take in the otherworldly scenery, the monument's raison d'être is archaeological—more than a hundred sand-and-gravel ridges along the coast hold artifacts that speak to some 9,000 years of human activity. ■

National Park Service Visitor Information Center
www.nps.gov/nwak or www.nps.gov/kova
✉ 154 2nd Ave.
☎ 907/442-3760 or 907/442-3890 in winter (Northwest Arctic Headquarters)
🕐 Closed Aug.–late May

Dalton Highway

After crossing the Arctic Circle, the Dalton Highway runs another 300 miles (480 km) north to the Arctic Ocean.

🅐 217 C3–C4

Bureau of Land Management Northern Field Office
www.blm.gov
✉ 1150 University Ave., Fairbanks, AK 99709
☎ 907/474-2200 or 800/437-7021

THOUGH IN ITS STRICTEST SENSE NOT THE BUSH, THIS road *is* wild and beautiful. It's also long and rough, passing through boreal forest, across tundra, and beyond the Arctic Circle to the North Slope and the Arctic Ocean. Also known as the Haul Road, the Dalton Highway was built in the mid-1970s to provide construction access to the northern stretch of the trans-Alaska oil pipeline. It runs 414 miles (667 km), from Mile 73.1 on the Elliott Highway (84 miles/135 km north of Fairbanks) to Deadhorse.

Big gravel-flinging trucks still service the oil fields along this highway. If you see one coming, pull over and pray for the safety of your windshield. Emergency supplies should include replacement headlights and belts, two full-size, mounted spare tires, coolant, plenty of food and water, blankets, and sleeping bags. Also carry extra gas, as service stations are scarce along this route. Always drive with your headlights on.

If you'd rather have someone else do the driving, several companies run vans and tours up the Dalton *(for information, contact Fairbanks Convention & Visitors Bureau, tel 907/456-5774, www.explorefairbanks.com).*

The route north begins along a stretch of forest where birders have logged more than a hundred species. At Mile 55.5 the road crosses the 2,290-foot **Yukon River Bridge;** to learn about the pipeline and Alaska's longest river, stop by the **Yukon Crossing Visitor Contact Station** *(closed early Sept.–late May).*

Around Mile 95 the scenery shifts from varied spruce forest to wildflower-dotted tundra. Pause at the **Finger Mountain BLM Wayside** (Mile 98) to stroll the short interpretive nature trail.

The Dalton crosses the **Arctic Circle** at Mile 115; interpretive signs enhance the **Arctic Circle BLM Wayside.** Sixteen miles (26 km) farther, **Gobblers Knob** offers a stellar view where the sun never sets at the summer solstice.

At Mile 175, **Coldfoot** (pop. 11), provides gas, lodging, tours and flightseeing. Visit the **Arctic Interagency Visitor Center** *(tel 907/678-5209, closed Labor Day–Memorial Day)* for details about surrounding public lands.

Above the tree line at Mile 244.7, the road crests the high point of the drive—4,800-foot **Atigun Pass,** in the striking

Brooks Range. Watch for Dall sheep and grizzlies as you descend to the tundra-covered **North Slope.** Millions of birds nest and breed here, including tundra swans, arctic terns, long-tailed jaegers, spectacled eiders, and snowy owls. You may also spot caribou and musk oxen.

The highway ends at Mile 414 in the oil town of **Deadhorse.** To venture the last few miles across the oil fields to the Arctic Ocean, you must join a tour. Grizzlies have been hanging around Deadhorse in recent years, so exercise caution while walking around the area. ■

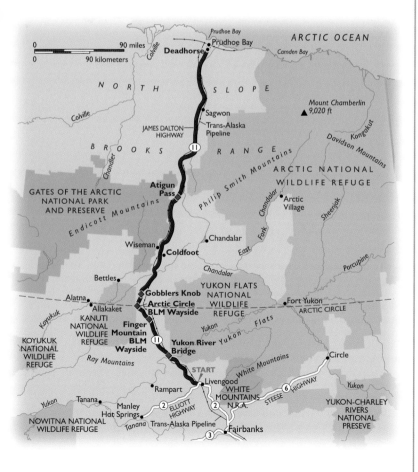

Winter in Alaska

Granted, sometimes the stereotype about the brutality of Alaska's winters is accurate. In the Interior occasional inversions shove thermometers deep below zero; it was once so cold in Fairbanks that an auto tire shattered on the ground after falling off a truck. Winter storms along the Gulf of Alaska and other coastal zones often lash the shoreline with gale-force winds and buckets of rain. As for the far north, near the Arctic Ocean, well, let's just note that folks up there routinely leave their vehicles running in winter—their cars might not otherwise start. And then there's

the darkness. Above the Arctic Circle, which encompasses about a third of Alaska, the sun never rises above the horizon in midwinter, while southern regions get a measly five to six hours of daylight during each revolution of the Earth.

That's the bad news. The good news for winter travelers is that the stereotype applies more to the extremes. For most of the winter in most of Alaska the weather is tolerable. Take Anchorage—February the average high temperature is 25° F (-4° C). Not quite tropical, to be sure, but not much different from

The otherworldly aurora borealis is a highlight for many winter visitors.

and wait it out, running the engine and heater about ten minutes every hour, not continuously—and be sure to crack a downwind window and keep the exhaust pipe clear of snow to avoid carbon monoxide poisoning. For more safety tips, consult www.arh.noaa.gov/essd/safety/winter05 .htm. Be sure to get information about road conditions and impending weather for the routes you plan to travel.

AURORA BOREALIS

Now, to be honest, less-than-unbearable weather is hardly a big selling point. Why then *do* people visit Alaska in winter?

Many come to catch the aurora borealis (aka northern lights), which shimmies across the night sky in colossal, ever-shifting bands of light. Auroras occur when solar flares send streams of charged particles into the Earth's magnetic field, where they react with atmospheric gases to create those radiant colors. Onlookers watch, mesmerized, as undulating yellow-green streamers suddenly swell to drape the whole sky. Sometimes blues, purples, and pinks dance into the picture. On rare occasions the aurora is wholly red. Among the state's accessible regions, the Fairbanks area offers the best northern lights viewing. Some lodges and tour operators cater to aurora-watchers with such amenities as heated, glassed-in rooms or hot tubs from which to soak up the lights, snowcapped peaks, alpenglow, and other phenomenal winter features.

WINTER ACTIVITIES

Others take part in winter activities, notably skiing. Some even try night skiing while watching the northern lights. The biggest downhill ski area is Mount Alyeska, about 40 miles south of Anchorage, near the town of Girdwood. Alaska's second and third largest cities, Fairbanks and Juneau, also host downhill ski areas. Cross-country skiing abounds, including maintained trails just outside cities and towns. Guides and heli-skiing operators will take the willing and able deep into the backcountry.

Minnesota or Montana. Anchorage also gets much less precipitation in the winter than in the summer. Ditto for the Interior. The Southeast does get drenched in winter, but its proximity to the Pacific moderates temperatures. Bottom line, winter in Alaska offers a lot for visitors, and they shouldn't be afraid of the weather.

That said, motorists should respect the winter weather. Use common sense and don't head into a storm along a backroad in an '89 Yugo with a quarter tank of gas and no blankets, extra clothing, food, or water. Consider bringing a small bag of sand to pour onto the snow beneath your tires for traction should you get mired. If you are caught in a blizzard while driving, pull over

Sled dogs of renowned musher Jeff King rocket forward at the start of the Iditarod.

If you'd rather have someone else do the work, try a dogsledding tour. Mushers statewide maintain kennels full of howling huskies. Visitors can also watch dogsled races, from short runs on a track to the granddaddy of all races, the Iditarod, in which mushers and their teams cover some 1,050 miles from Anchorage to Nome. The race kicks off the first Saturday in March.

Alaskans engage in dozens of additional activities to ward off cabin fever during those cold, dark winter months. Among them is the well-known Fairbanks' Festival of Native Arts, in February or March, which draws dancers, musicians, and artisans from settlements throughout the state, as well as Russia, Canada, and Japan. Another must-see is Anchorage's celebrated Fur Rendez-vous, a two-week-plus, extravaganza that defies categorization. Among the many eclectic elements that make up the Fur Rondy: dogsled races, a dog weight pull, snowshoe softball, ice bowling, curling, a snow sculpture contest, and an oyster-shucking contest, fireworks, a carnival, horse-drawn carriage rides, bingo, a motor-cycle show, a masque ball, a chess tourna-ment, an antique tractor show, a mutt show, a weiner-eating contest, and, of course, a fur auction.

This breadth of imagination to spice up winter spreads far beyond Anchorage. Small communities across the state stage simple diversions that often morph into larger events as restless souls from neighboring towns attend. Cordova's Ice Worm Festival, for example, kicks off on the first weekend in February with a parade led by a 100-foot (30 m) ice worm. The Bering Sea Ice Golf Classic, in Nome, is held on the third Saturday in March; using bright-orange golf balls and old shotgun shells for tees, golfers trudge across the frozen sea in boots and parkas—no plaid slacks here—to challenge the makeshift course. Seward gets into the act on the third weekend in January with the Polar Bear Jump Off. Though it includes such normal activities as a seafood feed and basketball tourney, the Jump Off is defined by a waiter/waitress contest, oyster slurping, the ugly fish toss, and the dog weight pull—winners haul well over a ton. The highlight, though, comes when a host of costumed lunatics plunge into Resurrection Bay, whose water is about one degree shy of being ice.

Finally, if the northern lights, winter sports, and a host of activities still haven't sold you on Alaska as a winter destination, consider one last fact: no mosquitoes. ∎

Kobuk Valley National Park

SANDWICHED BETWEEN TWO MOUNTAIN RANGES, KOBUK
Valley National Park offers 1.8 million acres (730,000 ha) of roadless,
trailless wilderness. Kobuk lies above the Arctic Circle at the northern boundary of the boreal forest, where scrawny spruces and birch-
es survive amid the vast tundra. Though few visitors make it to this
park, Alaska Natives use it for subsistence fishing and hunting, so
please be respectful of any cabins, camps, or nets you may find.

**Kobuk Valley
National Park**
www.nps.gov/kova
🗺 217 B3
☎ 907/442-3890

To reach the park, either charter
a plane in Kotzebue or Nome
or take a scheduled flight into
one of several Inupiat villages
on the Kobuk River—say,
Ambler or Kiana—and air taxi
or boat in from there. Guided
tours often raft a portion of
the **Kobuk River,** the park's
main artery. Closer to the headwaters the river offers serious
whitewater, but the lower river
is a relaxed drift. While floating
down the river or hiking its
margins, watch for grizzlies,
caribou, and golden eagles.

Anglers cherish the river for its
arctic char, grayling, and spirited
giant sheefish.

A 1.5-mile (2.4 km) hike
from the river is the park's central feature, **Great Kobuk
Sand Dunes,** a 25-square-mile
(65 sq km) mini Sahara whose
golden dunes rise to 100 feet/30
m (remote dunes to the south
reach 500 feet/152 m). Millennia
ago upriver glaciers ground parts
of the Brooks Range into sand,
which gradually tumbled down
the Kobuk and blew into the
dune fields you see today. ■

**The Great Kobuk
Sand Dunes rise
amid the tundra
and boreal forest
of Kobuk Valley
National Park.**

Gates of the Arctic National Park & Preserve

Gates of the Arctic National Park & Preserve
www.nps.gov/gaar
🗺 217 B4 & 225

Fairbanks Headquarters
www.nps.gov/gaar
✉ 201 1st Ave.
☎ 907/457-5752 or 907/678-2004
🕐 Closed weekends

Bettles Ranger Station/Visitor Center
☎ 907/692-5494

Arctic Interagency Visitor Center
✉ Coldfoot
☎ 907/678-5209
🕐 Closed Labor Day– Mem. Day

FOR TRAVELERS EAGER TO EXPLORE ALASKA'S GREAT northern wilderness but unready to delve into the Bush on their own, Gates of the Arctic is the perfect solution. Nearly four times bigger than Yellowstone and utterly undeveloped, the park comprises an enormous expanse of wild Alaska. "It seemed as if time had dropped away a million years and we were back in a primordial world," wrote Robert Marshall, famed explorer and conservationist, when he hiked this region in the 1930s.

Today you'll find the same saw-tooth mountains, the same pure rivers, and the same array of wolves, grizzlies, eagles, beavers, caribou, and other animals. But thanks to its designation as a national park, Gates of the Arctic is much more accessible than in Marshall's time. Visitors can get plenty of information about the park, and outfitters and guides organize a variety of tours.

A demanding hike accesses the park from the **Dalton Highway** (see p. 224–225), but most people fly from Fairbanks into the small gateway community of **Bettles,** which hosts a Park Service visitor center and several outfitters. From there small planes make the short hop into the park.

The prospect of trudging over tussocks and tundra convinces most people to traverse the park down one of its many rivers via raft, canoe, or kayak. The **North Fork Koyukuk** involves a few tricky obstacles, though no appreciable rapids. A floatplane can drop you at **Summit Lake** (or lakes near **Redstar Creek**), from which you'll drift past waterfalls, glacial valleys, and mountains, including **Frigid Crags** and **Boreal Mountain,** the peaks Marshall dubbed the "Gates of the Arctic." (The Arctic ecosystem starts north of the Brooks Range.)

Pause for a few hikes, and after four or five days and 100 miles (160 km) you'll float into Bettles.

A designated Wild and Scenic River, the **Alatna** descends the south slopes of the Brooks Range. The first couple of dozen miles below the headwaters involve rapids and sweepers (trees whose branches graze the river surface), so be sure to have experience or a guide at the helm. Gorgeous scenery is your reward. Put in farther downriver for a gentle float past lush tundra into the forested lowlands. Most people take out at the village of **Allakaket,** on the Arctic Circle where the Alatna intersects the Koyukuk, and fly back to Bettles. Itineraries range between four and seven days.

Hardier souls may choose to tackle the **Noatak.** Though a relatively easy course, the usual run—from a put-in at **Lake Matcharak** to the village of **Noatak,** near the Chukchi Sea on the west coast—spans about 350 miles (565 km) and takes about two to three weeks. So the challenge is not white water but weeks of dealing with weather, bears, health issues, gear problems, etc. Consult with Park Service staff to find a trip that matches your fitness and experience, and be sure to exercise due caution even on guided trips. ■

Opposite: Trees and other flora are sparse this far north.

Arctic National Wildlife Refuge

Arctic National Wildlife Refuge

http://arctic.fws.gov

▲ 217 C4 & 225

✉ Visitor informatio:
U.S. Fish & Wildlife
Service, 101 12th
Ave., Room 236,
Fairbanks

☎ 907/456-0250 or
800/362-4546

THANKS TO THE LONG-RUNNING CONTROVERSY OVER whether to drill for oil in the Arctic National Wildlife Refuge (ANWR), this 19.3-million-acre (7.8 million ha) hunk of northeast Alaska has become the nation's most famous wildlife refuge. Yet few people know much about it, and far fewer have ever been there.

ANWR is a tough place to get to (think little charter planes landing on gravel bars), a tough place to get around in (think trailless hiking and wilderness river running), and a tough place to get along with (think mosquitoes, days of fog, and bears). Ah, but the payoff is as big as the place. The refuge boasts the greatest diversity of flora and fauna of any park or refuge in the circumpolar Arctic. Look for wolves, moose, musk oxen, Dall sheep, and all three species of bear—grizzly, black, and polar. And don't forget the famous Porcupine caribou, all 123,000 of them, or the millions of birds representing 177 species.

The best hiking is in the **Brooks Range,** which reaches its widest point—110 miles (177 km) north to south—as it arcs through the refuge. Outfitters drop off trekkers on riverbanks or dry ridges, often in the company of guides—the Park Service works with more than three dozen authorized operators.

River running is increasingly popular, particularly on the **Kongakut,** the **Canning** (and its tributary, the **Marsh Fork**), the **Hulahula,** and the **Sheenjek.** The first three run north from the Brooks Range to the Arctic Ocean, though most trips stop short of the sea. Float down the Kongakut at the right time and you'll encounter herds of migrating caribou.

The Sheenjek flows south to the Porcupine River from the region's highest peaks, which top 9,000 feet (2,740 m). Mostly smooth with just a few Class II rapids, this Wild and Scenic River passes rocky pinnacles and lowland forests; watch for grizzlies, moose, beavers, and waterfowl. A series of visits to the Sheenjek area in the mid-1950s inspired conservationists Olaus and Margaret "Mardy" Murie to lobby for establishment of the refuge, which happened in 1960. ∎

Caribou herds

Many people know about Porcupine caribou due to the controversy over plans to drill for oil in the Arctic National Wildlife Refuge and whether such operations would harm the herd. At about 123,000 strong, it's an impressive herd, too, though far from being Alaska's largest. That honor goes to the Western Arctic herd, made up of almost 500,000 caribou. Altogether about a million caribou spend at least some of their time in Alaska. Some cross into Canada for part of the year; such long migrations are typical for these footloose critters. One radio-collared caribou walked 3,000 miles (4820 km) in a single year—the longest measured migration of any land mammal. ∎

Barrow

BARROW MAY NOT BE AT THE END OF THE EARTH, BUT IT IS unquestionably at the northern end of the United States—on the Arctic Ocean 375 miles (600 km) north of the Arctic Circle. This is hardcore land of the midnight sun, with the sun remaining above the horizon from May 10 to August 2—82 days straight.

In such a remote place visitors aren't surprised to find whale bones leaning against walls or seal meat drying on racks outside bunkerlike houses. Less expected are SUVs, racquetball courts, and the nearly $80-million high school. This town of 4,351 people, more than 60 percent of whom are Inupiat Eskimos, maintains a balance between the modern and the traditional.

Begin your visit by simply strolling the beach fronted by Stevenson Street to gape at the **Arctic Ocean.** (The sea off Barrow remains frozen ten months out of the year; even in high summer you'll spot drifting pack ice along the shore.) On the west end stand remnants of ancestral whalebone-and-sod houses—the Inupiat have lived here for at least 1,500 years.

Next, stop by the excellent new **Inupiat Heritage Center,** which displays artifacts and offers traditional craft demonstrations. Affiliated with the New Bedford Whaling National Historical Park in Massachusetts, the museum centers on whaling. In the 19th and 20th centuries New England whalers worked these waters with Inupiat help. Don't miss the featured exhibit, "The People of Whaling." The museum gift shop sells high-quality Inupiat crafts, including parkas and etched baleen.

Last but not least, take one of the guided tours of the town and vicinity, which feature historic sites, contemporary culture, and wildlife. Millions of birds, including snowy owls, nest and breed around Barrow, and polar bears roam the area. ■

A warmly dressed couple watches the sun set over the Arctic Ocean.

Barrow
🅐 217 B4
Visitor information
www.cityofbarrow.org
☎ 907/852-5211

Inupiat Heritage Center
www.nps.gov/inup
www.northslope.org/IHCSite
✉ 5421 North Star St.
☎ 907/852-4594
🕐 Closed weekends
💲 $$

Nary a tree to be seen on the tundra at Woolley Lagoon, on the Seward Peninsula.

More places to visit in the Bush

BERING LAND BRIDGE NATIONAL PRESERVE

Between 30,000 and 10,000 years ago the peopling of the Western Hemisphere began here, on the western tip of the Seward Peninsula, 55 miles (89 km) from Siberia. With much of the world's water locked up in ice, the shallow stretch of the Bering Sea between these two points lay exposed. Theory has it that as game animals wandered across, humans from Asia followed.

Most of the preserve's 2.8 million acres (1.1 million ha) are mosquito-infested tundra. Sane visitors will find the rolling hills of the Interior more conducive to hiking. Try the old lava flows around **Imuruk Lake** and the five maar (crater) lakes in the **Devil Mountains-Cape Espenberg** area.

To learn flight details to this preserve, stop by or contact the **visitor center** in Nome, which showcases woolly mammoth bones and a seven-foot (2.1 m) tusk. The most popular fly-in destination is **Serpentine Hot Springs,** which centers on a wooden tub in the steamy bathhouse and a bunkhouse-style public-use cabin that sleeps up to 20 people. Between soaks you can roam amid granite tors on the nearby ridges and watch for wildlife, including the occasional stray bird from Asia. 🗺 217 A3 ☎ 907/443-2522, www.nps.gov/bela

ST. LAWRENCE ISLAND

If you stand on the shore in **Gambell,** one of two main towns on St. Lawrence, and stretch your hand out west, you'll nearly penetrate Russian airspace. Okay, that's a slight exaggeration, but Gambell is much closer to Russia than to mainland Alaska. On a clear day you can easily see across the 38 intervening miles of the Bering Strait to mainland Asia. It's no wonder nearly all of the island's 1,358 residents, half of whom live in Gambell, are Siberian Yupik and speak Siberian Yupik as a first language (though they speak English, too).

Subsistence living remains common on this 95-mile-long (153 km) island; residents use traditional walrus-hide umiak boats to hunt walrus, bowhead whales, and seals. They're also known for their intricate ivory carvings, which visitors can purchase. The other 710 people, who live 39 miles (63 km) away in the town of **Savoonga,** supplement their hunting, fishing, and carving by herding some 10,000 reindeer, which were introduced to the island in 1900.

To meet these distinctive people and see the island's wildlife and striking scenery, catch a flight from Nome. For information on tours and lodging in Gambell, contact the **Sivuqaq Native Corporation.** 🗺 217 A3 ☎ 907/985-5826 ■

Travelwise

**Travelwise informaton
  236-240**
Planning your trip **236**
Getting around **236–238**
Practical advice **238–240**
Hotels & restaurants 241–260
Shopping 261–262
Entertainment 263
Activities 264–265

**Kayaks beached at the
mouth of Reid Glacier**

TRAVELWISE INFORMATION.

PLANNING YOUR TRIP

WHEN TO GO

Conventional wisdom dictates traveling to Alaska in summer to avoid harsh winter weather. In addition, many hotels, restaurants, and attractions reduce their hours or close altogether from mid-September to mid-May. That said, a growing number of visitors sing the praises of Alaska winters. They wax poetic about the peace and quiet, lack of crowds, joys of dog mushing, beauty of the snow, and dazzling displays of the northern lights.

Peak season runs from mid-May to mid-September. However, weather and other factors vary widely from region to region. In Fairbanks, for instance, July and August are the wettest months, whereas those months are among the driest in the Southeast.

When you check on weather, also ask about mosquitoes and other biting bugs—often the greater concern. In many areas the best combination of warm temperatures, low rainfall, and fewer biting bugs occurs from mid-May to early June and mid-August to early September.

If you plan to visit the Southeast, also factor in ships that cruise the Inside Passage, inundating small towns with passengers. Some travelers appreciate the company, but if you want to avoid the crowds, experience decent weather, and find most facilities open, visit the region between mid-May and early June or in early to mid-September.

WHAT TO TAKE

If you're planning a trek into the backcountry, you should largely know what you'll need—if not, reconsider going. But you may overlook a few nonstandard items, such as head nets or bear-proof food canisters. It's best to consult with the staff at a public lands office or your outfitter for more specifics.

Anyone planning to spend time outdoors should bring a light rainsuit, a waterproof cap or hat, sunglasses, and layers of warm, breathable, moisture-wicking clothing. If you're headed someplace like the Arctic coast or the Aleutians or planning a winter visit, pack additional tops and bottoms, plus a heavy coat and gloves. If you're going to a wet region, consider bringing rubber boots or buy a pair when you arrive. Otherwise, take hiking boots or sturdy walking shoes.

Also bring protection against biting insects—repellent, head nets, mosquito jackets, or whatever the locals advise. If you plan to visit in winter, you can skip the repellent.

Alaska is arguably the most informal of states. In small towns don't be surprised if you see someone in a flannel shirt, jeans, and knee-high rubber boots seated at a fancy restaurant. However, a number of restaurants, hotels, bars, resorts, and clubs, especially in Anchorage, require spiffier attire, though very seldom does it rise to the level of a jacket and tie for men or the equivalent for women.

GETTING AROUND

AIR TRAVEL

Ted Stevens Anchorage International Airport is Alaska's air transportation hub (tel 907/266-2525, www.dot.state .ak.us/anc). It lies 3 miles (4.8 km) southwest of downtown. Other major airports include **Fairbanks International Airport** (tel 907/474-2500 or 907/479-7407, www.dot.state .ak.us/faiiap), 3 miles (4.8 km) southwest of downtown, and **Juneau International Airport** (tel 907/789-7821), 9 miles (14.5 km) northwest of downtown.

Because this state has so few roads relative to its size, airplanes of all sorts and sizes play a prominent role. Remote Arctic

towns like **Kotzebue** offer daily jet service. More remote and smaller settlements, like **Adak,** in the Aleutians, welcome twice weekly Alaska Airlines flights. Smaller airlines with smaller planes—20-seaters or so—regularly service many otherwise isolated communities. Check with a travel agent, local visitor center, or chamber of commerce about flight availability to your chosen destinations.

Bush planes
Bush planes—commonly three- to six-passenger propeller planes, some on wheels or tundra tires, some on floats, and some on skis—offer scheduled flights or are available for charter. Bush planes can go almost anywhere, landing on lakes, riverbed gravel bars, beaches, and even glaciers. However, they are expensive—perhaps $200 to $600 an hour for the plane. Hours add up quickly.

Some travelers harbor concerns about small plane travel that are entirely appropriate. Crashes do occur now and then in Alaska, usually due to foul weather. While even cautious, experienced pilots with shipshape planes sometimes have accidents, more crashes stem from careless operators who are cavalier about dangerous weather or proper maintenance.

Choosing a reliable operator is more art than science, but you can take several steps to improve your odds. If the National Park Service, a cruise ship company, or other discerning entity regularly uses the operator, it's likely among the best. If the company is recommended by the local chamber of commerce and has been around for a decade or two and can demonstrate a good safety record, it's also a good bet. Don't be embarrassed to ask a company about its safety record or its pilots' levels of experience (though, of course, you'll have to take any replies with a grain of salt). Use your instincts and common sense, too. If you encounter a one-man operation out of a shack, and the pilot is downing vodka shots when you walk in, walk right back out. You can also search for an operator's safety record on the National Transportation Safety Board website (www.ntsb.gov).

As a passenger on a chartered flight, you also play an important safety role. First, urge your pilot to err on the side of caution if the weather seems risky. Pay attention to the safety lecture at the start of the flight and take note of the location of flotation devices, survival kit, etc. Bring along survival gear of your own, such as clothing that will keep you warm and dry if the pilot has to make an emergency landing in the wilderness. If you're carrying bear spray or compressed gas for a backpacking stove, ask the pilot to store it safely. With regard to comfort and convenience: Bring earplugs in case the pilot doesn't supply ear protection and carry your gear in small- to medium-size soft bags, not big, hard-shelled suitcases. Small planes adhere to space and weight restrictions and cargo and passengers must properly balance.

BUS TRAVEL
Public buses and shuttles are scarce in Alaska, though tour buses are common. Ask at local visitor centers or browse the Alaska Travel Industry Association website (www.travel alaska.com) for a listing of bus-tour companies.

BOAT TRAVEL
Alaska encompasses islands galore, more coastline than the lower 48 combined, and long navigable rivers that meander through roadless expanses. Thus, it's not surprising that boat travel is a popular option. Large cruise ships account for the lion's share, each year hauling hundreds of thousands of people to and around Alaska. These 2,000- to 3,000-passenger behemoths are balanced by

smaller cruise ships that accommodate up to 250 passengers.

Overseeing the state ferries, the **Alaska Marine Highway System** (P.O. Box 25535, Juneau, AK 99802 or 605 W. 4th Ave., Anchorage, AK 99501, tel 907/272-7116 or 800-642-0066, www.ferryalaska.com) is the other big player, transporting tens of thousands of people along the southeastern and south–central coasts, even into the Aleutians. Providing access to 32 Alaskan communities, the AMHS is an essential resource for exploring the Inside Passage.

If you want to transport your vehicle from the lower 48 to Alaska, start on the Washington State or British Columbia ferries and cross to Prince Rupert, B.C., where you can pick up the Alaska Marine Highway.

Operating on a much smaller scale are water taxis, which can take travelers to places not served by the cruise ships or ferries. While a few water taxis operate on more or less regular schedules, nearly all are for hire, just like a city cab. Weather and tide allowing, they'll drop you off at a little fishing village, a remote trailhead, or a public lands cabin. Water taxis are especially common in the Southeast and in Kachemak Bay. To locate water taxis, contact the local visitor center or chamber of commerce. Be sure to ask a few questions to make sure your water taxi company is reliable.

CAR TRAVEL
Most people who drive to Alaska cross over from Canada via the the **Alaska Highway**—aka the Alcan. (Another road, the **Top of the World Highway,** is rough gravel, provides few facilities, and is closed by snow for much of the year.) The Alaska Highway is paved and offers ample services, though it still passes through wilderness for most of its 1,390 miles (2,238 km) between Dawson Creek, B.C., and Delta Junction, Alaska. Travelers who'd like to drive the highway only one direction can close the loop

by taking their vehicle one way on the ferry.

While most of Alaska lacks roads, south–central and parts of the Interior include a handful—most of them paved, all of them scenic. However, scenery means you're driving in remote, wild country, so bring emergency gear, including ample clothing, food, water, spare tires, and tools in case you get stuck. To check road conditions and other driving information, dial 511 or visit http://511.alaska.gov.

Rental cars
Major airports host car-rental agencies, though sometimes you can get better rates from agency offices outside the airport. In popular parts of Alaska, summer gets very busy, so book months in advance. Rental cars are often available in towns that remain inaccessible by road, though not necessarily from major agencies. While a passenger car will suffice for most highways, you may need a 4WD, high-clearance vehicle on gravel highways and other roads.

TRAIN TRAVEL
Train travel in Alaska is limited, but the two existing options both follow scenic routes. In fact, the **White Pass & Yukon Route,** which runs between Skagway and Fraser, Bennett Lake, and Whitehorse, Canada, is primarily a tourist train (see pp. 88–89).

Primary train service is run by the state-owned **Alaska Railroad** (tel 907/265-2494 or 800/544-0552, www.alaskarail road.com or www.akrr.com). In summer it makes daily runs between Anchorage, Fairbanks, and Seward; a 7-mile (11 km) spur leads from Portage through the tunnel to Whittier.

Passengers can opt for first-class cars—offered by the railway and private tour companies. Visitors also can take such unique trains as the **Hurricane Turn Train,** which runs several days a week between Talkeetna and Hurricane—55 miles (89 km) one way, most along the beautiful Susitna River. The Hurricane is one of the nation's last flag-stop trains. Locals living in remote cabins or backpackers emerging from the forest can flag it down and hop on board.

PRACTICAL ADVICE

MAPS

State and city maps are available from local tourism offices and visitor centers. If you'd like more details of the entire state, try the *Alaska Atlas & Gazetteer* (by DeLorme Mapping). All public lands are plotted on broad-scale map brochures or detailed topographic maps. Contact the Alaska Public Lands Information Center for assistance.

SAFETY

Wild place that Alaska is, safety concerns revolve around the outdoors. Bears, for example, top the list of worries for most people (see pp. 134–135).

Though thousand-pound predators tend to grab one's attention, hypothermia is actually a greater menace. A day hike can turn deadly if you go out in shorts and a cotton sweatshirt in 50°F (10°C) weather and get soaked in a storm. Likewise, canoeing can quickly become a disaster if the wind comes up and you capsize in icy water. Be aware of weather-related concerns and prepare accordingly.

In an emergency, dial 911 to summon police, medical, or fire department help. (In some rural areas it is necessary to dial "0".) Some roads include emergency phones and contact stations.

TAXES & TIPPING

Rules for tipping waitresses, taxi drivers, hotel staff, etc., follow those elsewhere in the U.S.—15 to 20 percent for waitstaff, 10 to 15 percent for taxi drivers, and $1–5 per day for hotel maids. Guidelines for tipping tour operators are less standardized, but if you're on a small, personalized trip, a tip for good service is

appropriate—perhaps 10 percent of the overall cost.

Shoppers will be happy to learn that Alaska has no state sales tax, though some boroughs impose their own taxes.

TIME

Nearly all the state lies in the Alaska time zone, one hour earlier than Pacific time—except for the western two-thirds of the Aleutian Islands, which observe Hawaiian-Aleutian time, two hours earlier than Pacific time.

TRAVELERS WITH DISABILITIES

A largely wild and rural state, Alaska can be a difficult travel destination for those with disabilities. Major tour companies and government operations generally offer reasonable access and appropriate facilities. But in small towns and remote villages travelers with disabilities will encounter many obstacles. For more information, contact Access Alaska (tel 907/248-4777 or 800/770-4488 in Anchorage, 907/479-7940 or 800/770-7940 in Fairbanks, or 907/357-2588 in Wasilla, www.accessalaska.org).

VISITOR INFORMATION

The main statewide tourism information entity is the **Alaska Travel Industry Association** (2600 Cordova St., Suite 201, Anchorage, AK 99503, tel 907/929-2842, www.alaskatia.org or www.travelalaska.com). Before leaving home, ask the association to mail you its vacation planner, which is full of useful information.

Other useful information can be gathered from: **Alaska Public Lands Information Centers** (605 W. 4th Ave., Suite 105, Anchorage, AK 99501, tel 907/271-2737, or 250 Cushman St., Suite 1A, Fairbanks, AK 99701, tel 907/456-0527).

The **Southeast Alaska Discovery Center** (50 Main St, Ketchikan, AK 99901, tel 907/228-6220, or P.O. Box 359, Tok, AK 99780, tel 907/883-5667, www.nps.gov/aplic/) interagency

offices allow visitors one-stop shopping for information on state and federally managed public lands. Recreation permits and reservations for backcountry cabins may also be made here. The **Alaska Natural History Association** has outlets in each of these locations, selling natural history books, maps, and guides to all areas of Alaska. Fee for Ketchikan office in summer only.

WEBSITES

Helpful websites include www.travelalaska.com, www.alaska.com, and www.everythingalaska.com. Many other sites focus on specific destinations and activities, including:

www.nps.gov (National Park Service)
www.nps.gov/aplic (Alaska Public Lands Information Centers)
www.r7.fws.gov (U.S. Fish & Wildlife Service, Alaska region)
www.alaskastateparks.org (Alaska State Parks)
www.blm.gov (Bureau of Land Management)
www.fs.fed.us/r10/chugach or www.fs.fed.us/r10/tongass (Forest Service, Chugach and Tongass National Forests, Alaska Region)
www.state.ak.us (State of Alaska travel and recreation info).

YEARLY EVENTS

JANUARY

Kuskokwim 300 Bethel, mid-to late Jan., tel 907/543-3300, www.k300.org. Premier mid-distance sled-dog race with world-class mushers.

Polar Bear Jump Off Seward, 3rd weekend, tel 907/224-5230. The main event is the plunge (Sat.), when costumed folks leap into icy Resurrection Bay. Other events include the ugly fish toss, ice bowling, and a sled-dog race.

Anchorage Folk Festival Anchorage, two weekends in mid- to late Jan., tel 907/566-2334, www.anchoragefolkfestival.org. More than 120 acts take to the stages. While many are folk performers, genres also include jazz, bluegrass, klezmer, and Celtic. All concerts and workshops are free.

FEBRUARY
Alaska Ski for Women Anchorage, Super Bowl Sunday, tel 907/279-9581, www.alaskaskiforwomen.org. This benefit is the country's biggest cross-country ski event for women. Largely for laughs, with skiers dressed in hula skirts and old prom dresses.
Cordova Ice Worm Festival Cordova, early Feb., tel 907/424-7260, www.iceworm.com. Features fireworks, musical performances, food, and the parade, led by a 140-foot (43 m) ice worm.
Tent City Days Wrangell, early Feb., tel 907/874-3699, www .wrangell.com. Commemorates gold seekers who established a tent city in Wrangell around 1900. Features a long-john contest, bed races, the telling of tall tales, and a beard contest.
Yukon Quest International Sled Dog Race Fairbanks (even years) or Whitehorse, Yukon Territory (odd years), mid-Feb., tel 907/452-7954 or 867/668-4711 (Canada), www.yukonquest.com. A 1,000-mile (1,610 km) sled-dog race that follows gold rush trails and mail routes.
Fur Rendezvous Anchorage, mid-Feb. to early March, tel 907/274-1177, www.furrondy.net. Alaska's biggest winter festival offers three weeks of diversions, from a fur auction to the World Ice Bowling Championship.

MARCH
World Ice Art Championships Fairbanks, end of Feb. through late March, tel 907/451-8250, www.icealaska.com. The finest ice artists converge to create elaborate sculptures.
Festival of Native Arts Fairbanks, usually 1st Thurs. to Sat., tel 907/474-7181. Alaska Natives convene to perform and to display their arts and crafts.
Iditarod Trail Sled Dog Race From Anchorage to Nome, starts 1st Sat., tel 907/376-5155 or 907/248-6874, www.iditarod

.com. The granddaddy of all sled-dog races.
Bering Sea Ice Golf Classic Nome, 3rd Sat., tel 907/443-6624, www.nomealaska.org. A benefit tournament held on a makeshift six-hole course atop the frozen Bering Sea. Golfers use bright orange balls and spent shotgun shells for tees.

APRIL
Alaska Folk Festival Juneau, early to mid-April, tel 907/463-3316, www.juneau.com/aff/. Weeklong celebration of folk music draws about 450 musicians to Juneau from all over. Shows are free. Informal jam sessions are held around town.
Cama'i Dance Festival Bethel, early to mid-April, tel 907/543-2911, www.bethelarts .com. The festival attracts 400 to 500 dancers to revel in traditional dance. Many of the participants are Yupik Eskimo dancers.

MAY
Copper River Delta Shorebird Festival Cordova, early May, tel 907/424-7260, www.cordovachamber.com. Celebrates the arrival of millions of shorebirds at Copper River Delta. All sorts of workshops and birding trips.
Kachemak Bay Shorebird Festival Homer, early May, tel 907/235-7740, www.homeralaska .org/shorebird/htm. Birders can spot a hundred species a day. Includes workshops, field trips, boat tours, and sea kayak trips.
Little Norway Festival Petersburg, weekend closest to May 17, tel 907/772-4636, www .petersburg.org/visitor/littlenorway.html. Locals commemorate their Norwegian roots, the start of spring, U.S. Armed Forces Day, and the opening of the commercial fishing season. You'll find food, music, and a big parade featuring Norwegian costumes.
Juneau Jazz & Classics Juneau, late May, tel 907/463-3378, wwwjazzandclassics.org. World-class artists perform on Juneau stages during this

nine-day event, which includes blues, as well as jazz and classical.
Kodiak Crab Festival Kodiak, late May, tel 907/486-4782 or 800/789-4782, www.kodiak.org /crabfest/html. Five-day festival features crab fixed any way you can imagine. Also offers golf, tennis, fencing, and table tennis tournaments, as well as maritime poetry, Russian folk dancing, and a Native arts bazaar.

JUNE
Sitka Summer Music Festival Sitka, early June, tel 907/277-4852 (in June, tel 907/747-6774), www.sitkamusicfestival.org. This three-week chamber music series attracts world-class performers.
Colony Days Palmer, mid-to late June, tel 907/745-2880, www.palmerchamber.org. A parade, a street dance, wagon rides, craft fairs, and other activities commemorate Palmer's beginnings as a farming colony.
Midnight Sun Baseball Game Fairbanks, June 20/21/22, tel 907/451-0095, www.goldpanners.com/midnight_sun_game .html. On the summer solstice baseball teams start playing as the sun dips at 10:30 p.m. and continue till it rises high again.
Doyon, Limited Yukon 800 Fairbanks, late June, tel 907/456-6554, www.yukon800.com. In this "longest, toughest, roughest speedboat race in the world," contestants roar along 800 miles of the Chena, Tanana, and Yukon Rivers for two days.

JULY
Mount Marathon Race Seward, July 4, tel 907/224-8051, www.sewardak.org. Since about 1915, runners starting at sea level in Seward have raced 1.5 miles (2.4 km) up this 3,000-foot (914 m) mountain and back. The race draws 900 participants and tens of thousands of onlookers.
Moose Dropping Festival Talkeetna, 2nd weekend, tel 907/746-5000 or 907/733-2330. Moose scat is used in the Moose Dropping Toss. Another event is the Mountain Mother Contest,

in which competitors perform such feats as teetering across a 20-foot (6m) log wearing hip waders, holding two bags of groceries, and carrying a ten-pound (4.5 kg) doll on their backs.
World Eskimo-Indian Olympics Fairbanks, mid- to late July, tel 907/452-6646, www.weio.org. Alaska Native athletes gather for four days of competition in traditional events that derive from survival skills.
Golden Days Fairbanks, weekend closest to July 22, tel 907/452-1105, www.fairbanks chamber.org. For five days residents and visitors revel in summer via a huge parade, pancake breakfasts, a river regatta, the Rubber Duckie Race, and historical reenactments.
Southeast Alaska State Fair Haines, late July to mid-Aug., tel 907/766-2476, www.seakfair.org.

AUGUST
Tanana Valley State Fair Fairbanks, early Aug., tel 907/452-3750, www.tananavalleyfair.org.
Tanana Valley Sandhill Crane Festival Fairbanks, mid-Aug., tel 907/452-5162, www.creamers field.org. A celebration of the cranes that flock to Creamer's Field during fall migration.
Alaska State Fair Palmer, late Aug.-early Sept., tel 907/745-4827, www.alaskastatefair.org.

SEPTEMBER
Kodiak State Fair & Rodeo Kodiak, Labor Day weekend, tel 907/486-6380, www.kodiak.org.
Alaska Airlines' Autumn Classics Anchorage, mid- and late-Sept., tel 907/277-4852, www.sitkamusicfestival.org. Part of the Sitka Summer Music Festival, these two weekends of top chamber music take place in Anchorage.

OCTOBER
Make It Alaskan Festival Anchorage, 1st weekend, tel 907/279-0618, http://miafestival .com. Hundreds of Alaska artists and craftspeople gather to sell their wares.

Alaska Day Festival Sitka, mid-Oct., tel 907/747-5940, www.sitka.org. Commemorates the transfer of Alaska from Russia to the U.S., on October 18, 1867. Tours of historic sites, traditional Russian dancing, and a ball reflect the theme.
Alaska Federation of Natives Convention Location varies, mid- to late Oct., tel 907/274-3611, www.nativefeder ation.org. This weeklong event is the biggest Alaska Native gathering of the year, hosting 4,000 to 5,000 delegates. Many events, such as the arts and crafts fair and dance presentations, are open to the public.

NOVEMBER
WhaleFest Sitka, early Nov., tel 907/747-7964, www.sitkawhale fest.org. As humpback whales congregate in nearby waters, Sitka celebrates with whale-watching tours, slide shows, and workshops.
Alaska Bald Eagle Festival Haines, usually 2nd weekend, tel 907/766-3094, http://bald eaglefestival.org. Attracts bird experts, artists, and entertainers for several days of lectures, photography workshops, and guided eagle-viewing tours.
Athabascan Fiddlers Festival Fairbanks, mid-Nov., tel 907/474-5503, www.explorefairbanks .com. Celebrating the many Athabascan who took up fiddle playing and gave it a Native twist. Fiddle music takes center stage at this foot-stomping festival.

DECEMBER
Winterfest Talkeetna, each weekend, tel 907/733-2330, www.talkeetna-chamber.org. Celebrates December with arts, food, music, and goofy contests, notably the Bachelor's Auction and Wilderness Women Contest.
Ivory Jacks Invitational Golf Tourney Fairbanks, weekend nearest Dec. 21, tel 907/451-9401. On a weekend day near the winter solstice, golfers slog it out in the snow on a special five-hole course.

FURTHER READING
Updated and published annually for nearly six decades, The Milepost is a large-format, 784-page book that describes what you'll find along every road in Alaska, including advertisements for lodges, outfitters, and attractions. The beauty of The Milepost is that it pinpoints locations to the tenth of a mile and offers practical information about road conditions, activities, and the like.
   From the same publisher, the regularly updated Alaska Wilderness Guide covers remote villages and settlements, national and state parks, other public lands, attractions, and activities.
   Classics about Alaska still merit a read, such as John Muir's Travels in Alaska, written in 1915. A generation later, in 1944, naturalist Adolph Murie wrote The Wolves of Mount McKinley. Murie followed up in 1961 with the broader study, A Naturalist in Alaska. Margaret Murie penned another classic, Two in the Far North, in 1968. But arguably the single best book ever written about traveling in Alaska is John McPhee's Coming into the Country, published in 1977.
   Alaska: Saga of a Bold Land (2003), by Walter Borneman, is a good general history, as is Alaska: An American Colony (2002), by Stephen Haycox. Many books focus on narrower aspects of Alaska's past, such as Wager with the Wind: The Don Sheldon Story (1982), by James Greiner, which shares tales of a pioneer bush pilot. Tappan Adney's The Klondike Stampede (1994) captures the adventure of the Klondike gold rush. One notable account of Alaska Native history is The Epic of Qayaq: The Longest Story Ever Told by My People (1995), by Lela Kiana Oman, which includes traditional stories of the Inupiat.
   Alaska Native writers have produced fascinating chronicles of recent and contemporary life, and resident authors also have used fiction and poetry to examine life in Alaska (see p. 46).

HOTELS & RESTAURANTS

Alaska's hotels and restaurants share a few traits that travelers should note. To begin with, they're generally more expensive than their counterparts in the lower 48. Many hotels and restaurants open only for the summer season—generally mid-May to mid-September. Even those that stay open year-round often close for extended periods in winter. Smaller travel-oriented businesses—remote lodges, rafting outfits, tour boats—may keep unpredictable hours and often set their seasons based on weather, perhaps opening later in May or staying open later in September. Access for disabled travelers is decent in cities or popular tourist areas, but spotty in rural areas. Check access with your destination or check the Access Alaska website (www.accessalaska.org).

ACCOMMODATIONS

Accommodations in Alaska range from posh urban hotels and luxurious wilderness lodges through mid-range local hotels and bed-and-breakfasts to hostels and public-use cabins. Be aware that harsh weather, high costs, and isolation pose a burden to hostelries in remote areas, so they may not be as tidy as you might expect, but they still may be wonderful places. The following accommodations lie close to attractions listed in this book or are destinations in themselves.

Reservations

It's best to make reservations early, particularly during peak season, because some places book months in advance. Reservations also are advised when traveling to remote areas that have few options.

Lodging chains

Though major chains have made inroads, Alaska still has far fewer of these than in the rest of the U.S. For the most part the local places are fine, even outstanding, and offer a richer experience. But quality varies widely, so ask visitor centers for suggestions, especially out in the Bush.

Bed-and-breakfasts

Bed-and-breakfasts are prevalent —related organizations include the Bed & Breakfast Association of Alaska, www.alaskabba.com; Anchorage Alaska Bed & Breakfast Association, tel 907/272-5909 or 888/584-5147, www.anchorage-bnb.com; Fairbanks Association of Bed & Breakfasts, www.ptialaska .net/~fabb; Kenai Peninsula Bed & Breakfast Association, www.kenaipeninsulabba.com; Bed & Breakfast Association of Alaska INNside Passage Chapter, www.accommodations-alaska .com; and Mat-Su Bed & Breakfast Association, www.alaskabnb hosts.com.

Hostels

Alaska boasts dozens of hostels where travelers of all ages and backgrounds can find rooms or bunks at bargain rates. Guests may have to deal with such restrictions as day-time closures, separate dorm rooms for men and women, and curfews. It's best to bring your own sleeping bag or linens, though bedding is often available for rent. To learn more about Alaska hostels, go to www .hostels.com.

Wilderness lodges

Hundreds of lodges dot Alaska's backcountry, enabling non-backpackers to experience the wilds. Access to many of these lodgings is limited to plane or boat. While most are geared to fishers, a growing number offer a broader focus on ecology, wildlife-watching, and scenery, providing such activities as flightseeing, hiking, canoeing, rafting, and a host of winter activities. Because they're remote, often luxurious, and provide gourmet cuisine, many wilderness lodges are extremely expensive, running perhaps $300 to $500 (and up) a day per person. That often includes meals, guides, and gear, and sometimes includes transportation to the lodge.

Camping

While backcountry camping opportunities are practically limitless, Alaska has relatively few developed campgrounds. In the lower 48, national parks, national forests, and state parks usually offer the best shot at developed sites, but in Alaska such lands include few or no campgrounds. For information on where to camp contact the Alaska Public Lands Information Centers (tel 907/271-2737, www.nps.gov /aplic). Ask about the hundreds of remote public-use cabins, especially on Forest Service and Alaska State Park lands.

RESTAURANTS

Alaska eateries vary widely. Often, they are quite informal, pitching together people in work boots or outdoor gear with those in suits and ties. Most provide huge servings. And they serve seafood, lots and lots of fresh seafood, even in the Interior. There doesn't seem to be any dish Alaskans won't add halibut to.

HOW TO USE THESE LISTS

The hotels and restaurants listed here have been grouped first according to their region, then alphabetically within their price category. Prices, phone numbers, closing dates, and other data change often; check important information with the businesses in which you're interested. Reservations are advised.

The letter L is used for lunch, D for dinner.

Credit cards

If a business accepts at least three major credit cards, it gets the credit card symbol. If it accepts one or two, those cards are listed using these abbreviations: AE (American Express), MC (Mastercard), or V (Visa).

HOTELS & RESTAURANTS

◼ SOUTHEAST ALASKA

KETCHIKAN

🏨 🍴 WESTCOAST CAPE FOX LODGE
$$$
800 VENETIA WAY
TEL 907/225-8001 or
866/225-8001
FAX 907/225-8286
www.capefoxcorp.com/cflodge
.html
Ketchikan's most elegant
hotel boldly announces its
Northwest Native flavor out
front with a circle of six
totems. Inside is a large
collection of Tlingit and
Haida art and artifacts.
Beneath massive beams in
the lobby are overstuffed
chairs, a library, and a stone
fireplace. The rooms are
spacious, with hilltop views
of either Tongass Narrows
or Deer Mountain. Those
seated in the **Heen Kahidi
Dining Room** will take in
floor-to-ceiling views of
downtown and the marina
while savoring seafood, steak,
pasta, and chicken dishes.
🛈 72 rooms, 2 suites 🅿
🚭 ⬌ 🅂 All major cards

🏨 MADAME'S MANOR
$$-$$$
324 CEDAR ST.
TEL/FAX 907/247-2774 or
877/531-8159
www.madamesmanor.com
A sumptuous Victorian bed-
and-breakfast in the historic
Nob Hill section of Ketch-
ikan, with views of the town
and harbor. From the china
to the Waterford crystal,
antique furniture, and fine
breakfasts, this place has
class. The deck overlooking
Tongass Narrows is an
appealing perch during tea.
🛈 3 suites, 2 apartments
🅿 🚭 3 ⬌ 🅂
🅂 All major cards

🍴 ANNABELLE'S KEG & CHOWDER HOUSE
$$
326 FRONT ST.
TEL 907/225-6009
On the ground floor of
the historic Gilmore Hotel,
Annabelle's has been on
Ketchikan's waterfront since
1927. Annabelle herself is
no longer with us, but her
casual Victorian restaurant
continues to serve several
kinds of chowder and beer—
as the name promises—plus
fresh seafood (try the halibut
Olympia), steaks, prime rib,
and chicken. The restaurant
is split between the down-
home lounge and somewhat
fancier parlor (no smoking).
Both are local hangouts with
a friendly atmosphere.
🪑 120 🚭 🅂 All major
cards

WRANGELL

🏨 RAIN HAVEN PRIVATE FLOATING LODGE
$$$
TEL 907/874-2549
www.rainwalkerexpeditions.com
/rainhaven.html
This custom houseboat
provides a unique Alaska
experience for up to five
guests. It features a full galley
(stocked with staples), a hot
shower, and a bathroom, plus
extras like featherbeds and
a library. You can board it
dockside near Wrangell and
enjoy its amenities or meet
the houseboat anchored in a
remote location, where your
neighbors are bears, hump-
back whales, and eagles
(kayak or canoe provided for
shore access). Safety gear
includes a marine radio and
other equipment.
🛈 1 boat (sleeps 5)

🏨 BRUCE HARDING'S OLD SOURDOUGH LODGE
$$-$$$
1104 PENINSULA AVE.
TEL 907/874-3613 or
800/874-3613
FAX 907/874-3455
www.akgetaway.com
On the docks, this pretty

HOTELS
An indication of the maxi-
mum high-season cost of a
double room with breakfast is
given by $ signs. Rooms may
often be available for less
than the indicated price.

$$$$$	Over $300
$$$$	$200–$300
$$$	$120–$200
$$	$80–$120
$	Under $80

RESTAURANTS
An indication of the cost
of a three-course dinner,
including interesting rather
than the cheapest menu
options, is given by $ signs.
Less expensive meals will be
available. Drinks are excluded.

$$$$$	Over $75
$$$$	$50–$75
$$$	$35–$50
$$	$20–$35
$	Under $20

lodge is made from hand-
milled Alaska red cedar. The
rooms aren't luxurious, but
they're comfortable and offer
touches like Alaska Native
art, handmade quilts, and
harbor views. Guests can get
three home-cooked squares,
featuring, of course, sourdough bread.
🛈 16 🚭 🅂 All major cards

PETERSBURG

🏨 SCANDIA HOUSE
$$-$$$
110 N. NORDIC DR.
TEL 907/772-4281 or
800/722-5006
FAX 907/772-4301
www.scandiahousehotel.com
This European-style hotel is
immaculate. Though it has
been a fixture in downtown
Petersburg since 1905, it was
completely rebuilt following
a 1994 fire. The exterior
rosemaling reflects the
town's Norwegian roots.
Ample rooms have a bright,
contemporary feel.
🛈 33 🅿 🚭 ⬌
🅂 All major cards

COASTAL COLD STORAGE
$
306 N. NORDIC DR.
TEL 907/772-4177 or 877/257-4767 (outside Alaska)
Petersburg is a fishing town, and Coastal Cold Storage gives visitors a chance to enjoy the fruits of that industry. Primarily a place for anglers to bring their catch for processing, this company runs a retail shop where you can buy fresh halibut beer bits, fish chowder, scallops, crab, and other seafood.
Closed D / All major cards

SITKA

ROCKWELL LIGHTHOUSE
$$$-$$$$
VIA 1315 HALIBUT POINT RD.
TEL/FAX 907/747-3056
This four-story home was built in the shape of a lighthouse, and, indeed, its rooftop light meets Coast Guard specs. It sits on an island in Sitka Sound about a mile from town—the owner will run guests out in a skiff, or they can do it themselves. The views are incredible, the decor nautical (think wood and brass), and it does have an interior spiral staircase, just like a real lighthouse. Up to eight people can sleep in the four rooms, but no matter the size of your party, you must rent the whole house. For summer visits you may need to reserve up to a year in advance.
4 / None

ALASKA OCEAN VIEW BED & BREAKFAST INN
$$-$$$
1101 EDGECUMBE DR.
TEL 907/747-8310 or 888/811-6870
FAX 907/747-3440
www.sitka-alaska-lodging.com
This elegant two-story shoreline house commands views of Sitka Sound and Mount Edgecumbe. The airy rooms with private baths include such modern amenities as DVD/VCR players and data ports. Some rooms have sofas, fireplaces, and whirlpool baths.
3 / All major cards

SITKA HOTEL
$-$$
118 LINCOLN ST.
TEL 907/747-3288
FAX 907/747-8499
www.sitkahotel.com
Here since the late '30s, the Sitka was recently renovated. Rooms are modest, but they and the lobby offer Victorian charm. Some have private baths; some share baths down the hall. There's also a restaurant and the nautically named Bilge Bar.
60 / All major cards

SOMETHING SPECIAL

LUDVIG'S BISTRO
Ludvig's is hands-down the best restaurant in Sitka and one of the best in Alaska. Though small and informal, it turns out superb, imaginative food, such as wild paella à la Andalucia, which features saffron rice, prawns, scallops, clams, calamari, and chicken and chorizo sausage mixed with vegetables and spices. Check out the daily specials; the chefs continually invent new dishes, taking advantage of the fresh seafood. The food's Mediterranean accent is reflected in the warm yellows and coppers that brighten this amiable bistro. In addition to elaborate dinners, Ludvig's serves simple (and excellent) lunches and Spanish-style tapas in the afternoons. Reservations recommended. The bistro closes for long periods in fall and winter.
$$-$$$$
256 KATLIAN ST.
TEL 907/966-3663
www.ludvigsbistro.com
25 / Closed Sun. & Mon. / All major cards

BACK DOOR CAFÉ
$
104 BARRACKS ST.
TEL 907/747-8856
The official address is on Barracks Street, but you actually have to slip down an alley to reach the Back Door's main entrance—hence the name. A favorite local hangout, especially among the literary and artistic set, this café is loud and lively. It offers make-your-own bagel sandwiches, coffee drinks, and the claim to fame: great baked goods. Try the cranberry-walnut scones or poppy-seed cake.
35 / All major cards

JUNEAU

PEARSON'S POND LUXURY INN & ADVENTURE SPA
$$$-$$$$$
4541 SAWA CIRCLE
TEL 907/789-3772 or 888/658-6328
FAX 907/790-1965
www.pearsonspond.com
This exquisite log house is tucked into the woods on a pond close to Mendenhall Glacier, a few miles north of downtown. With fireplaces, whirlpool tubs for two, outdoor hot tubs, an indoor fountain, and flowers everywhere, the inn aims for a romantic mood. The "adventure spa" portion of the inn's name is manifested by yoga on the deck, massages, exercise equipment, and the many activities available nearby, such as mountain biking, paddling around the pond, hiking, and winter sports and activities.
5 suites, 2 off-site condos / All major cards

SOMETHING SPECIAL

ALASKA'S CAPITAL INN
This B&B just turned 100 and has never looked better, having been restored in 2003.

Built in 1906 by gold rush pioneer John Olds, this four-story mansion perches atop a hillside with a grand waterfront view. The historic building is complemented by period antiques, notably the array of beds, including a carved king sleigh bed and an oak spindle bed. The inn also features VCRs, high-speed Internet access, and an outdoor hot tub. The top floor has been converted into a single elegant room, the Governor's Suite. Reserve early for summer stays.

$$$-$$$$
113 W. 5TH ST.
TEL 907/586-6507 or
888/588-6507
FAX 907/586-6508
www.alaskacapitalinn.com
[i] 7 [S] [cards] All major cards

[H] WESTMARK BARANOF [R] HOTEL
$$$-$$$$
127 N. FRANKLIN ST.
TEL 907/586-2660 or
800/544-0970
FAX 907/586-8315
www.westmarkhotels.com
/juneau.php
The understated rich woods, the embroidered chairs, and the old-money atmosphere in the grand lobby suggest power, and since its opening in 1939 this downtown landmark has indeed been a home away from home for legislators, lobbyists, and corporate execs. It offers a wide range of rooms. To escape street noise and for better views, ask for a room on the upper floors. The Baranof has two restaurants: one casual, the other a place to close big deals, aptly named the **Gold Room.**
[i] 196 [P] [S] [arrow]
[cards] All major cards

[H] SENTINEL ISLAND LIGHTHOUSE
$$
TEL 907/586-5338
The accommodations may be rustic in this 34-foot (10 m)

decommissioned lighthouse, but it has a great location—on a six-acre (2.4 ha) island about 25 miles (40 km) northwest of downtown. Guests can watch breaching whales, wave at passing ferries, and stroll the island. There are six bunks, a tent platform, and basic cooking and bathroom facilities. The lighthouse is operated by the Gastineau Channel Historical Society, which rents it at a reasonable rate, but don't overlook the fact that you'll have to pay a bit to get out to the island by charter boat, helicopter, or sea kayak.
[i] 6

SOMETHING SPECIAL

[R] FIDDLEHEAD RESTAURANT & BAKERY/DI SOPRA
This establishment comprises two restaurants: downstairs the Fiddlehead Restaurant & Bakery, upstairs Di Sopra. The Fiddlehead is casual and serves breakfast, lunch, and dinner in a room lighted by stained glass. Care for Alaska fisherman's pie, halibut tacos, or shrimp-and-halibut quesadillas? Don't neglect the bakery, known for breads like chocolate chip cherry brioche and desserts like interstellar chocolate love cake. For dinner only, Di Sopra's is an elegant, candlelit room with mountain views. Start with truffled elk carpaccio or baked cambozola cheese and enjoy an entrée of fisherman's stew in fennel-and-saffron broth.
$-$$$
429 W. WILLOUGHBY AVE.
TEL 907/586-3150
FAX 907/586-1644
www.thefiddlehead.com
[seats] 35 in Fiddlehead,
60 in Di Sopra [P] [S]
[cards] All major cards

[R] HANGAR ON THE WHARF
$-$$$
2 MARINE WAY, NO. 106

TEL 907/586-5018
www.hangaronthewharf.com
In a made-over hangar where Alaska Airlines got its start, the Hangar still roars on occasion as floatplanes take off from the channel not 50 feet (15 m) from the front door. An energetic crowd often jams this place—perhaps for the beer list that tops a hundred varieties. You'll find the expected pub fare, but the Hangar also serves finer dishes, such as pepper scallops, jambalaya, coconut prawns, and a cognac pork plate. On a sunny day the patio overlooking the water is a pleasure.
[seats] 175 [P] [S] [cards] All major cards

[R] THANE ORE HOUSE SALMON BAKE
$$
4400 THANE RD.
TEL 907/586-3442
One of Alaska's oldest and most authentic salmon bakes occupies a waterfront building 4 miles (6 km) south of downtown—take the free shuttle. All-you-can-eat salmon, of course, but also halibut, barbecued ribs, baked beans, corn bread, and salad.
[seats] 200 [P] [closed] Closed in winter [S] [cards] MC, V

[R] THE HISTORIC SILVERBOW INN
$
120 2ND ST.
TEL 907/586-4146 or
800/586-4146
FAX 907/586-4242
www.silverbowinn.com
The Silverbow is one of Alaska's idiosyncratic gems. First, it's a bakery—Alaska's oldest, having baked its first loaf of sourdough bread in the 1890s. In addition to fresh breads, the bakery produces scrumptious chocolate cheesecakes, peanut butter mousse cakes, and honest-to-God New York bagels. Second, the Silverbow is an excellent

breakfast and lunch place, featuring imaginative salads, sandwiches, and soups, mostly for takeout but also to munch at its few tables or in the outdoor beer garden. Third, the Silverbow is a downtown inn, with six small but nice rooms upstairs. Fourth, the Silverbow is a social center, with a large room for live music, dinner theater, and first-run independent and art films.
🛏 20 🅿 🚫 Closed D 🚭
🎴 All major cards

ADMIRALTY ISLAND

🏨 THAYER LAKE LODGE
$$$$$
TEL 907/789-5646 or 907/788-3203 (summer), 907/247-8897 or 707/928-5523 (winter)
FAX 907/247-7053
www.thayerlakelodge.com
The Nelsons built this lodge by hand in the mid-1950s, and the family still owns it. It's one of the few old-time wilderness lodges not geared primarily toward anglers. The Nelsons also reach out to greenhorns, offering to guide them. The lodge generally requires a six-day stay, which the lodge will tailor to fit the party's desires—Admiralty Island's famous brown bears, the lush rain forest, fishing for salmon, canoeing Thayer Lake, or learning to kayak. The two cabins include kitchens, hot showers, flush toilets, and fireplaces, and each sleeps up to five people.
🛏 2 cabins 🅿 🚫 Closed in winter 🚭 🎴 MC, V

GLACIER BAY/GUSTAVUS

🏨 BEAR TRACK INN
🍴 $$$$$
255 RINK CREEK RD.
TEL 907/697-3017 or 888/697-2284
FAX 907/697-2284
www.beartrackinn.com
This luxurious spruce-log inn sits on acres of wildflower meadows and forest facing

Icy Strait. The lobby features a 30-foot (9 m) ceiling, a stone fireplace, and hand-crafted furnishings throughout, including not one but two moose-antler chandeliers. The rooms are spacious and contain "rustic-fancy" appointments. The restaurant serves guests morning, noon, and night and nonguests for dinner, which features a range of fare, from steak and seafood to caribou and musk ox. The inn offers a full menu of outings, as well.
🛏 14 🅿 🚫 Closed in winter 🚭 🎴 All major cards

🏨 GLACIER BAY COUNTRY INN
$$$$$
TEL 907/697-2288 or 800/628-0912
FAX 907/697-2289
www.glacierbayalaska.com
The inn sits on 160 acres (65 ha) of rain forest and meadows 4 miles (6 km) out of Gustavus on the road to Bartlett Cove. You can't miss this three-story log castle replete with dormers, gables, cupolas, and porches. Around the main building are five cabins, a gazebo, and the organic vegetable garden that provides for the inn's renowned meals. Inside are five theme rooms, a library, and the dining room, where guests savor such simple treasures as wild berries picked from the adjacent forest, tea-smoked breast of duck, and salmon en croute with green peppercorn sauce. The innkeepers have a passion for fishing and offer many angling excursions, though they'll also take you hiking or whale-watching.
🛏 10 🅿 🚫 Closed in winter 🚭 🎴 All major cards

SOMETHING SPECIAL

🏨 GUSTAVUS INN AT
🍴 GLACIER BAY

This might not be the swankiest lodge nor the fanciest restaurant in the Glacier Bay orbit, but many think it's the best. Personal and informal, the place bears the imprint of its owners, whose family has been running it for nearly four decades. They know the area and can tell guests where to pick wild strawberries or find the best spot to hook a Dolly Varden. Daily they drive people to Bartlett Cove and the national park visitor center to go on naturalist-led hikes. They also prepare notable food for their guests and, at fixed-price ($$) family-style dinners, for the public. Much of that food comes from the inn's enormous garden or surrounding meadows and forest.
$$$$$
MILE 1, GUSTAVUS RD.
TEL 907/697-2254 or 800/649-5220
FAX 907/697-2255
www.gustavusinn.com
🛏 11 🅿 🚫 Closed in winter 🚭 🎴 All major cards

🏨 ANNIE MAE LODGE
$$-$$$$
TEL 907/697-2346 or 800/478-2346
www.anniemae.com
One of the few places in the Glacier Bay area that stays open year-round, this pretty, two-story lodge sits in a meadow on the Good River, a five-minute walk from the coast. The views from the veranda take in forest and mountains and the river. The price includes three ample and tasty meals a day and transportation from Juneau. The staff can arrange almost any outing.
🛏 11 🅿 🚫 🎴 All major cards

🏨 GLACIER BAY LODGE
$$-$$$$
179 BARTLETT COVE RD.
TEL 907/697-4000, 907/264-4600, or 888/229-8687

HOTELS & RESTAURANTS

FAX 907/258-3668
www.visitglacierbay.com
This massive-timbered lodge boasts two unique privileges. One, it's the only lodging inside Glacier Bay National Park. Two, the park visitor center is in the lodge, so guests can take advantage of all the park's organized activities, notably guided hikes, kayak trips, and naturalist-led boat tours of the bay. But the lodge offers more than location. It is a comfortably rustic place virtually surrounded by old-growth rain forest and offers guests and park visitors alike a good restaurant, a popular bar, mountain bike and fishing gear rentals, a gift shop with authentic Alaska Native arts and crafts, and a large stone fireplace that holds great appeal after a day out amid the glaciers.
🛈 50 🅿 🕒 Closed in winter 🚫 🖸 All major cards

HAINES

🏨 HOTEL HÄLSINGLAND
🍴 $-$$
13 FORT SEWARD DR.
TEL 907/766-2000 or 800/542-6363
FAX 907/766-2060
www.hotelhalsingland.com
Listed on the National Register of Historic Places, the Hälsingland once served as the commanding officer's quarters at Fort Seward—the historic military facility. The lovely old Victorian has been updated without losing any of its charm. The hotel also harbors one of the best eateries in Haines, the **Commander's Room Restaurant,** which relies on its cook's garden for herbs and greens and on the Chilkoot Inlet for fresh seafood. Dishes tend toward the innovative, such as seared wild Alaska salmon in a rhubarb-ginger chutney.
🛈 60 🅿 🕒 Closed early

Nov.–early May (restaurant closes mid-Sept.) 🚫 🖸 All major cards

SKAGWAY

🏨 THE HISTORIC SKAGWAY INN
$$-$$$
655 BROADWAY AT 7TH
TEL 907/983-2289 or 888/752-4929
FAX 907/983-2713
www.skagwayinn.com
This inn occupies one of the Klondike Gold Rush National Historical Park buildings. Built in 1897, it began life as a brothel, and each room is named after one of the original working girls. In 2004 the owners remodeled the inn, restoring its Victorian glory with cast-iron beds and period antiques. Breakfast is served downstairs in **Olivia's Restaurant** (open to the public for lunch and dinner).
🛈 10 🅿 🕒 Closed in winter 🚫 🖸 All major cards

🏨 THE WHITE HOUSE
$$-$$$
475 8TH AVE. AT MAIN ST.
TEL 907/983-9000
FAX 907/983-9010
www.atthewhitehouse.com
Built in 1902 by a gambler and saloon owner, who apparently did well at both professions, this large, two-story white clapboard house is in a quiet residential neighborhood two blocks from Skagway's main drag. This Victorian beauty has aged well and still boasts much of the original woodwork. Rooms are furnished in period antiques, and the beds are graced by fine hand-made quilts.
🛈 10 🅿 🚫 🖸 All major cards

🍴 THE STOWAWAY CAFÉ
$$-$$$
205 CONGRESS WAY
TEL 907/983-3463
This dockside café fittingly

HOTELS
An indication of the maximum high-season cost of a double room with breakfast is given by $ signs. Rooms may often be available for less than the indicated price.
$$$$$	Over $300
$$$$	$200–$300
$$$	$120–$200
$$	$80–$120
$	Under $80

RESTAURANTS
An indication of the cost of a three-course dinner, including interesting rather than the cheapest menu options, is given by $ signs. Less expensive meals will be available. Drinks are excluded.
$$$$$	Over $75
$$$$	$50–$75
$$$	$35–$50
$$	$20–$35
$	Under $20

serves a lot of fresh seafood. Try the hot scallop-and-bacon salad or the prawns with Gorgonzola. The café also offers landlubber dishes, such as steaks, Thai curry, or smoked ribs. The Stowaway is very popular with locals and travelers, so reservations are recommended.
🪑 40 🅿 🕒 Closed in winter 🚫 🖸 All major cards

ANCHORAGE & MAT-SU

ANCHORAGE

SOMETHING SPECIAL

🏨 HOTEL CAPTAIN
🍴 COOK
Though national hotel chains have moved into Anchorage in force, the venerable Captain Cook remains at the top of the heap. The building encompasses an entire block with three sky-scraping towers. In homage to its namesake explorer the hotel pursues a nautical theme in its rooms. Amenities include a

dozen shops, an athletic center, a business center, and four restaurants. The best of the latter is the **Crow's Nest Restaurant,** also one of the city's finest restaurants. As the name implies, it nests atop one of the towers and commands grand views of the Chugach Mountains and, appropriately, Cook Inlet. It's especially noted for its 10,000-bottle wine cellar.

$$$$-$$$$$
939 W. 5TH AVE.
TEL 907-276-6000 or
800/843-1950
FAX 907/343-2298
www.captaincook.com
[i] 547 [P] [⇄] [📺] [🏊]
[🅢] [🅢] All major cards

🏨 THE HISTORIC ANCHORAGE HOTEL
$$$$
330 E. ST.
TEL 907/272-4553 or
800/544-0988
FAX 907/277-4483
www.historicanchoragehotel.com
This small downtown hotel has a big history. Beloved humorist Will Rogers and pioneer aviator Wiley Post slept here two days before they died in a tragic plane crash near Barrow. Alaska's most renowned painter, Sydney Laurence, lived in the hotel for years and created many of his masterful landscapes in a studio in the lobby. This 1916 building has been nicely renovated, with dark cherrywood furnishings and contemporary amenities like high-speed Internet and large-screen digital TVs. Check out the photos in the upstairs hallways.
[i] 26 [P] [🅢] [⇄]
[🅢] All major cards

🏨 INLET TOWER HOTEL 🍴 & SUITES
$$$-$$$$
1200 L ST.
TEL 907/276-0110 or
800/544-0786
FAX 907/258-4914
www.inlettower.com

Completed in 1951, this 14-story building on the edge of downtown was Alaska's first skyscraper, and its views of Cook Inlet and the Chugach Mountains remain wonderful. After a recent large-scale remodeling, the place has a light, clean, modern feel and many new amenities, including spacious suites, large-screen TVs, and top-end linens. It also houses **Mick's at the Inlet,** a fine restaurant with an elegant air.
[i] 180 [🛏] 100 [P] [🅢] [⇄]
[🅢] [🅢] All major cards

🏨 15 CHANDELIERS B&B INN
$$$
14020 SABINE ST.
TEL 907/345-3032
FAX 907/345-3990
www.15chandeliers.com
Yes, chandeliers dangle everywhere—and there's a lot of everywhere in this 7,000-square-foot (630 sq m) mansion with a vast lawn and flower-bedecked backyard patio. Public rooms are spacious and elegant; especially notable is the grand, double winding staircase. Each of the five distinctive rooms flaunts a theme, such as the Prussian Room and the Scottish Room. Above the bed in the Captain Room is a painting of a stereotypical sea dog wearing a white cap and smoking a pipe.
[i] 5 [P] [🅢] [🅢] All major cards

🏨 COPPER WHALE INN
$$-$$$
440 L ST.
TEL 907/258-7999 or
888/942-5346
FAX 907/258-6213
www.copperwhale.com
This tidy little inn sits on a hillside on the west end of downtown, from which it commands views of Cook Inlet, the Alaska Range, and the Mount Spurr volcano. Note the binoculars on the windowsill. They're for

scanning the waters below for seals or beluga whales, which are dear to innkeeper and marine biologist Tony Carter. His vocation also explains the striking photos of Alaska's natural charms that adorn the inn's walls. This big 1939 home has been well kept, from the brass-trimmed fireplace and original pine floors to the lush flower gardens.
[i] 15 [P] [🅢] [🅢] All major cards

SOMETHING SPECIAL

🍴 THE MARX BROS. CAFÉ
The owners bill their renowned restaurant as serving "innovative contemporary cuisine." That phrase hardly captures the flavor of halibut baked in a macadamia-nut crust with a coconut curry sauce and mango chutney or wild Alaska salmon basted with sun-dried tomato butter. The desserts aren't bad, either—the white chocolate coffee tower, for instance, consists of chocolate cake topped with white chocolate espresso mousse with a chocolate glaze and amaretto crème anglaise. The remarkably high quality stems in part from an intimate focus—no lunch and only about 60 dinners a night, five nights a week, in this charming little 1916 wood frame house with inlet views.
$$$$-$$$$$
627 W. 3RD AVE.
TEL 907/278-2133
FAX 907/258-6279
www.marxcafe.com
[i] 46 [P] [🕐] Closed Sun. & Mon. in summer, Mon. & Tues. in winter [🅢] [🅢] All major cards

🍴 RISTORANTE ORSO
$$$-$$$$
737 W. 5TH AVE. AT G ST.
TEL 907/222-3232
www.orsoalaska.com
Pass through the lively downstairs bar and step

upstairs into a quiet realm of Oriental rugs, reddish walls, and a striking slate-framed fireplace. This Tuscan inn setting suits the osso buco (braised lamb) and the gemelli pasta sautéed in garlic cream sauce with scallops, clams, mussels, shrimp, and rockfish. Orso serves many traditional Italian pasta dishes, and at times the Alaska influence emerges, as with the smoked salmon chowder. Reservations advised.
🛏 120 🅿 🕒 Closed L Sat. & Sun. 🚫 🏧 All major cards

🍴 SACKS CAFÉ & RESTAURANT
$$$-$$$$
328 G ST.
TEL 907/274-4022 or 907/276-3546
FAX 907/276-3548
www.sackscafe.com
As soon as you set eyes on the coral-colored exterior and bright Southwestern interior, you'll sense that the food at Sacks will be creative, even playful. It doesn't fit into any standard category, but you won't care when you start your meal with a seared calamari spinach salad or crab and scallop cakes with pico de gallo and honey chipotle aioli. Then move on to an entrée of grilled king salmon in a sashimi marinade and soy maple glaze or organic free-range chicken grilled and stuffed with prosciutto, spinach, caramelized onion, and manchego cheese. A tapas bar serves those who wish to graze. Sacks is a popular lunch spot. Reservations recommended for lunch and dinner.
🛏 84 🚫 🏧 All major cards

🍴 DOWNTOWN DELI & CAFÉ
$-$$
525 W. 4TH AVE.
TEL 907/276-7116
The busy Downtown Deli is

an Anchorage tradition. The sourdough pancakes are made from starter that dates back to sourdough a gold miner gave to the deli in 1939. Alaska-influenced dishes include reindeer stew and grilled salmon. Also available are such traditional deli foods as chicken soup, with either noodles or homemade matzo balls. Try the Alaska Sampler appetizer, which features smoked halibut, lox cream-cheese dip, and reindeer sausage.
🛏 50 🚫 🏧 All major cards

🍴 MOOSE'S TOOTH PUB & PIZZERIA
$-$$
3300 OLD SEWARD HWY.
TEL 907/258-2537
FAX 907/258-7361
www.moosestooth.net
This midtown brew pub and pizza place ranks high in the hearts and stomachs of Anchorage residents. The pizza ranges from the ordinary to the odd, such as eggplant parmesan; this being Alaska, salmon and halibut are popular toppings. The repertoire of beers is impressive and includes local north country brews, such as Polar Pale Ale, Northern Light Amber, and Pipeline Stout.
🛏 180 🅿 🚫 🏧 All major cards

🍴 NEW SAGAYA'S CITY MARKET/MIDTOWN MARKET & LAROMA DELI
$-$$
900 W. 13TH AVE.
TEL 907/274-6173 or 800/764-1001
3700 OLD SEWARD HWY.
TEL 907/561-5173
FAX 907/561-2042
www.newsagaya.com
These two stores are primarily groceries that carry regular items but specialize in fresh seafood and ethnic foods, including Thai, Korean, Chinese, and Hispanic. The not-so-well-kept secret is

that people looking for a ready meal can find all sorts of food to eat at the inside and outside tables or take-out counters. Among the choices are Asian food, lattes, deli sandwiches, excellent baked goods, salads, and great fresh seafood.
🅿 🚫 🏧 All major cards

🍴 THAI KITCHEN
$-$$
3405 E. TUDOR
TEL 907/561-0082
FAX 907/563-6868
www.thaikitchenalaska.com /home.html
Though this Thai restaurant, Anchorage's first, is hidden in a strip mall, guests will remember the food. Locals crowd into the dining room to eat authentic Thai classics, like pad Thai and green curries, as well as less typical dishes, like jungle beef. If you can't decide what to order off the long menu, try the Thai Kitchen Platter, a heaping sampler of appetizers.
🛏 60 🅿 🕒 Closed L Sat. & Sun. 🏧 All major cards

TURNAGAIN ARM

SOMETHING SPECIAL

🏨 ALYESKA PRINCE 🍴 HOTEL
This is Alaska's foremost large luxury resort. Every room has such top-drawer amenities as heated towel racks, fluffy robes, a refrigerator, and an in-room safe. Imagine the extras in the 1,275-square-foot (115 sq m) Royal Suite—a mere $1,700 per night. For a memorable dining experience, take the tram up to the **Seven Glaciers Restaurant**, atop the ski slopes. Along with the views, which include seven hanging glaciers, diners can savor mesquite-grilled salmon, buffalo strip loin, or pesto-roasted scallop bisque.
$$$$-$$$$$
1000 ARLBERG AVE.
(GIRDWOOD)

TEL 907/754-1111 or
800/880-3880
FAX 907/754-2200
www.alyeskaresort.com
[i] 307 [P] [S] [↕] [📹] [≋]
[≋] All major cards

▯ DOUBLE MUSKY INN
$$$-$$$$
MILE 0.3 CROW CREEK RD.
(GIRDWOOD)
TEL 907/783-2822
FAX 907/783-5520
www.doublemuskyinn.com
This place is an idiosyncratic
cross between a fine restau-
rant and a rowdy roadhouse,
with a Cajun-Louisiana-
meets-Alaska accent. The
place gets crowded and the
service slow, but it kind of
works with the laid-back
attitude. The Cajun-meets-
Alaska blend leads to dishes
that are mouthwatering
and often eye watering
(i.e., spicy). Try the authen-
tic shrimp étouffee or the
lobster kabobs. The Double
Musky has also gained a
national reputation for
fine steaks, especially its
pepper steak.
[⇆] 85 [P] [⏲] Closed Mon. &
six weeks in late fall [S]
[≋] All major cards

MAT-SU

▦ COLONY INN
▯ $$-$$$
325 E. ELMWOOD AVE.
(PALMER)
TEL 907/746-3330
FAX 907/746-3330
Teachers who came to the
region during the Great
Depression used the Colony
Inn building as their dorm.
A good renovation has given
the place a refined though
not luxurious country-inn
atmosphere, with such
modern amenities as VCRs
and data ports. In summer
a homey restaurant on the
ground floor (famed for its
blue-ribbon pies) serves
breakfast and lunch daily and
dinner on Friday and Satur-

day nights. Reservations and
check-ins are handled a few
blocks away at the Valley
Hotel (606 S. Alaska St.).
[i] 12 [P] [S] [≋] All major
cards

▦ HATCHER PASS
▯ LODGE
$$-$$$
MILE 17 HATCHER PASS RD.
(PALMER-FISHHOOK RD.)
TEL 907/745-5897 or
907/745-1200
www.hatcherpasslodge.com
Near Hatcher Pass summit,
this A-frame lodge and
scattered cabins nestle amid
alpine tundra and rugged
mountains. Guests come to
cross-country ski and admire
the views or to hike and
admire the views. The lodge
sits at the entry road to
Independence Mine State
Historical Park. Cabins
include chemical toilets and
water, while the lodge
provides showers. A decent
restaurant in the lodge
serves three meals a day.
[i] 12 [P] [S] [≋] All major
cards

▦ PIONEER RIDGE BED &
BREAKFAST
$$-$$$
2221 YUKON DR.
TEL 907/376-7472 or
800/478-7472
FAX 907/376-7470
www.pioneerridge.net
Pioneer Ridge rises amid the
wide-open rural spaces of
the Mat-Su outside Wasilla;
you'll need driving directions
from the owners or website
to find it. As you approach,
watch for this 10,000-square-
foot (900 sq m) colony barn.
Once part of the Fairview
Dairy, it has been converted
into a bed-and-breakfast.
This B&B augments its
authentic old-Alaska char-
acter with such decor as a
wall-mounted moosehead
and antler chandeliers. Each
room reflects an Alaska
theme, like the Denali Room,
bedecked with snowshoes

and crampons.
[i] 7 [P] [S] [📹]
[≋] All major cards

▯ EVANGELO'S
TRATTORIA
$-$$$
301 PARKS HWY.
(MILE 40, WASILLA)
TEL 907/376-1212
Evangelo's spacious, comely
interior includes banquet and
conference facilities. The
food is a pleasant surprise,
from the fine salad bar and
good pizzas to such
elaborate fare as garlic-
sauteed shrimp in a white-
wine butter sauce. Evangelo's
also serve a calzone so big
you'll have to put more air in
your car tires if you take it
with you.
[i] 200 [P] [S] [≋] All major
cards

▯ CADILLAC CAFÉ
$-$$
MILE 49 PARKS HWY. AT
SYLVAN RD.
TEL 907/357-5533
Attached to a gas station, this
diner-type place doesn't put
on any airs. It just serves
good, robust food, including
hefty hamburgers, South-
western food, homemade
pies, and both ordinary and
unusual pizzas baked in a
wood-fired oven.
[⇆] 30 [P] [S] [≋] All major
cards

▯ VAGABOND BLUES
$
642 S. ALASKA ST. (PALMER)
TEL 907/745-2233
On the main drag in old
downtown Palmer, this café
seems like something you'd
find on an urban corner in
San Francisco. The healthful,
vegetarian fare includes pasta
salads, bagel sandwiches, and
large portions of homemade
soup served in hand-painted
bowls created by a local
artist. Another highlight is
dessert, particularly the
strawberry pie. Local
performers fill the place with

HOTELS & RESTAURANTS

live music some evenings.
 70 🅿 Ⓢ

🍴 VALLEY BISTRO
$
300 E. HERNING AVE.
(WASILLA)
TEL 907/357-5633
This appealing bistro
occupies a former general
store built in 1920; it's even
owned by the local historical
society. Historic photos of
old Wasilla line the walls, and
many of the furnishings are
antiques. Swing by the bistro
in the morning to grab a
scone and an espresso, or
stop by at lunch for its tasty
sandwiches and salads.
45 🅿 Ⓢ 🔇 All major
cards

KENAI PENINSULA

SEWARD

🏨 KENAI FJORDS
WILDERNESS LODGE
$$$$$
TEL 907/224-8068 or
800/478-8068
FAX 907/777-2888
www.kenaifjords.com
This lodge is on Fox Island,
near the mouth of Resur-
rection Bay, 14 miles (23 km)
from Seward. To stay there,
guests must sign on for a trip
with Kenai Fjords Tours (see
p. 264). Trips include the one-
hour boat ride to the lodge,
an overnight in a pretty cabin
on a pretty bay, a salmon bake, dinner,
breakfast the next day, and a
full-day boat tour of Kenai
Fjords National Park. Guests
are welcome to extend their
stays in the cabins.
ⓘ 8 🕐 Closed in winter
🔇 All major cards

🏨 HOTEL EDGEWATER
$$$–$$$$
200 5TH AVE.
TEL 907/224-2700 or
888/793-6800
FAX 907/224-2701
www.hoteledgewater.com

The new arrival among
downtown Seward hotels
reflects its recent vintage
with data ports and an up-to-
date business center. It
retains at least one time-
honored Alaska service,
however—freezer space for
guests' fish. The Edgewater
also offers such high-end
amenities as a spa and a fine
art shop.
ⓘ 76 🅿 Ⓢ 🔇 ⬆
🔇 All major cards

🏨 HOTEL SEWARD
$$$–$$$$
221 5TH AVE.
TEL 907/224-2378 or
800/655-8785
FAX 907/224-3112
www.alaskaone.com/hotelseward
Guests may appreciate this
hotel's historical gold rush
atmosphere or its nice
rooms and many amenities,
but above all this establish-
ment offers a great location
in Seward's comfy old
downtown. Practically next
door to the famous Alaska
SeaLife Center, it's about a
block from the waterfront
and overlooks the mountains
and lovely Resurrection Bay.
ⓘ 38 🅿 Ⓢ ⬆
🔇 All major cards

🏨 VAN GILDER HOTEL
$$$
308 ADAMS ST.
TEL 907/224-3079 or
800/204-6835
FAX 907/224-3689
www.vangilderhotel.com
This 1916 hotel lacks some
of the newer amenities, but it
compensates with Victorian
charm and good service.
Except for the four suites,
the rooms are small, but
they're spotless and offer
nice touches like brass beds
and period antiques. The
parlor features a player piano
and a collection of Alaska-
themed books. Throughout
are historic photos with
informative captions.
ⓘ 24 🅿 Ⓢ 🔇 All major
cards

🍴 CHINOOKS
WATERFRONT
RESTAURANT
$$–$$$
1404 4TH AVE.
TEL 907/224-2207
FAX 907/224-2414
www.chinookswaterfront.com
Sure, diners can get beef or
pasta at Chinooks and a
great view of the harbor
from the upstairs dining
room, but that's not what
brings in the crowds. People
come to lunch and dinner for
fresh and plentiful seafood.
For a serious seafood fix, try
the halibut filet stuffed with
crab and shrimp or the
seafood sauté, a sampler
plate that groans under the
weight of crab, halibut,
salmon, prawns, scallops,
and mussels.
100 🅿 🕐 Closed
Nov.–April Ⓢ
🔇 All major cards

🍴 CHRISTO'S PALACE
$$–$$$
133 4TH AVE.
TEL 907/224-5255

FAX 907/224-2699
It's easy for travelers exploring downtown Seward to walk by the unprepossessing exterior of Christo's and wonder if the word "palace" is a joke, but step inside and you'll understand. The interior is elegant, almost opulent: dark polished wood, vaulted ceilings, fine furnishings, and a beautiful mahogany bar thought to date back to the 19th century. Incongruously, the restaurant is known especially for its pizza, but Christo's also serves a wide variety of other dishes, ranging from Greek to Italian, Mexican to seafood.
🛏 102 🅿 🚭 🚫 All major cards

🍽 RAY'S WATERFRONT
$$-$$$
1316 4TH AVE.
TEL 907/224-5606
FAX 907/224-3861
Ray's is a Seward landmark. For many years anglers have come to this harborside restaurant after a day on the water. Most likely it's the straightforward but top-notch seafood that packs them in (on busy days expect long waits). Ray's signature dish is its seafood chowder. Dining areas have appealing views of the harbor.
🛏 175 🅿 🕐 Closed mid-Oct.–late April
🚭 🚫 All major cards

SOLDOTNA

🏨 ASPEN HOTEL
$$$
326 BINKLEY CIRCLE
TEL 907/260-7736 or
866/308-7848
FAX 907/260-7786
www.aspenhotelsak.com
This new hotel sits on a bluff overlooking the Kenai River in Soldotna, one of the world's most famous salmon-fishing areas. Part of a small Alaska chain, it lacks charm, but its rooms are spotless, bright, spacious, and well

appointed (refrigerators, microwaves, VCRs, data ports).
🛏 63 🚭 🅿 ⬍ 🚿
🚫 All major cards

🍽 DUCK INN
$-$$
43187 KALIFORNSKY
BEACH RD.
TEL 907/262-1849
FAX 907/262-4588
The Duck Inn offers just about everything but duck—from steaks to seafood, chicken to pizza. It's known for its creative hamburgers and for halibut fresh from Cook Inlet. If you've been out combat fishing all day, you'll appreciate the soft lighting and soothing music. The inn also provides a small hostelry and a lounge.
🛏 60 🅿 🚭 🚫 All major cards

KENAI

🏨 KENAI LANDING
🍽 $$-$$$$
2101 BOWPICKER LANE
TEL 907/335-2500
FAX 907/335-2505
www.kenailanding.com
Built in the 1920s, this former cannery complex was recently transformed into a contemporary resort. Accommodations range from immaculate but smallish rooms, with bathrooms down the hall in the former women's quarters—the "Hen House"—to remodeled former fishermen's bunkhouses turned into three-bedroom cottages. The resort includes docks, a theater, more than 25 shops, nature trails, a restaurant, and even a remnant seafood-processing plant.
🛈 44 🅿 🕐 Closed mid-Sept.–mid-May 🚭 🚫 All major cards

🍽 CHARLOTTE'S BAKERY
$
115 S. WILLOW ST.
TEL 907/283-2777

Charlotte Legg runs the kind of bakery that locals can't get enough of. The food is good and varied, the room bright and appealing, and the prices very reasonable. The bakery turns out berry pastries, cookies, and other sugary treats to have with tea or take home. It also produces the fragrant bread for Charlotte's excellent sandwiches. The eat-in section offers salads (using greens from her garden) soups, omelets, and sourdough pancakes.
🛏 70 🅿 🕐 Closed early–mid-Jan. 🚭 🚫 MC, V

🍽 SAL'S KLONDIKE DINER
$
44619 STERLING HWY.
TEL 907/262-2220
This classic roadside diner looks touristy but has a heart of gold. Locals frequent the joint as much as travelers. They come for the tasty food, generous portions, and fast, attentive service. The diner is open 24/7, and it's cheap. The menu includes burgers, sandwiches, fish and chips, and the other usual suspects, plus halibut and salmon. The staff bakes fresh pies and bread every day.
🛏 100 🅿 🚭 🚫 All major cards

HOMER

SOMETHING SPECIAL

🏨 ALASKA ADVENTURE CABINS
This property sprawls atop Baycrest Hill—the high point north of Homer—and views of the Cook Inlet and far beyond are incredible, to say the least. The two handsome, three-story cabins cling to the hillside, but what really catches the eye are the caboose and the boat. The Moose Caboose is a 54-foot Pullman car that has been remade into a gorgeous, if long and skinny, two-level structure with

amenities like kitchens, a fireplace, gleaming hardwood floors, satellite TVs, two full baths, a big picture window, and a 30-foot deck. The Double Eagle is a former shrimp boat with a bright, polished interior, fine furnishings, two bedrooms, a kitchen, a living room, two and a half baths, and three decks.
$$$$
2525 STERLING HWY.
TEL 907/223-6681 or
907/278-2784
www.alaskaadventurecabins.com
[i] 4 [P] [S] [&] All major cards

🏨 ALASKAN SUITES
$$$-$$$$
42485 STERLING HIGHWAY
TEL 907/235-1972 or
888/239-1972
FAX 907/235-7641
www.alaskansuites.com
Fantastic views. That's the first thing you'll notice on this property high on a hillside just west of Homer. Should you spot soaring bald eagles, you'll probably be looking down on them. When you do finally notice the accommodations, you'll find stand-alone log cabins (plus a cottage that sleeps eight) with back decks about 30 feet (9 m) from the bluff. The interiors are spacious (they sleep five) and luxurious, with a long list of amenities, including tiled bathrooms, a small refrigerator, a satellite TV, a sofa, and a La-Z-Boy recliner.
[i] 6 [P] [S] [&] All major cards

🏨 CHOCOLATE DROP INN
$$$
57745 CLOVER AVE.
TEL 907/235-3668 or
800/530-6015
FAX 907/235-3729
www.chocolatedropinn.com
Six miles (10 km) east of Homer, the Chocolate Drop sits on a slice of rural land that overlooks Kachemak

Bay. Views encompass much of the bay, the distant Kenai Mountains, four glaciers, and the eponymous Chocolate Drop peak. Rooms are light, spacious, and well furnished. Guests can soak in a sauna or in a hot tub on the deck. The innkeepers are known for their breakfasts and treats, such as reindeer sausage and seafood omelets.
[i] 6 [P] [S] [&] MC, V

🏨 OLD TOWN BED & BREAKFAST
$-$$
106 W. BUNNELL ST.
TEL 907/235-7558
www.oldtownbedandbreak
fast.com
This B&B occupies the second floor of a building that dates back to 1936. It served for decades as Homer's trading post. (The first floor is home to the Bunnell Street Art Gallery, one of Homer's finest; see p. 262.) Near the beach, it offers one large apartment for four. Sea breezes and ocean views set the mood. Rooms include such amenities as a cherrywood four-poster bed, hardwood floors, a handmade Alaska wildflower quilt, and antique chairs. Breakfast is catered by a neighboring café.
[i] 4 [P] [S] [&] MC, V

🍴 HOMESTEAD RESTAURANT
$$-$$$$
MILE 8.2 EAST END RD.
TEL 907/235-8723
www.homesteadrestaurant.net
This former roadhouse has moved up in the world, serving elaborate cuisine in an art-filled room—though the walls are still those of a log cabin. Enjoy seafood, steak, prime rib, or rack of lamb as you appreciate views of Kachemak Bay and distant mountains and glaciers. Reservations recommended.
[+] 60 [P] [S] [&] All major cards

🍴 CAFÉ CUPS
$$-$$$
162 W. PIONEER AVE.
TEL 907/235-8330
This eatery is nothing if not whimsical; look for the four mammoth teacups that adorn the exterior. The intimate interior features plants, flowers, and dark wood—and excellent food. The chef produces a wide range of dishes, from simple and cheap to elaborate and expensive, with an emphasis on seafood. Ask about the specials.
[+] 30 [P] [⊘] Closed Sun.
[S] [&] MC, V

🍴 FAT OLIVES RESTAURANT
$-$$
276 OLSON LANE
TEL 907/235-8488
Noisy, cheerful, and informal, Fat Olives is a welcoming place, just like an Italian bistro ought to be. The familiar, high-quality food is welcoming, too, with something for everybody: wood-fired pizzas, fresh seafood, roasted chicken, calzones, salads, beef, and many appetizers.
[+] 60 [P] [S] [&] All major cards

🍴 FRESH SOURDOUGH EXPRESS
$-$$
1316 OCEAN DR.
TEL 907/235-7571
www.freshsourdoughexpress.com
Offering one of the best values in Alaska, this pleasant dining room serves breakfast, lunch, or dinner consisting of savory, healthful (often organic) food. Portions are large and the price small (for Alaska). Try the reindeer grill, an outstanding pizza, or the halibut hoagie. The bakery creates all its own fresh items from original recipes, including Puffin Muffins, Moose Mounds, Obscene Brownies, and wonderful sourdough bread.

🛏 250 🅿 🕐 Closed in
winter 🚭 🏧 MC, V

ACROSS KACHEMAK BAY

SOMETHING SPECIAL

🏨 KACHEMAK BAY WILDERNESS LODGE

As one should expect at a lodge this expensive, the owners and staff provide luxury and personal attention—to a maximum of 12 guests. But it's the owners' strong conservation ethic that makes this a world-class wilderness hideaway. They'll whisk you by boat to watch sea otters, seals, and whales, lead hikes through rain forests and alpine meadows in the adjacent state park, guide tide-pooling excursions in their bay, lead kayaks to seabird rookeries, and hire floatplanes to view brown bears. As for the rustic luxury…the four cabins, some with two bedrooms, are simply gorgeous, and guests can relax in a sod-roof sauna, an outdoor hot tub, or a solarium. Sophisticated food rounds out the experience.Guests arrive by boat from Homer on Monday and leave Friday. Reserve early.
$$$$$
CHINA POOT BAY
TEL 907/235-8910
FAX 907/235-8911
www.alaskawildernesslodge.com
ℹ 4 cabins 🕐 Closed Oct.–April 🚭

🏨 QUIET PLACE LODGE
$$$$$
HALIBUT COVE
TEL 907/235-1800 or
907/296-2212 (summer)
FAX 907/235-1800
www.quietplace.com
The lodge and three upscale cabins are tucked away in the tiny community of Halibut Cove, where a handful of artists and fishermen live without roads, connected by a boardwalk and their boats. Lodge guests can lounge on the deck and watch the sea

otters, stroll the meandering boardwalk, hike to a nearby glacier, explore in a kayak or rowboat, or go beachcombing. Four-day packages include three fine meals a day. Reserve early.
ℹ 3 🅿 🕐 Closed in winter
🚭 🏧 MC, V

🏨 TUTKA BAY WILDERNESS LODGE
$$$$$
TUTKA BAY
TEL 907/235-3905 or
800/606-3909
FAX 907/235-3909
www.tutkabaylodge.com
This lodge defines rustic luxury: cabins with floor-to-ceiling windows and fine furnishings; fine food with an emphasis on Alaska seafood; and extras like a hot tub gazebo and a sauna. Still, the surroundings steal the show. The forest, the mountains, the bay, the sea otters outside your window—these things make a stay here truly memorable. The lodge leads or arranges all sorts of excursions, some of which cost extra. Access is by boat or plane from Homer. Reserve early.
ℹ 3 cabins, 2 suites
🕐 Closed mid-Sept.–mid-May 🚭 🏧 All major cards

🏨 PETERSON BAY LODGE
$$$
PETERSON BAY
TEL 907/235-7156 or
866/899-7156
www.petersonbaylodge.com
This pretty lodge features a full menu of ecotours, including kayaking, fishing, hiking, and wildlife-watching, but the highlight of a stay here is getting a feel for daily life in the Alaska wilderness. The owners live in the main building, run an oyster farm as well as the lodge, and are happy to chat about their lifestyle. Some guests volunteer to help with the oysters and enjoy that even more

than the outings and fine dinners. Guests stay in eco-cabins—large log-and-canvas structures set on hillside platforms with great views. Reserve early.
ℹ 4 cabins 🚭 🕐 Closed in winter 🏧 MC, V

🏨 ALASKA DANCING EAGLES BED & BREAKFAST
$$–$$$
165 MAIN ST. AT WATER ST., SELDOVIA
TEL 907/234-7627 (summer) or
907/360-6363 (winter)
www.dancingeagles.com
On a small point at the end of Main Street, this waterfront property overlooks the boat harbor and the mouth of Seldovia Slough. Guests can rent the whole lodge, which sleeps ten. The adjacent cabin, which sleeps six, is a remodeled boat-house that rests on pilings. This informal place is rustic in a pleasant, natural way.
ℹ 2 🅿 🕐 Closed Labor Day–Memorial Day 🚭
🏧 All major cards

SOMETHING SPECIAL

🍴 THE SALTRY
The caught-that-morning fresh seafood, home-baked breads, greens right from the garden, intricate sushi, an array of microbrews, the artsy room, and the reasonable prices are all a marvel. When the restaurant is full, the population nearly triples in tiny Halibut Cove, where a boardwalk on pilings substitutes for main street and people use kayaks and rowboats instead of cars. Unless you're staying in town, you'll have to book passage on the M.V. *Danny J.*, and they'll make your lunch or dinner reservations.
$$–$$$
HALIBUT COVE
TEL 907/235-7847 or
800/478-7847
www.centralcharter.com (follow links to Halibut Cove)

🎴 50 🚫 Closed Labor Day
—Memorial Day 🚫 🐾
MC, V

ALASKA PENINSULA & THE ALEUTIANS

KATMAI NATIONAL PARK & PRESERVE

🏨 BROOKS LODGE
$$$$$
KATMAI NATIONAL PARK
TEL 907/243-5448 or
800/544-0551
FAX 907/243-0649
www.katmainationalpark.com
The hub of big, remote, and
supremely wild Katmai
National Park, Brooks Camp
is also home to the main
building and adjacent 16
cabins that make up Brooks
Lodge. Most people come to
watch the renowned brown
bears fishing for salmon on
the Brooks River; others
come to do some fishing
themselves or to see the
Valley of Ten Thousand
Smokes. The cabins aren't
fancy, but they're modern
and offer private toilets,
heat, and electricity. Most
guests arrange package deals
from Anchorage through an
outfit called Katmailand Inc.
(tel 800/544-0551, www
.katmailand.com).
ⓘ 16 cabins 🚫 🚫 Closed
mid-Sept.–May 🐾 MC, V

SOMETHING SPECIAL

🏨 HALLO BAY
BEAR CAMP
Surrounded by Katmai
National Park, scenic Hallo
Bay is one of Alaska's premier
brown bear viewing spots, yet on
a typical night only about a
dozen people stay here. The
owners of this remote enclave
limit access to protect the bears.
Hallo Bay's approach to bear
viewing depends on keeping the
brown bears utterly wild and
uninterested in the humans who
walk into their midst. That's

right, walk right among them.
While Hallo Bay's safety record
is perfect, this method isn't for
everyone, and you should
explore it further before going.
Up to four guests sleep on cots
in heated structures that
resemble canvas Quonset huts.
$$$$$
KATMAI NATIONAL PARK
TEL 907/235-2237 (Homer)
FAX 907/235-9461
www.hallobay.com
ⓘ 5 🚫 Closed Oct.–
April 🚫

KODIAK

🏨 BEST WESTERN
🍴 KODIAK INN
$$$
236 W. REZANOF DR.
TEL 907/486-5712 or
888/563-4254
FAX 907/486-3430
www.kodiakinn.com
Yes, it's just a chain motel,
but hostelries are few and
expensive in Kodiak, and this
one is newly refurbished and
situated downtown with
views of St. Paul Harbor. It
hosts one of Kodiak's best
eateries, the Chart Room,
good for seafood and steaks.
ⓘ 80 🅿 🚻 📺 🚫 Closed
in winter 🚫 🐾 All major
cards

🍴 2ND FLOOR
RESTAURANT
$$-$$$
116 W. REZANOF DR.
TEL 907/486-8555
Alaska's Pacific Rim makes a
showing at this fine Japanese
restaurant on the second
floor above a Chinese
restaurant. The tempura
dishes are first rate, and
many of the sushi ingredients
came off the Kodiak docks.
🎴 100 🅿 🚫 Closed L Sat.
& Sun. 🚫 🐾 MC, V

🍴 EL CHICANO
$-$$
103 CENTER ST.
TEL 907/486-6116
Surprisingly authentic

Mexican food for this far
north of the border. All
portions are hungry-
fisherman big, but if you
want *really* big, go for the
license-plate burrito, which
truly shares the dimensions
of a license plate (with
more depth, of course).
🎴 60 🅿 🚫 Closed Mon.
in winter 🚫

🍴 KING'S DINER
$
1941 MILL BAY RD.
TEL 907/486-4100
A loud, busy, fun place where
both local families and men
wearing the commercial
fisherman's uniform—rubber
boots and hooded sweat-
shirts—load up at breakfast
on sourdough pancakes, at
lunch on cheeseburgers, and
at dinner on seafood and
prime rib.
🎴 50 🅿 🚫 🐾 MC, V

ALEUTIAN ISLANDS

🏨 GRAND ALEUTIAN
🍴 HOTEL
$$$-$$$$

---

498 SALMON WAY
TEL 907/581-3844 or
866/581-3844
FAX 907/581-7150
www.grandaleutian.com
This fairly luxurious, executive-style hotel seems out of place out here in the remote wilds of the Aleutians, as though it drifted in from Anchorage. It offers bright, spacious rooms decorated with local and regional art and amenities such as Internet hookups and an extra vanity and sink. The hotel includes a fine restaurant (see following entry), a café, a lounge, and a sports bar and grill.
🚪 114 🅿 🚫 🔁 🚫All major cards

🍴 CHART ROOM
$$-$$$
498 SALMON WAY
(GRAND ALEUTIAN)
TEL 907/581-3844 or
800/891-1194
www.grandaleutian.com
Downright posh, the Chart Room serves cuisine that befits its views of the surrounding waters—among the world's best fishing grounds. Salmon, shrimp, crab, halibut, and other seafood figure in most dishes. Locals also frequent this restaurant, especially on lavish "special" nights: a Wednesday night seafood buffet, a Friday night barbeque on the deck, and a Sunday brunch. Reservations recommended.
🚪 100 🅿 🕐 Closed L, except Sun. brunch 🚫 🔁
🚫 All major cards

■ PRINCE WILLIAM SOUND & AROUND

VALDEZ

🏨 ASPEN HOTEL
$$$
100 MEALS AVE.
TEL 907/835-4445
FAX 907/835-2437
www.aspenhotelsak.com
Part of a small hotel chain (in

five Alaska cities), the Aspen offers a generic experience but amenities not found in most small-town lodgings, including wireless Internet, VCRs, a business center, a pool, a spa, an exercise room, and a decent continental breakfast.
🚪 103 🅿 🚫 🔁 🚫 🚫
🚫 All major cards

🏨 WILD ROSES BY THE SEA B&B RETREAT
$$$
629 FIDDLEHEAD LANE
TEL 907/835-2930
www.bythesea.alaska.net
Rose's bed-and-breakfast sits at the edge of the forest atop Blueberry Hill, a mile (1.6 km) out of Valdez. Views of the sound, the mouth of Mineral Creek Canyon, and the Chugach Mountains are grand. One of the rooms is a suite with a Jacuzzi, while another is a one-room apartment with a private entrance.
🚪 3 🅿 🚫 🚫MC, V

🍴 ALASKA'S BISTRO
$$-$$$
100 FIDALGO DR.
TEL 907/835-5688
FAX 907/835-4240
www.alaskasbistro.com
Connected to the Best Western, this restaurant serves sophisticated food with a Mediterranean flair. While the wide-ranging menu includes imaginative beef, chicken, and pork dishes and unusual pizzas, seafood is the star. Try the locally famous chef's paella, with fish right off the docks, or the shrimp and scallops sautéed in a sauce of Spanish saffron, cream, and sherry. This choice location overlooks the bay and small-boat harbor.
🚪 100 🅿 🚫 🚫All major cards

🍴 MIKE'S PALACE
$-$$
201 N. HARBOR DR.

TEL 907/835-2365
With its harbor views, varied food, cheerful atmosphere, and good prices, Mike's is, not surprisingly, a local favorite. You can get lasagna, enchiladas, steak, seafood, Greek gyros, veal, and Mike's highly regarded pizza.
🚪 80 🚫 🚫All major cards

CORDOVA

🏨 ORCA ADVENTURE LODGE
$-$$$
2 MILES (3 KM) NORTH OF TOWN
TEL 907/424-7249 or
866/424-6722
FAX 907/424-3579
www.orcaadventurelodge.com
If you like to play outdoors, this is the place for you. At the head of Orca Inlet, the lodge provides easy access to the mountains, forest, and sea. For $140 a night guests can stay overnight, while just $15 more gets them three meals a day and access to kayaks, fishing gear, canoes, and mountain bikes. The lodge also offers ice climbing, rafting, and heli-skiing excursions. Rooms are set in a renovated historic cannery.
🚪 34 🅿 🕐 Closed Nov.– Dec. 🚫 🚫All major cards

🏨 CORDOVA ROSE LODGE
$$
1315 WHITSHED RD.
TEL 907/424-7673
www.cordovarose.com
This lodge comes by its nautical theme honestly; it's built on an old barge anchored beside a lighthouse at the mouth of Odiak Slough. Guests can scan the slough for birds and otters or gaze across the harbor at the distant mountains and islands. Everyone has free run of a sauna and library, and some of the rooms have access to a kitchen and deck with a

HOTELS & RESTAURANTS

barbeque. Less than half a mile (.8 km) from downtown.
🛏 12 🅿 🚫 🚭 MC, V

🏨 NORTHERN NIGHTS INN
$-$$
500 3RD ST.
TEL 907/424-5356
FAX 907/424-3291
www.northernnightsinn.com
A great bargain, this grand, centrally located 1908 house features spacious rooms furnished with antiques and such amenities as entertainment centers, kitchens, private entrances, and great views of the water. You also get the attention of the innkeeper, a friendly and knowledgeable dynamo.
🛏 4 🅿 🚫 🚭 All major cards

🍴 BAJA TACO
$
NICHOLOFF ST. AT THE HARBOR
TEL 907/424-5599
For years this café's owners came north from Mexico in summer to run a popular food stand out of a small converted school bus. Success led to expansion into a small café with a pleasant deck—though they still use a converted bus (albeit a larger one) as the kitchen. Try the fish tacos—what could be better in a commercial fishing hub?
🪑 40 🅿 🕐 Closed Oct.–mid-April 🚫

🍴 KILLER WHALE CAFÉ
$
507 1ST AVE.
TEL 907/424-7733
A busy gathering place, this café occupies the back of a fine little book-and-music store. Serves traditional breakfast and a good selection of soups, sandwiches, and salads for lunch. Locals are partial to the Killer Whale's cheesecake.
🪑 30 🕐 Closed D & Sun. 🚫

PRINCE WILLIAM SOUND

🏨 PRINCE WILLIAM SOUND LODGE
$$$$$
ELLAMAR
TEL 907/248-0909 (Anchorage) or 907/440-0909 (cell)
www.alaska.net/~pwslodge
This remote cluster of log buildings is tucked into a forested little bay in the Tatitlek Narrows, 25 floatplane miles (40 km) from Valdez. The lodge offers ocean fishing for halibut, hiking, Native village visits, whale-watching, fly-fishing, bird-watching, and serious loafing. The rooms are handsome and the food excellent. How about balsamic pepper steak followed by carrot macadamia cake with crème fraiche for dessert?
🛏 5 🕐 Closed mid-Sept.–April 🚫

WRANGELL–ST. ELIAS NATIONAL PARK

🏨 ULTIMA THULE LODGE
$$$$$
WRANGELL–ST. ELIAS NP
TEL 907/688-1200
www.ultimathulelodge.com
This cozy lodge lies deep in the heart of Wrangell–St. Elias National Park. Flown in for a minimum of four nights, guests spend their days exploring the wilds by flightseeing, hiking, fishing, camping, glacier trekking, dogsledding, or wildlife-watching.
🛏 6 🕐 Closed Oct.–mid-March 🚫

🏨 COPPER RIVER PRINCESS WILDERNESS LODGE
$$$
MILE 102 RICHARDSON HWY. (COPPER CENTER)
TEL 907/822-4000 or 800/426-0500
FAX 907/822-4480
www.princesslodges.com
One of a chain of luxury lodges set in beautiful parts of Alaska, the Copper River Princess sits above the confluence of the Copper and Klutina Rivers. Overlooking Wrangell–St. Elias, with great views of towering peaks, the Princess assumes a ritzy hunting lodge theme and offers a lot of amenities.
🛏 85 🅿 🕐 Closed mid-Sept. to mid-May 🚫 🚭 🚭 All major cards

McCARTHY/KENNICOTT

🏨🍴 KENNICOTT GLACIER LODGE
$$$-$$$$
KENNICOTT
TEL 907/258-2350 or 800/582-5128
FAX 907/248-7975
www.kennicottlodge.com
In the middle of Wrangell–St. Elias, this reproduction of a historic mine building sits amid a ghost town—the site of the old Kennecott copper mill. This lovely wooden building features a full-length front porch for gazing at the surrounding mountains, woods, and glaciers. The restaurant serves fresh, hearty food and is open to the public as well as guests. Reservations recommended.
🛏 25 🕐 Closed mid-Sept. to mid-May 🚫 🚭 All major cards

🏨 McCARTHY LODGE
$$$
DOWNTOWN MCCARTHY
TEL 907/554-4402
FAX 907/554-4404
www.mccarthylodge.com
This lodge comprises two facilities: a backpacker hotel for budget travelers and, across the street, Ma Johnson's, a nicely restored 1916 building that blends historic elegance with a hint of funkiness. Extras include a restaurant, a bar, and a shuttle service that takes visitors to the mill site and the glacier.
🛏 6 🕐 Closed in winter 🚫 🚭 MC, V

■ INTERIOR

TALKEETNA

🏨 DENALI OVERLOOK INN
$$$-$$$$
MILE 8.5 TALKEETNA SPUR RD.
TEL 907/733-3555
www.denalioverlook.com
Atop a bluff 5 miles (8 km) south of Talkeetna, this striking inn deserves its name; the views of Mount McKinley and the Alaska Range are spectacular. The new building itself reminds one of a mountain: three stories tall, with a sharply peaked roof and gables and big windows everywhere. The interior design features spacious rooms and odd angles in the 52-foot (16 m) Great Room.
🛏 5 rooms, 1 cabin 🅿
🕐 Closed mid-Dec.–mid-Jan.
🚭 🚫 MC, V

🏨 TALKEETNA CABINS
$$$
N. C ST. AT MAIN ST.
TEL 907/733-2227 or
888/733-9933
www.talkeetnacabins.org
Hand built by the owners, these three new log cabins are pretty on the outside and spacious and well appointed inside. Each includes a kitchen, living room, and full bath. The cabins lie near the river on the edge of historic Talkeetna. The owners also rent a three-bedroom house.
🛏 3 cabins, 1 house 🅿 🚭

🍴 CAFÉ MICHELE
$$-$$$$
MILE 13.7 TALKEETNA SPUR RD.
TEL 907/733-5300
FAX 907/733-5302
www.cafemichele.com
On the edge of down-home Talkeetna, this French bistro (the owner/chef is indeed French) seems to belong somewhere else—say, Paris. Its sophisticated menu has earned the café a reputation

as one of Alaska's best fine-dining experiences. Try the signature king salmon with a soy/ginger/garlic/sesame oil sauce or the shrimp, scallops, and vegetables in a Madras curry-coconut sauce. When possible, the chef uses local organic produce.
🍴 35 🅿 🕐 Closed in winter 🚭 🚫 MC, V

🍴 TALKEETNA ROADHOUSE
$-$$
MAIN ST. BETWEEN B & C STS.
TEL 907/733-1351
www.talkeetnaroadhouse.com
This café/bakery is classic Talkeetna, in a historic building where locals and visitors have gathered for hearty meals, strong coffee, and famed cinnamon rolls since 1944. Upstairs are eight basic rooms for rent.
🍴 50 🕐 Closed D 🚭 🚫 MC, V

DENALI NATIONAL PARK

SOMETHING SPECIAL

🏨 CAMP DENALI
Deep in the heart of Denali National Park, this lodge understands its priorities. Sure, the cabins scattered across the hillside are a cozy delight and the meals are excellent, but Camp Denali focuses on the park, the grand wilderness that surrounds it. Guests can choose from among several naturalist-led outings on such topics as tundra wildflowers, glaciers, and wildlife, and each evening visiting authorities host pre-sentations on various aspects of the park. Camp Denali is the only park lodge with views of the Great One.
$$$$$
DENALI NATIONAL PARK
TEL 907/683-2290
FAX 907/683-1568
www.campdenali.com
🛏 17 🕐 Closed mid-Sept.–early June 🚭

🏨 DENALI CROW'S NEST
$$$
MILE 238.5 PARKS HWY.
TEL 907/683-2723 or
888/917-8130
FAX 907/683-2323
www.denalicrowsnest.com
The Crow's Nest is perched high on the flank of Sugarloaf Mountain, overlooking the development that crowds the entrance to Denali National Park. That lofty position provides both quiet and fantastic views from its cluster of airy, bright cabins. Facilities include a good steak-chili-pasta-burger restaurant.
🛏 39 🅿 🕐 Closed Oct.–mid-May 🚭 🚫 MC, V

🍴 THE PERCH
$$-$$$
MILE 224 PARKS HWY.
TEL 907/683-2523 or
888/322-2523
www.denaliperchresort.com
As its name suggests, the Perch is on a hill (actually, a glacial moraine) amid the treetops. Customers sit back and enjoy the views as they dine on beef, seafood, vegetarian dishes, pasta, and game such as caribou medallions with Portobello mushrooms. Famous for its bread, which it supplies to other restaurants, the Perch lies about 13 miles (21 km) south of the park.
🍴 50 🅿 🕐 Closed Sun.–Thurs. in winter 🚭 🚫 All major cards

🍴 MCKINLEY CREEKSIDE CAFÉ
$-$$
MILE 224 PARKS HWY.
TEL 907/683-2277 or
888/533-6254
FAX 907/683-1558
www.mckinleycabins.com
A casual family dining spot that provides much better food than most such places, the Creekside is known for its varied and enormous breakfasts; try the Mountain Woman's (or Man's)

HOTELS & RESTAURANTS

Breakfast. The vast lunch and dinner menus range from chili to halibut, soups to sandwiches, and salmon to burgers, salads, steaks, and Cajun linguine.

⬛ 40 🅿 🚫 🕐 Closed in winter 💳 All major cards

FAIRBANKS

🏨 WEDGEWOOD 🍴 RESORT
$$$-$$$$
212 WEDGEWOOD DR.
TEL 907/452-1442 or 800/528-4916
FAX 907/451-8184
www.fountainheadhotels.com
Bordering Creamer's Field Migratory Waterfowl Refuge and hosting the Alaska Bird Observatory, this large, intown luxury resort feels more like a country place. The Wedgewood's one- and two-bedroom suites feature kitchens, living rooms, and dining rooms and are tastefully decorated. Here is the warm and inviting Zach's restaurant. Also on the resort property is the summers-only **Bear Lodge** hotel, with 157 spacious rooms.

ℹ️ 297 🚫 🚭 💳 All major cards

🏨 AURORA EXPRESS
$$-$$$
1540 CHENA RIDGE RD.
TEL 907/474-0949 or 800/221-0073
FAX 907/474-8173
www.aurora-express.com
This bed-and-breakfast comprises seven railroad cars set permanently on 700 feet (213m) of track amid a spruce forest on the property. Dating back as far as 1924, the cars have been converted into elegant lodgings that would befit an 1890s railroad magnate. One of the sleepers is divided into four suites, while each of the three other cars rents in its entirety. Breakfast is served in the dining car.

ℹ️ 4 🚫 🕐 Closed early Sept.–late May 💳 MC, V

🏨 BRIDGEWATER HOTEL
$$-$$$
723 1ST AVE.
TEL 907/452-6661 or 800/528-4916
FAX 907/452-6126
www.fountainheadhotels.com
On the Chena River, in the midst of historic downtown Fairbanks, this quiet, refined boutique hotel offers a European feel. Generous service and the fact that the hotel is kept so shipshape place it among the town's finest. Try to reserve one of the corner rooms facing the river.

ℹ️ 94 🅿 🕐 Closed in winter 🚫 🚭 💳 MC

🏨 CLOUDBERRY LOOKOUT
$$
310 YANA CT.
TEL 907/479-7334
FAX 907/479-7134
www.mosquitonet.com/~cloudberry
This bed-and-breakfast features a solarium, a music room with grand piano, a library of Alaska-themed books, antiques throughout, a network of trails for snowshoeing or hiking, and views of a neighboring lake and the surrounding forest. But the hands-down highlight is the aurora borealis viewing tower.

ℹ️ 4 🚫 🕐 Closed Nov.–late Feb. 🅿 💳 All major cards

🍴 PIKE'S LANDING
$$-$$$$
4438 AIRPORT WAY
TEL 907/479-7113
www.pikeslanding.net
Another Fairbanks institution on the banks of the Chena, Pike's is noisy and crowded, just the way patrons like it. The luxurious fine-dining room will fill your steak and lobster needs, after which

---

HOTELS
An indication of the maximum high-season cost of a double room with breakfast is given by $ signs. Rooms may often be available for less than the indicated price.

$$$$$	Over $300
$$$$	$200–$300
$$$	$120–$200
$$	$80–$120
$	Under $80

RESTAURANTS
An indication of the cost of a three-course dinner, including interesting rather than the cheapest menu options, is given by $ signs. Less expensive meals will be available. Drinks are excluded.

$$$$$	Over $75
$$$$	$50–$75
$$$	$35–$50
$$	$20–$35
$	Under $20

---

you can mingle with the masses on the enormous summertime deck, which serves about 400 people at a time and has its own dock. Pike's is known for its Sunday brunch and desserts.

⬛ 530 🅿 🕐 Closed L Sat. 🚫 🚭 💳 All major cards

🍴 THE PUMP HOUSE
$$-$$$$
796 CHENA PUMP RD. (MILE 2)
TEL 907/479-8452
www.pumphouse.com
A National Historic Monument, this favorite Fairbanks restaurant is a converted early-1900s mining pump station. The sprawling lawn and deck on the Chena River are traditional spots for basking in the warm Interior summer sun. Seafood is first among equals on the lengthy menu, which also features beef, pork, chicken, pasta, vegetarian, and game with a wild berry demi-glace.

⬛ 220 🅿 🚫 🚭 💳 All major cards

HOTELS & RESTAURANTS

🍴 GAMBARDELLA'S PASTA BELLA
$$
706 2ND AVE.
TEL 907/457-4992
www.gambardellas.com
A warm, homey downtown restaurant beloved by locals, Gambardella's has a genuine Italian feel and menu. The Italian sausage and bread are made on the premises, and the lasagna boasts a nationwide reputation, with ten layers of fresh pasta, ricotta cheese, and that homemade sausage.
🔢 200 🅿 🕐 Closed L Sun. 🚭 🚗 All major cards

🍴 BUN ON THE RUN
$
3480 COLLEGE RD.
(IN PARKING LOT BY BEAVER SPORTS)
This wildly popular white-and-pink trailer in a parking lot dishes out food that is fast but wonderful—and cheap. Two sisters run the place, and they're especially adept at baking. Among the winners are coconut bars, muffins, cinnamon rolls, brownies, and calzones.
🅿 🕐 Closed Sept.–May

CHENA HOT SPRINGS ROAD

🏨 CHENA HOT SPRINGS RESORT
$-$$$$
MILE 56.6 CHENA HOT SPRINGS RD.
TEL 907/451-8104 or 800/478-4681
FAX 907/451-8151
www.chenahotsprings.com
The sprawling resort at the end of this beautiful road centers on outdoor and indoor hot springs, but activities are many and varied, including hiking, canoeing, horseback riding, mountain biking, and flightseeing. Guests can also take a carriage ride, go gold panning, ride in a cart pulled by sled dogs, or visit the ice museum and ice bar—not to

mention all the winter activities. Accommodations range from tents and yurts to rustic/swanky lodge rooms.
ℹ 80 rooms, 10 cabins 🅿 🚭 🚗 All major cards

🍴 TWO RIVERS LODGE
$$$
MILE 16 CHENA HOT SPRINGS RD.
TEL 907/488-6815
FAX 907/488-9761
www.tworiverslodge.com
In this historic log building superb contemporary dishes abound. The diverse menu covers all bases, from basic grilled fish or steaks to red curry prawns, crispy duck, pheasant apricot, and other imaginative concoctions. On sunny days the wood-fired oven on a deck overlooking the lake bakes excellent foccacia and pizza.
🔢 90 🅿 🕐 Closed L 🚭 🚗 All major cards

THE BUSH

DILLINGHAM

🏨 THAI INN
$$-$$$
119 E ST., W
TEL 907/842-7378
www.thaiamerican.com
Accommodations in this remote town are basic—except for this incongruous inn that brings a little piece of Thailand to the Alaska Bush. Perched atop the highest inhabited point in Dillingham, the B&B offers great views of the bay and mountains. Rooms feature hand-carved teak furniture from Thailand, Thai art, and other Thai decor. The Royal Orchid Suite is especially huge and luxurious.
ℹ 8 🅿

BETHEL

🏨 BENTLEY'S PORTER HOUSE BED & BREAKFAST

$$-$$$
624 1ST AVE
TEL 907/543-3552
FAX 907/543-3230
Rooms in this big, friendly B&B in downtown Bethel explore an eclectic array of themes, including rural English and African. Ask for one overlooking the Kuskokwim River. The rooms share about half as many baths.
ℹ 30 🅿 🚭 🚗 All major cards

🏨 PACIFICA GUEST HOUSE
$$-$$$
1220 HOFFMAN HWY.
TEL 907/543-4305
FAX 907/543-3403
Pacifica offers quiet, modern rooms (some with shared baths) in three buildings. Alaska Native art beautifies most of the rooms and public spaces. A café in the adjacent solarium serves good seafood and vegetarian fare.
ℹ 30 🅿 🚭 🚗 All major cards

NOME

🏨 AURORA INN
$$$-$$$$
302 E. FRONT ST.
TEL 907/443-3838 or 800/354-4606
www.aurorainnome.com
While this attractive new hotel may lack character, it does boast many amenities. Some rooms offer views of the Bering Sea, while the executive suites feature full kitchens and bay windows. Go in search of the sauna should things get a bit chilly.
ℹ 68 🅿 🚭 ⬆ 🚗 All major cards

🏨 NOME NUGGET INN
$$$
FRONT ST. & BERING AVE.
TEL 907/443-4189 or 877/443-2323
FAX 907/443-5966
Right on the Bering Sea, this fun place is stuffed with gold rush memorabilia and kitsch,

HOTELS & RESTAURANTS

although the plain guest rooms lack the spirit of the public spaces. Attached to the inn is one of Nome's most popular hangouts, **Fat Freddie's,** where guests can mingle and chat with locals while scarfing down burgers and chowder.

🛈 47 🅿 Ⓢ 🄰 All major cards

KOTZEBUE

🏨 NULLAGVIK HOTEL
🍴 $$$
308 SHORE AVE.
TEL 907/442-3331
FAX 907/442-3340
www.nullagvik.com
To plant this modern hotel north of the Arctic Circle took some doing, such as erecting it on pilings. The decor reflects Kotzebue's predominant Inupiat Eskimo culture. In the hotel restaurant (which often closes in winter), guests can savor such dishes as reindeer sausage, steaks, and seafood. This is the town's tourism hub, so reserve early.

🛈 75 Ⓢ 🄰 All major cards

DALTON HIGHWAY/ DEADHORSE

🏨 PRUDHOE BAY HOTEL
🍴 $$$
DEADHORSE
TEL 907/659-2449
FAX 907/659-2752
www.prudhoebayhotel.com
Think mobile home on steroids and you'll have an accurate picture of this hotel's style. Here on the Arctic Ocean, near the end of the Dalton Highway, most of the clientele are oil- field workers. While some of the rooms are spartan, a few provide TVs and phones. The hotel can also rent you a vehicle or arrange a tour of the oil fields. Its cafeteria is among the few eateries in Deadhorse.

🛈 170 🅿 Ⓢ 🄰 All major cards

GATES OF THE ARCTIC NATIONAL PARK & PRESERVE

SOMETHING SPECIAL

🏨 FINIAKUK LAKE WILDERNESS LODGE
This exclusive fly-in lodge provides rustic luxury 6 miles (10 km) from Gates of the Arctic National Park, one of the world's wildest and most remote places. The hand-built log lodge is a spacious marvel that even has electricity and hot water, thanks to solar and wind power. You can canoe, hike, fish, and watch for the abundant wildlife, including caribou, grizzlies, moose, and wolves. If you want even more remoteness, the owners can fly you (and a guide) to either of two cabins deep within the park. Winter stays are also possible.

$$$$$
INIAKUK LAKE
TEL 907/479-6354 or
877/479-6354
FAX 907/474-2096
www.gofarnorth.com
🛈 5 rooms, 2 cabins Ⓢ 🄰 MC, V

🏨 PEACE OF SELBY WILDERNESS
$$$$$
SELBY LAKE
TEL 907/672-3206
www.alaskawilderness.net
This isolated lodge within the national park offers the chance to get really far away from it all and see the Arctic wilderness and wildlife. The handsome main lodge was handcrafted from white spruce logs felled on the site. The expansive and nicely furnished loft is rented as a single unit. When it's time to bathe, guests use the outdoor, wood-fired hot tub by the lake. The lodge's other units consist of four rustic cabins at far-flung sites within the park.

🛈 1 room, 4 cabins Ⓢ 🄰 None

BARROW

🏨 KING EIDER INN
$$$-$$$$
1752 AHKOVAK ST.
TEL 907/852-4700
FAX 907/852-2025
www.kingeider.net
This new, well-appointed, contemporary hotel comes as a surprise in the nation's northernmost town, beside the Arctic Ocean. Rooms are spacious, bright with blond pine furniture, and replete with modern amenities; about half have kitchenettes. The Presidential Suite features a stone fireplace, a kitchen, a pine-log four-poster bed, and a Jacuzzi.

🛈 19 Ⓢ 🄰 All major cards

🏨 TOP OF THE WORLD HOTEL
$$$
1200 AGVIQ ST.
TEL 907/852-3900 or
800/882-8478
FAX 907/852-6752
www.topoftheworldhotel.com
A fixture in downtown Barrow since the 1970s, this aptly named hotel is also the town's tourism hub. All the rooms are clean and decent, particularly those in the new wing; try for one with an ocean view. Ask about walking tours, sightseeing excursions, and Inupiat Eskimo cultural programs.

🛈 50 🅿 Ⓢ 🄰 All major cards

🍴 PEPE'S NORTH OF THE BORDER
$$-$$$
1204 AGVIK ST.
TEL 907/852-8200
North of the border, indeed. Next door to the Top of the World Hotel, Pepe's is a local gathering place that serves up Mexican and American food and conversation galore. In addition to the flautas and soft tacos, you can get steak and lobster.

🛗 220 🅿 Ⓢ 🄰 All major cards

SHOPPING

Most Alaska artisans draw from a deep-seated intimacy with the outdoors when creating their arts and crafts. This bond with the natural world also influences such products as clothing, books, and food. Works by Alaska Natives often carry on ancient traditions, sometimes with a modern twist.

SOUTHEAST ALASKA

ARTS, CRAFTS & GIFTS
Alaska Indian Arts Historic 13 Fort Seward Dr., Haines, tel 907/766-2160. Carved totems, prints, silverwork, and other traditional Northwest Coast Native items.
Juneau Artists Gallery 175 S. Franklin St., Juneau, tel 907/586-9891. Local artists operate this gallery, selling work that spans a wide range of media, including quilts, watercolors, fused art glass, and Ukrainian art.
Raven's Journey 439 S. Franklin St., Juneau, tel 907/463-4686. A shop that sells such authentic arts and crafts as masks, ivory carvings, intricately woven grass baskets, and dolls. Lots of Tlingit work, but other Northwest Native art and Inupiat and Yupik Eskimo items, too.
Sea Wolf/Whale Rider Galleries Fort Seward Parade Grounds, Haines, tel 907/766-2540. The gallery and studio of Native son and artist Tresham Gregg, whose diverse work includes totems, bronzes, jewelry, and wall sculptures.
Soho Coho Contemporary Art & Craft Gallery 5 Creek St., Ketchikan, tel 907/225-5954 or 800/888/4070. Owner/operator Ray Troll exhibits and sells his fishy art, but he also designs funny T-shirts and calendars. The gallery also displays the work of other local artists.

BOOKS & MAPS
The Observatory 200 N. Franklin St., Juneau, tel 907/586-9676. This bookstore specializes in maps and books about Alaska and other Arctic regions—more than 3,000 titles and other items all told.
Old Harbor Books 201 Lincoln St., Sitka, tel 907/747-8808. A local institution in Sitka, this bookseller carries an impressive number of books that deal with Alaska topics.
Parnassus Books 5 Creek St., Ketchikan, tel 907/225-7690. On a boardwalk above the water in the Creek Street district, this pleasantly cluttered store offers fine collections of books on Alaska, art, and women.

FOOD
Taku Smokeries 550 S. Franklin St., Juneau, tel 907/463-3474 or 800/582-5122. Taku smokes salmon, and visitors can both watch the process and taste the results. In addition to hot-smoked sockeye, you can buy sockeye lox, smoked salmon spread, and other fishy products.
Theobroma Chocolate Company Sitka, tel 907/966-2345 or 888/985-2345. A local man set up this chocolate factory in the old pulp mill and now sells his superb chocolates as fast as he can make them. While he doesn't have his own store, local merchants stock his products.

ANCHORAGE & MAT-SU

ARTS, CRAFTS, & GIFTS
Alaska Glass Gallery 423 G St., Anchorage, tel 907/279-4527. This artist-owned gallery displays dazzling glass vases, bowls, and abstract sculptures.
Anchorage Museum of History & Art 121 W. 7th Ave., Anchorage, tel 907/343-4326. This large, excellent downtown museum is arguably the finest in Alaska, and the gift shop shares that reputation. A great place to buy a souvenir.
Alaska Native Heritage Center 8800 Heritage Center Dr., Anchorage, tel 907/330-8000 or 800/315-6608. The state's premier institution devoted to Alaska Natives. Its on-site gift shop offers a diverse array of authentic items.
Alaska Native Medical Center 4315 Diplomacy Dr., Anchorage, tel 907/729-1122. Virtually unknown to visitors, this medical center's gift shop is probably the best place in the city to get good deals on first-rate authentic Alaska Native works.
Aurora Fine Art Gallery 737 W. 5th Ave., Anchorage, tel 907/274-0234. One of many fine downtown galleries, the Aurora features both traditional and contemporary works—some ranging into the multi-thousands, although more affordable pieces are available.

BOOKS
Cook Inlet Book Company 415 W. 5th Ave., Anchorage, tel 907/258-4544 or 800/240-4148. Claiming to have the world's largest selection of Alaska-themed books, this downtown bookstore also carries a full range of general books.
Title Wave Books 1360 W. Northern Lights Blvd., Anchorage, tel 907/278-9283 or 888/598-9283. The state's largest independent bookseller, this store boasts a half million titles.

CLOTHING
Oomingmak 604 H St., Anchorage, tel 907/272-9225 or 888/360-9665. Some 250 Alaska Native women belong to Oomingmak, the Musk Ox Producers' co-operative. They hand-knit expensive, luxurious qiviut into marvelous hats, scarves, and tunics.

GENERAL MERCHANDISE
Saturday Market 3rd Ave. & E St., Anchorage, tel 907/272-5634. Name notwithstanding, this sprawling outdoor market is held on both Saturdays and Sundays in summer. Hundreds of vendors sell all sorts of arts, crafts, and food.

KENAI PENINSULA

ARTS, CRAFTS, & GIFTS
Bunnell Street Gallery 106 W. Bunnell St., Suite A, Homer, tel 907/235-2662. This nonprofit institution occupies the Inlet Trading Post, where curious browsers can contemplate the works of some 40 artists, many of them local.

Experience Gallery On the boardwalk, Halibut Cove, tel 907/296-2215. This quaint space is literally a community of artists, most of whom also display their works, which range from pottery to paintings, jewelry, and other pieces.

Fireweed Gallery 475 E. Pioneer Ave., Homer, tel 235-3411. This pretty gallery offers a variety of high-end Alaska art. Look for such unusual works as wildlife sculptures fashioned out of fossilized whale flipper finger bones.

Inua—The Spirit of Alaska Cannery Row Boardwalk, Homer, tel 907/235-6644. This shop sells fine Alaska Native crafts, particularly from the re-mote Inupiat and Yupik Eskimo villages of western Alaska. Customers can buy fossilized walrus jawbone carvings, baleen baskets, knives, reindeer hides, antler carvings, and totem poles.

Kenai Fine Arts Center 816 Cook Ave., Kenai, tel 907/283-7040. This center houses the Peninsula Art Guild, an organization of visual artists that displays and sells paintings, pottery, sculptures, fiber art, and other works.

Resurrect Art Coffeehouse Gallery 320 3rd Ave., Seward, tel 907/224-7161. Set in a historic building that once housed a Lutheran church, this favorite local hangout offers espresso, tasty pastries, and a healthy helping of local art, ranging from simple crafts to expensive paintings.

Resurrection Bay Galerie 500 4th Ave., Seward, tel 907/224-3212. This top-drawer fine art gallery displays serious contemporary paintings and sculpture—some with serious prices to match.

CLOTHING
Nomar 104 E. Pioneer Ave., Homer, tel 907/235-8363 or 800/478-8364, www.nomar alaska.com. Visitors who want no-nonsense, Alaska-tough apparel should try this store. Much of its gear and clothing is perfect for travelers who plan to spend time in the outdoors.

GENERAL MERCHANDISE
Alaska Wild Berry Products 528 E. Pioneer Ave., Homer, tel 907/235-8858. Founded in 1946, this small chain offers such Alaska specialties as canned salmon, honey, and, of course, its signature berry products, made from wild berries handpicked on the Kenai Peninsula.

Kenai Landing 2101 Bow-picker Lane, Kenai, tel 907/335-2500. This complex features galleries, a museum, and an indoor market with 40 vendors. Goods include pottery, fishing tackle, and specialty foods.

ALASKA PENINSULA

ARTS, CRAFTS, & GIFTS
Alutiiq Museum & Archaeological Repository 215 Mission Rd., Kodiak, tel 907/486-7004. In keeping with the repository's mission to ex-plore and preserve Alutiiq culture, the on-site gift shop sells consignment items—dolls, baskets, ivory carvings, masks—for Native artists and craftspeople.

Baranov Museum 101 Marine Way, Kodiak, tel 907/486-5920. The gift shop in this museum naturally carries classic Russian pieces, including icons, samovars, painted Easter eggs, nesting dolls, and lacquerware.

PRINCE WILLIAM SOUND

ART, CRAFTS, & GIFTS
Spirit Mountain Artworks Mile 33 Edgerton Hwy., Chitina, tel 907/823-2222. Though perched on the edge of remote Wrangell–St. Elias, this is one of Alaska's best galleries, featuring more than 100 Alaska artists.

BOOKS
Orca Book & Sound Co 507 1st St., Cordova, tel 907/424-5305. This legendary local bookstore offers rare, out-of-print, and first-edition books. It also serves as an art gallery; visitors can admire and buy.

INTERIOR

ARTS, CRAFTS, & GIFTS
Goose Lake Studio Mile 239 Parks Hwy. (Denali entrance), tel 907/683-2904 or 907/683-2570. Housed in a log cabin, this gallery displays works by Alaska artists, including owner Donna Gates King. Pieces include paintings, quilts, and pottery.

Judie Gumm Designs 3600 Main St., Ester (Fairbanks area), tel 907/479-4568. Using silver and beads to fashion such items as an aurora borealis pin, flying geese necklace, and salmon earrings, Gumm creates jewelry that seems more like sculpture.

Santa Claus House 101 St. Nicholas Dr., North Pole (Fairbanks area), tel 907/488-2200. The vast Santa Claus House sells everything virtually connected to Christmas.

Talkeetna Artisans Main St., Talkeetna, tel 907/733-4222. This gallery displays the mixed-media works of a dozen local artists. Pieces include pottery, oils, basketry, photography, stained glass, and digital art.

THE BUSH

ARTS, CRAFTS, & GIFTS
Arctic Trading Post Front & Bering Sts., Nome, tel 907/443-2686. Browse amid the T-shirts to find well-made Alaska Native crafts, including carved ivory and woven grass baskets.

Chukotka-Alaska 514 Lomen St., Nome, tel 907/443-4128. This small shop celebrates the Russia-Alaska connection by selling art and crafts from both sides of the Bering Sea.

ENTERTAINMENT

Summer or winter, Alaskans love events, and visitors are welcome to join the fun. In addition to transitory events, some cities and larger towns offer ongoing entertainment (often only in summer), such as music, theater, dance, comedy, and general carousing.

SOUTHEAST ALASKA

Days of '98 Show Eagles Hall, 6th & Broadway, Skagway, tel 907/983-2545, www.alaskan .com/daysof98. Chronicling the last days of 19th-century con man Soapy Smith's life, this musical comedy has been getting laughs for more than 70 years. Prior to the show, watch "The Vagabond of Verse," a tribute to famed far-north poet Robert Service, or indulge in mock gambling with "Soapy's money" at the roulette wheel or card table.
New Archangel Dancers Harrigan Centennial Hall, Sitka harbor, tel 907/747-5516, www .newarchangeldancers.com. This well-regarded, all-female group performs traditional Russian dances and stages frequent programs in downtown Sitka. They are a blaze of colorful costumes and bounding energy as they do the Cossack Horse-men's Dance or the Moldovian Suite. They also sing traditional Russian songs.
Perseverance Theatre 914 3rd St., Douglas (Juneau area), tel 907/364-2421, www.persever ancetheatre.org. Among the nation's finest regional theaters, PT mixes challenging classics with innovative, often edgy works. The classics range from *Death of a Salesman* to a rendition of *MacBeth* set in Tlingit culture and featuring an all-Native cast. Premieres of new works have included Paula Vogel's *How I Learned to Drive*.
Sheet'ka Kwaan Naa Kahidi Native Dancers 200 Katlian St., Sitka, tel 907/747-7290 or 888/270-8687, www.sitkatribal .com. In a handsome community center that local Tlingit built in downtown Sitka, the public can catch traditional performances, during which dancers wear resplendent Tlingit regalia.

ANCHORAGE & MAT-SU

Alaska Dance Theatre 2602 Gambell St., Anchorage, tel 907/277-9591, www.alaskadance theatre.org. Alaska's premier professional dance company and school performs both ballet and modern. It often collaborates with Alaska musical companies to bring in big-name dancers from outside the state.
Anchorage Opera 1507 Spar Ave., Anchorage, tel 907/279-2557, www.anchorageopera.org. Alaska's only professional opera company is one of the nation's best regional companies. Each year the troupe graces the performing arts center with three full-blown operas—usually the classics, sometimes with world-class guest singers.
Anchorage Symphony Orchestra 400 D St., Anchorage, tel 907/274-8668, www.anchoragesymphony.org. An accomplished company of some 80 professional musicians, the Anchorage Symphony plays several annual concerts in the performing arts center, often with prominent guests. It also gives children's concerts and other miscellaneous perfor-mances, such as playing the score to accompany a screening of Charlie Chaplin's silent film classic *City Lights*.
Chilkoot Charlie's 1071 W. 25th Ave., Anchorage, tel 907/279-1692, www.koots.com. Arguably Alaska's most famous nightspot, Koot's comprises ten separate bars. The rambling wooden building is often the scene of unbridled drinking, dancing, and loud music.
Fly by Night Club 3300 Spenard Rd., Anchorage, tel 907/279-7726, www.flybynight club.com. Run by the peculiar Mr. Whitekeys, this bar/music club sometimes draws big-name musicians. It's best known, however, for the *Whale Fat Follies*, a satirical revue that skewers all things Alaska.

KENAI PENINSULA

Pier One Theater on Homer Spit, Homer, tel 907/235-7333, www.pieronetheatre.org. Consistently intriguing and unpredictable, this esteemed theater stages a spectrum of plays and musical events. Visitors might catch an Edward Albee drama, a remake of *The Beggar's Opera*, a jazz harp trio, or a musical comedy covering a century of women's music.

INTERIOR

Blue Loon Mile 353.5 Parks Hwy., 3 miles south of Fairbanks, tel 907/457-5666, www.theblueloon.com. Fairbanks's one-of-a-kind, self-proclaimed "cultural epicenter," the Blue Loon offers excellent food, nationally known musical acts, comedy, dancing, and first-run movies (mainstream and art house), as well as a campfire area, RV park, and volleyball court. Special events include Monday Night Football on the giant screen, a hip-hop music fest, and a scholarly lecture series.
Malemute Saloon at Ester Gold Camp, Main St., Ester (Fairbanks area), tel 907/479-2500 or 800/676-6925. This historic gold rush saloon comes alive as boisterous crowds enjoy an evening show that revolves around the gold rush, Robert Service poems, and plenty of song and dance. It's silly but fun—and done well.
Palace Theatre & Saloon Pioneer Park, at Airport Way & Peger Rd., Fairbanks, tel 800/354-7274, www.akvisit.com. Nightly venue of the *Golden Heart Revue*, a lighthearted, costumed look at some of the leading figures of Fairbanks's gold rush past. You'll get a kick out of the Alaska fashion show, which is big on rubber boots.

ACTIVITIES

Alaska offers several hundred million acres of great outdoors to explore, not to mention a rich cultural legacy. Given all that raw material, it's not surprising that there are hundreds, perhaps thousands, of guides and tour companies willing and able to show you around. This section is a mere sampler of available operators. Most are good, and many are excellent, but don't hesitate to check out an outfit if you're unsure about its reliability. Stop in and ask at the nearest chamber of commerce, visitor center, or Alaska Public Lands Information Center.

SOUTHEAST ALASKA

BOAT TOURS
Breakaway Adventures
P.O. Box 2107, Wrangell, AK 99929, tel 907/874-2488 or 888/385-2488, www.breakaway adventures.com. The folks at Breakaway have been taking small groups up the mighty Stikine River since 1989, leading them through the maze of channels, showing them moose, glaciers, and bears, and stopping at the hot springs along the way. The new boats feature sliding windows on all sides for easy viewing and warmth when it's blustery. Breakaway also runs trips to LeConte Glacier and the Anan Bear Observatory.
***Esther G* Sea Taxi**
215 Shotgun Alley, Sitka, tel 907/747-6481, www.puffins andwhales.com. In Capt. Davey Lubin, passengers get a former commercial fisherman, experienced mariner, biologist, botanist, and conservation-minded educator who can share much about the wildlife and ecology of gorgeous Sitka Sound. He offers small, personal, customized tours to a maximum of six people.

HIKING & BACKPACKING
Gastineau Guiding 1330 Eastaugh Way, Juneau, tel 907/586-8231 or 907/586-2666, www.stepintoalaska.com. Leads a mix of active cruise ship passengers and independent travelers on hiking trips in the rain forest, across the alpine tundra, and to a glacier. Also offers sea kayaking, photo safari, and whale-watching excursions.

KAYAKING
Alaska Discovery
5310 Glacier Hwy., Juneau, tel 907/780-6226 or 800/586-1911, www.akdiscovery.com. Known for its sea kayaking trips—from easy outings with lessons for beginners to ten-day expeditions. How about a paddle to see the brown bears of Admiralty Island or rivers of ice in Glacier Bay? Also guides rafting, canoeing, and hiking trips and provides lodging.

SCENIC FLIGHTS
Southeast Aviation 1249 Tongass Ave., Ketchikan, tel 907/225-2900 or 888/359-6478, www.southeastaviation.com. The pilots of this small outfit will fly customers almost anywhere in Southeast Alaska; each has been flying the Inside Passage for more than 25 years. They specialize in flightseeing trips in six-passenger float-planes to beautiful Misty Fjords National Monument; trips range from a 30-minute introduction to 2.5 hours above the glaciers and rainforest–cloaked mountains.

TOURS & EXCURSIONS
Alaska Nature Tours
P.O. Box 491, Haines, AK 99827 tel 907/766-2876, http://kcd .com/aknature. This company's bus, van, boat, and hiking tours focus on the rich wildlife and fine scenery that envelop Haines, notably the Chilkat Bald Eagle Preserve, where more than 3,000 eagles gather in fall. Some tours lead from the shoreline, where you'll see whales, seals, and seabirds, to the alpine tundra, where you

may spot bears, marmots, or mountain goats.

Chilkat Guides Ltd., PO Box 170, Haines, AK, 99827, tel 888/292-7789, www.chilkat guides.com. For almost three decades, Chilkat has been leading raft trips and hikes through the Arctic National Wildlife Refuge and along the rivers of the Tatshenshini-Alsek World Heritage Site.

ANCHORAGE & MAT-SU

SCENIC FLIGHTS
Rust's Flying Service Lake Hood P.O. Box 190867, Anchorage, AK 99519, tel 907/243-1595 or 800/544-2299, www .flyrusts.com. Taking off from the world's busiest seaplane base, this decades-old company offers a bird's-eye view of south–central Alaska. Also runs bear-viewing trips and drops off passengers for hunting, fishing, and rafting adventures.

MOUNTAIN BIKING
Alaska Backcountry Bike Tours LLC P.O. Box 6754-JA, Palmer, AK 99645, tel 907/746-5018 or 866/354-2453, www .mountainbikealaska.com. Ideal for those seeking to bike Alaska but preferring some guidance. Rides range from a two-hour family jaunt on a municipal bike path to nine days of technical riding in the mountains of Chugach National Forest.

KENAI PENINSULA

BOAT TOURS
Kenai Fjords Tours Seward tel 907/276-6249 or 800/478-8068, www.alaskaheritagetours .com. Offers more than a dozen different boat tours of Resur-rection Bay and Kenai Fjords National Park. Watch for whales, seabird rookeries, sea otters, and calving glaciers. An asso-ciated outfit, **Mariah Tours,** runs much smaller boats (max. 16 passengers) for a more intimate look at the park.

CANOEING
Alaska Canoe & Campground 35292 Sterling Hwy., Sterling, tel 907/262-2331, www.alaskacanoetrips.com. For boat and gear rental, shuttles, and other services. Adjacent to the nearly two million acres (810,000 ha) of the Kenai National Wildlife Refuge, including the renowned Canoe Lakes Trails System.

HIKING & BACKPACKING
Center for Alaskan Coastal Studies P.O. Box 2225, Homer, AK 99603, tel 907/235-6667, www.akcoastalstudies.org. This nonprofit group educates visitors about Kachemak Bay and nearby lands. Its all-day natural history excursion begins with a boat tour across the bay, stops at a research center on the far shore, takes a hike through the rain forest, and finishes with outstanding tide-pooling. Ask about the kayaking option.

ALASKA PENINSULA & THE ALEUTIANS

BACKCOUNTRY EXPLORATION
Alaska Alpine Adventures, General Delivery, Port Alsworth, AK 99653, tel 877/525-2577 www.alaskaalpineadventures .com. Located near Lake Clark, Alaska Alpine Adventures specializes in trips exploring this hard-to-reach park and other remote destinations such as Katmai and Gates of the Arctic as well as the Alaska National Wildlife Refuge.

BEAR VIEWING
Hallo Bay Katmai National Park P.O. Box 2904, Homer, AK 99603, tel 907/235-2237, www.hallobay.com. Less than a dozen people at a time fly the 120 miles (190 km) from Homer to this utterly remote shoreline camp amid Katmai National Park. Guests spend anywhere from five hours to a week seeing the brown bears up close.

Sea Hawk Air Kodiak P.O. Box 3561, Kodiak, AK 99615, tel 907/486-8282 or 800/770-4295, www.seahawkair .com. Kodiak bears are the nation's largest brown bear species, and Sea Hawk Air takes people out to view them—safely—in Kodiak National Wildlife Refuge and Katmai National Park.

PRINCE WILLIAM SOUND & AROUND

BOAT TOURS
Stan Stephens Glacier & Wildlife Cruises 112 N. Harbor Dr., Valdez, tel 907/835-4731 or 866/867-1297, www .stanstephenscruises.com. The Stephens family has run tour boats across Prince William Sound since 1971. During the signature day trip to the massive Columbia Glacier, visitors often spot sea otters, puffins, and sea lions, as well as the occasional orca (killer whale) or humpback whale.

RIVER RUNNING
Alaska River Rafters Mile 13 Copper River Hwy., Cordova, tel 907/424-7238 or 800/776-1864, www.alaskarafters.com. Operating in Chugach National Forest and Wrangell–St. Elias National Park, this company runs everything from half-day to ten-day rafting trips. Starting outside Cordova, the half-day trip begins amid icebergs at the base of a glacier and crosses the wildlife-rich Copper River Delta.

SCENIC FLIGHTS
Wrangell Mountain Air No. 25, P.O. Box MXY, McCarthy, AK 99588, tel 907/554-4411 or 800/478-1160, www.wrangell mountainair.com. Even the longest flights can't take in all of 13.2-million-acre Wrangell–St. Elias National Park, but starting from this enclave amid the park, pilots manage to cover quite a distance. You may see the Bagley Icefield, the lofty peaks of the Wrangells, the Stairway Icefall, and all manner of wildlife.

INTERIOR

CLIMBING SCHOOLS
Alaska Mountaineering School, P.O. Box 566, 3rd St., Talkeetna, AK 99676, tel 907/733-1016, fax 907/733-1362, www.climbalaska.org. Offers multiday climbing courses as well as organizes climbing expeditions in Denali and throughout Alaska.

SCENIC FLIGHTS
Talkeetna Air Taxi P.O. Box 73, Talkeetna, AK 99676, tel 907/733-2218 or 800/533-2219, www.talkeetnaair.com. In small planes equipped with skis, you'll fly over the rugged Alaska Range and 45-mile-long (72 km) Kahiltna Glacier, passing between 14,573-foot (4,442m) Mount Hunter and 17,400-foot (5,300m) Mount Foraker on your way to circling the Great One—20,320-foot (6,194 m) Mount McKinley. You may spot climbers inching up its slopes. Some trips land on a glacier at the base of McKinley.

THE BUSH

SCENIC TOUR
Northern Alaska Tour Company P.O. Box 82991W, Fairbanks, AK 99708, tel 907/474-8600 or 800/474-1986, www.northernalaska.com. Using the 414 rugged and remote miles (667 km) of the Dalton Highway as its lifeline, this company makes the Arctic accessible. In 10-passenger vans or 25-passenger buses, visitors can take a one-day run up to the Arctic Circle and back. The classic trip features a flight to Prudhoe Bay, followed by a drive back down to Fairbanks.

TOURS & EXCURSIONS
Sourdough Outfitters, P.O. Box 26066, Bettles Field, AK 99726, tel 907/692-5252, www.sourdough.com. This three-decades old company offers dog-sledding on the North Slope in the winter and hiking, fishing, and rafting in the Brooks Range in summer.

INDEX

Bold page numbers
indicate illustrations

A

Adak Island 165
Admiralty Island National
Monument 90, **90**
Kootznoowoo Wilderness
90
Pack Creek 90
Afognak Island State Park
159
Ahtna 15
Alaska Bird Observatory
206
Alaska Botanical Garden 99
Alaska Chilkat Bald Eagle
Preserve 84
Alaska Highway 39
Alaska Islands & Ocean
Visitor Center 137–138
Alaska Marine Highway
(AMHS) 67–69, 164, 237
Alaska Maritime National
Wildlife Refuge 65, 127,
137, 162, 164–165, **165**
Adak Island 165
Chiswell Islands 127
St. Lazaria Island 65
St. Paul Island 165
Alaska Native Heritage
Center **107**, 107–108,
108
Alaska Natives **9**, 13–17, 33
Alaska Native art **100**,
100–101, **101**
see also specific groups
Alaska Peninsula and the
Aleutians 149–166
Alaska Maritime National
Wildlife Refuge 164–165
Alaska Peninsula &
Becharof National
Wildlife Refuges 166
Aleutian Islands 162–163
Birding on Attu Island 154
Chiniak Highway 160–161
Hotels & restaurants
254–255
Izembek National Wildlife
Refuge 166
Katmai National Park &
Preserve 155–157
Kodiak Island archipelago
158–159
Lake Clark National Park
& Preserve 152
map 150–151
McNeil River State Game
Sanctuary 153
Alaska Peninsula National
Wildlife Refuge 166
Alaska Rainforest Sanctuary
53
Alaska Range 28
Alaska Veterans
Memorial/POW-MIA Rest

Area 214
Alatna 230
Aleknagik 219
Aleut 15, 16, 150–151
Aleutian Islands 162–163
Church of the Holy
Ascension 162, 163
Unalaska Island 20, **162**,
163
Unimak Island **151**, **163**
Aleutian World War II
National Historic Area
163
Allakaket 230
Alpenglow at Arctic Valley
108
Alutiiq 15, 151, 168
Alyeska Highway 106
Anan Creek 57
Anan Wildlife Observatory
57
Anchorage 22, **22–23**, 27,
39, 45, 94–99
Anchorage Market &
Festival 96
*Aurora—Alaska's Great
Northern Lights* 98
downtown area **94–95**,
95–96
galleries and museums
97–99
gardens and parks 99
historic district 96–97
Kincaid Park 97
Lowenfels Family Nature
Trail 99
Oomingmak Co-op 98–99
Oscar Anderson House
96–97
Ship Creek 95, **96**
Tony Knowles Coastal
Trail 97, **99**
Wendler Building 96
Wildflower Trail 99
Anchorage and Mat-Su
91–116, **92**
Anchorage 94–99
Chilkoot Charlie's 116
Chugach State Park **91**,
99, 102–106
Hatcher Pass drive
114–115
Hotels & restaurants
246–250
history and description
92–93
map 92–93
Mat-Su Borough 110–113
Mr. Whitekey's Fly by
Night Club 116
North Anchorage
107–109
Turnagain Arm 102–106
Anchorage Coastal Wildlife
Refuge 102
Aniakchak Mountain 22
Annette Island 53
Anolic Unneengnuzinna
Aaluhguk 43

Arctic Circle 225
Arctic Interagency Visitor
Center 225
Arctic National Wildlife
Refuge 24, 232
Arctic Ocean 233, **233**
Arctic region 26
Arnold Espe Auditorium
207
Arts, 40–46, **40–41**, **42**, **43**,
44, **100**, 100–101, **101**
buying **100**, 100–101,
101
literature 46
native artists 43–45
performing arts 45–46
visual 40–43
Athabascan 14–15, 93, 168,
190
Attu Island 24, 38–39, 154
birding 154
Aurora borealis **226–227**,
227

B

Bald eagles 30, **47**
Barrow 24, **24**, 26, 233,
233
Bears **134**, **135**
Brown bears **18–19**,
155, 157
Kodiak bears 29
Polar bears 29, **29**, 222
viewing 28–29, 134–135,
135, 157
Becharof National Wildlife
Refuge 166
Behm Canal 54
Bennett, Lake 37
Bering land bridge 24,
32–33
map 32
Bering Land Bridge
National Preserve 234
Bethel 220
Bettles 230
Birds and birding **144–145**,
154, **174**
Blackstone Bay 176
Blind River Rapids
Boardwalk 59
Blind Slough Swan
Observatory 59
Blueberry Lake State
Recreation Site 178–179
Boat tours
see Cruise or Boat Tours
Bonanza Mine Trail 187
Bridal Veil Falls 89, **171**,
178
Brooks Falls 157
Brooks Range 27, 28, 39,
232
Bush, The 215–234
Arctic National Wildlife
Refuge 232
Barrow 233
Bering Land Bridge
National Preserve 234

Bethel 220
Dalton Highway 224–225,
230
description 216–217
Dillingham 218–219
Gates of the Arctic
National Park &
Preserve 230
Hotels & restaurants
259–260
Kobuk Valley National
Park 229
Kotzebue 223
map 217
Nome 221–222
St. Lawrence Island 234
Bush planes **167**

C

Caines Head State
Recreation Area 122–123
Canning River 232
Cantwell 193
Cape Krusenstern National
Monument 223
Castle Hill 60–61
Central 212
Chadwick, Jerah 46
Chena Hot Springs Road
209, 209–210
Chena River State
Recreation Area 209
Plain of Monuments 210
Chena River 204
Chenega 23–24
Chief Shakes Island 56–57
Chilkoot Lake State
Recreation Site 84
Chilkoot Pass 37, **37**
Chilkoot Trail 87
Chiniak Highway 160–161
Anton Larsen Bay 160
Buskin River State
Recreation Site 160
Fossil Beach 161
map 161
Russian River Bridge 161
Sargent Creek 160
Women's Bay 160
Chiswell Islands 127
Chitina River 181
Chugach Mountains 11, **91**
Chugach State Park **91**, 99,
102–106, 116, **116**
Hillside Trail System 116
Coldfoot 225
Colony Village 112
Cook, Capt. John 40, 78, 93,
168
Cooper Landing 148
K'beq Footprints
Heritage Site 148
Copper Center 188
Copper River **172**,
172–175, **173**, 181, 182
Copper River Highway
174–175
Alaganik Slough 175
Childs Glacier 175

Haystack Trail 175
Million Dollar Bridge 175
Sheridan Glacier 174
Cordova 172–174
downtown 173–174
harbor walk 172–173
Ilanka Cultural Center
173
Prince William Sound
Science Center 172
Cordova and Copper River
Delta 20, 172–175, **175**
Creamer's Field Migratory
Waterfowl Refuge 205
Creek Street, Ketchikan 52,
53
Crow Creek Mine 106
Cruises or boat tours
Boat tour Kachemak Bay
146–147
map 147
Cruising Misty Fiords 54–
55, **54**
map 55

D
Dall sheep 30
Dalton Highway **224**,
224–225, 230
Atigun Pass 225
Finger Mountain BLM
Wayside 224
map 225
Deadhorse 225
Deep Creek State
Recreation Area 148
Deer Mountain Tribal
Hatchery and Eagle
Center 52
Dena'ina 15, 93
Denali Highway 193, **193**
Denali National Park &
Preserve **2–3**, 12–13,
16–17, 194–201, **195**,
196, 198, 200, 201
drive 198-201
map 199
hiking 196–197, 200
Horseshoe Lake Trail 197
Kettle Lake **16–17**
map **197**
Mount Healy Overlook
Trail 197
McKinley, Mount **16–17**,
22, **26**, 28, **195**
Murie Science & Learning
Center 196
Park Road 194, 198–201
Savage River Loop Trail
197
Taiga Trail 197
visitor centers 196, 201
Wilderness Access
Center 198
Wonder Lake 201
Dillingham 20, 218–219,
219
Drives
Chiniak Highway 160–161

map 161
Denali Park Road
198–201
map 199
Hatcher Pass Drive
114–115
map 115
Richardson Highway
179–179, **178**
map 179
Dyea 37

E
Eagle Beach State
Recreation Area 76
Eagle River Nature Center
108–109, **109**
Albert Loop Trail 109
Rodak Nature Trail 109
Earthquakes 22–24
Eklutna 109
Eklutna Historical Park
109
Eklutna Lake Recreation
Area 109
St. Nicholas Russian
Orthodox Church 109,
Elliott Highway 213, **213**
Wickersham Dome
Trailhead 213
Ellis, William 40
Entertainment and activities
263–265
Exxon Valdez oil spill 39,
39, 169
Eyak 15, 168

F
Fairbanks 24, 26, 203–208,
203
Chena Indian Village 204
downtown 203–206
Georgeson Botanical
Garden 207–208
Pioneer Park 204–205
University of Alaska
206–208
Ferries
Alaska Marine Highway
67–69, 237
Gustavus 79
Kodiak to Unalaska
164–165
Petersburg to Wrangell
56
Russian River 148
Festivals and yearly events
227–228, 238–240
Fishhook Trail 114
Fishing **128, 129**
competitions 128–129
Flattop Mountain **91, 116**
Floatplanes **14–15**, 192
Fort Abercrombie State
Historical Park 159
Fort William H. Seward
National Historic
Landmark 83

G
Galleries
see Museums and
galleries
Gates of the Arctic
National Park & Preserve
230, **231**
Glacier Bay 35
Glacier Bay National Park
& Preserve 78–81, **78, 79**
Bartlett Cove 79–80, **79**
Bartlett Lake Trail 80
Bartlett River Trail 80
Forest Loop Trail 79–80
Gustavus 78–79
Johns Hopkins Glacier **78**
Johns Hopkins Inlet 81
Lamplugh Glacier 81
map 81
Margerie Glacier 81
Point Gustavus 80
Reid Glacier 81, **235**
Tarr Inlet 81
Glacier Gardens Rainforest
Adventure 74
Glacier/Juneau Veterans'
Memorial Highway 74–76
Auke Bay 76
Inspiration Point 76
Shrine of St. Therese 76
Glaciers 24
recession of 184–185
see also glaciers by name
Glen Alps 116
Gold Creek 36
Gold dredges 211, **212**,
214
Gold rushes 36–38
Golden eagles 30
Goldrush Cemetery 88
Great Alaskan Lumberjack
Show 51
Great Kobuk Sand Dunes
229, **229**
Gull Island 146, **147**
Gustavus 78–79

H
Haida 15
Haines 82–84
Alaska Indian Arts 83
Alaska Chilkat Bald Eagle
Preserve 84
Chilkat Center for the
Arts, Haines 83
Chilkoot Lake State
Recreation Site 84
Eagle Council Grounds
84
Fort William H. Seward
National Historic
Landmark 83
Hammer Museum 83
Seldon Museum and
Cultural Center 82
Totem Village 83
Valley of the Eagles 84
Halibut Cove 142
Harding Icefield 127

Harris, Richard 36
Hatcher Pass drive
114–115
Fishhook Trail 114
Gold Mint Trail 114
Independence Mine State
Historical Park 114–115
Little Susitna River 114
map 115
Heart of the Klondike
(poster) **36**
Hidden Creek Trail 131
History
first inhabitants 32–33
gold rushes 36–38
modern times 39
Russian influence 33–34
Seward's purchase
34–35, 34–36
World War II **38**, 38–39,
163
Homer 136–140, **136, 138**
Alaska Islands & Ocean
Visitor Center 137–138
Bishop's Beach 138
galleries and museums
138–139
Carl E. Wynn Nature
Center 140
outdoor activities
139–140
Horsetail Falls 178
Hotels and restaurants
241–260
House of Wickersham 71
Hulahula River 232
Humpback whales **28**, 30

I
Icy Bay 182
Iditarod National Historic
Trail 108
Iditarod Trail Sled Dog
Race Headquarters,
Wasilla 113, **113**
Independence Mine State
Historical Park 114–115
Inside Passage **66–67**,
66–69, **68–69**
Interior 24, 26, 189–214
Chena Hot Springs Road
209–210
Chicken 214
Denali Highway 193
Denali National Park &
Preserve 194–201
Denali State Park 214
description and history
190–191
Elliott Highway 213
Fairbanks 203–208
Hotels & restaurants
257–259
map 191
Nenana 202
Steese Highway
211–212
Talkeetna 192
Inuit **24**

Inupiat 14, 26, **43**
Inupiat Heritage Center, Barrow 233
Izembek National Wildlife Refuge 166

J
Jackson, Nathan **40–41**, 44–45
Johns Hopkins Glacier 78
Jumbo Mine **182**
Juneau 70–77, **70**,
Alaska State Capitol 71
Alaska State Museum, Juneau 72
Decker Gallery 73
Glacier/Juneau Veterans' Memorial Highway 74–76
historic downtown 70–71, 70–71
House of Wickersham 71
Juneau Artists Gallery 73
Juneau-Douglas City Museum 71
Mount Roberts **73**, 73–74
Perseverance Theatre, Juneau 46
Raven's Journey 73
Senate Building, 73
South Franklin Street 72–73
Juneau, Joe 36

K
Kachemak Bay **141**
boat tour 146, 146–147
map 147
Center for Alaskan Coastal Studies 141–142
China Poot Bay 147
Gull Island 146, 147
Peterson Bay 147
Peterson Bay Coastal Science Field Station 146
Kachemak Bay State Park 143
Grewingk Glacier Lake Trail 143
Poot Peak Trail 144
Kantner, Seth 46
Katmai National Park & Preserve **18–19, 25**, 155–157, **155, 156–157**
bear-watching **18–19**, 135, **135, 155**
Brooks Camp 155
Dumpling Mountain 155
Hallo Bay **156–157**, 157
Kulik Lake **14–15**
Naknek Lake 155
Three Forks Convergence 156
Ukak Falls Trail 156
Valley of Ten Thousand Smokes 156

Kayak Island 188
Kelliher-Combs, Sonya 43–44
Kenai 132–133
Holy Assumption of the Virgin Mary Church **132**, 133
Clam Gulch **133**
Kenai Landing 133
Visitors & Cultural Center 132
Kenai Fjords National Park & Preserve **124**, 124–127, **126**
Alaska Maritime National Wildlife Refuge 127
Exit Glacier 126, 127
Harding Icefield 127
Holgate Glacier 127
map 125
Overlook Trail 127
Kenai Lake 148
Kenai National Wildlife Refuge 130–131
Bear Mountain Trail 131
Hidden Creek Trail 131
Keen Eye Trail 130
Skilak Lake Loop Road 131, **131**
Skilak Wildlife Recreation Area 131
Swan Lake Canoe Route 130–131
Swanson River Canoe Route 131
Kenai Peninsula 117–148
bear-watching 134–135
description and history 118–119
Cooper Landing 148
fishing 128–129
Hotels & restaurants 250–254
Homer 136–140
Kachemak Bay 141–147
Kenai 132–133
Kenai Fjords National Park 124–127
Kenai National Wildlife Refuge 130–131
map 119
Ninilchik 148, **148**
Resurrection Pass Trail 148
Seward 120–123
Kenai River Flats 133
Kennecott Mines 187
Kennicott
see McCarthy/Kennicott
Kennicott Glacier Lodge **186–187**, 187
Kennicott River 181
Ketchikan 12–13, **12–13**, 24, **50**, 50–53
Alaska Eagle Arts 51
Alaska Rainforest Sanctuary 53
Creek Street 52, **53**
Deer Mountain Tribal

Hatchery and Eagle Center 52
Lumberjack Show 51
Saxman Native Village and Totem Park 52–53
Soho Coco 51
Southeast Alaska Discovery Center 51
Star Building 50–51
Tongass Highway 52–53
Tongass Historical Museum 52
Totem Bright State Historical Park **42**, 53
Totem Heritage Center 52
waterfront 50, **50–51**, 51–52
Kettle Lake **16–17**
Kigluaik Mountains 222
King Salmon 155
Kiska 38–39
Klondike gold rush 36–38
Klondike Gold Rush National Historical Park 85, 86, **86–87**
Kluane National Park, Yukon, Canada 80, 90
Kobuk Valley National Park 229
Boreal Mountain 230
Frigid Crags 230
Kodiak 18, 20, 24, 158–159, 160, **160**
Fort Abercrombie State Historical Park 159
Holy Resurrection Russian Orthodox Church 159
St. Herman Theological Seminary 159
Kodiak Island Archipelago 158–159
Chiniak Highway 160–161
map 161
Kodiak National Wildlife Refuge 159
Kongakut River 232
Kotzebue 223, **223**
Kuroshio (Japan Current) 24

L
Lake Clark National Park & Preserve 152, **152**
Tanalian Falls Trail 152
Tazimina Lakes 152
Telaquana Trail 152
Turquoise Lake 152
Twin Lakes 152
Two Lakes 152
Land and landscape 22–31
Laurence, Sydney **40–41**
LeConte Glacier 57
Leutze, Edward (painting) **34–35**
Lincoln Street, Sitka **60–61**, 61–63
Lindeman, Lake 37

Literature 46
Little Susitna River 114
Lookout Park 82
Lost Creek 183
Lowe River 178
Lowell Point State Recreation Site 122
Lutak Highway 84
Chilkoot Lake State Recreation Site 84
Lutak Inlet 84
Tanani Point 84
Lynn Canal **82**

M
Malaspina Glacier 36–37
Manley Hot Springs 213
Marathon, Mount 122
Margerie Glacier **68–69**, 81
Marsh Fork River 232
Mat-Su Borough **110–111**
Farm Loop Road 112
Palmer 110–113
Wasilla 113
Matcharak, Lake 230
McCarthy/Kennicott 186–187
Root Glacier Trail 187
McDonald Spit 145
McKinley, Mount **1, 16–17**, 22, **26**, 28, **195**
McNeil River State Game Sanctuary 135, 153, **153**
Mendenhall Glacier 74–75, **74–75, 77**
East Glacier Loop 76
Photo Point Trail 75
Trail of Time 76
Metlakatla 53
Michelson, Mount 28
Midnight sun 26–27
Misty Fiords National Monument **54**, 54–55
map 55
Punchbowl Cove 52
Mitkof Highway 59
Moose 11, **140, 190**
viewing 29–30, 130
Mountain goats 30
Muir, John 35
Muir Glacier 35
Museums and galleries
Alaska Aviation Heritage Museum, Anchorage 99
Alaska Eagle Arts 51
Alaska Experience Center, Anchorage 98
Alaska Gallery, Anchorage 98
Alaska Glass Gallery, Anchorage 97
Alaska State Museum, Juneau 72
Alaska State Railroad Museum, Nenana 202
Alutiiq Museum and Archaeological Repository, Kodiak 159
Anchorage Museum of

History & Art 97–98, **98**
Anchorage Museum of History and Art 41
Artist Cove Gallery, Sitka 62
Aurora Fine Art Gallery, Anchorage 97
Aurora Ice Museum, Chena 210
Baranov Museum, Kodiak 159
Bunnell Street Gallery, Homer 138
Carrie M. McLain Memorial Museum, Nome 222
Circle District Historical Society Museum, Central 212
Clausen Memorial Museum, Petersburg 59
Colony House Museum, Palmer 111
Cooper Landing Museum, 148
Cordova Historical Museum 173
Cove Gallery, Halibut Cove 143
Decker Gallery, Juneau 73
Dorothy Page Museum, Wasilla 113
Experience Fine Art Gallery, Halibut Cove 143
Fairbanks Ice Museum 204, **204**
Fireweed Gallery, Homer 138
Gallery of Alaska, Fairbanks 207
Gallery Row, Homer 138
George I. Ashby Memorial Museum, Copper Center 188
Hammer Museum, Haines 83
Heritage Library Museum 99, Anchorage
Imaginarium, Anchorage 98
International Gallery of Contemporary Art, Anchorage 97
Isabel Miller Museum, Sitka 62
Juneau Artists Gallery, Juneau 73
Juneau-Douglas City Museum , Juneau 71
Knik Museum & Sled Dog Musher's Hall of Fame, Wasilla 113
Maxine & Jesse Whitney Museum, Valdez 171
McCarthy-Kennicott Museum 187

Museum of Alaska Transportation & Industry, Wasilla 113
Museum of the Aleutians, Unalaska 163
Museum of the North, Fairbanks 40, **205**, 206
Picture Alaska Art Gallery, Homer 139
Pratt Museum, Homer 139, **139**
Ptarmigan Arts, Homer 138–139
Resurrect Art Coffee House Gallery, Seward 122
Resurrection Bay Galerie, Seward 122
Rose Berry Alaska Art Gallery, Fairbanks 207
Sam Fox Museum, Dillingham 218
Seldon Museum and Cultural Center, Haines 82
Seward Museum 122
Sheldon Jackson Museum, Sitka 63–64, **64**
Skagway Museum, Skagway 87
Soho Coho 51
Stephan Fine Arts Gallery, Anchorage 97
Talkeetna Historical Society Museum 192
Tongass Historical Museum 52
Valdez Museum 170–171
Western & Arctic Coasts Gallery, Fairbanks 207
Wrangell Museum 56
Yupiit Piciryarait Cultural Center & Museum, Bethel 220
Musk Ox Farm **112,** 112–113
M.V. *Sea Life Discovery* 65, **65**

N
Nabesna 183
Nabesna River 181
Nabesna Road 182–183
Nenana 202, **202**
Alfred Starr Nenana Cultural Center 202
Nenana River 193
New Eddystone Rock 54
Ninilchik 148
Nizina River 181
Noatak 230
Noatak National Preserve 223
Nome 36, **221**, 221–222
North Anchorage 107–108
North Slope 27, 39, 225
Novarupta Volcano 22, 157
Nunamiut 14

P
Palmer 110–113
Pamyua 45, **45**
Park Road, Denali 194, 198–201
map 199
Paxson 193
Performing arts 45–46
Perseverance Theatre, Juneau 46
Peter the Great, Tsar (Russia) 33, **33**
Petersburg **20**, 48, **56**, 58–59, **58, 59**
Mitkof Highway 59
Sing Lee Alley 58, 59
Sons of Norway Hall 59
Petroglyph Beach State Historic Site 57, **57**
Pinnell Mountain National Recreation Trail 212
Planning your trip 236
Polychrome Pass, Denali **198**, 201
Port Alsworth 152
Portage Glacier 106, **185**
Portage Valley 106
Potter Marsh 102, **103**
Potter Creek Viewpoint & Trail 104
Potter Section House 104
Pribilof Islands 164, **164**, **215**
St. Paul Island 165
Prince William Sound **2-3**, 22, 176–177, **177**
Barry Arm 176
Blackstone Bay 176
College Fjord 176
Columbia Glacier 177
Esther Passage 176
Exxon Valdez oil spill 39, **39**
Harriman Fjord 176
Valdez Arm 176–177
Valdez Narrows 177
Prince William Sound & around 167–188, **177**
Cordova 172–174
Copper River Delta 172–175, **175**
description and history 168–169
Hotels & restaurants 255–257
map 168–169
McCarthy/Kennicott 186–187
Prince William Sound 167–168
Richardson Highway 178–179
Valdez 170–171, **170**, 176
Wrangell-St. Elias National Park & Preserve **180–181**, 180–183
Prince William Sound

Community College 171
Public use cabins 59
Punchbowl Cove **52**, 54

R
Rain forests 27, **158**
Rainbow Falls Trail 57
Rainbow Glacier **184–185**
Rendezvous Peak 108
Restaurants and hotels 241–260
Resurrection Bay **118**
Resurrection Pass Trail 148
Richardson Highway 178–179, **179**
Keystone Canyon 178
Thompson Pass **178**, 179
Tonsina River 179
Valdez Goat Trail 178
Worthington Glacier State Recreation Site 179
Roberts, Mount Interpretive Trail 74, **76**
tramway 73, 73–74
Rudyerd Bay 54
Rudyerd Island 54
Rufus Creek 182
Russell Fiord Wilderness 90
Russian Old Believers 18
Russian River 148

S
Safety Sound 222
Savoonga 234
Saxman Native Village and Totem Park **4, 44.** 52–53
Schoppert, James 43
Seabird Theater 137
Seldovia 145
Otterbahn Trail 145
Outside Beach 145
Seldovia Village Tribe 145
Senate Building, Juneau 73
Serpentine Hot Springs 234
Service, Robert 46
Seward 23, 120–123
Alaska SeaLife Center 120–121, **123**
downtown 120, 121–122
Seward Community Library 121–122
waterfront 120–121, **121**
Seward Highway **104**
Bird Point Scenic Overlook 105–106, **106**
Seward's purchase 34–36
Sheenjek River 232
Shopping 261–262
Shuyak Island State Park 159
Sitka 60–65, **60–61, 62, 63**
Alaska Raptor Center 63
Artist Cove Gallery 62
Castle Hill 60–61
Isabel Miller Museum 62
Lincoln Street **60–61,** 61–63

New Archangel Dancers 63
Sheet'ka Kwaan Naa Kahidi Tribal Community House 61–62
Sheldon Jackson Museum, Sitka 63–64, **64**
Starrigavan Recreation Area 64–65
Sitka National Historic Park **63**, 63–64
St. Michael's Cathedral **60–61**, 62
Tlingit Fort Site 63
Visitor Center and Southeast Alaska Indian Cultural Center 63
Sitka Sound 65
Skagway 37, **85**, 85–87
Arctic Brotherhood Hall 86
Chilkoot Trail 87
Klondike Gold Rush National Historical Park 85, 86, 86–87
Skagway Museum 87
White Pass & Yukon Route railroad 85–86, 88–89
map 89
Slana 182
Sled dogs **189**, 208, **228**
South Klondike Highway 87
Southeast Alaska 47–90
Admiralty Island National Monument 90
Glacier Bay National Park & Preserve 78–81
Haines 82–84
Hotels & restaurants 242–244
Inside Passage 48, 66–69
Juneau 70–77
Ketchikan 12–13, 24, 50–53
map 48–49
Misty Fiords National Monument 54–55
Petersburg 58–59
Sitka 60–65
Skagway 85–87
Tatshenshini and Alsek Rivers 90
Tongass NF 48
White Pass and Yukon Route 88–89
Yakutat 90
Goldrush Cemetery 88
Wrangell 56–57
Yakutat 90
Southeast Alaska Discovery Center 51
S.S. *Northwestern* 163
St. Elias Mountains 28
St. Michael's Cathedral **60–61**, 62
St. Nicholas Chapel, Kenai 133
St. Nicholas Russian

Orthodox Church, Seldovia 145
Star Building 51
Starrigavan Recreation Area 64–65
Estuary Life Trail 64
Forest and Muskeg Trail 64–65
Mosquito Cove Trail 64–65
Statehood 39
Steese Highway **211**, 211–212
Central 212
Chatanika Gold Camp 211–212
Nome Creek Valley Gold Panning Area 212
Twelve-mile Summit Wayside 212
Stikine River 57
Summit Lake 230
Summit Lake State Recreation Site 115

T

Talkeetna 192
Talkeetna Historic District 192
Tanana 15
Tangle Lakes 193
Tatshenshini-Alsek Provincial Park, B.C. Canada 80, 90
Telegraph Creek 57
Tetlin National Wildlife Refuge 188
Thomas Basin Boat Harbor 51
Three Forks Convergence 156
Tlingit 15
Tlingit Fort Site 63
Togiak National Wildlife Refuge 218
Tomka, Kat 43
Tongass Highway 52–53
Tongass National Forest 59
bear-watching 135
Rainbow Falls Trail 57

Starrigavan Recreation Area 64–65
Tony Knowles Coastal Trail, Anchorage 97, **99**
Totem Bight State Historical Park **4**, **42**, 53
Totem Heritage Center 52
Totem poles **4**, **40–41**, **42**, 44, 52, 53, 83
Train rides
Hurricane Turn 192
White Pass & Yukon Route railroad 88–89
map 89
Trans-Alaska pipeline **21**, 39, 179, 211
Travel information 236–240
Tsimshian 15, 53
Turnagain Arm 102–106
Turnagain Arm Trail **92**

U

Ukak Falls Trail 156
Ukak River 156
Ukinrek Maars 166
Unalaska Island 20, **162**
Unangan 15, 150–151
Unimak Island **151**, **163**
University of Alaska 206–208
Geophysical Institute 208
International Arctic Research Center 208
Large Animal Research Station 208
Upper Chatanika River State Recreation Site 212

V

Valdez 23, 170–171, 176
Dock Point Trail 171
Mineral Creek Trail 171
Shoup Bay Trail 171
Valley of Ten Thousand Smokes 156
Varnell, Donald **44**
Vogel, Paula 46

W

Walrus Islands State Game

Sanctuary **216**, 219
Round Island 219
Wasilla 113
Webber, John 40
White Mountains National Recreation Area 213
White Pass & Yukon Route railroad 85–86, 88–89
Bridal Veil Falls 89,
Goldrush Cemetery 88
Inspiration Point 89
map 89
Rocky Point 88
Tunnel Mountain 89
White Pass Summit 87, 89
Whittier 176
Wickersham Dome Trailhead 213
Wolves 30
Wood-Tikchik State Park 219
Woolley Lagoon **234**
Wrangell **56**, 56–57
Chief Shakes Island 56–57
Petroglyph Beach State Historic Site 57, **57**
Rainbow Falls Trail 57
Root Glacier **169**
Wrangell Museum 56
Wrangell Mountains 28
Wrangell-St. Elias National Park & Preserve 80, 90, 168, **180–181**, 180–183
backcountry 181–182
map 183
Nabesna Road 182–183
Trail Creek 183
visitor center 180

Y

Yakutat 90
Yakutat Bay 37, 182
Yukon Delta National Wildlife Refuge 220, **220**
Yukon River Bridge 224
Yupik 14

Z

Ziegler, Eustace 41–43

ILLUSTRATIONS CREDITS

All photos by Michael Melford, except the following;

22-23, Bettmann/CORBIS; 24, Galen Rowell/CORBIS; 29, Norbert Rosing/NGS Image Collection; 33, Archivo Iconografico, S.A./CORBIS; 34-35, Bettmann/CORBIS; 36 and 37, courtesy The Library of Congress; 38, CORBIS; 39, Gary Braasch/CORBIS; 43, Bates Littlehales/NGS Image Collection; 45, Adam Rountree/Getty Images; 46, Stewart Allison; 68-69, Ron Niebrugge/Graham/Accent Alaska.com; 96, Ken Graham/Accent Alaska.com; 153, Galen Rowell/CORBIS; 182, Didier Lindsey/Graham/Accent Alaska.com; 214, Ray Hafen/Graham/Accent Alaska.com; 220, Wolfgang Kaehler/CORBIS; 228, Paul A. Souders/CORBIS; 229, Hugh Rose/Accent Alaska.com; 233, Galen Rowell/CORBIS; 234, Matthias Breiter/Accent Alaska.com.

One of the world's largest nonprofit scientific and educational organizations, the National Geographic Society was founded in 1888 "for the increase and diffusion of geographic knowledge." Fulfilling this mission, the Society educates and inspires millions every day through its magazines, books, television programs, videos, maps and atlases, research grants, the National Geographic Bee, teacher workshops, and innovative classroom materials. The Society is supported through membership dues, charitable gifts, and income from the sale of its educational products. This support is vital to National Geographic's mission to increase global understanding and promote conservation of our planet through exploration, research, and education.

For more information, please call 1-800-NGS LINE (647-5463) or write to the following address:

National Geographic Society
1145 17th Street N.W.
Washington, D.C. 20036-4688
U.S.A.

Visit the Society's Web site at www.nationalgeographic.com.

Special Offer! Order today and get one year of National Geographic Traveler, the magazine travelers trust, for only $14.95. Call 1-800-NGS-LINE and mention code TRAC3A6.

Travel the world with National Geographic Experts:
www.nationalgeographic.com /ngexpeditions

Published by the National Geographic Society
John M. Fahey, Jr., *President and Chief Executive Officer*
Gilbert M. Grosvenor, *Chairman of the Board*
Nina D. Hoffman, *Executive Vice President,*
    President, Books and School Publishing
Kevin Mulroy, *Senior Vice President and Publisher*
Marianne Koszorus, *Design Director*
Kristin Hanneman, *Illustrations Director*
Elizabeth L. Newhouse, *Director of Travel Publishing*
Cinda Rose, *Art Director*
Carl Mehler, *Director of Maps*
Barbara A. Noe, *Series Editor*

Staff for this book:
Caroline Hickey, *Project Manager*
Kay Kobor Hankins, *Designer*
John C. Anderson, *Illustrations Editor*
David Lauterborn and Jane Sunderland, *Editors*
Leah Boltz, *Researcher*
Lise Sajewski, *Editorial Consultant*
XNR Productions, *Map Research, and Production*
R. Gary Colbert, *Production Director*
Mike Horenstein, *Production Manager*
Teresa Neva Tate, *Illustrations Specialist*
Carolinda E. Averitt, Dana Chivvis, and Steven D. Gardner, *Contributors*

Rebecca Hinds, *Managing Editor*

Artwork by Maltings Partnership, Derby, England

ISBN-10: 0-7922-5371-X
ISBN-13: 978-0-7922-5371-6

Printed and bound by Cayfosa Quebecor, Barcelona, Spain
Color separations by Quad Graphics, Alexandria, VA.

Visit the society's Web site at http://www.nationalgeographic.com.

The information in this book has been carefully checked and to the best of our knowledge is accurate. However, details are subject to change, and the National Geographic Society cannot be responsible for such changes, or for errors or omissions. Assessments of sites, hotels, and restaurants are based on the author's subjective opinions, which do not necessarily reflect the publisher's opinion. The publisher cannot be responsible for any consequences arising from the use of this book.

For information about special discounts for bulk purchases, please contact National Geographic Books Special Sales: ngspecsales@ngs.org

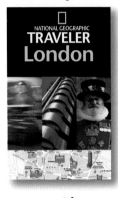
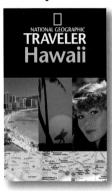